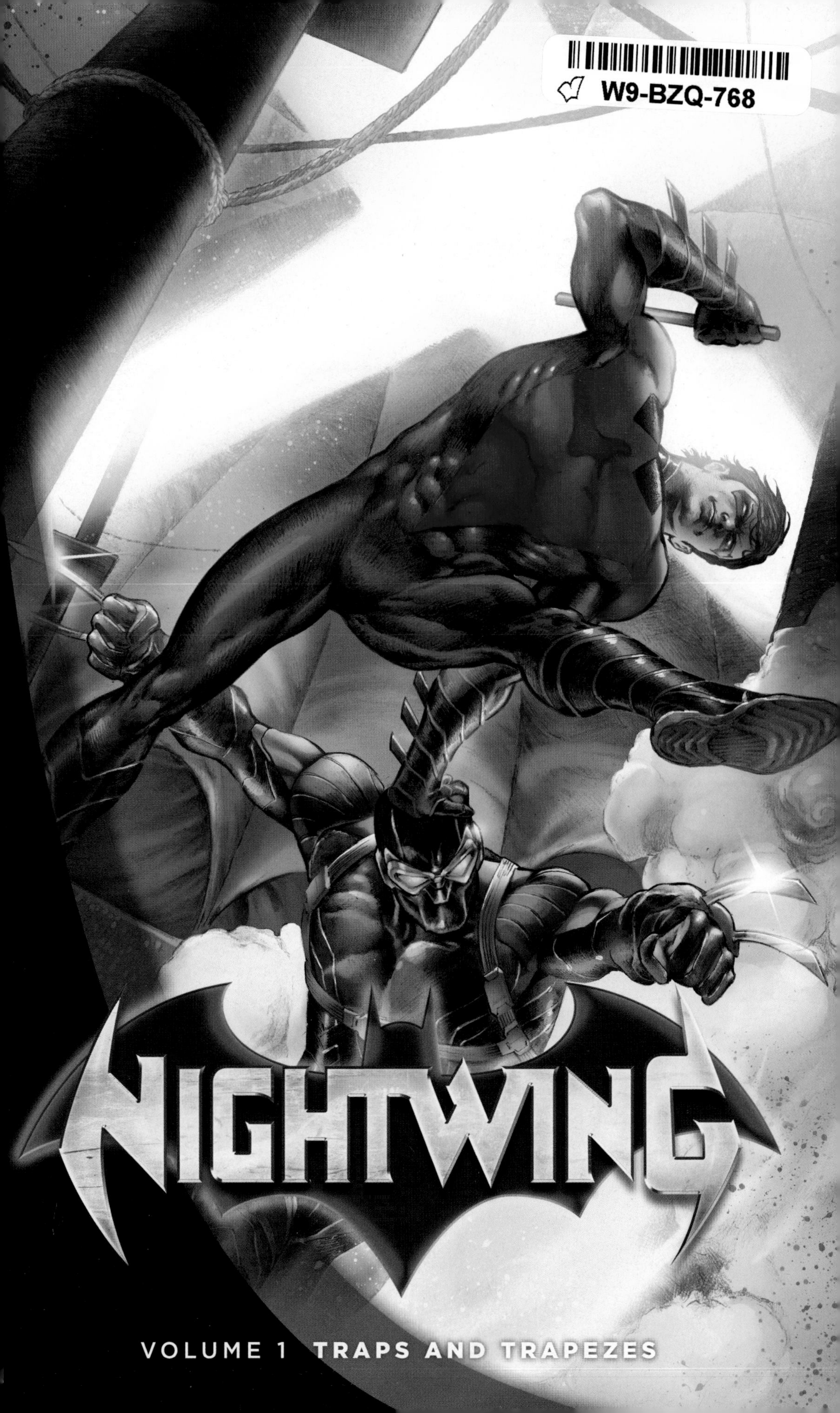
NIGHTWING
VOLUME 1 TRAPS AND TRAPEZES

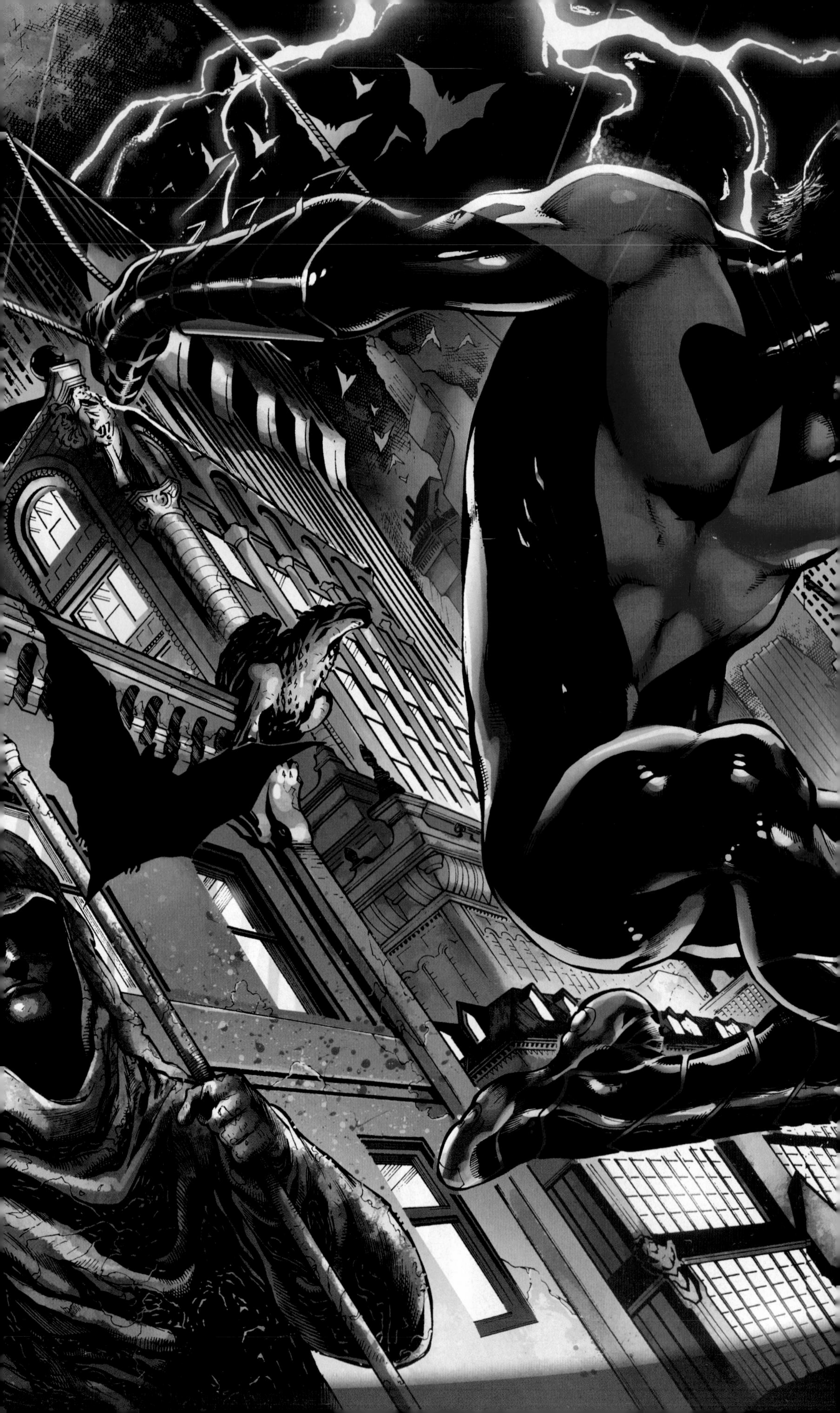

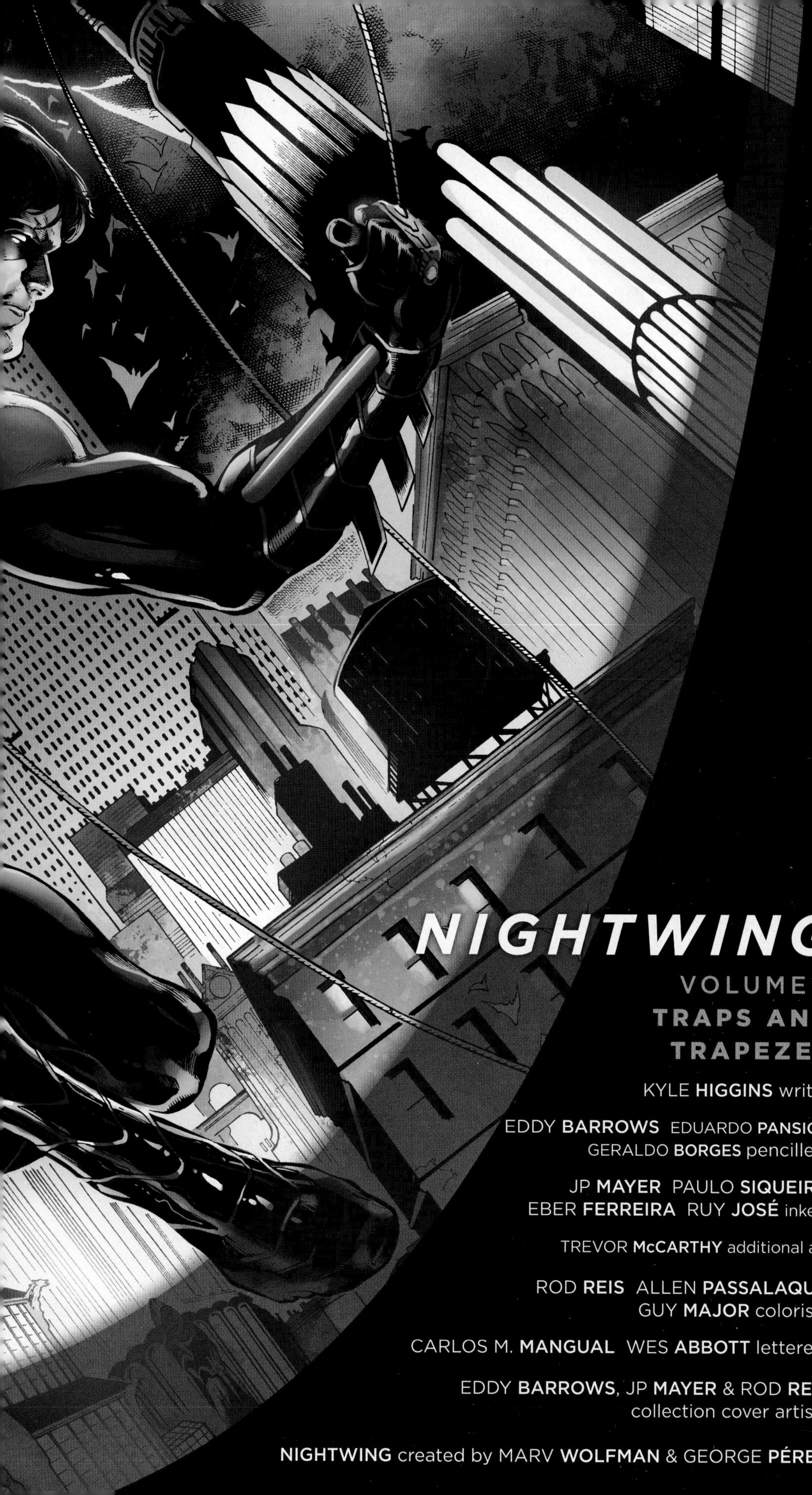

NIGHTWING

VOLUME 1
TRAPS AND TRAPEZES

KYLE **HIGGINS** writer

EDDY **BARROWS** EDUARDO **PANSICA**
GERALDO **BORGES** pencillers

JP **MAYER** PAULO **SIQUEIRA**
EBER **FERREIRA** RUY **JOSÉ** inkers

TREVOR **McCARTHY** additional art

ROD **REIS** ALLEN **PASSALAQUA**
GUY **MAJOR** colorists

CARLOS M. **MANGUAL** WES **ABBOTT** letterers

EDDY **BARROWS**, JP **MAYER** & ROD **REIS**
collection cover artists

NIGHTWING created by MARV **WOLFMAN** & GEORGE **PÉREZ**

BOBBIE CHASE Editor – Original Series KATIE KUBERT Assistant Editor – Original Series
ROWENA YOW Editor ROBBIN BROSTERMAN Design Director – Books
ROBBIE BIEDERMAN Publication Design

BOB HARRAS VP – Editor-in-Chief

DIANE NELSON President DAN DIDIO and JIM LEE Co-Publishers
GEOFF JOHNS Chief Creative Officer
JOHN ROOD Executive VP – Sales, Marketing and Business Development
AMY GENKINS Senior VP – Business and Legal Affairs NAIRI GARDINER Senior VP – Finance
JEFF BOISON VP – Publishing Operations MARK CHIARELLO VP – Art Direction and Design
JOHN CUNNINGHAM VP – Marketing TERRI CUNNINGHAM VP – Talent Relations and Services
ALISON GILL Senior VP – Manufacturing and Operations HANK KANALZ Senior VP – Digital
JAY KOGAN VP – Business and Legal Affairs, Publishing JACK MAHAN VP – Business Affairs, Talent
NICK NAPOLITANO VP – Manufacturing Administration SUE POHJA VP – Book Sales
COURTNEY SIMMONS Senior VP – Publicity BOB WAYNE Senior VP – Sales

NIGHTWING VOLUME 1: TRAPS AND TRAPEZES

DC Comics, 1700 Broadway, New York, NY 10019
A Warner Bros. Entertainment Company.
Printed by RR Donnelley, Salem, VA, USA. 3/14/13. Second Printing.

ISBN: 978-1-4012-3705-9

SUSTAINABLE FORESTRY INITIATIVE

Certified Chain of Custody
At Least 20% Certified Forest Content
www.sfiprogram.org
SFI-01042
APPLIES TO TEXT STOCK ONLY

Library of Congress Cataloging-in-Publication Data

Higgins, Kyle.
Nightwing volume 1 : traps and trapezes / Kyle Higgins, Eddy Barrows.
p. cm.
"Originally published in single magazine form in Nightwing 1-7."
ISBN 978-1-4012-3705-9
1. Graphic novels. I. Barrows, Eddy. II. Title. III. Title: Traps and trapezes.
PN6728.N55H54 2012
741.5'973—dc23
2012022429

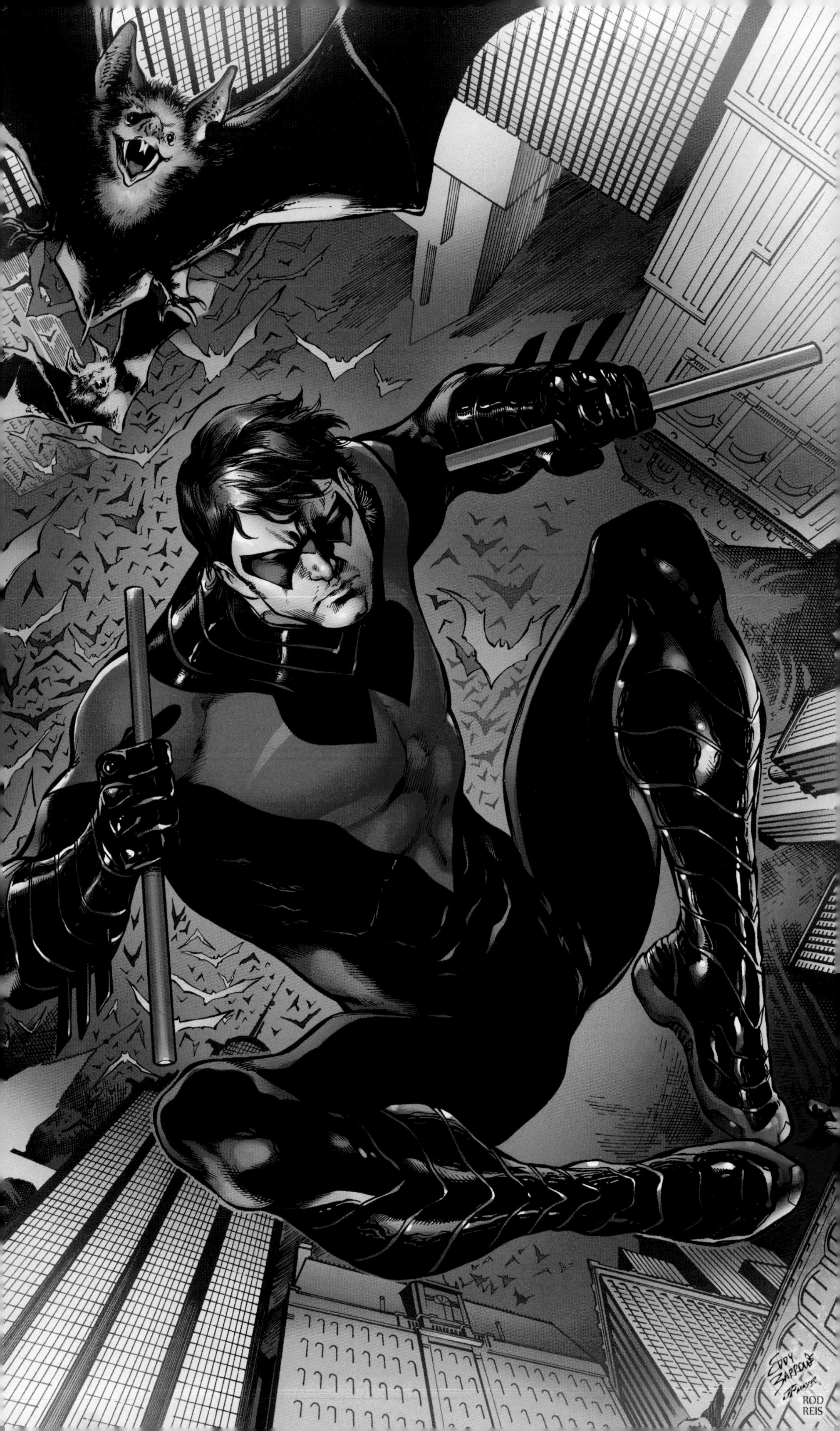
EDDY BARROWS
JPMAYER
ROD REIS

KYLE HIGGINS writer EDDY BARROWS penciller JP MAYER inker cover art by Eddy Barrows, JP Mayer & Rod Reis

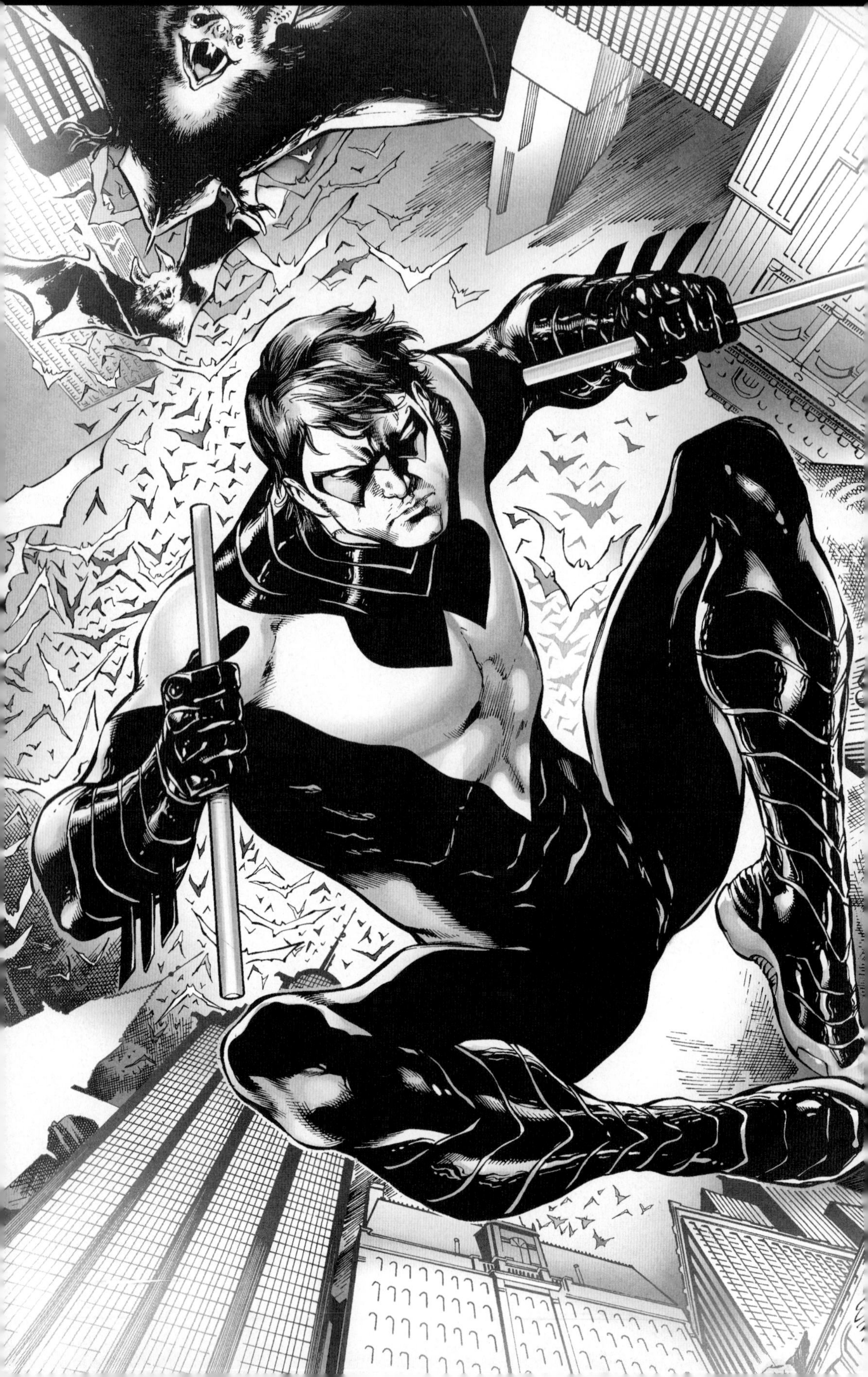

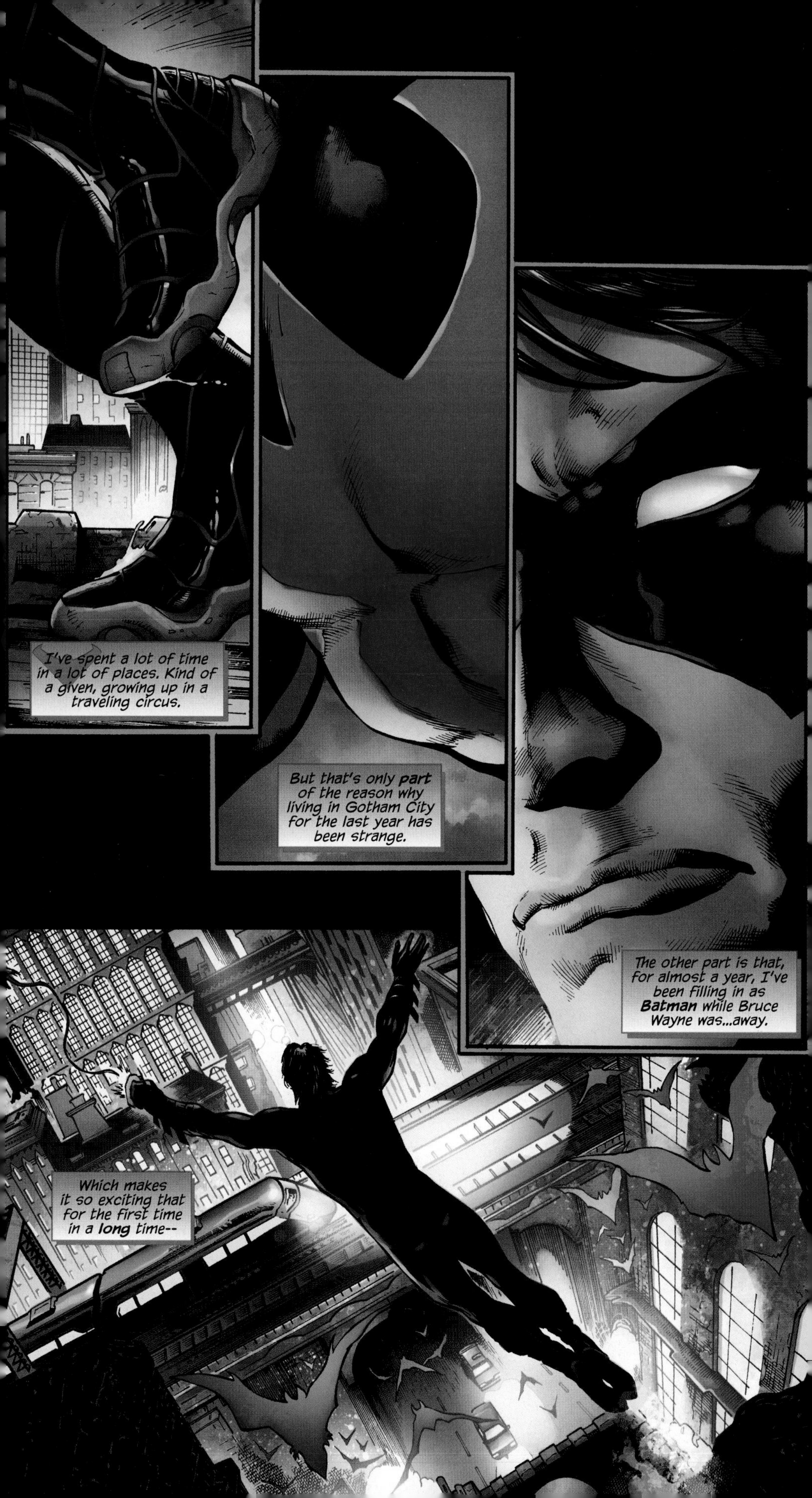
I've spent a lot of time in a lot of places. Kind of a given, growing up in a traveling circus.
But that's only part of the reason why living in Gotham City for the last year has been strange.
The other part is that, for almost a year, I've been filling in as Batman while Bruce Wayne was...away.
Which makes it so exciting that for the first time in a long time--

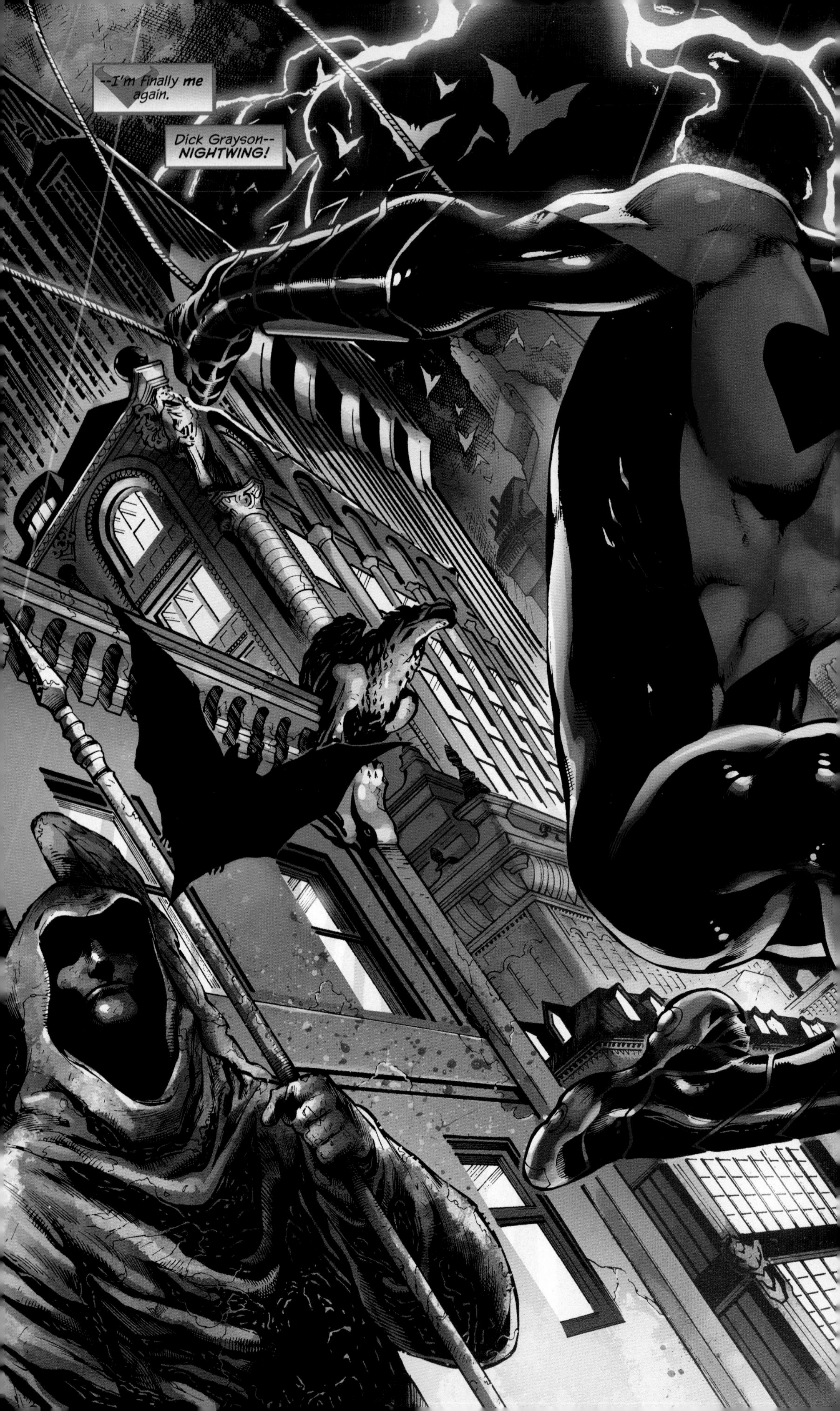
--I'm finally me again.
Dick Grayson--
NIGHTWING!

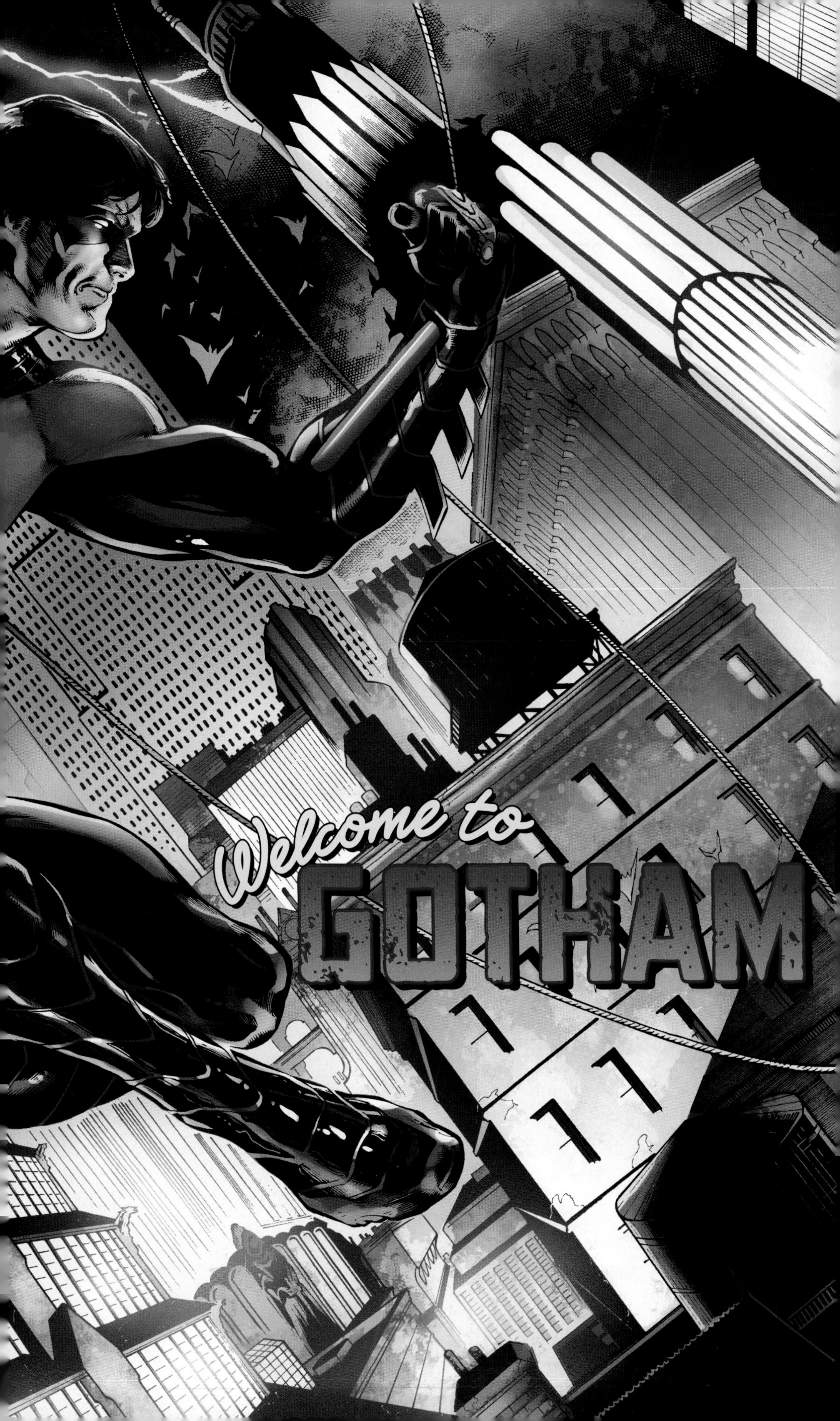
Welcome to
GOTHAM

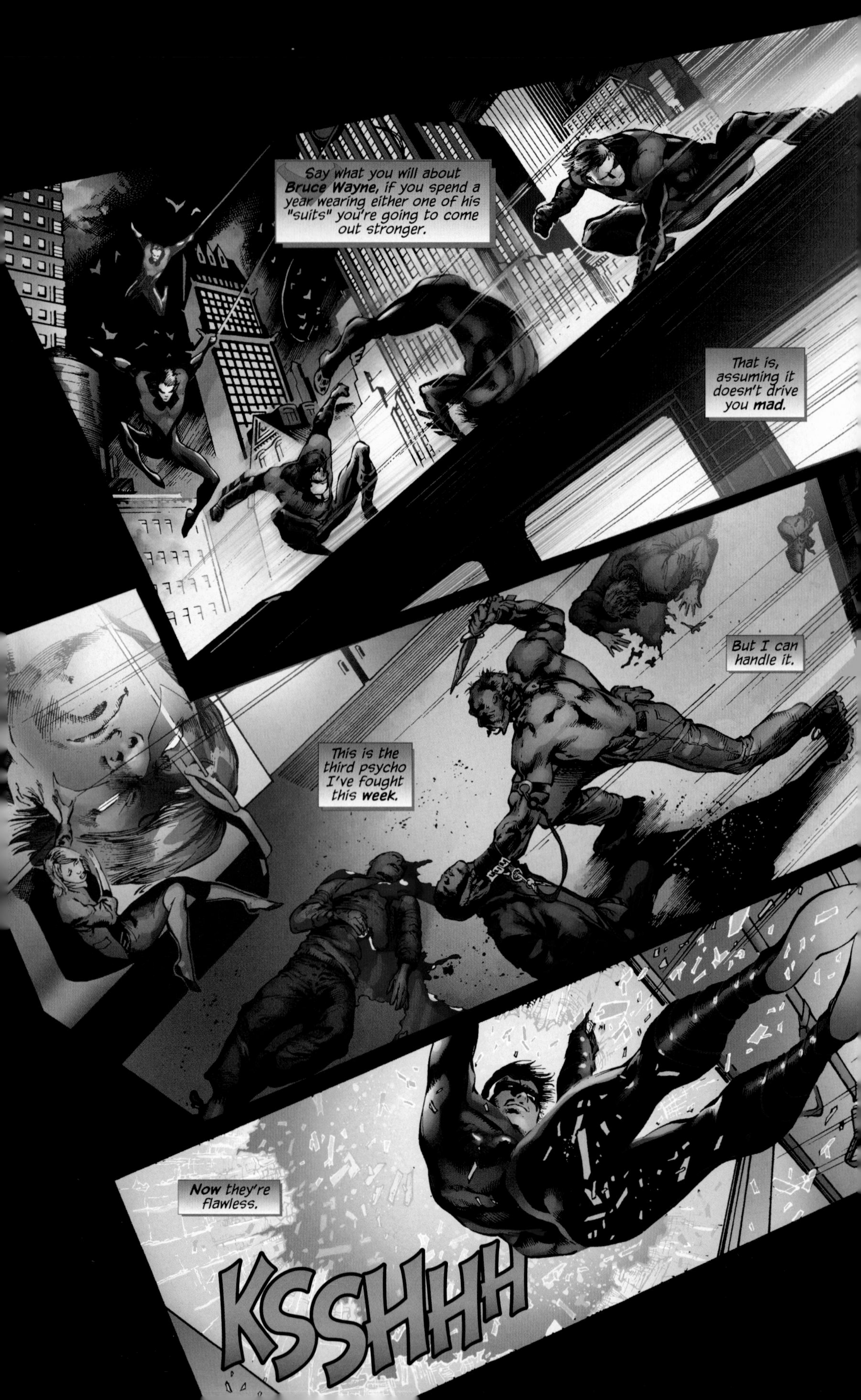

Say what you will about Bruce Wayne, if you spend a year wearing either one of his "suits" you're going to come out stronger.
That is, assuming it doesn't drive you mad.
But I can handle it.
This is the third psycho I've fought this week.
Now they're flawless.
KSSHHH

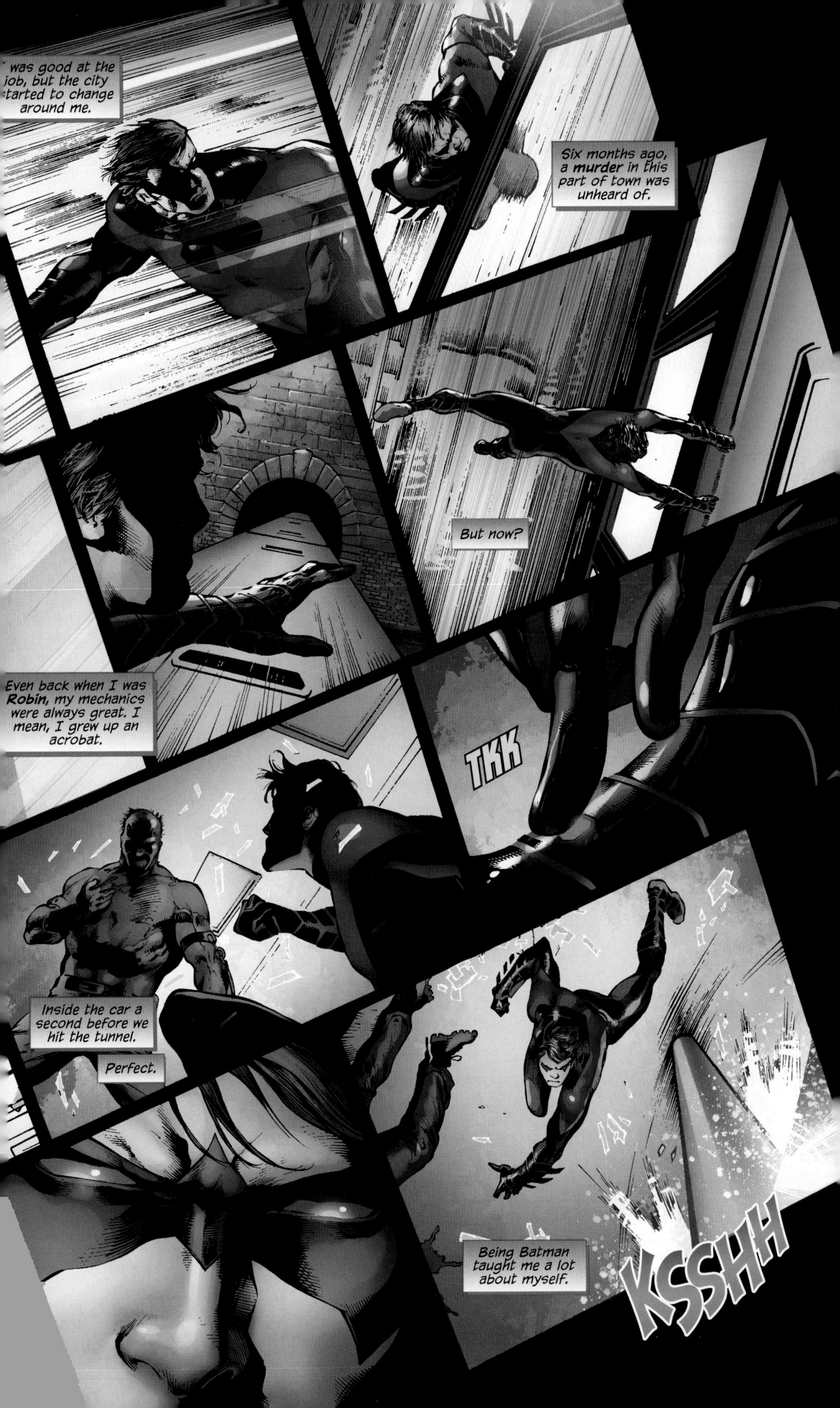

I was good at the job, but the city started to change around me.
Six months ago, a murder in this part of town was unheard of.
But now?
Even back when I was Robin, my mechanics were always great. I mean, I grew up an acrobat.
TKK
Inside the car a second before we hit the tunnel.
Perfect.
Being Batman taught me a lot about myself.
KSSHH

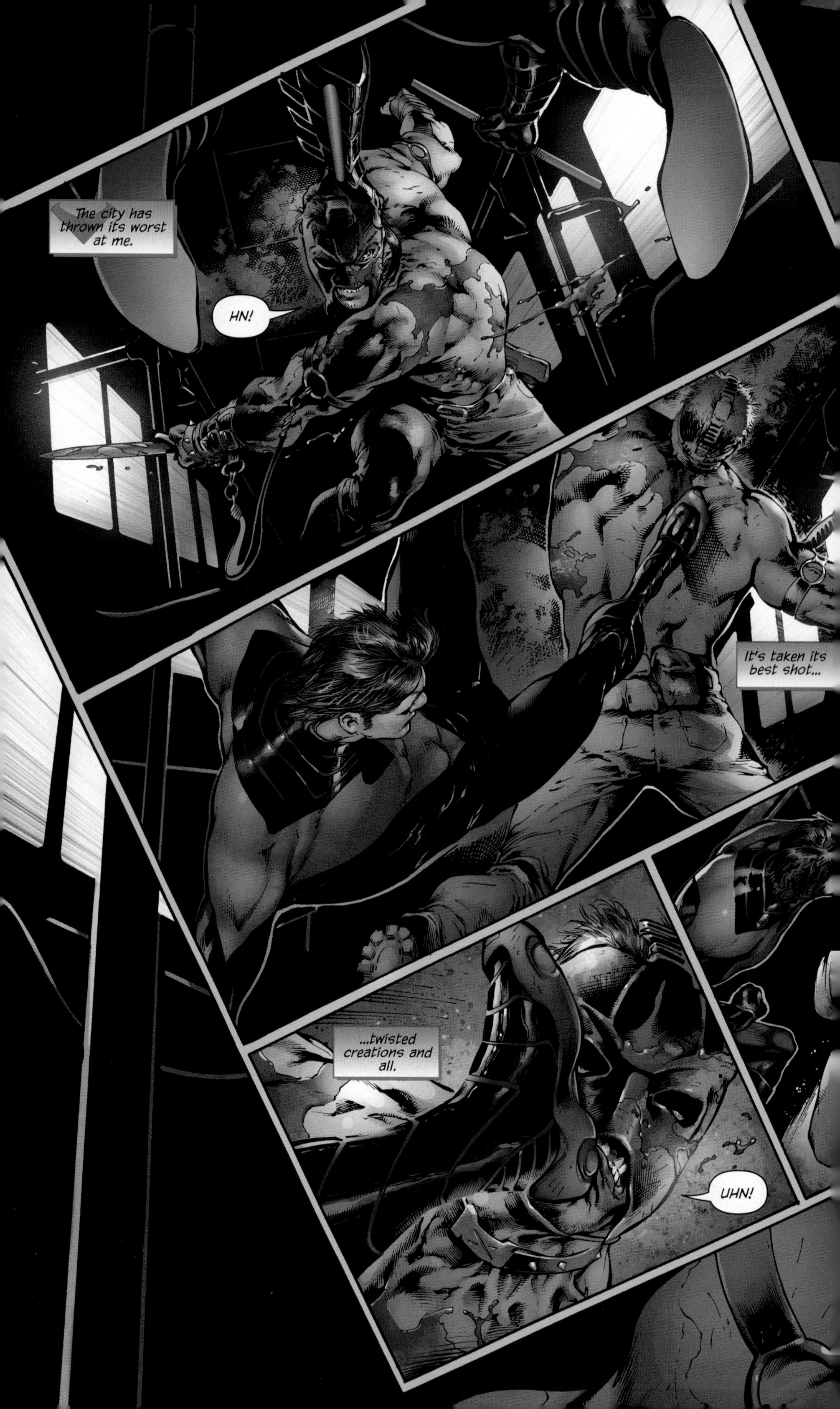
The city has thrown its worst at me.
HN!
It's taken its best shot...
...twisted creations and all.
UHN!

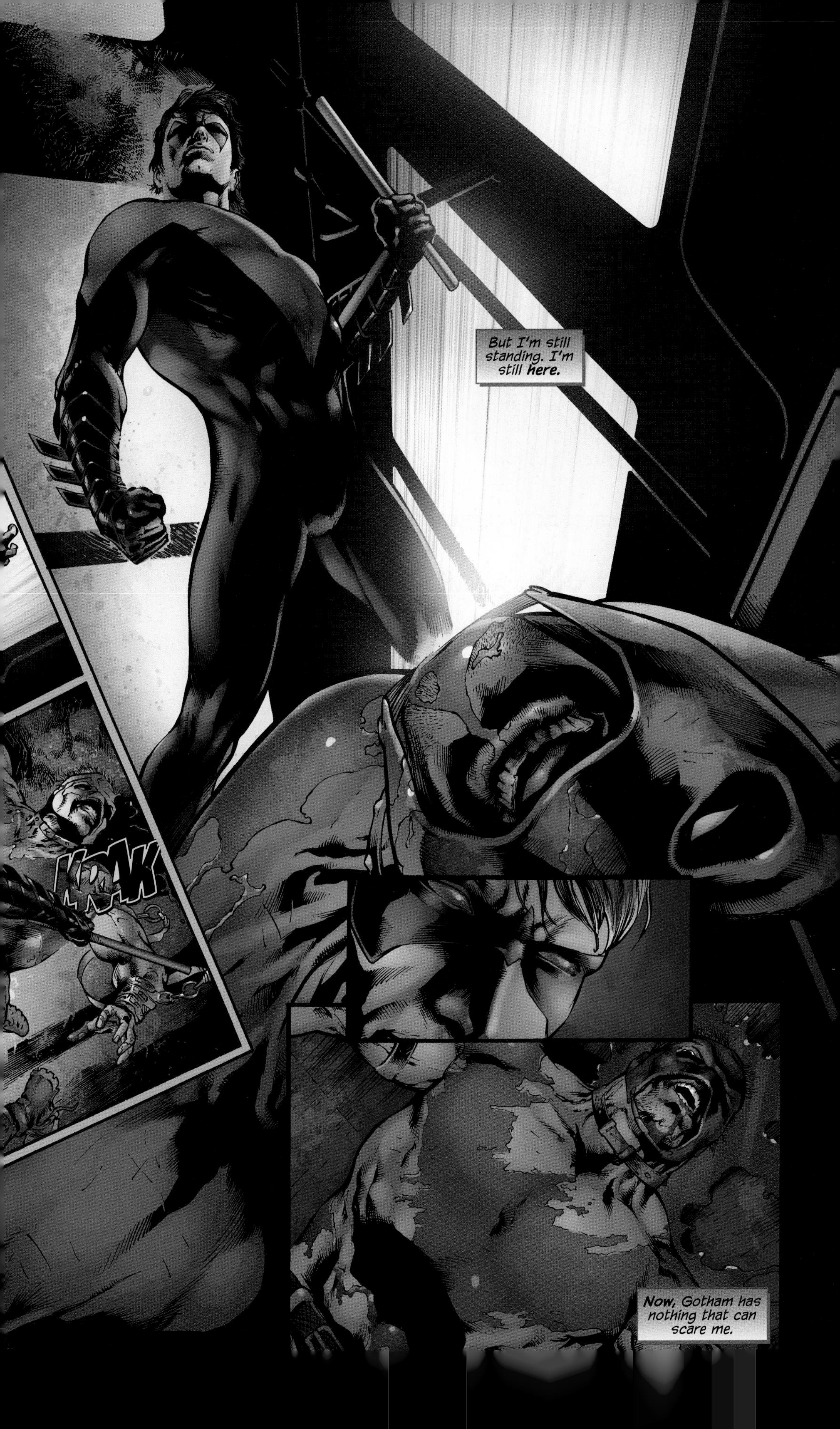
But I'm still standing. I'm still here.
KRAK
Now, Gotham has nothing that can scare me.

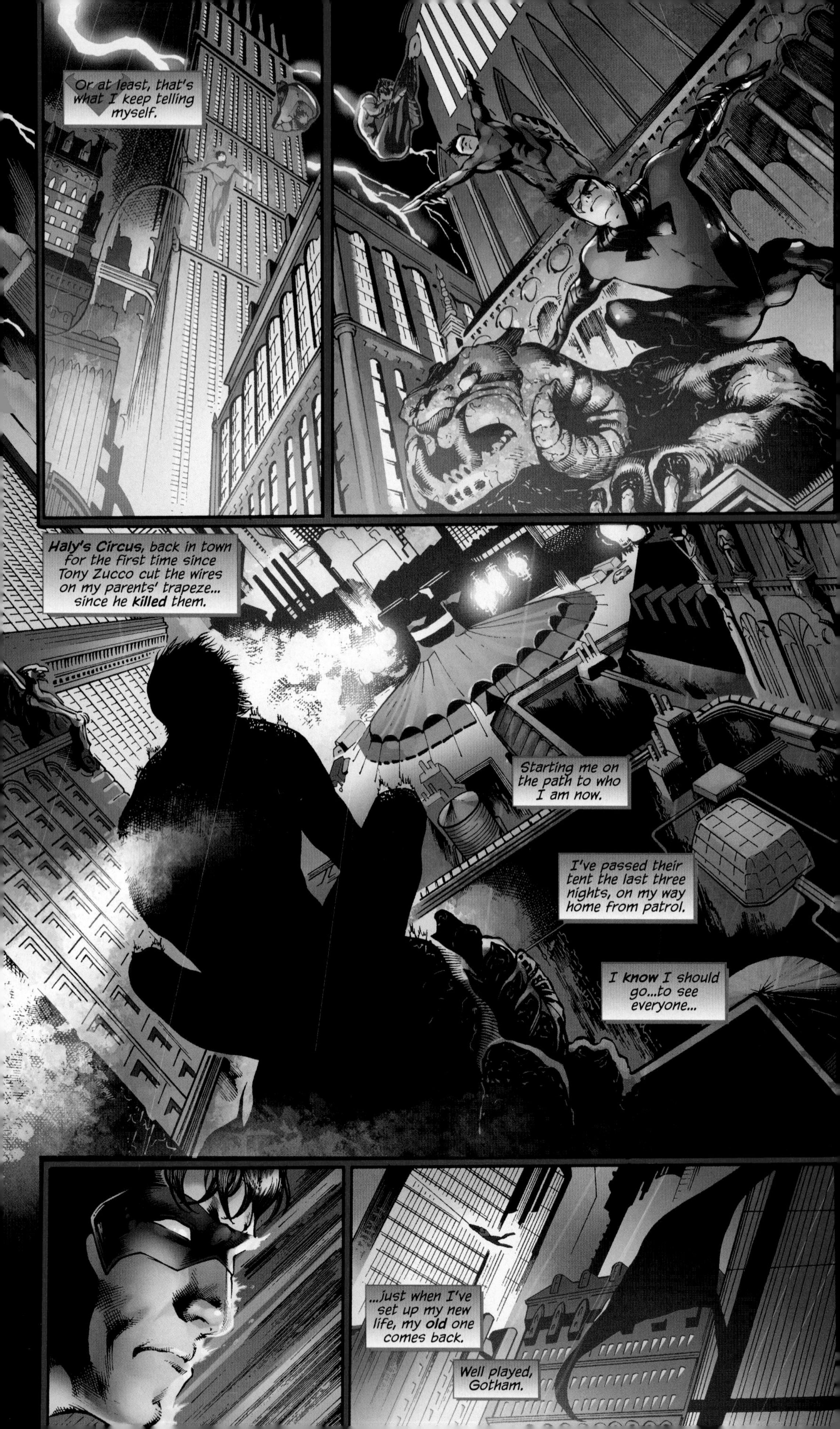
Or at least, that's what I keep telling myself.
Haly's Circus, back in town for the first time since Tony Zucco cut the wires on my parents' trapeze... since he killed them.
Starting me on the path to who I am now.
I've passed their tent the last three nights, on my way home from patrol.
I know I should go...to see everyone...
...just when I've set up my new life, my old one comes back.
Well played, Gotham.

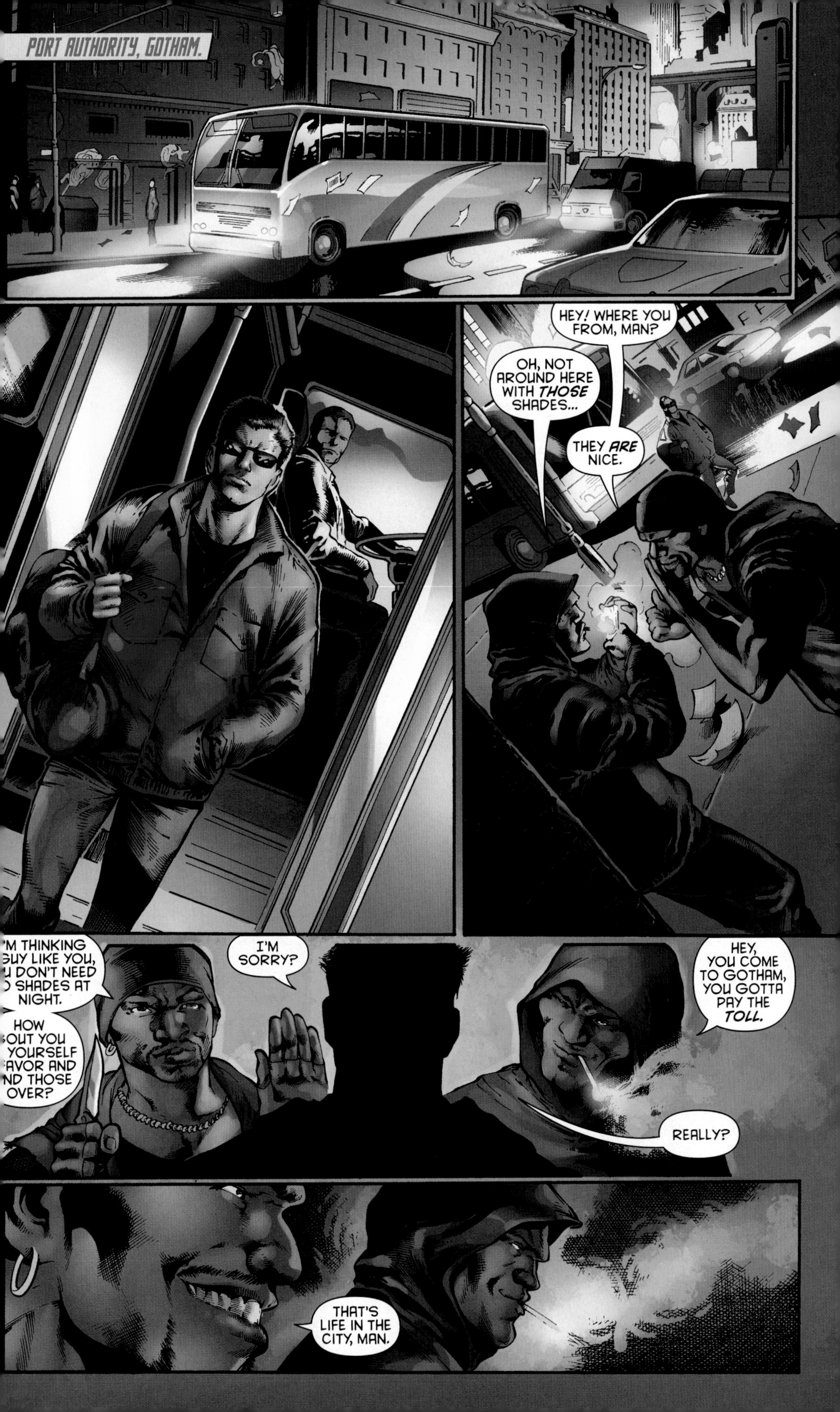
PORT AUTHORITY, GOTHAM.
HEY! WHERE YOU FROM, MAN?
OH, NOT AROUND HERE WITH THOSE SHADES...
THEY ARE NICE.
'M THINKING GUY LIKE YOU, U DON'T NEED O SHADES AT NIGHT.
HOW OUT YOU YOURSELF AVOR AND ND THOSE OVER?
I'M SORRY?
HEY, YOU COME TO GOTHAM, YOU GOTTA PAY THE TOLL.
REALLY?
THAT'S LIFE IN THE CITY, MAN.

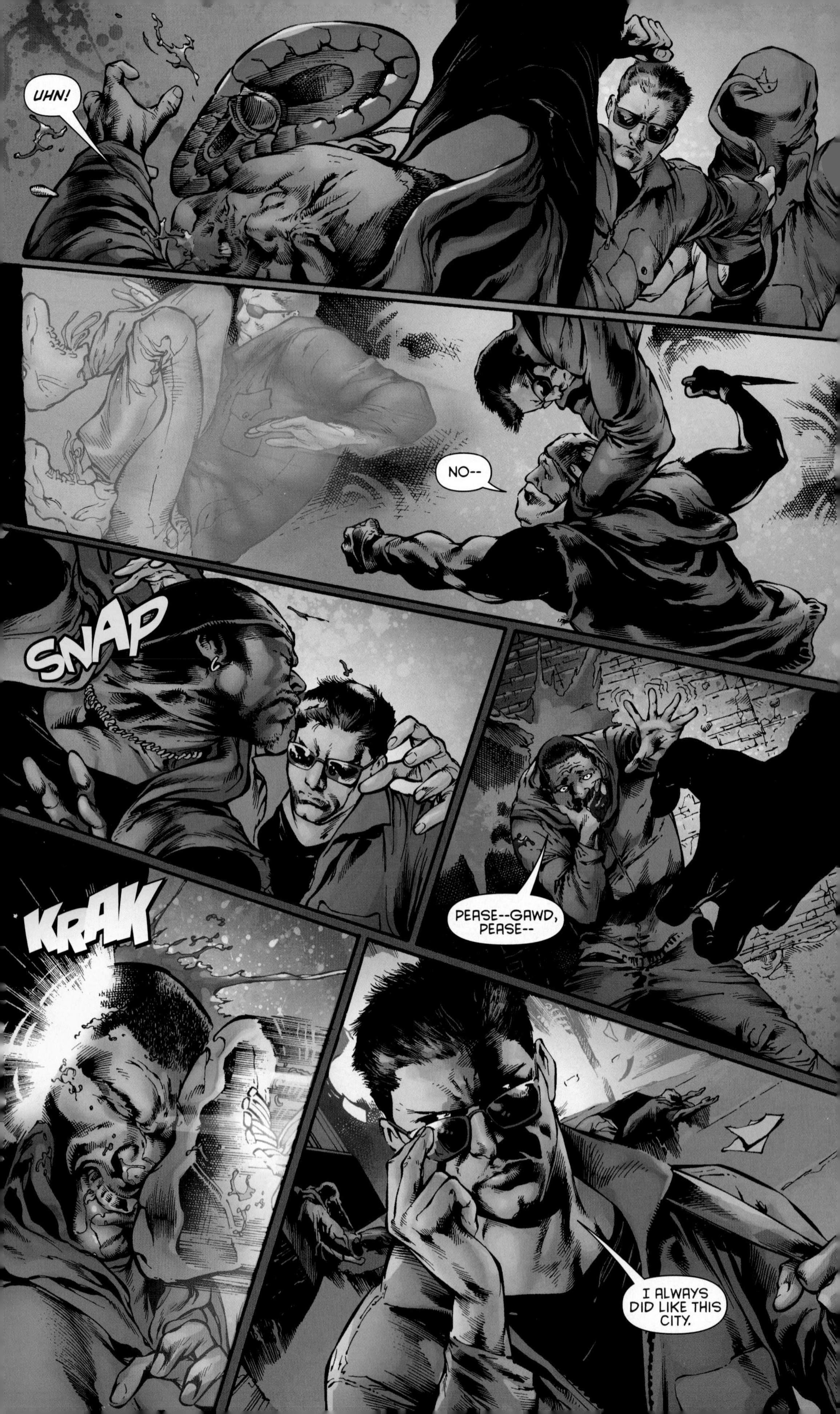
UHN!
NO--
SNAP
PEASE--GAWD, PEASE--
KRAK
I ALWAYS DID LIKE THIS CITY.

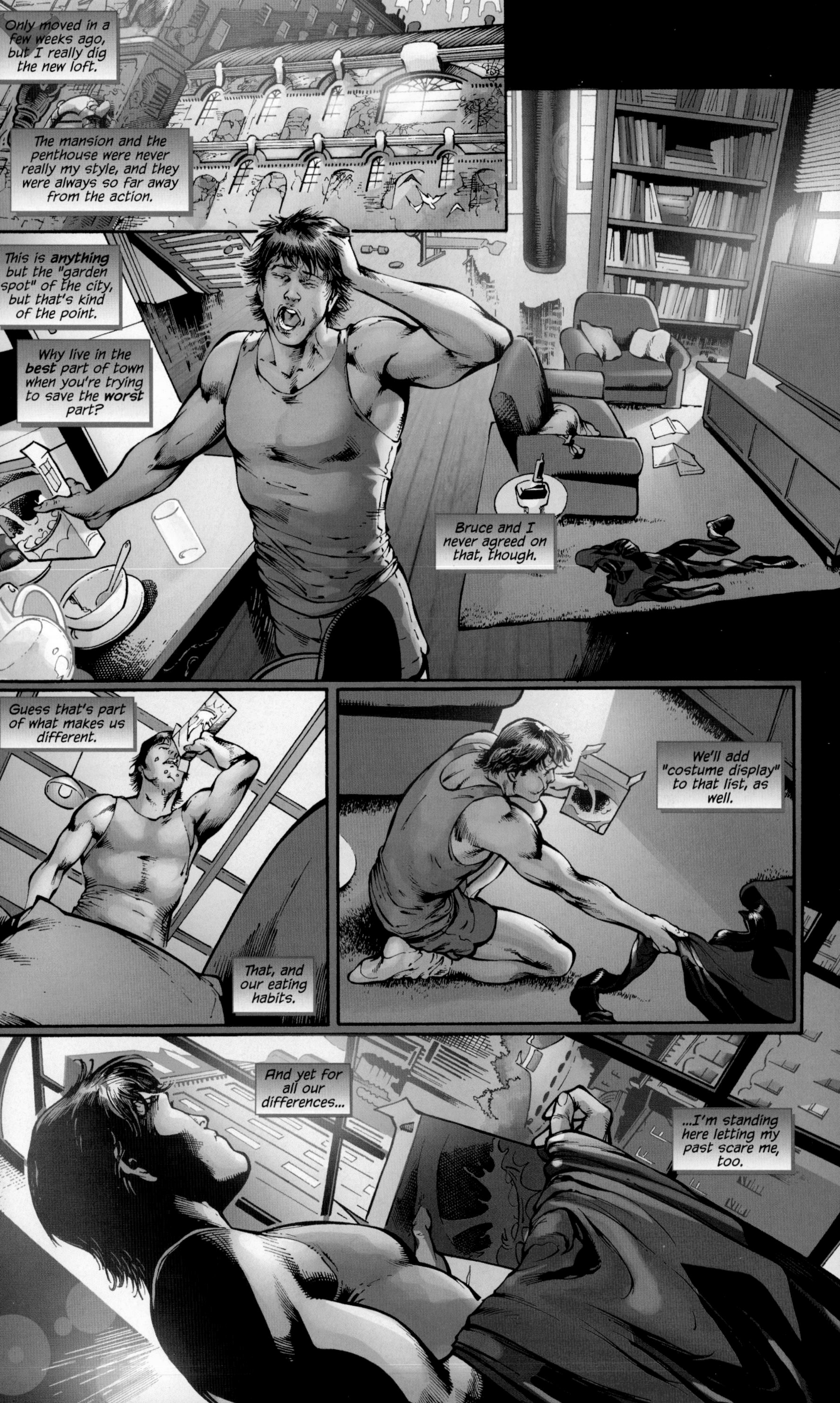

Only moved in a few weeks ago, but I really dig the new loft.
The mansion and the penthouse were never really my style, and they were always so far away from the action.
This is **anything** but the "garden spot" of the city, but that's kind of the point.
Why live in the **best** part of town when you're trying to save the **worst** part?
Bruce and I never agreed on that, though.
Guess that's part of what makes us different.
That, and our eating habits.
We'll add "costume display" to that list, as well.
And yet for all our differences...
...I'm standing here letting my past scare me, too.

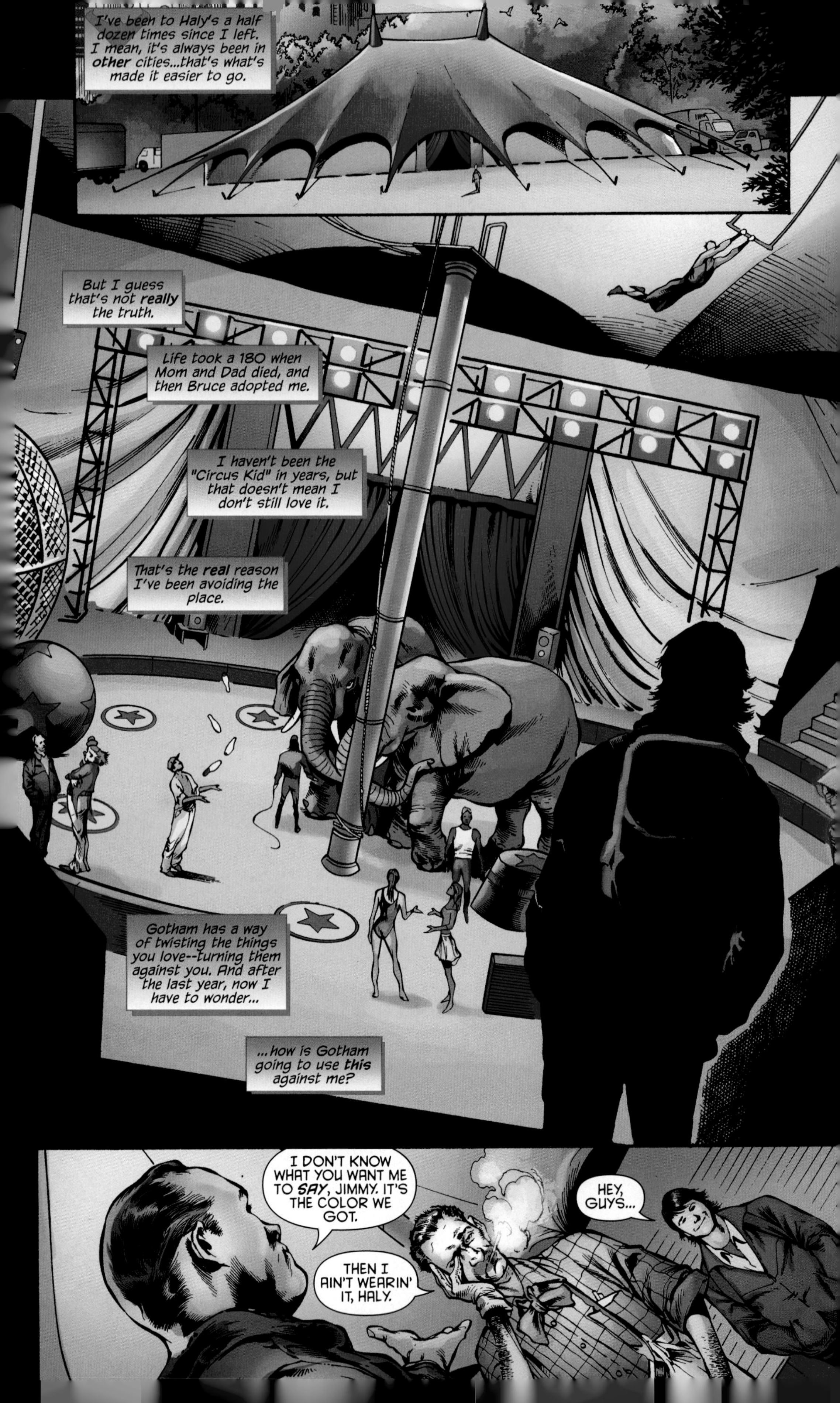

I've been to Haly's a half dozen times since I left. I mean, it's always been in other cities...that's what's made it easier to go.
But I guess that's not really the truth.
Life took a 180 when Mom and Dad died, and then Bruce adopted me.
I haven't been the "Circus Kid" in years, but that doesn't mean I don't still love it.
That's the real reason I've been avoiding the place.
Gotham has a way of twisting the things you love--turning them against you. And after the last year, now I have to wonder...
...how is Gotham going to use this against me?
I DON'T KNOW WHAT YOU WANT ME TO SAY, JIMMY. IT'S THE COLOR WE GOT.
THEN I AIN'T WEARIN' IT, HALY.
HEY, GUYS...

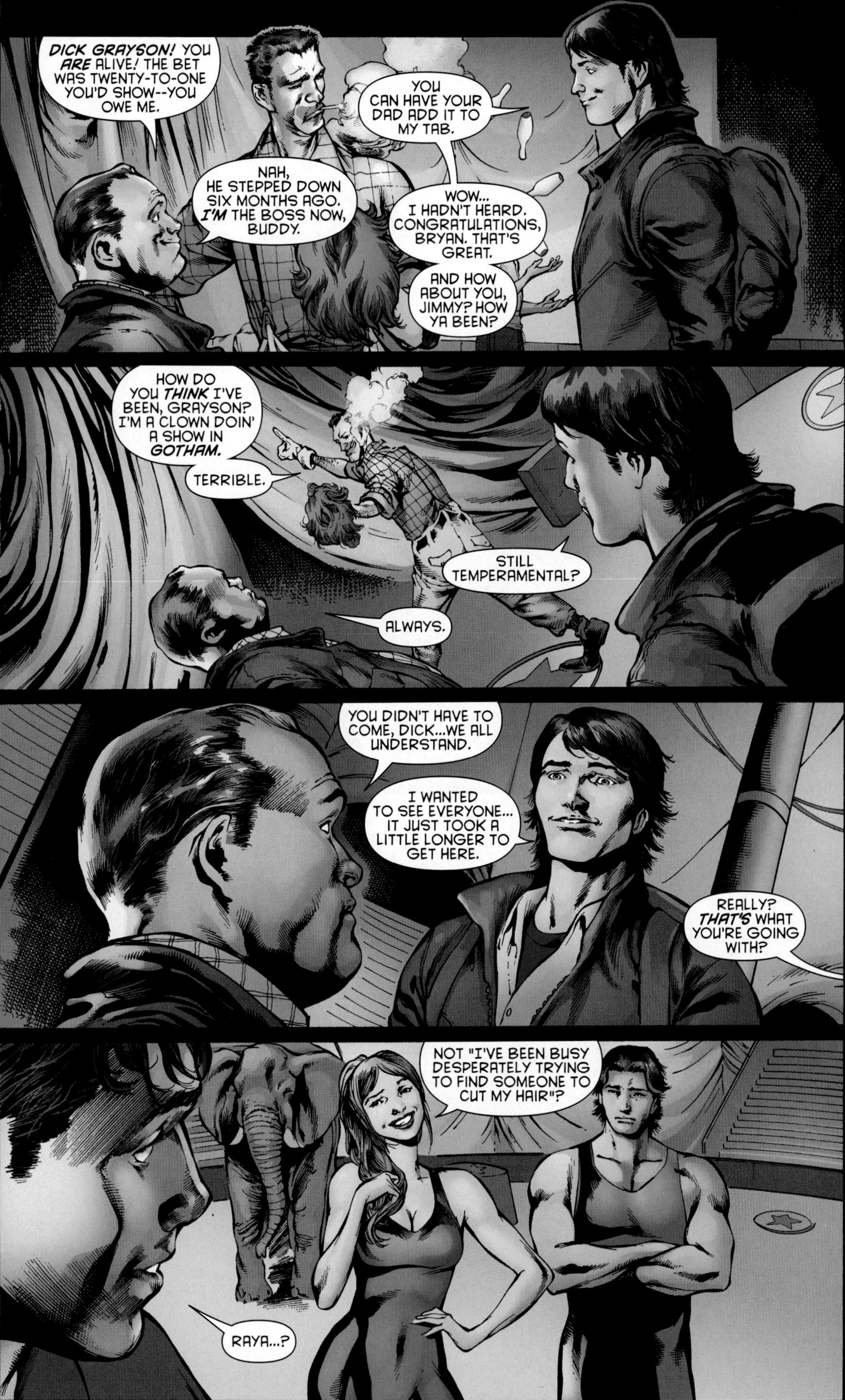
DICK GRAYSON! YOU ARE ALIVE! THE BET WAS TWENTY-TO-ONE YOU'D SHOW--YOU OWE ME.
YOU CAN HAVE YOUR DAD ADD IT TO MY TAB.
NAH, HE STEPPED DOWN SIX MONTHS AGO. I'M THE BOSS NOW, BUDDY.
WOW... I HADN'T HEARD. CONGRATULATIONS, BRYAN. THAT'S GREAT.
AND HOW ABOUT YOU, JIMMY? HOW YA BEEN?
HOW DO YOU THINK I'VE BEEN, GRAYSON? I'M A CLOWN DOIN' A SHOW IN GOTHAM.
TERRIBLE.
STILL TEMPERAMENTAL?
ALWAYS.
YOU DIDN'T HAVE TO COME, DICK...WE ALL UNDERSTAND.
I WANTED TO SEE EVERYONE... IT JUST TOOK A LITTLE LONGER TO GET HERE.
REALLY? THAT'S WHAT YOU'RE GOING WITH?
NOT "I'VE BEEN BUSY DESPERATELY TRYING TO FIND SOMEONE TO CUT MY HAIR"?
RAYA...?

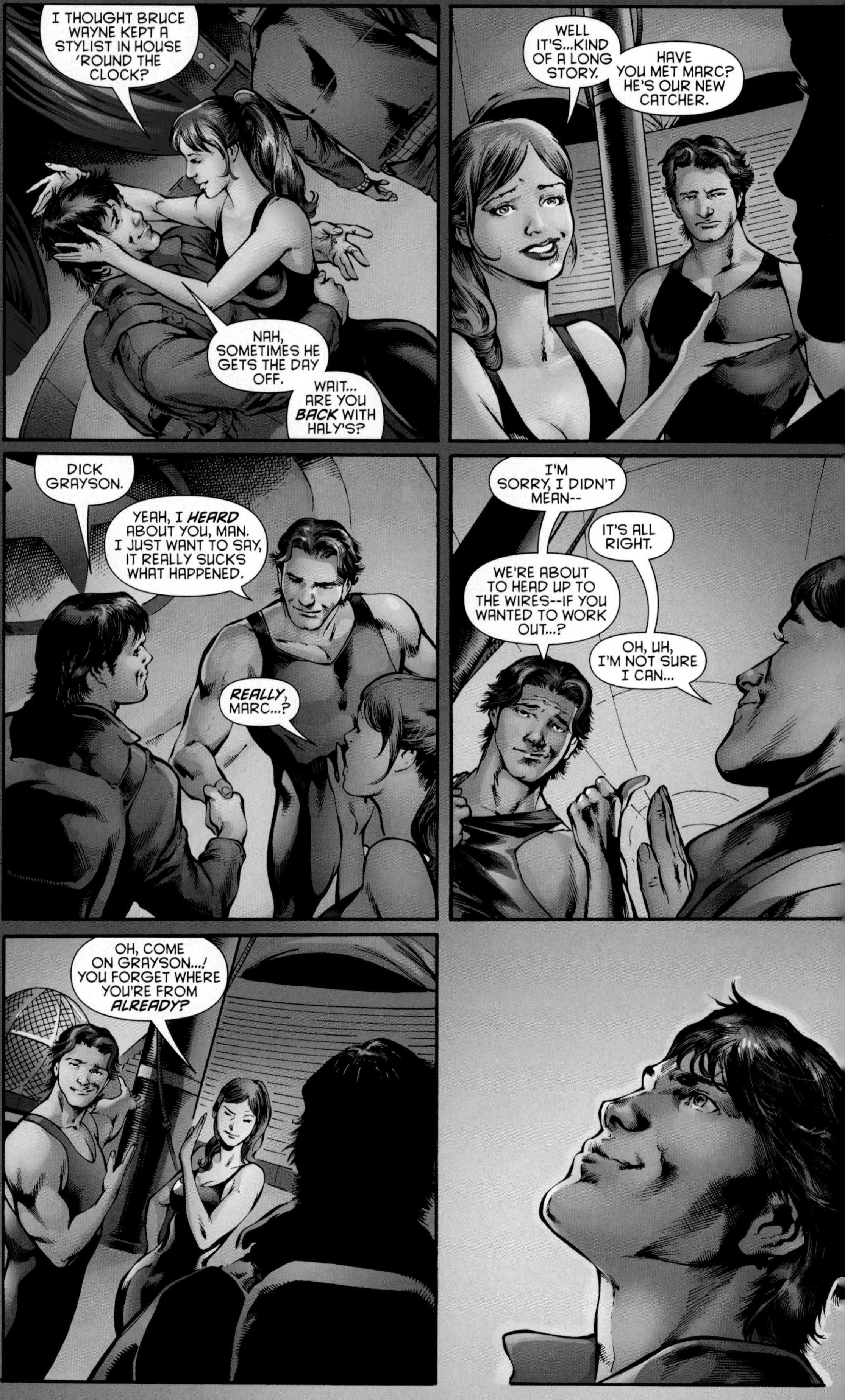
I THOUGHT BRUCE WAYNE KEPT A STYLIST IN HOUSE 'ROUND THE CLOCK?
NAH, SOMETIMES HE GETS THE DAY OFF.
WAIT... ARE YOU BACK WITH HALY'S?
WELL IT'S...KIND OF A LONG STORY.
HAVE YOU MET MARC? HE'S OUR NEW CATCHER.
DICK GRAYSON.
YEAH, I HEARD ABOUT YOU, MAN. I JUST WANT TO SAY, IT REALLY SUCKS WHAT HAPPENED.
REALLY, MARC...?
I'M SORRY, I DIDN'T MEAN--
IT'S ALL RIGHT.
WE'RE ABOUT TO HEAD UP TO THE WIRES--IF YOU WANTED TO WORK OUT...?
OH, UH, I'M NOT SURE I CAN...
OH, COME ON GRAYSON...! YOU FORGET WHERE YOU'RE FROM ALREADY?

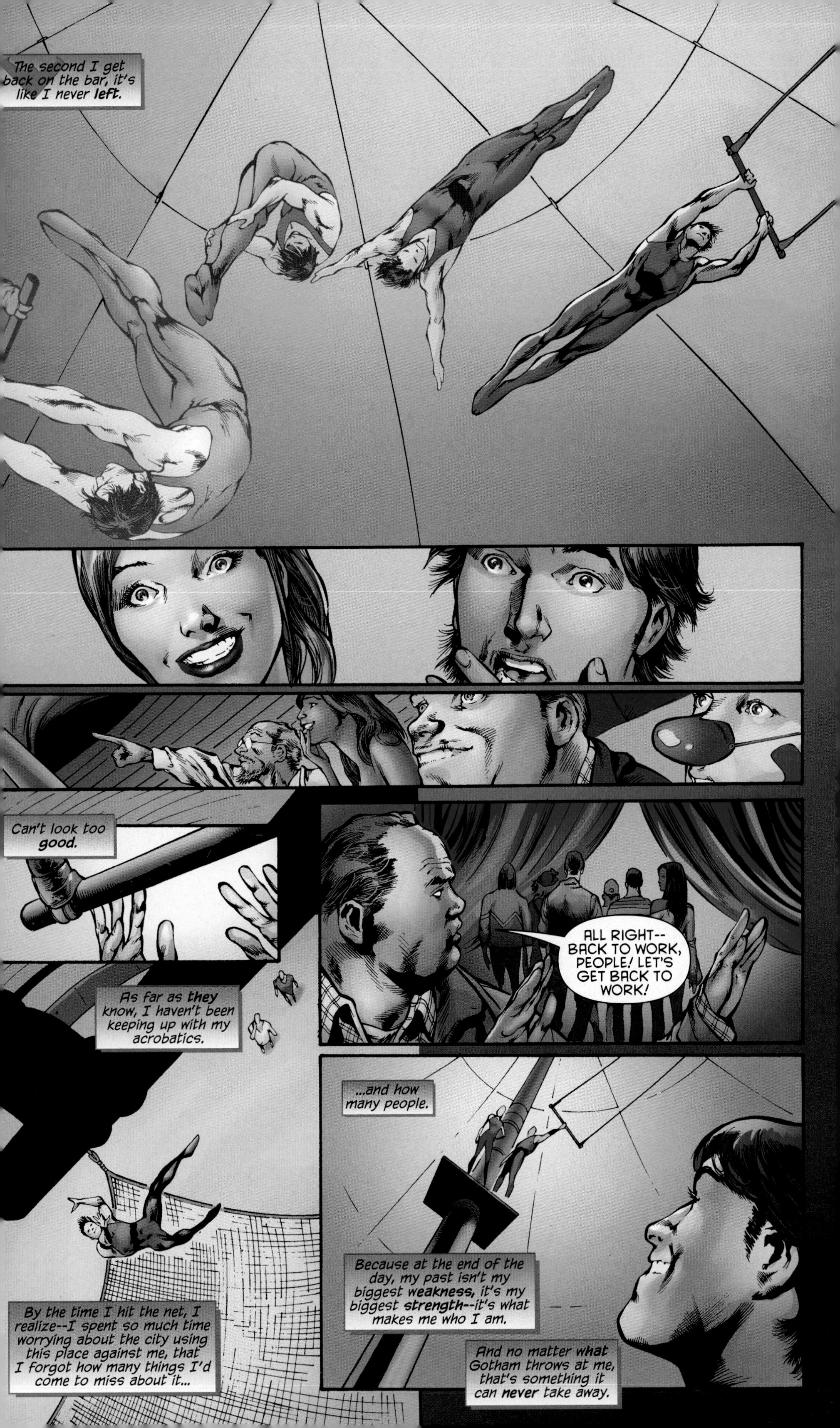
The second I get back on the bar, it's like I never left.
Can't look too good.
As far as they know, I haven't been keeping up with my acrobatics.
ALL RIGHT-- BACK TO WORK, PEOPLE! LET'S GET BACK TO WORK!
...and how many people.
By the time I hit the net, I realize--I spent so much time worrying about the city using this place against me, that I forgot how many things I'd come to miss about it...
Because at the end of the day, my past isn't my biggest weakness, it's my biggest strength--it's what makes me who I am.
And no matter what Gotham throws at me, that's something it can never take away.

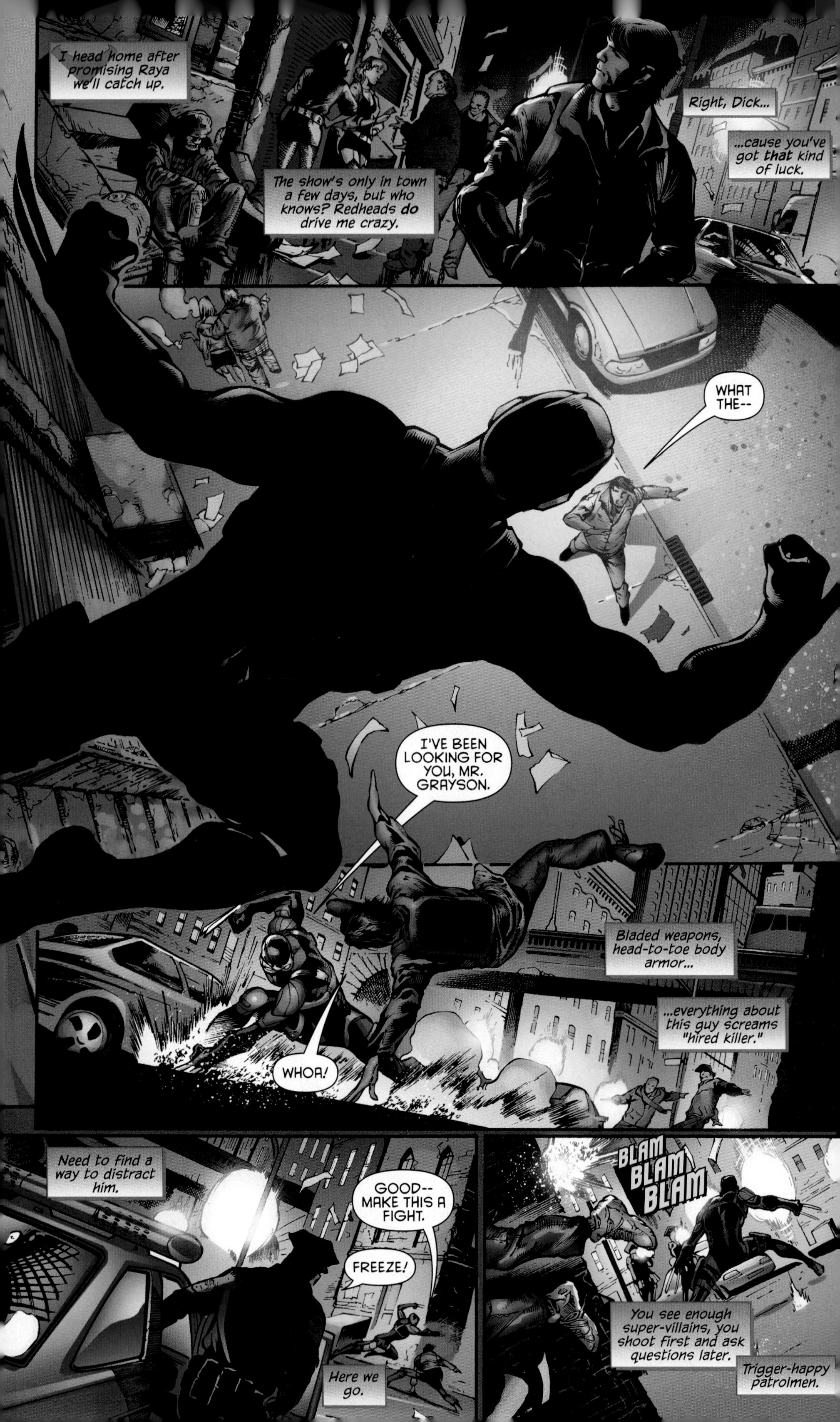

I head home after promising Raya we'll catch up.
The show's only in town a few days, but who knows? Redheads do drive me crazy.
Right, Dick...
...cause you've got that kind of luck.
WHAT THE--
I'VE BEEN LOOKING FOR YOU, MR. GRAYSON.
Bladed weapons, head-to-toe body armor...
...everything about this guy screams "hired killer."
WHOA!
Need to find a way to distract him.
GOOD-- MAKE THIS A FIGHT.
FREEZE!
Here we go.
BLAM BLAM BLAM
You see enough super-villains, you shoot first and ask questions later.
Trigger-happy patrolmen.

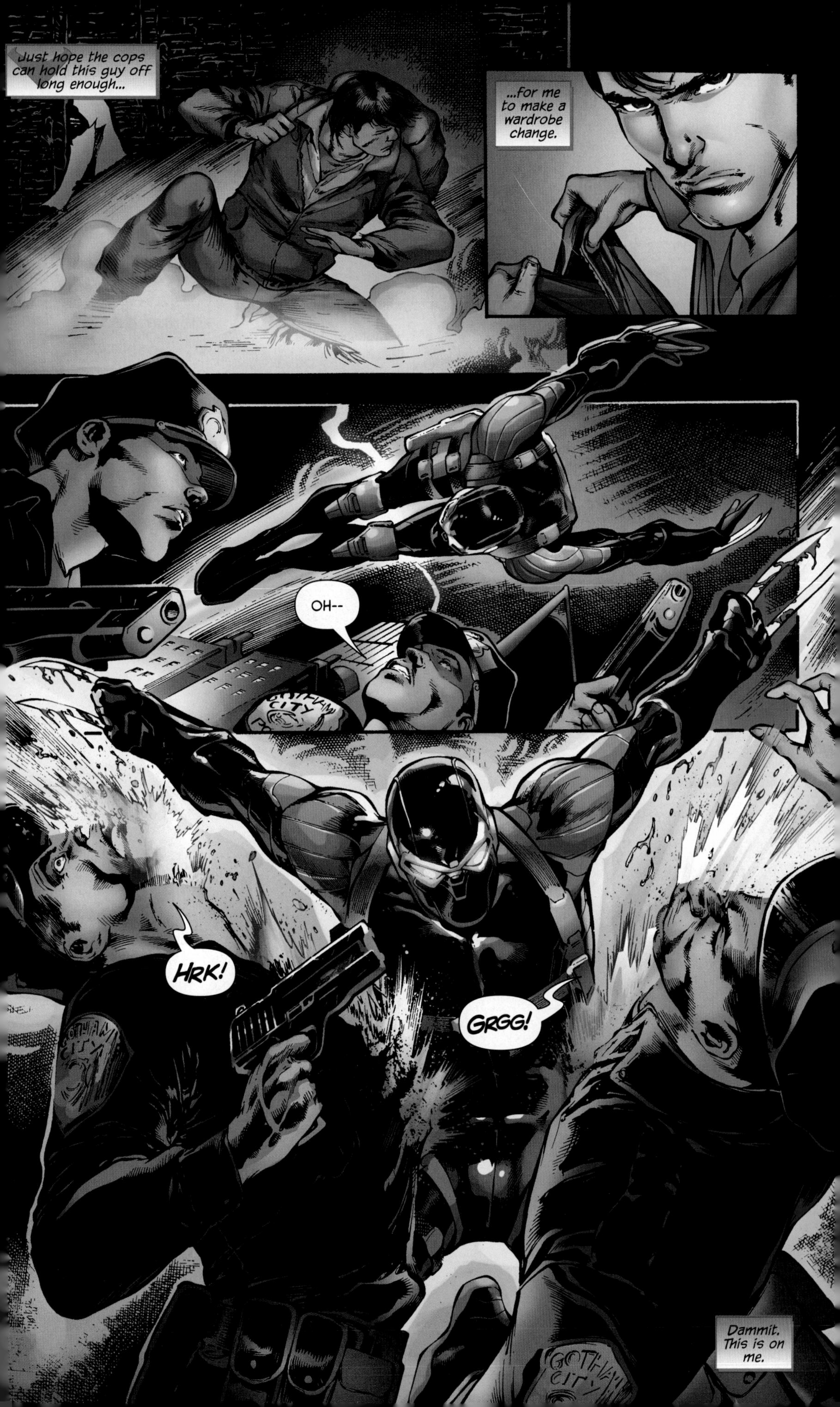
Just hope the cops can hold this guy off long enough...
...for me to make a wardrobe change.
OH--
HRK!
GRGG!
Dammit. This is on me.

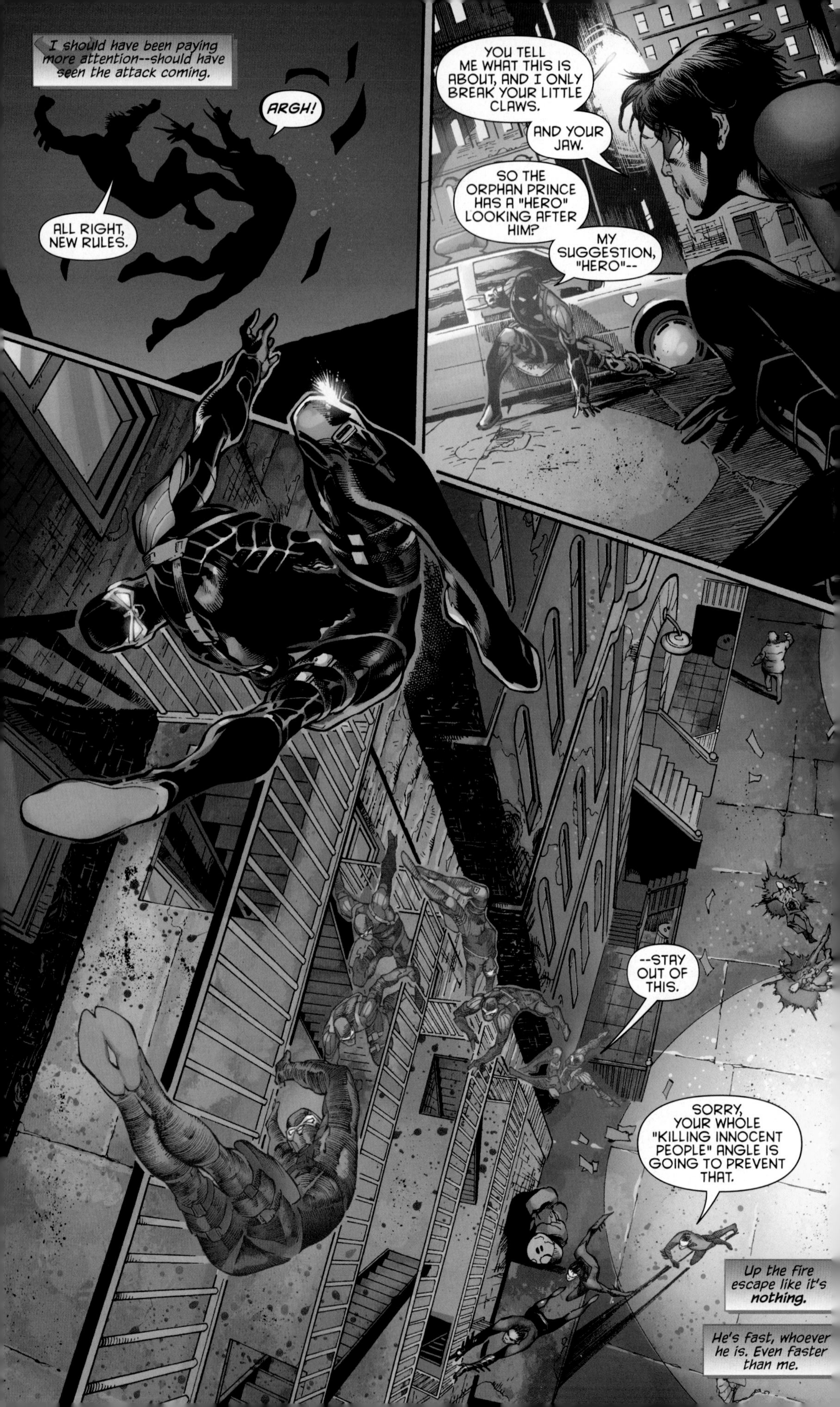

I should have been paying more attention--should have seen the attack coming.
ARGH!
ALL RIGHT, NEW RULES.
YOU TELL ME WHAT THIS IS ABOUT, AND I ONLY BREAK YOUR LITTLE CLAWS.
AND YOUR JAW.
SO THE ORPHAN PRINCE HAS A "HERO" LOOKING AFTER HIM?
MY SUGGESTION, "HERO"--
--STAY OUT OF THIS.
SORRY, YOUR WHOLE "KILLING INNOCENT PEOPLE" ANGLE IS GOING TO PREVENT THAT.
Up the fire escape like it's **nothing.**
He's fast, whoever he is. Even faster than me.

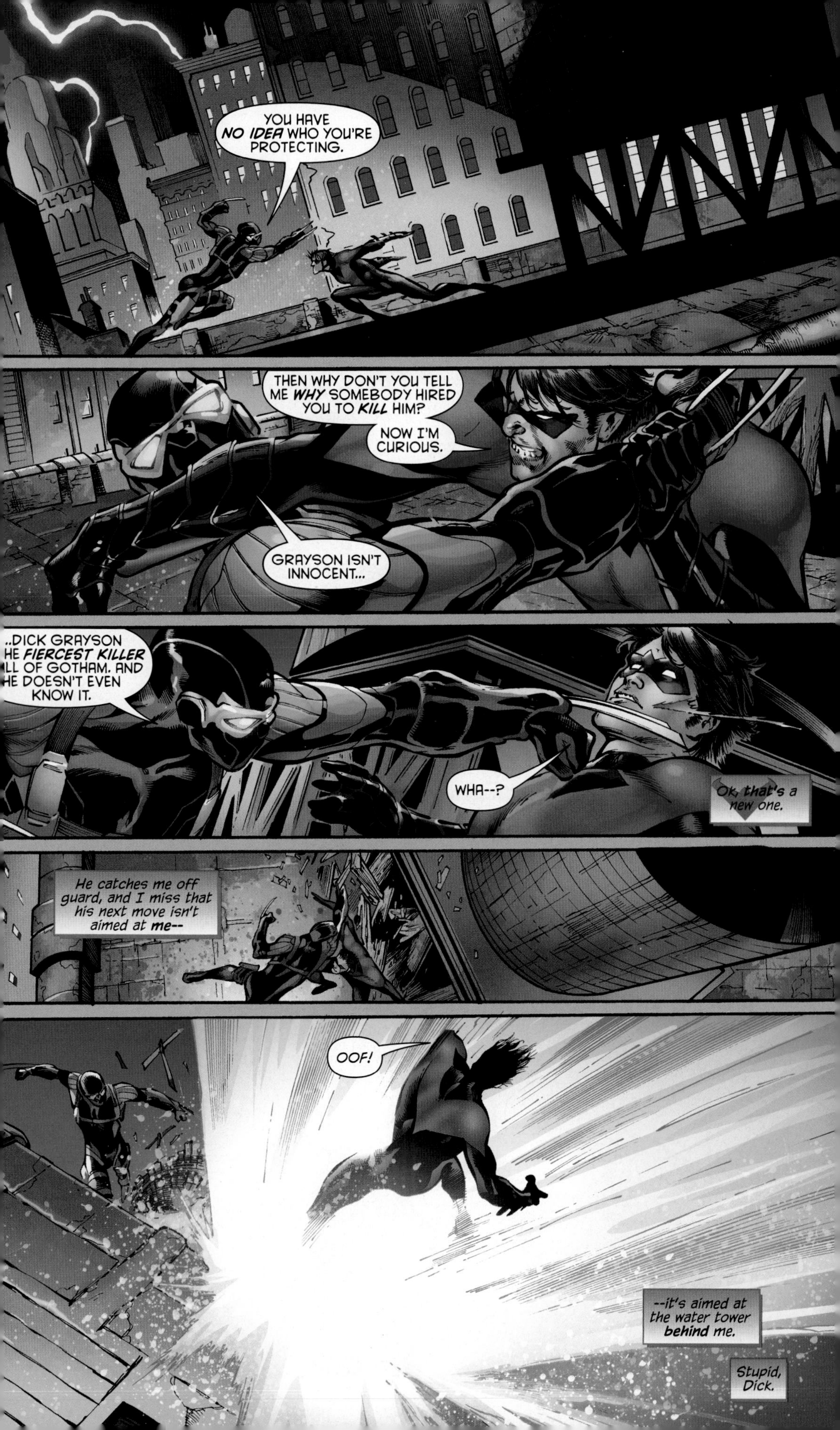
YOU HAVE NO IDEA WHO YOU'RE PROTECTING.
THEN WHY DON'T YOU TELL ME WHY SOMEBODY HIRED YOU TO KILL HIM?
NOW I'M CURIOUS.
GRAYSON ISN'T INNOCENT...
..DICK GRAYSON HE FIERCEST KILLER LL OF GOTHAM. AND HE DOESN'T EVEN KNOW IT.
WHA--?
Ok, that's a new one.
He catches me off guard, and I miss that his next move isn't aimed at me--
OOF!
--it's aimed at the water tower behind me.
Stupid, Dick.

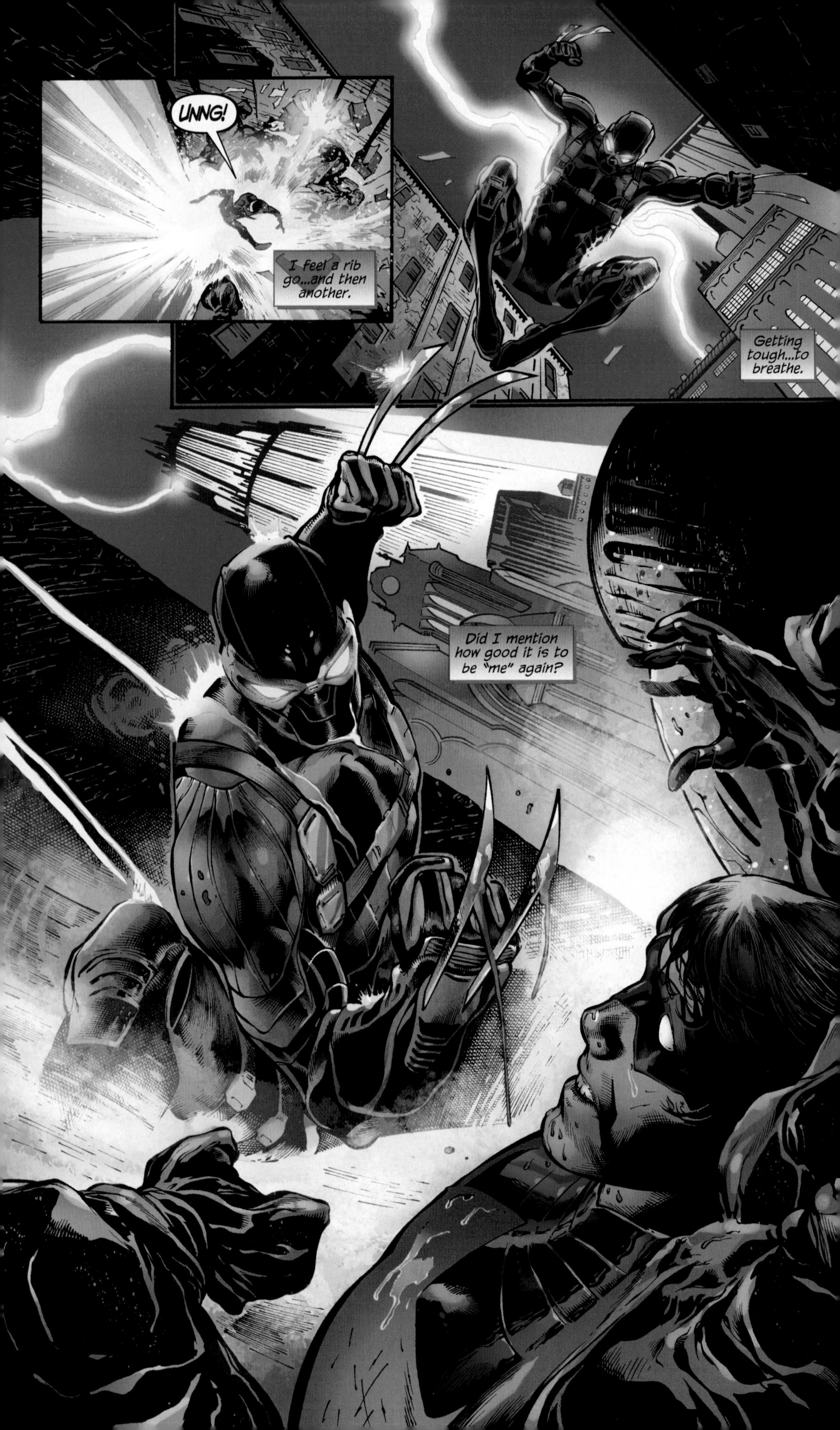
UNNG!
I feel a rib go...and then another.
Getting tough...to breathe.
Did I mention how good it is to be "me" again?

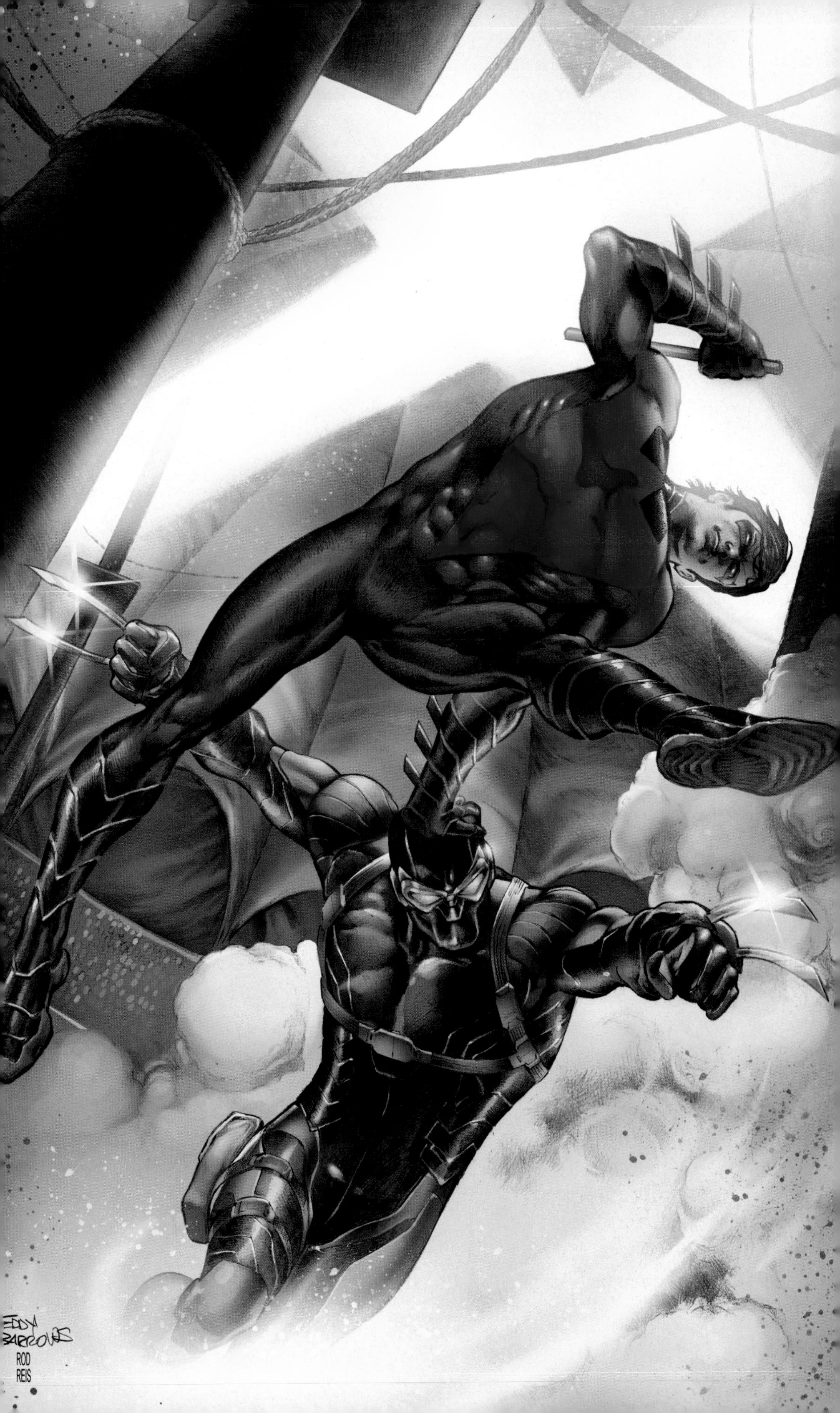
EDDY BARROWS
ROD REIS

KYLE HIGGINS writer EDDY BARROWS penciller JP MAYER & PAULO SIQUEIRA inkers cover art by Eddy Barrows & Rod Reis

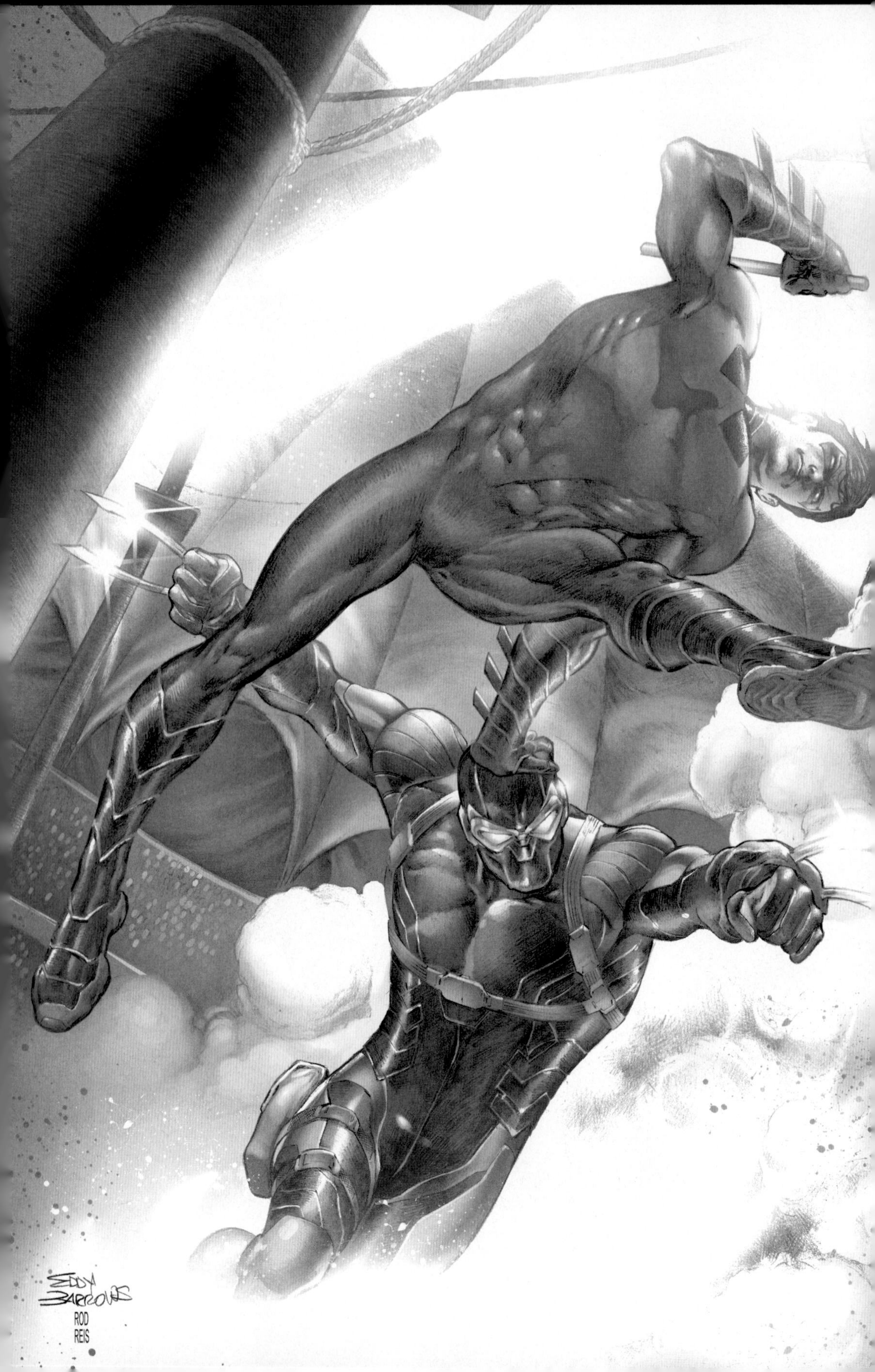
EDDY BARROWS
ROD REIS

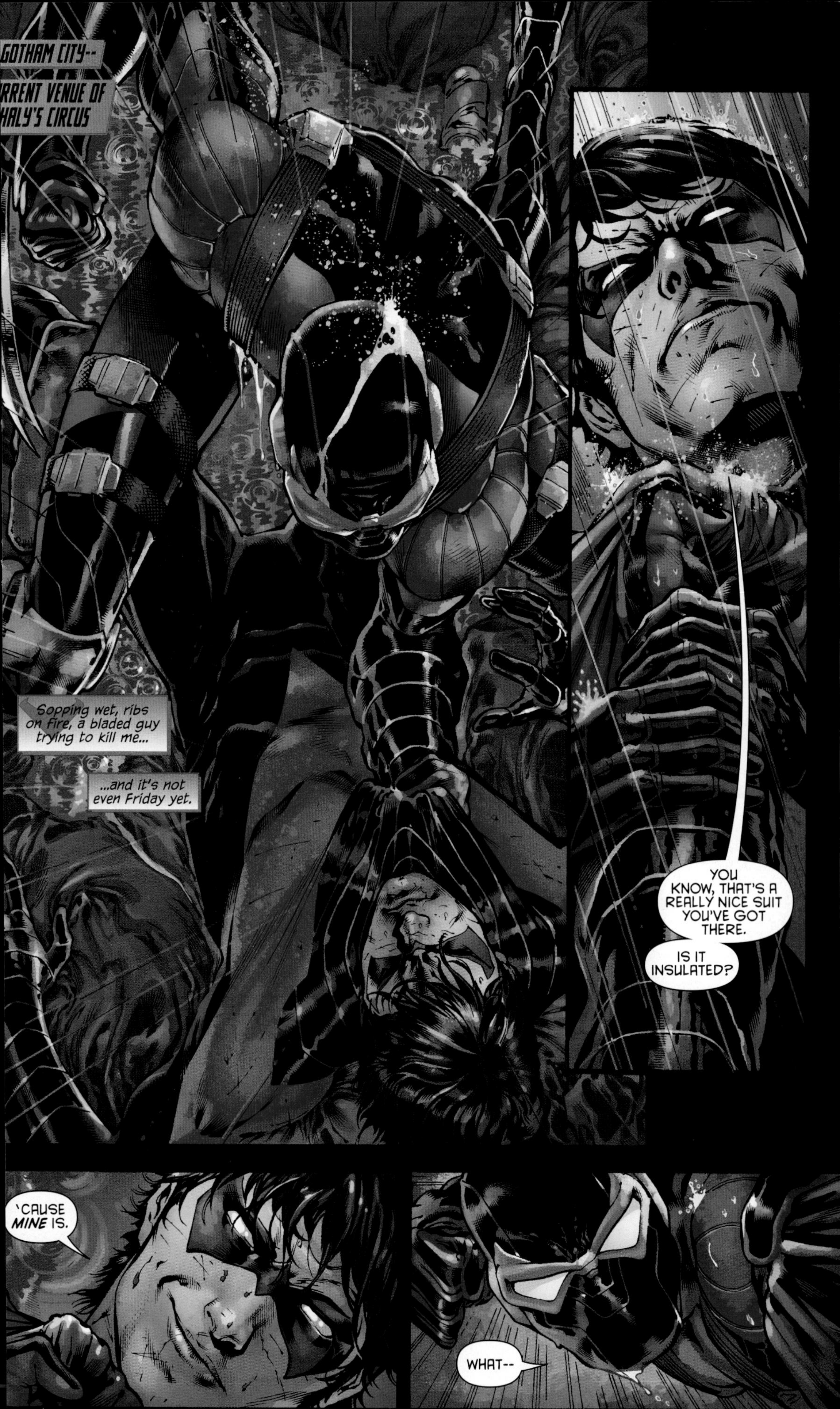

GOTHAM CITY--
RRENT VENUE OF HALY'S CIRCUS
Sopping wet, ribs on fire, a bladed guy trying to kill me...
...and it's not even Friday yet.
YOU KNOW, THAT'S A REALLY NICE SUIT YOU'VE GOT THERE.
IS IT INSULATED?
'CAUSE MINE IS.
WHAT--

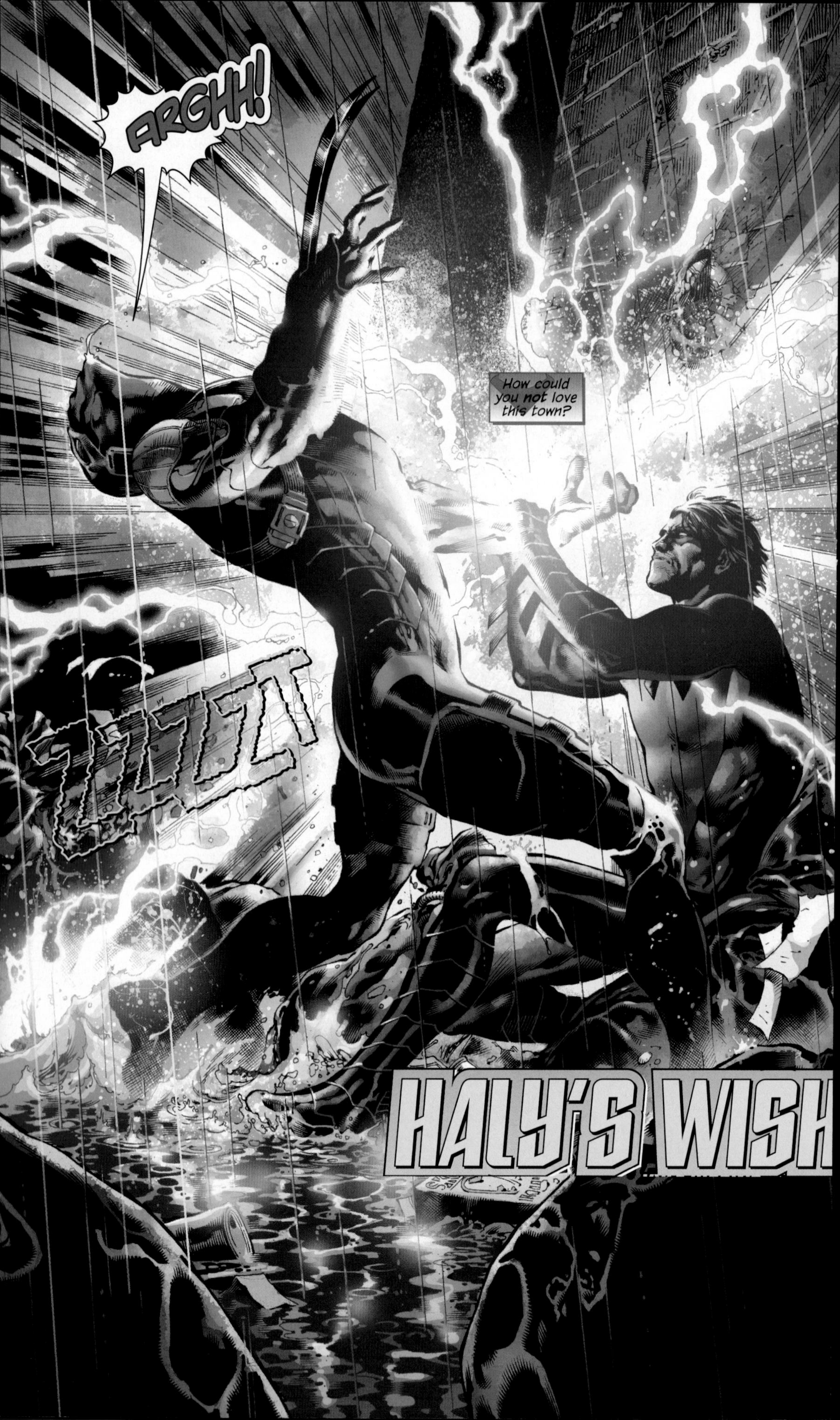
ARGHH!
How could you not love this town?
ZZZZZT
HALY'S WISH

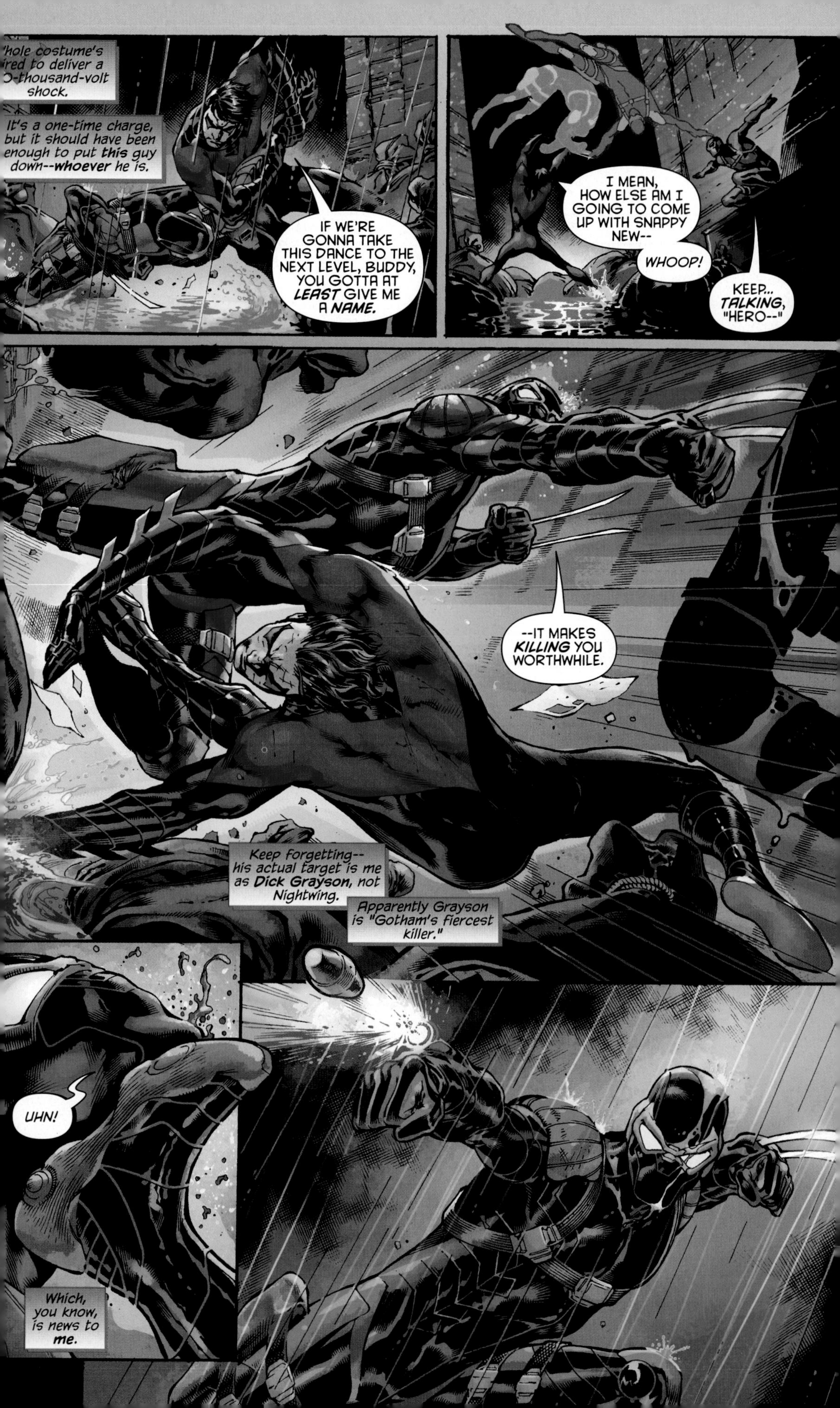

'hole costume's
ired to deliver a
0-thousand-volt
shock.
It's a one-time charge, but it should have been enough to put **this** guy down--**whoever** he is.
IF WE'RE GONNA TAKE THIS DANCE TO THE NEXT LEVEL, BUDDY, YOU GOTTA AT ***LEAST*** GIVE ME A ***NAME.***
I MEAN, HOW ELSE AM I GOING TO COME UP WITH SNAPPY NEW--
WHOOP!
KEEP... ***TALKING***, "HERO--"
--IT MAKES ***KILLING*** YOU WORTHWHILE.
*Keep forgetting--his actual target is me as **Dick Grayson**, not Nightwing.*
Apparently Grayson is "Gotham's fiercest killer."
UHN!
*Which, you know, is news to **me**.*

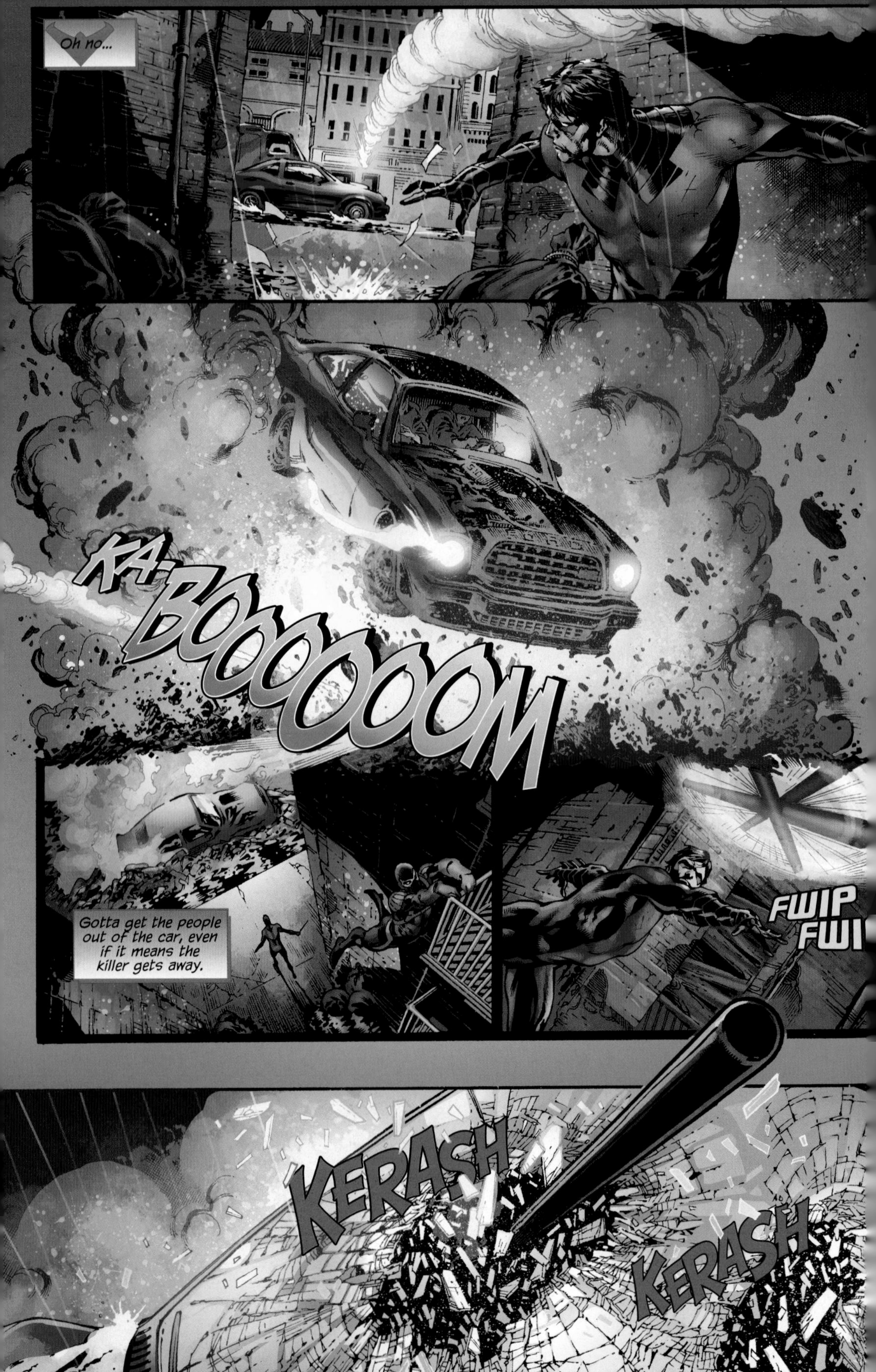
Oh no...
KA-BOOOOOOM
Gotta get the people out of the car, even if it means the killer gets away.
FWIP
FWI
KERASH
KERASH

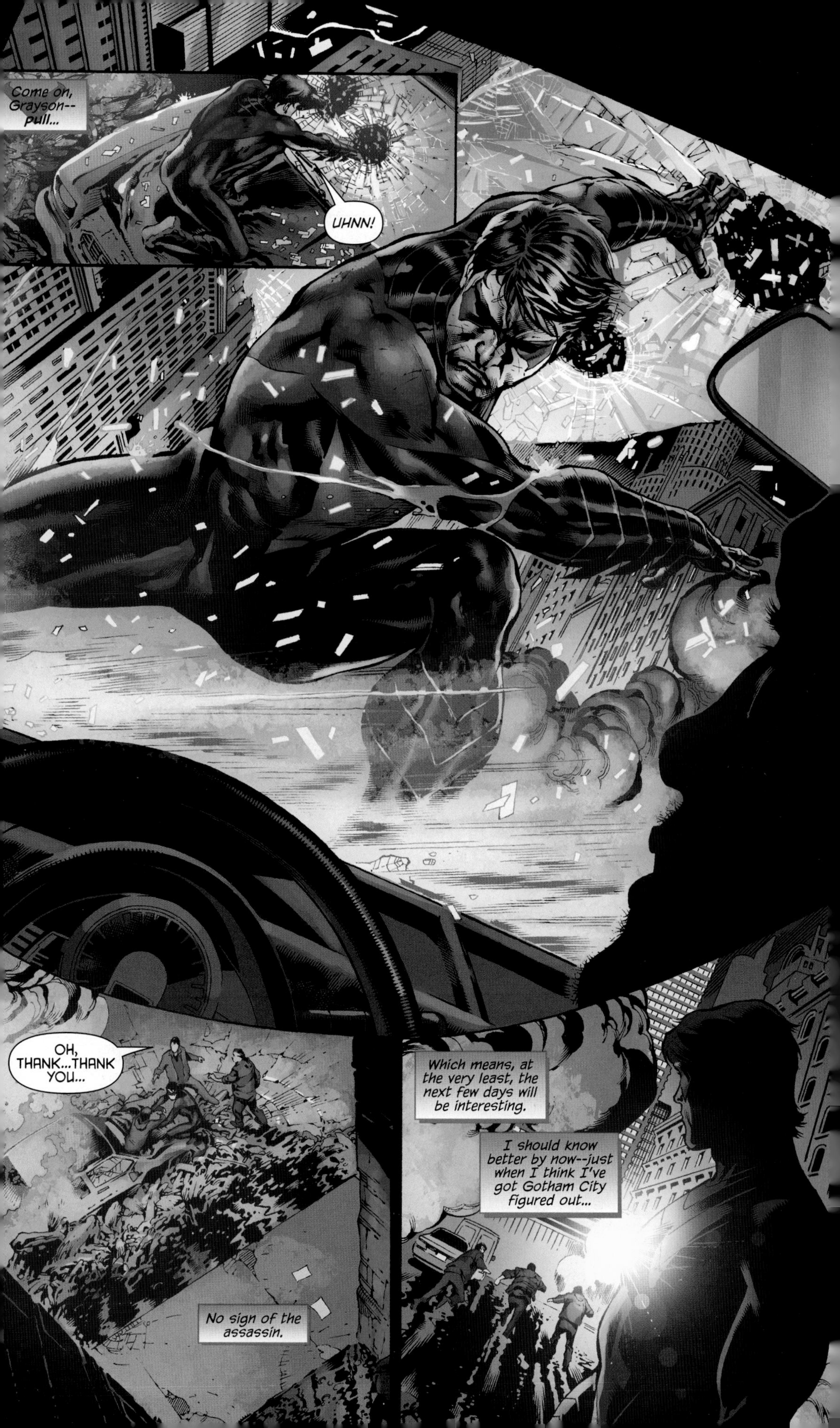
Come on, Grayson-- pull...
UHNN!
OH, THANK...THANK YOU...
No sign of the assassin.
Which means, at the very least, the next few days will be interesting.
I should know better by now--just when I think I've got Gotham City figured out...

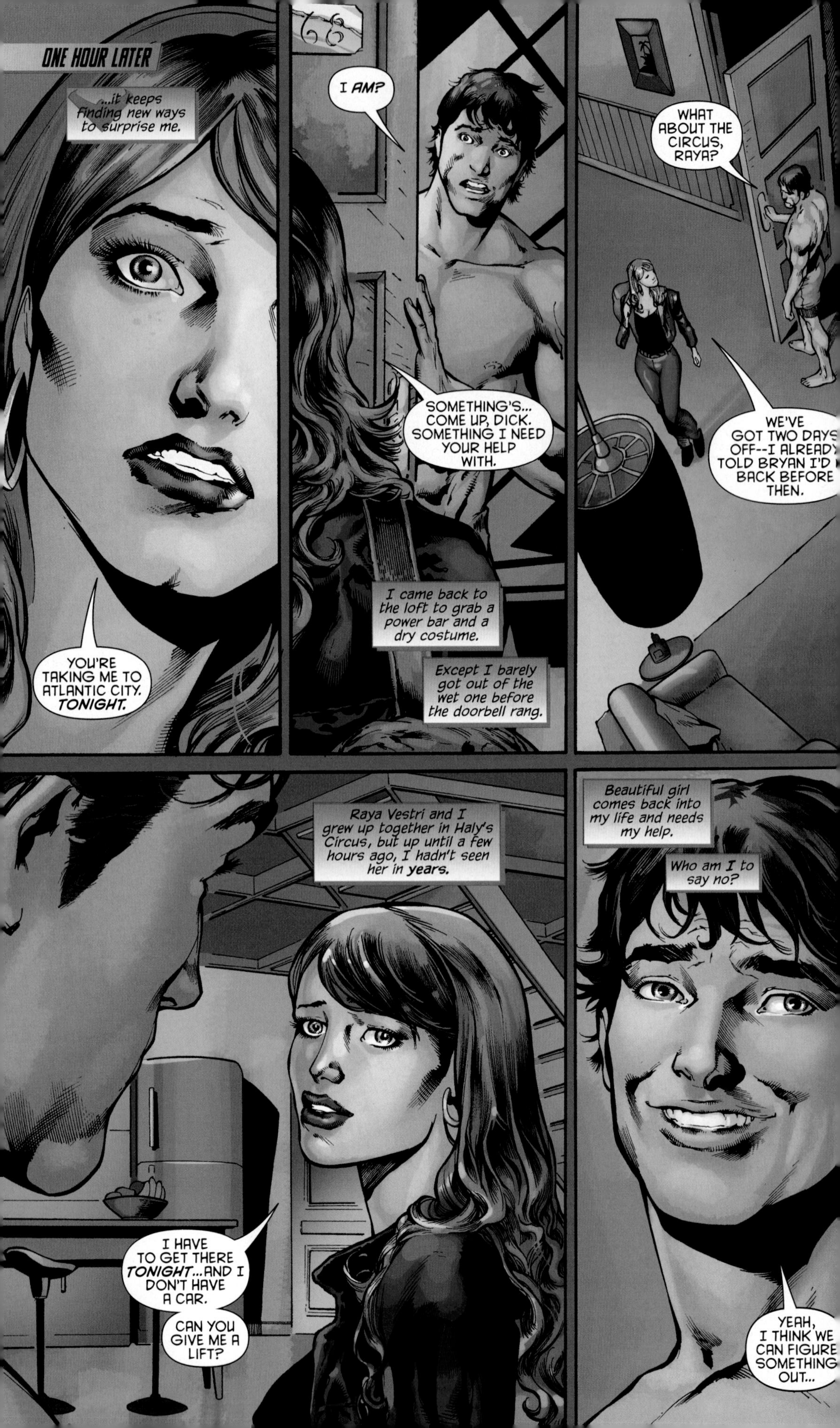
ONE HOUR LATER
...it keeps finding new ways to surprise me.
YOU'RE TAKING ME TO ATLANTIC CITY. TONIGHT.
I AM?
SOMETHING'S... COME UP, DICK. SOMETHING I NEED YOUR HELP WITH.
I came back to the loft to grab a power bar and a dry costume.
Except I barely got out of the wet one before the doorbell rang.
WHAT ABOUT THE CIRCUS, RAYA?
WE'VE GOT TWO DAYS OFF--I ALREADY TOLD BRYAN I'D BACK BEFORE THEN.
Raya Vestri and I grew up together in Haly's Circus, but up until a few hours ago, I hadn't seen her in years.
I HAVE TO GET THERE TONIGHT...AND I DON'T HAVE A CAR.
CAN YOU GIVE ME A LIFT?
Beautiful girl comes back into my life and needs my help.
Who am I to say no?
YEAH, I THINK WE CAN FIGURE SOMETHING OUT...

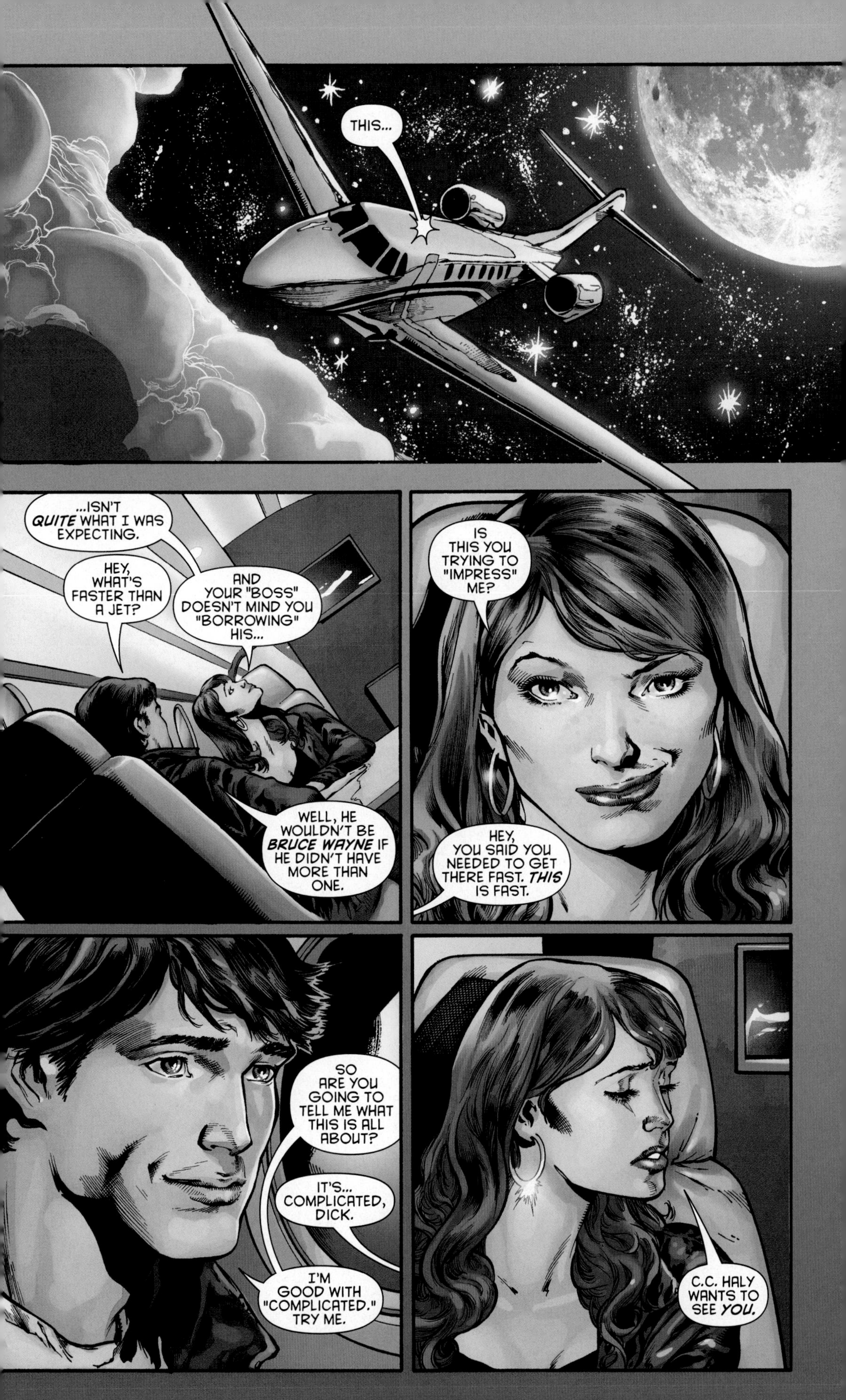
THIS...
...ISN'T QUITE WHAT I WAS EXPECTING.
HEY, WHAT'S FASTER THAN A JET?
AND YOUR "BOSS" DOESN'T MIND YOU "BORROWING" HIS...
WELL, HE WOULDN'T BE BRUCE WAYNE IF HE DIDN'T HAVE MORE THAN ONE.
IS THIS YOU TRYING TO "IMPRESS" ME?
HEY, YOU SAID YOU NEEDED TO GET THERE FAST. THIS IS FAST.
SO ARE YOU GOING TO TELL ME WHAT THIS IS ALL ABOUT?
IT'S... COMPLICATED, DICK.
I'M GOOD WITH "COMPLICATED." TRY ME.
C.C. HALY WANTS TO SEE YOU.

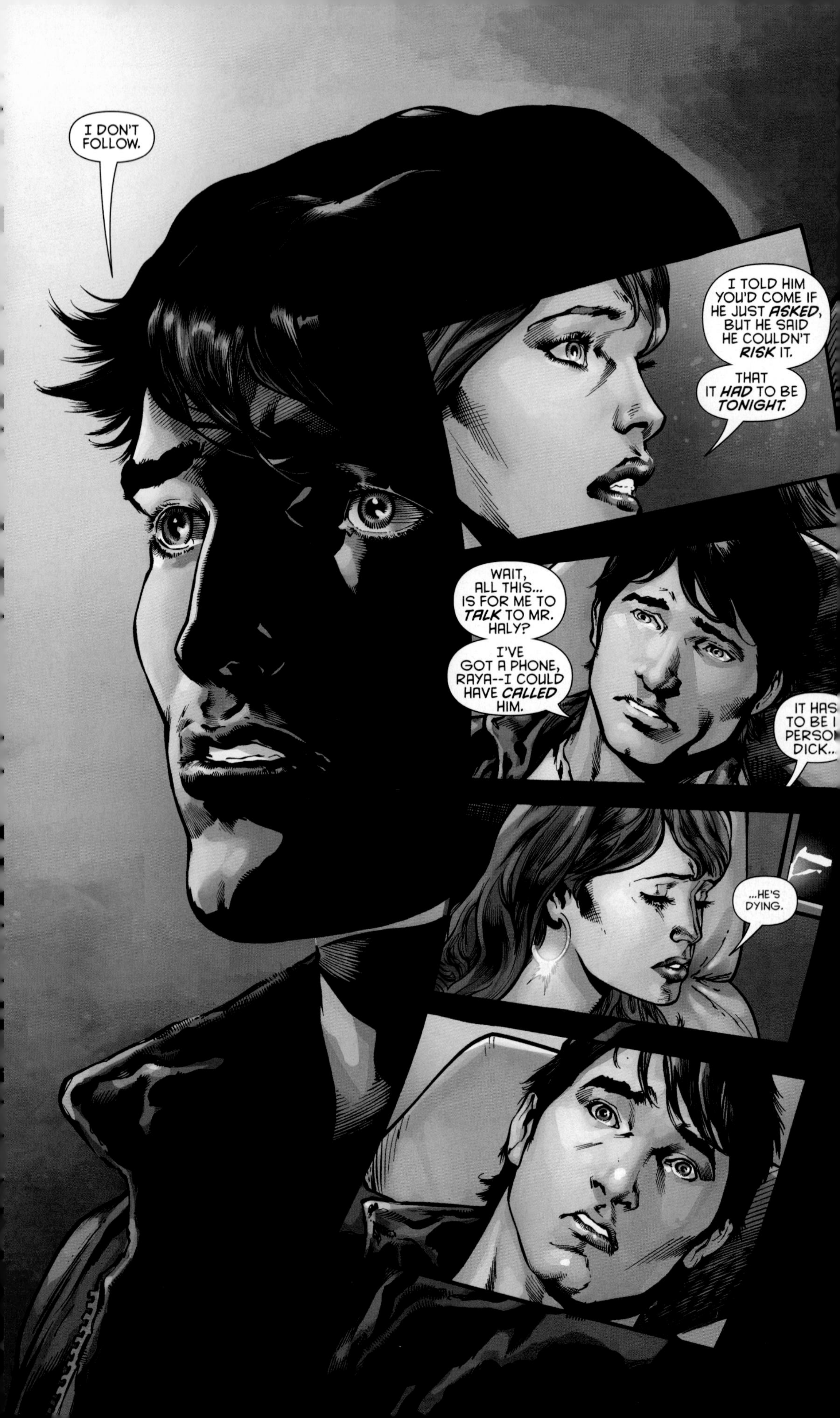
I DON'T FOLLOW.
I TOLD HIM YOU'D COME IF HE JUST ASKED, BUT HE SAID HE COULDN'T RISK IT.
THAT IT HAD TO BE TONIGHT.
WAIT, ALL THIS... IS FOR ME TO TALK TO MR. HALY?
I'VE GOT A PHONE, RAYA--I COULD HAVE CALLED HIM.
...HE'S DYING.

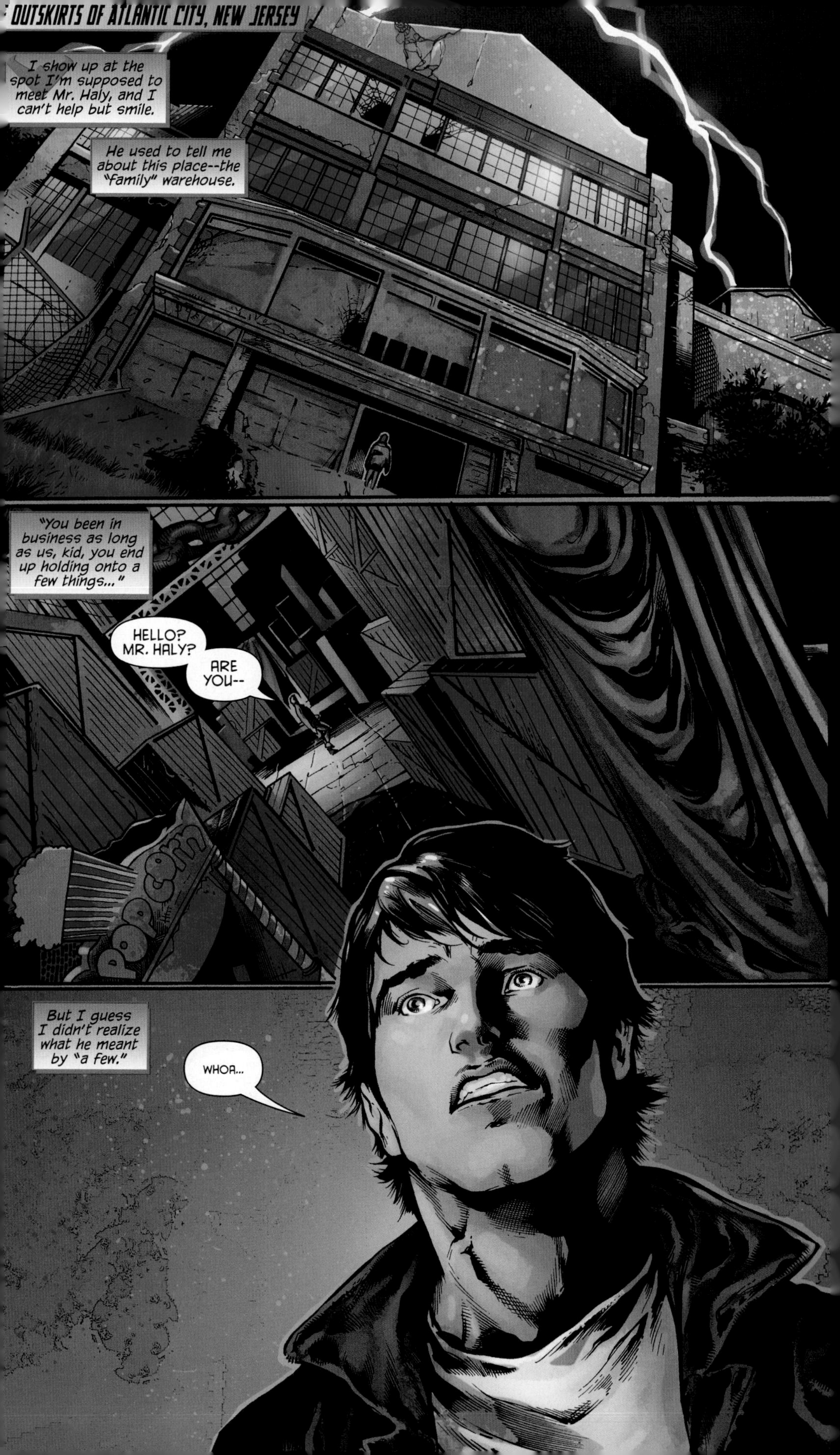

OUTSKIRTS OF ATLANTIC CITY, NEW JERSEY
I show up at the spot I'm supposed to meet Mr. Haly, and I can't help but smile.
He used to tell me about this place--the "family" warehouse.
"You been in business as long as us, kid, you end up holding onto a few things..."
HELLO? MR. HALY?
ARE YOU--
POPCORN
But I guess I didn't realize what he meant by "a few."
WHOA...

MR. HALY...?

SORRY HOW THIS ALL CAME TOGETHER, DICKIE, BUT I DON'T HAVE MUCH TIME. DAMN *TUMOR'S* EATING ME FROM THE INSIDE...

...AND I NEED TO MAKE SURE YOU HAVE *THIS* BEFORE THE CANCER FINISHES THE JOB...

THE DEED... TO EVERYTHING ON THE ROAD, AND EVERYTHING HERE. IT'S ALL *YOURS*, KID.

WHAT? HOW DO YOU KNOW...?

WHAT? MR. HALY...I CAN'T--

CAN'T WHY? BECAUSE YOU'RE TOO BUSY AS A BIG-TIME "HERO" NOW?

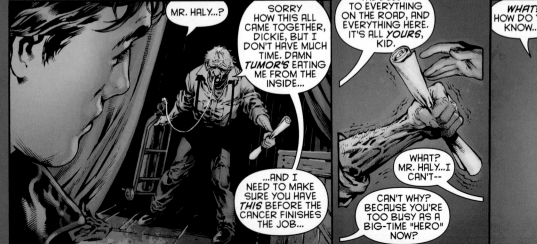

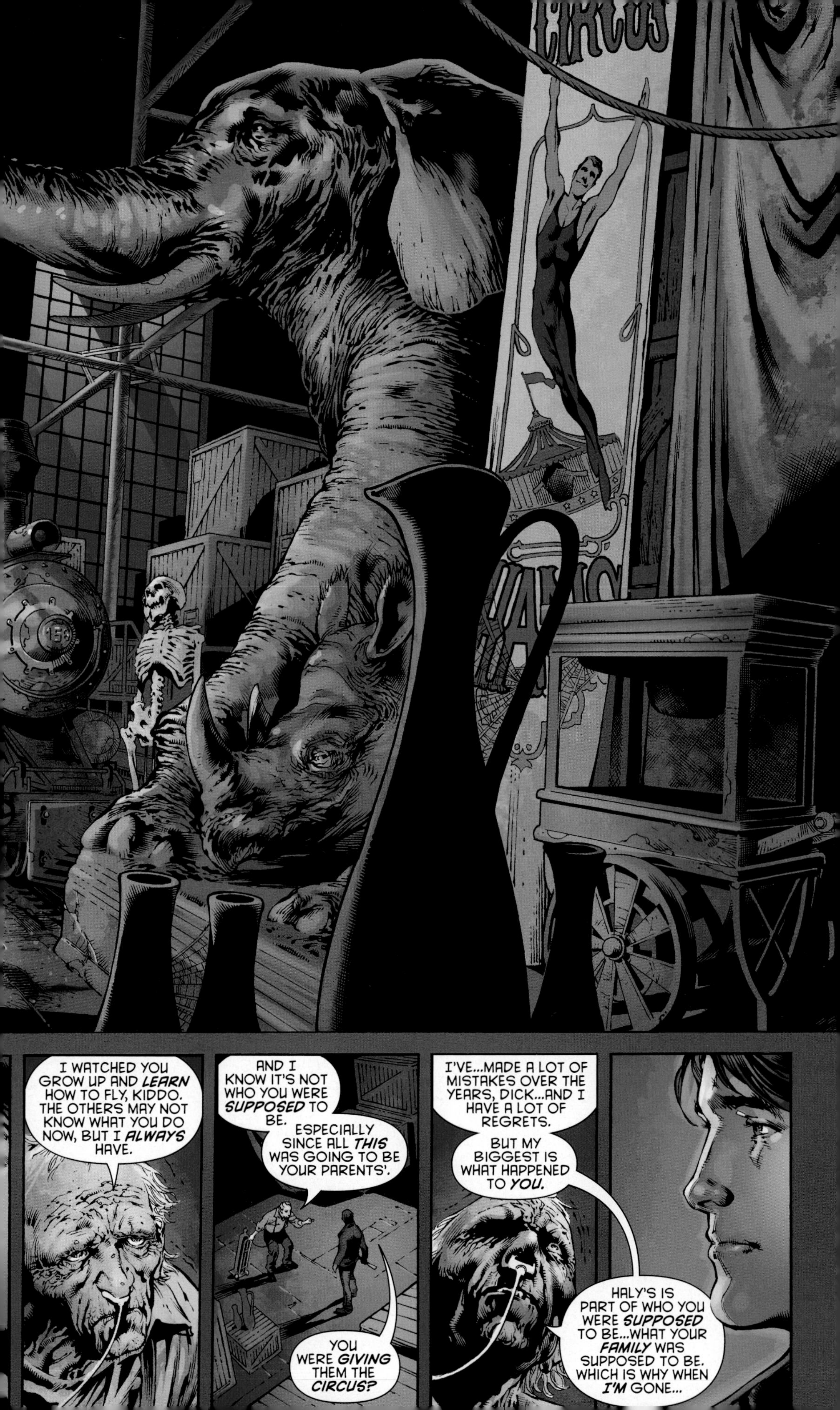
CIRCUS
I WATCHED YOU GROW UP AND *LEARN* HOW TO FLY, KIDDO. THE OTHERS MAY NOT KNOW WHAT YOU DO NOW, BUT I *ALWAYS* HAVE.
AND I KNOW IT'S NOT WHO YOU WERE *SUPPOSED* TO BE.
ESPECIALLY SINCE ALL *THIS* WAS GOING TO BE YOUR PARENTS'.
YOU WERE *GIVING* THEM THE *CIRCUS?*
I'VE...MADE A LOT OF MISTAKES OVER THE YEARS, DICK...AND I HAVE A LOT OF REGRETS.
BUT MY BIGGEST IS WHAT HAPPENED TO *YOU.*
HALY'S IS PART OF WHO YOU WERE *SUPPOSED* TO BE...WHAT YOUR *FAMILY* WAS SUPPOSED TO BE. WHICH IS WHY WHEN *I'M* GONE...

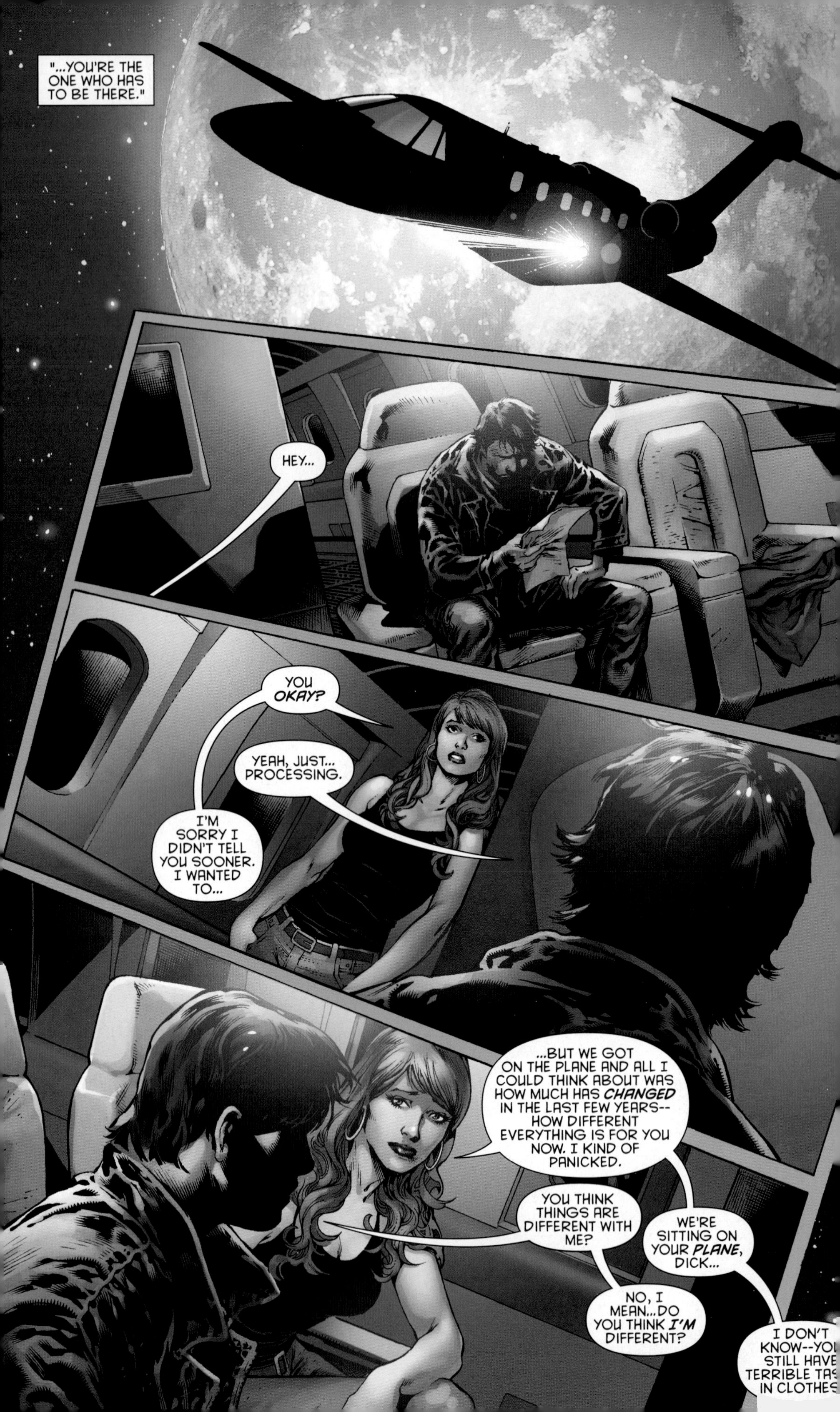
"...YOU'RE THE ONE WHO HAS TO BE THERE."
HEY...
YOU *OKAY?*
YEAH, JUST... PROCESSING.
I'M SORRY I DIDN'T TELL YOU SOONER. I WANTED TO...
...BUT WE GOT ON THE PLANE AND ALL I COULD THINK ABOUT WAS HOW MUCH HAS *CHANGED* IN THE LAST FEW YEARS--HOW DIFFERENT EVERYTHING IS FOR YOU NOW. I KIND OF PANICKED.
YOU THINK THINGS ARE DIFFERENT WITH ME?
WE'RE SITTING ON YOUR *PLANE*, DICK...
NO, I MEAN...DO YOU THINK *I'M* DIFFERENT?
I DON'T KNOW--YO STILL HAVE TERRIBLE TAS IN CLOTHES

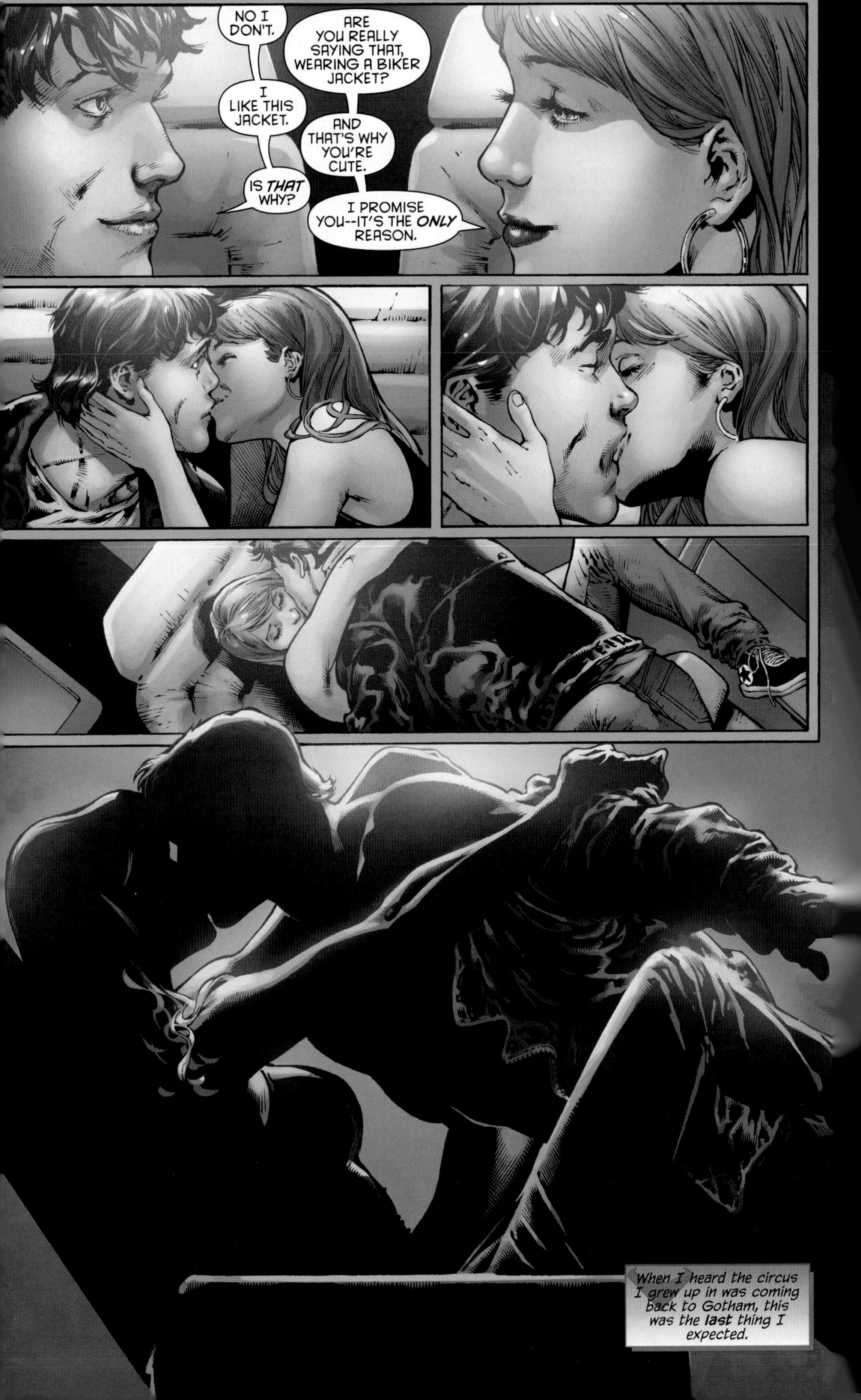

NO I DON'T.
ARE YOU REALLY SAYING THAT, WEARING A BIKER JACKET?
I LIKE THIS JACKET.
AND THAT'S WHY YOU'RE CUTE.
IS *THAT* WHY?
I PROMISE YOU--IT'S THE *ONLY* REASON.
When I heard the circus I grew up in was coming back to Gotham, this was the **last** thing I expected.

Raya...Mr. Haly...me *involved* with the circus again...

...my head is already swimming.

Everything feels familiar and different...all at the same time.

I guess that's the thing about revisiting your past.

It's easy for it to become your *present*.

CALL FOR YOU--GOT ROUTED UP HERE.

But is that such a *bad* thing?

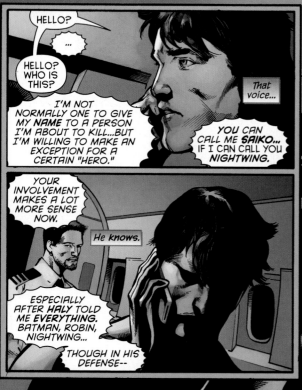

HELLO?

...

HELLO? WHO IS THIS?

I'M NOT NORMALLY ONE TO GIVE MY *NAME* TO A PERSON I'M ABOUT TO KILL...BUT I'M WILLING TO MAKE AN EXCEPTION FOR A CERTAIN "HERO."

That voice...

YOU CAN CALL ME *SAIKO*... IF I CAN CALL YOU *NIGHTWING*.

YOUR INVOLVEMENT MAKES A LOT MORE SENSE NOW.

He knows.

ESPECIALLY AFTER *HALY* TOLD ME *EVERYTHING*. BATMAN, ROBIN, NIGHTWING...

THOUGH IN HIS DEFENSE--

--PAIN IS QUITE A POWE. MOTIVATOR

WHAT DO YOU WANT?

FOR YOU TO WATCH ME KILL THE OLD MAN, DICK... RIGHT NOW.

THAT IS, C COURSE, UNL YOU CAN ST ME?

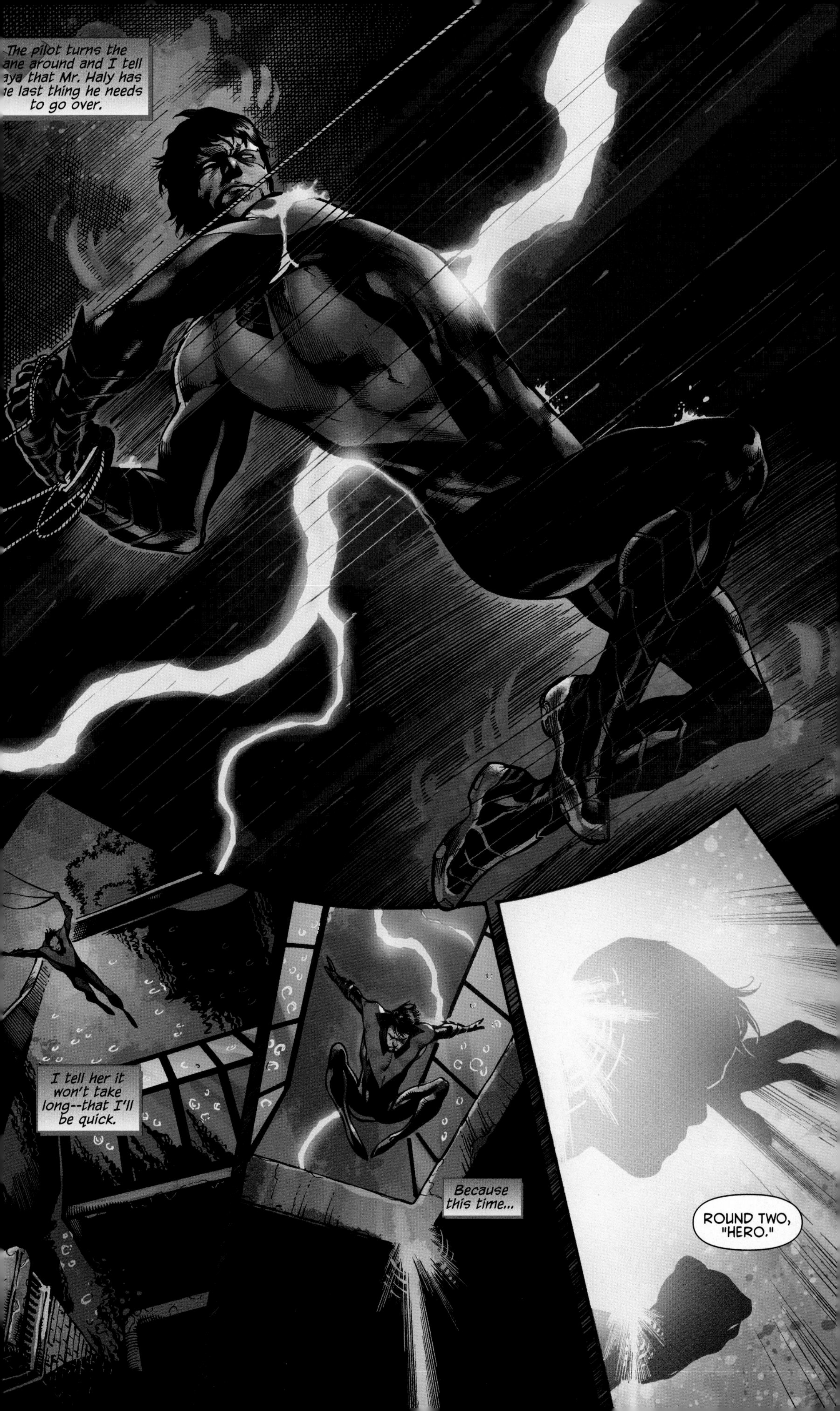
The pilot turns the
ane around and I tell
aya that Mr. Haly has
e last thing he needs
to go over.
I tell her it
won't take
long--that I'll
be quick.
Because
this time...
ROUND TWO,
"HERO."

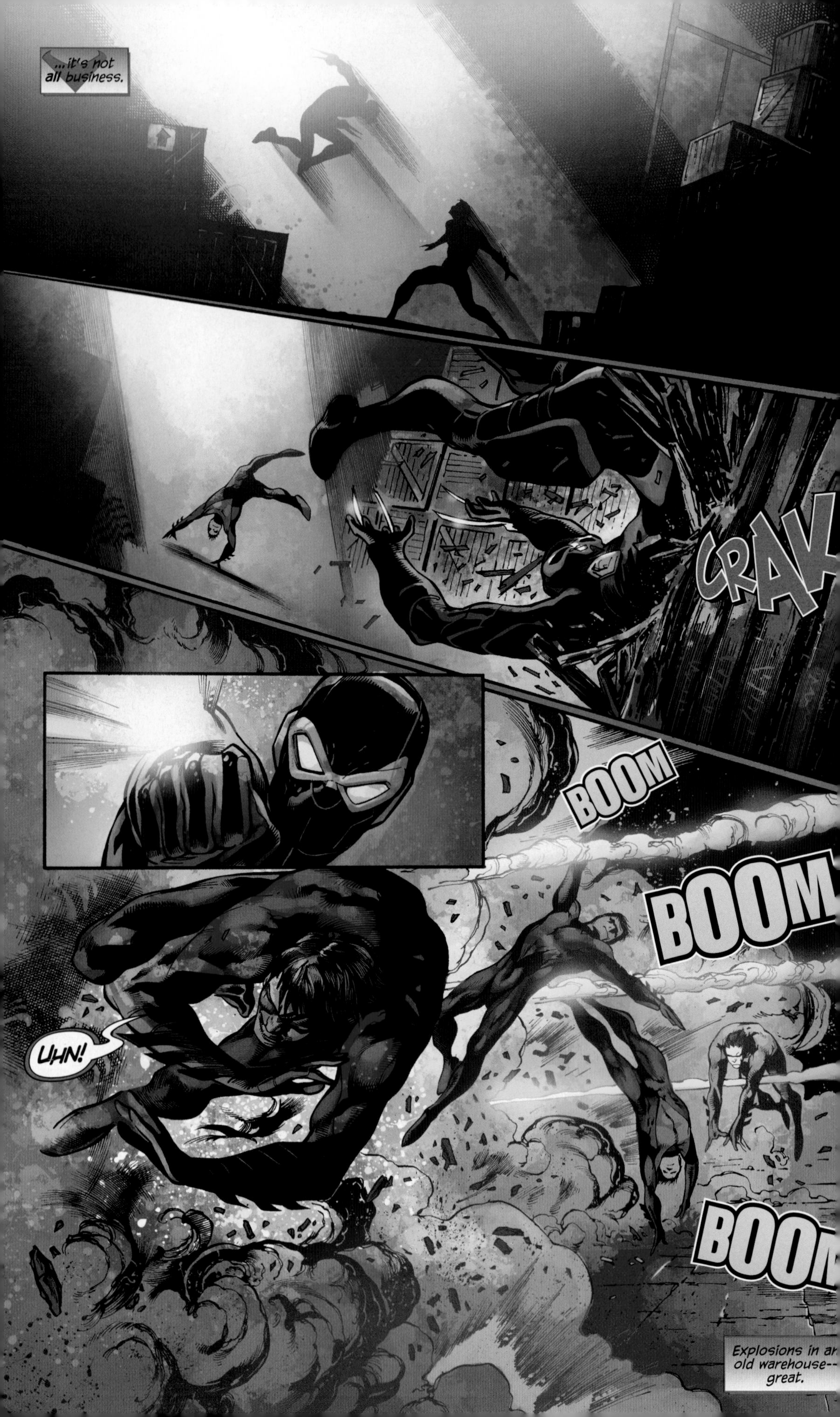
...it's not all business.
CRAK
BOOM
BOOM
UHN!
BOOM
Explosions in an old warehouse-- great.

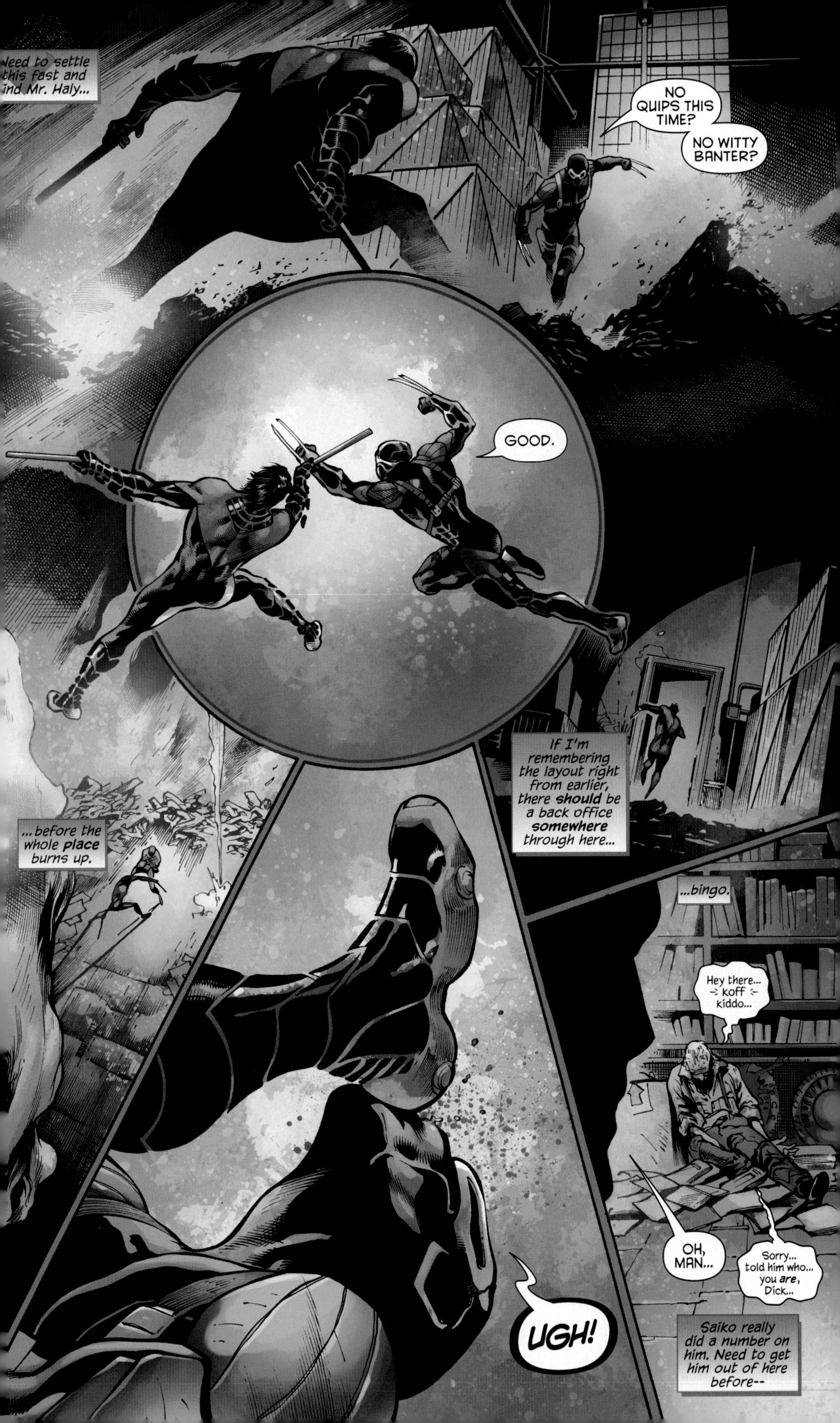
Need to settle this fast and find Mr. Haly...
NO QUIPS THIS TIME?
NO WITTY BANTER?
GOOD.
...before the whole place burns up.
If I'm remembering the layout right from earlier, there should be a back office somewhere through here...
...bingo.
UGH!
Hey there... koff kiddo...
OH, MAN...
Sorry... told him who... you are, Dick...
Saiko really did a number on him. Need to get him out of here before--

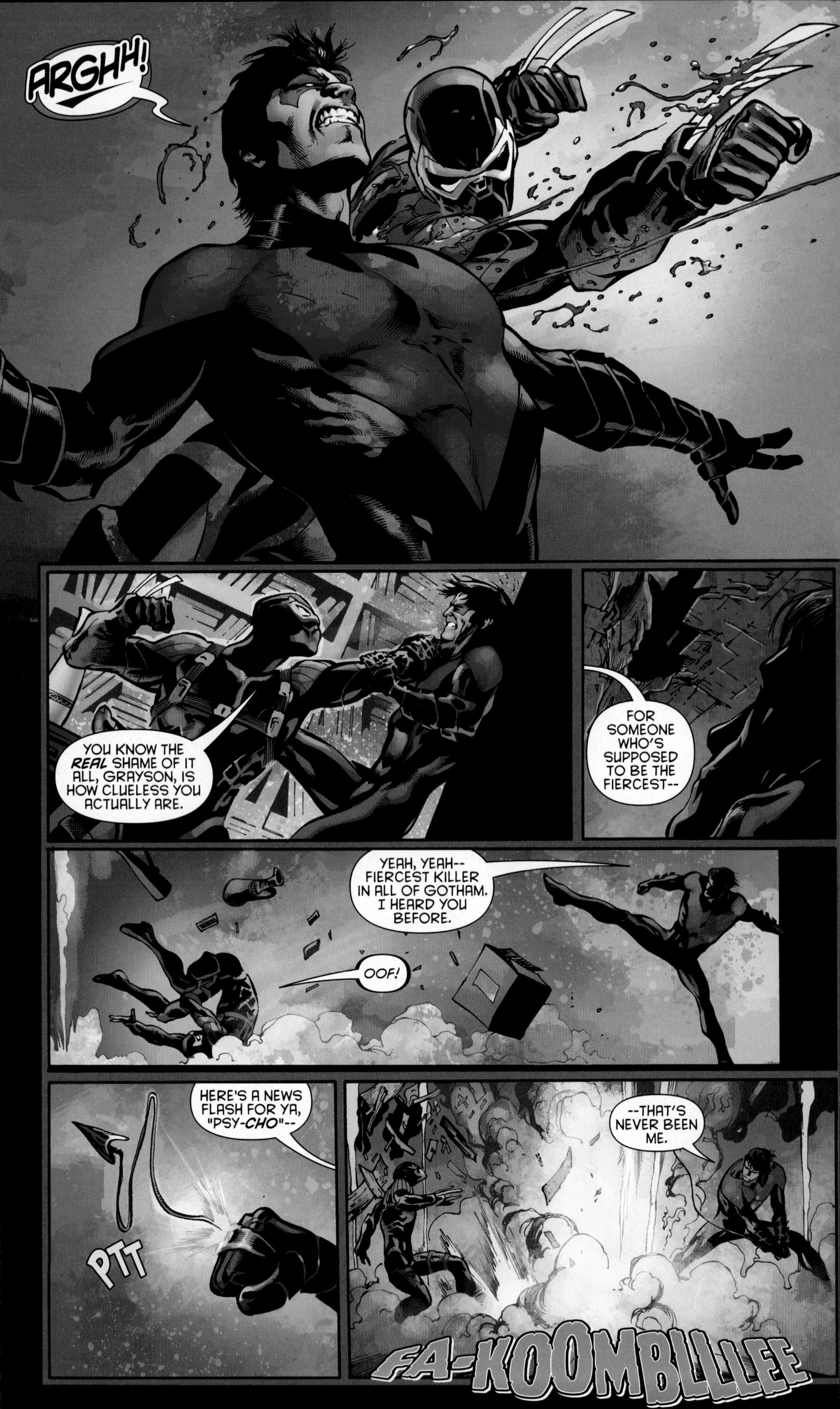

ARGHH!
YOU KNOW THE *REAL* SHAME OF IT ALL, GRAYSON, IS HOW CLUELESS YOU ACTUALLY ARE.
FOR SOMEONE WHO'S SUPPOSED TO BE THE FIERCEST--
YEAH, YEAH-- FIERCEST KILLER IN ALL OF GOTHAM. I HEARD YOU BEFORE.
OOF!
HERE'S A NEWS FLASH FOR YA, "PSY-*CHO*"--
PTT
--THAT'S NEVER BEEN ME.
FA-KOOMBLLLEE

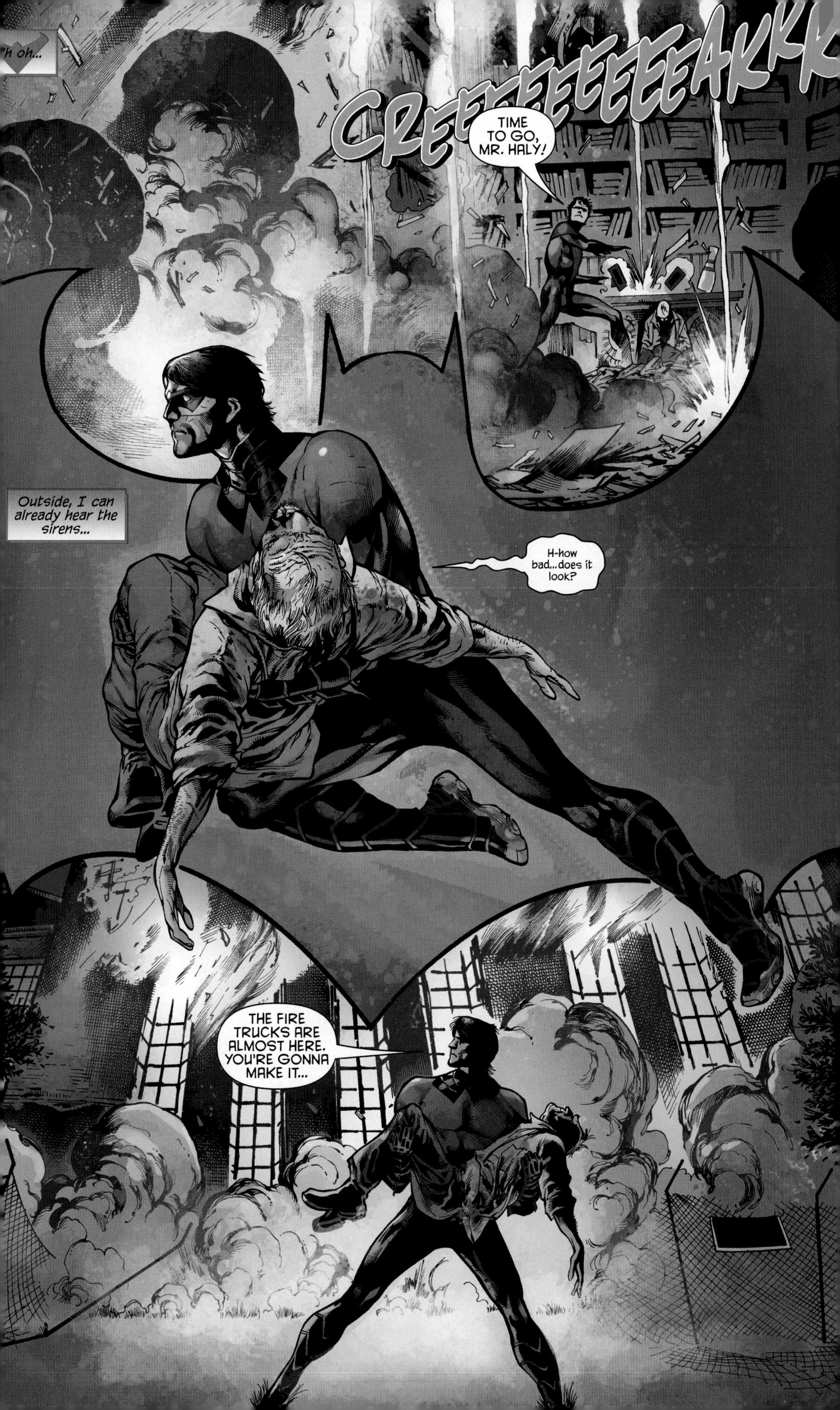
'h oh...
CREEEEEEEEEAKKK
TIME TO GO, MR. HALY!
Outside, I can already hear the sirens...
H-how bad...does it look?
THE FIRE TRUCKS ARE ALMOST HERE. YOU'RE GONNA MAKE IT...

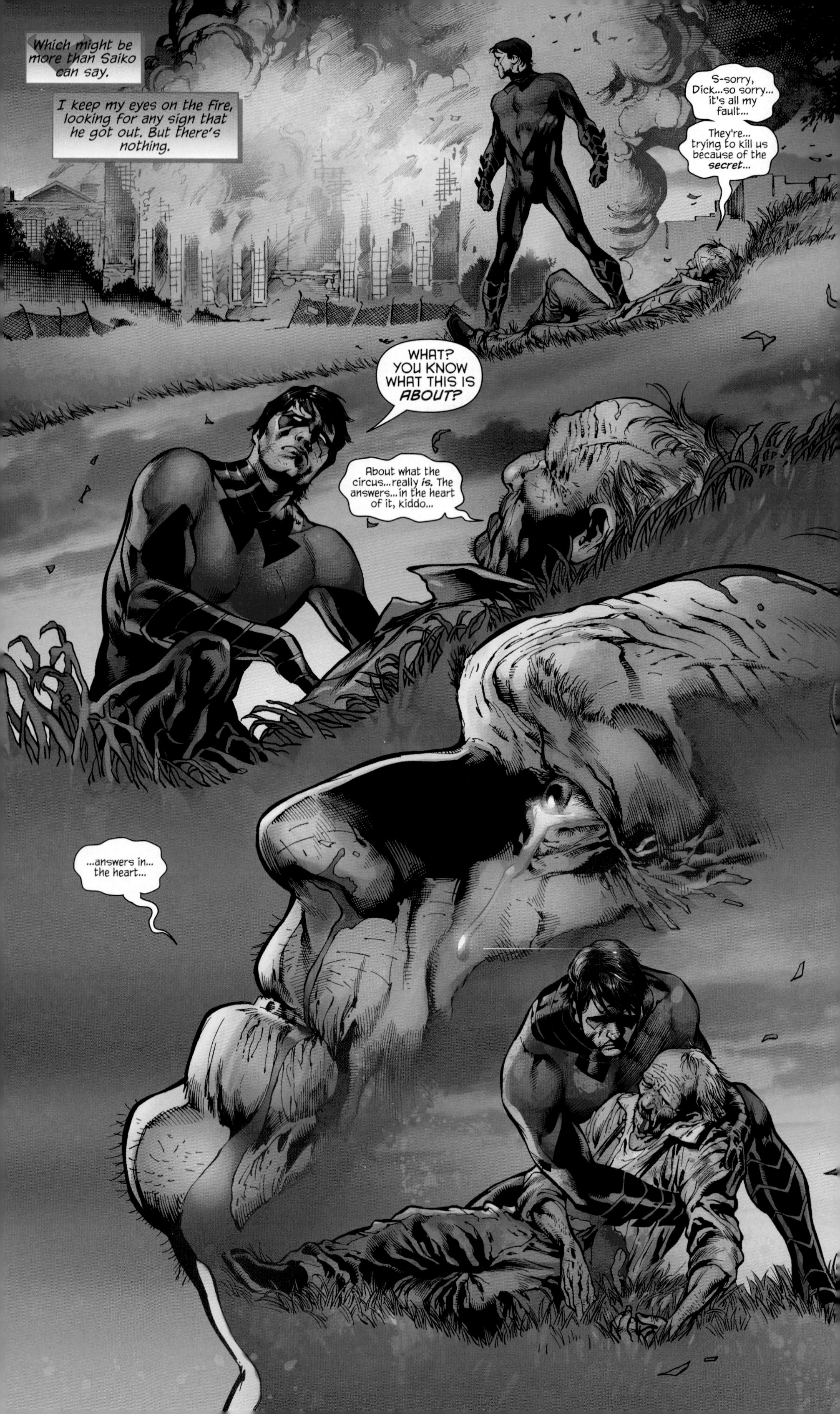

Which might be more than Saiko can say.
I keep my eyes on the fire, looking for any sign that he got out. But there's nothing.
S-sorry, Dick...so sorry... it's all my fault...
They're... trying to kill us because of the *secret*...
WHAT? YOU KNOW WHAT THIS IS *ABOUT?*
About what the circus...really *is*. The answers...in the heart of it, kiddo...
...answers in... the heart...

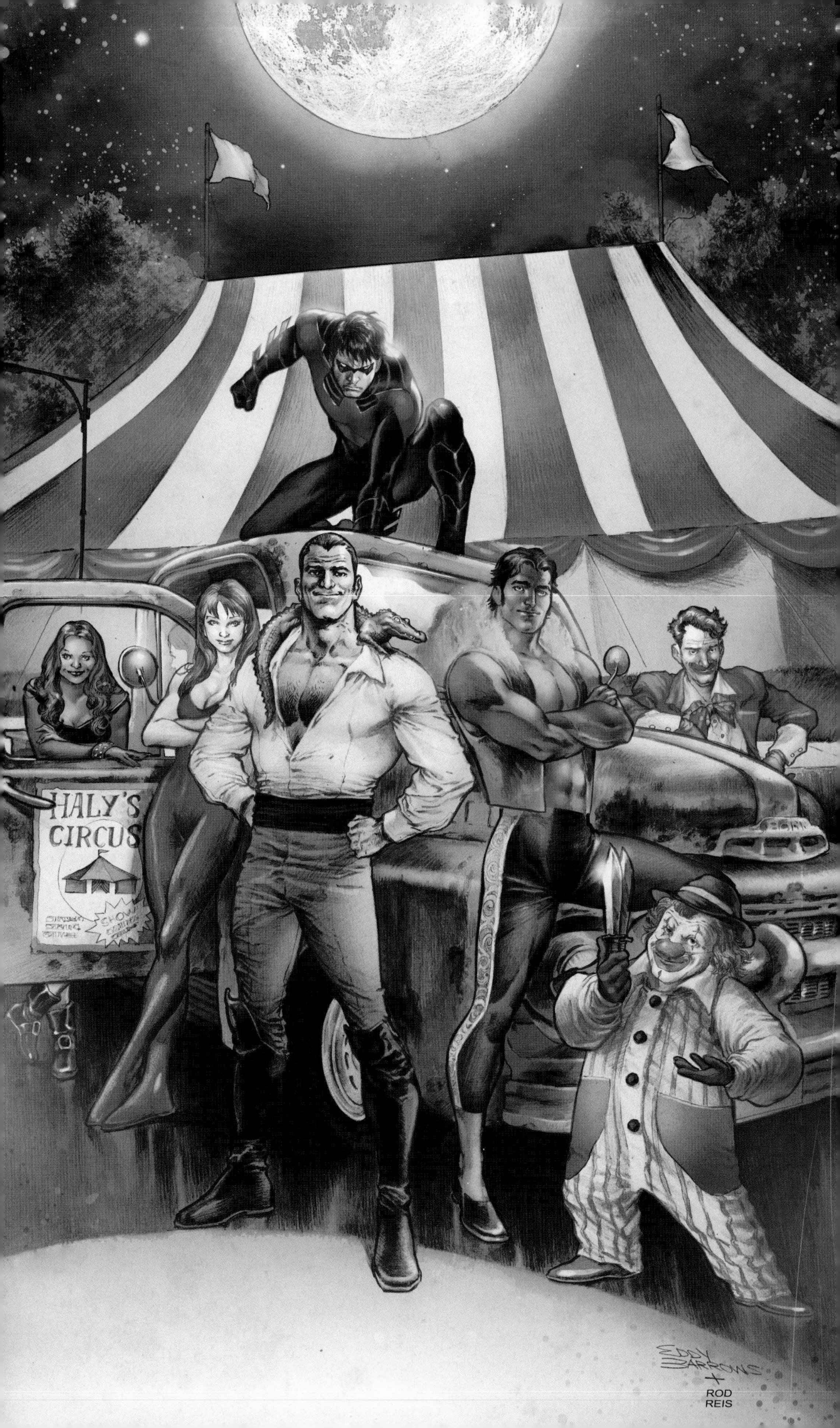
HALY'S
CIRCUS
EDDY BARROWS
+
ROD
REIS

KYLE HIGGINS writer EDDY BARROWS & EDUARDO PANSICA pencillers JP MAYER, PAULO SIQUEIRA & EBER FERREIRA inkers
cover art by Eddy Barrows & Rod Reis

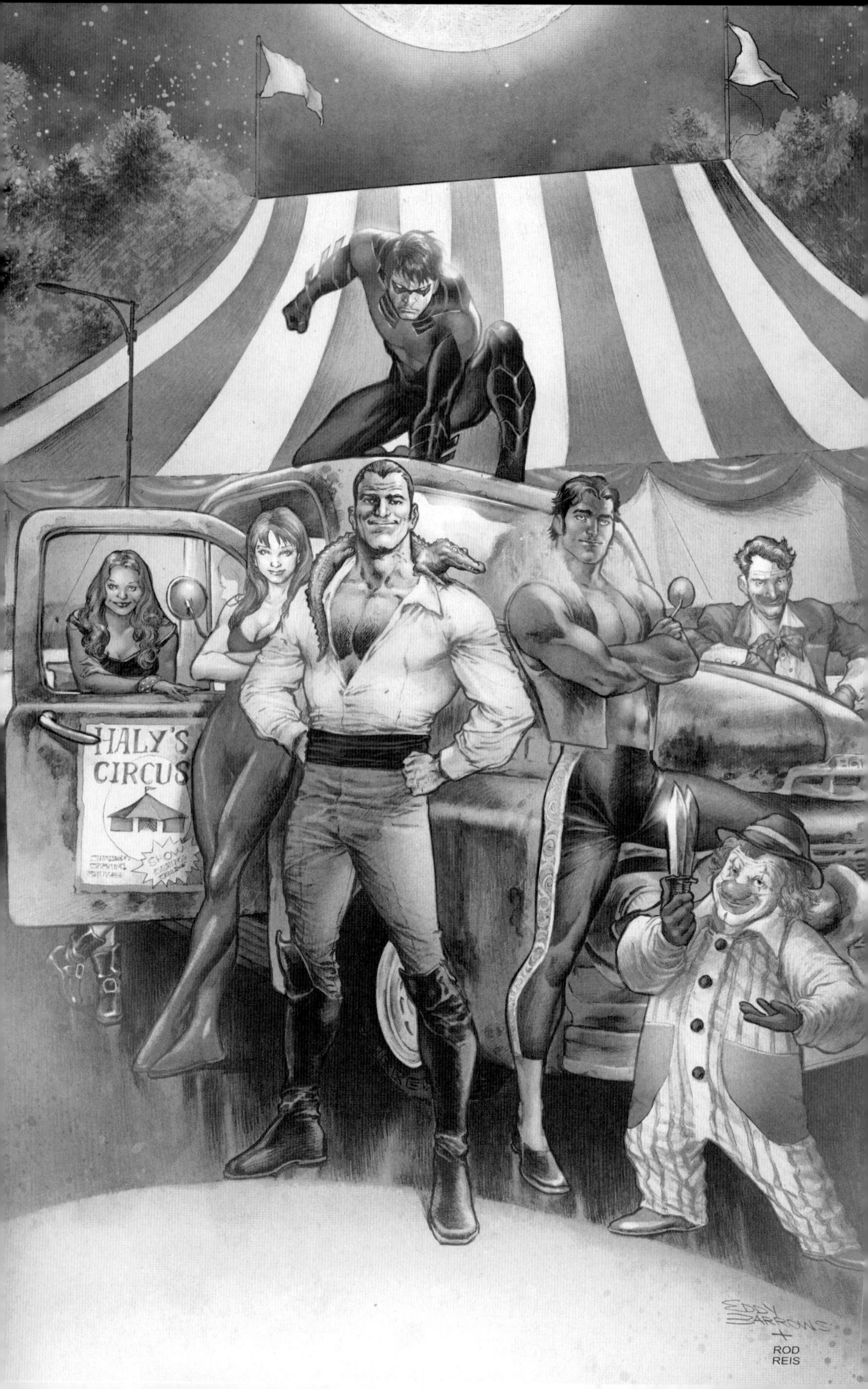
HALY'S
CIRCUS
SHOW
EDDY BARROWS
+
ROD
REIS

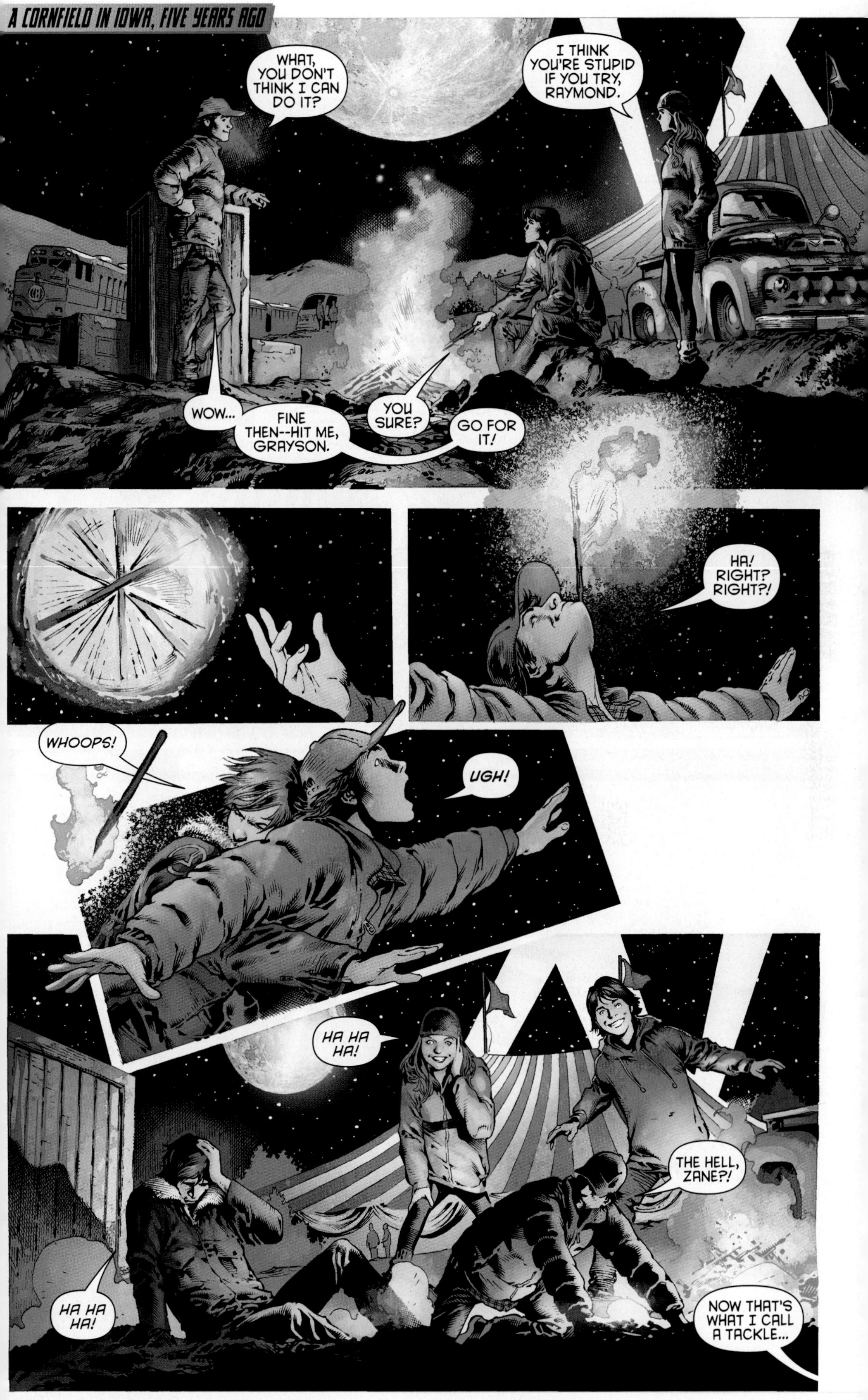
A CORNFIELD IN IOWA, FIVE YEARS AGO
WHAT, YOU DON'T THINK I CAN DO IT?
I THINK YOU'RE STUPID IF YOU TRY, RAYMOND.
WOW...
FINE THEN--HIT ME, GRAYSON.
YOU SURE?
GO FOR IT!
HA! RIGHT? RIGHT?!
WHOOPS!
UGH!
HA HA HA!
THE HELL, ZANE?!
HA HA HA!
NOW THAT'S WHAT I CALL A TACKLE...

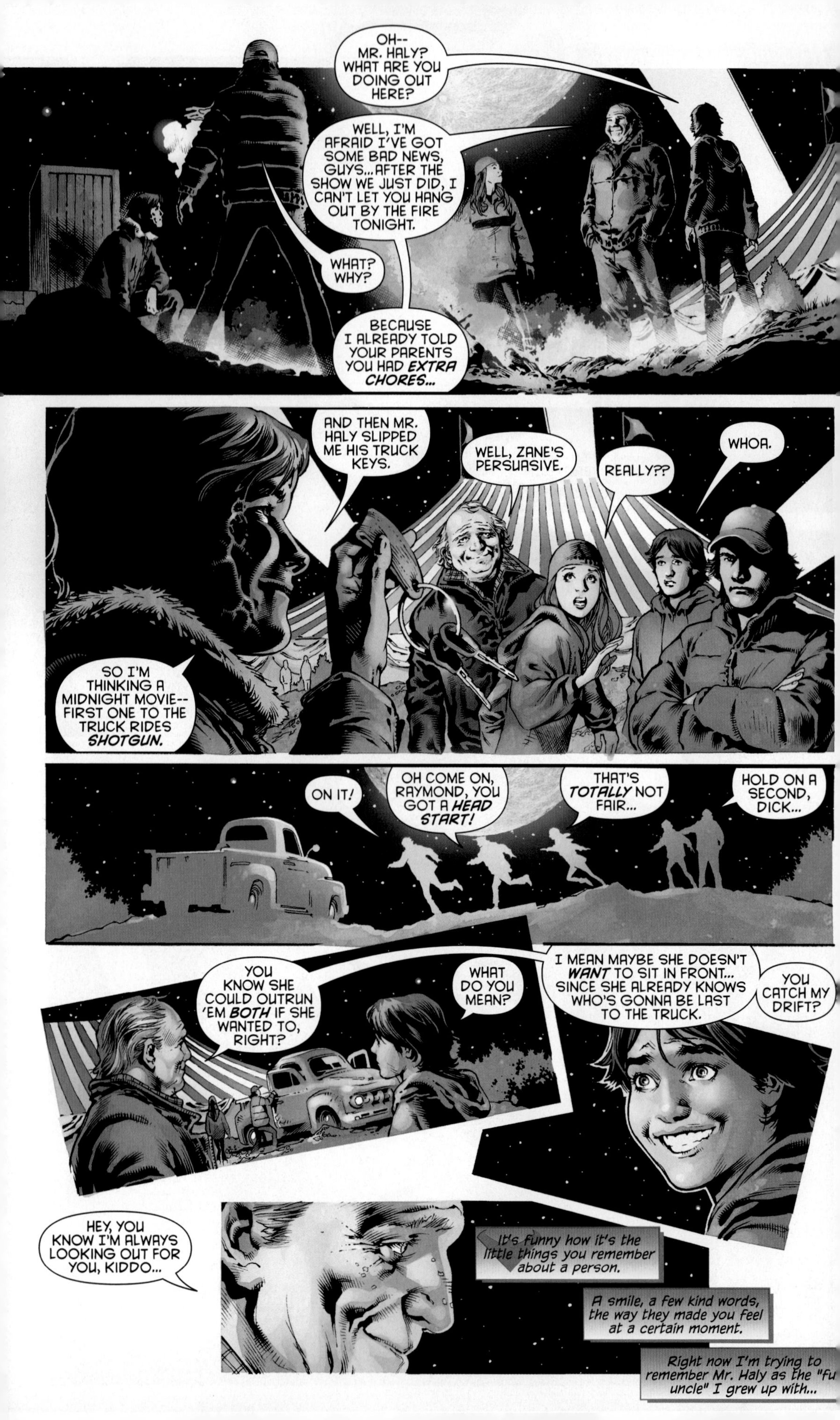
OH-- MR. HALY? WHAT ARE YOU DOING OUT HERE?
WELL, I'M AFRAID I'VE GOT SOME BAD NEWS, GUYS... AFTER THE SHOW WE JUST DID, I CAN'T LET YOU HANG OUT BY THE FIRE TONIGHT.
WHAT? WHY?
BECAUSE I ALREADY TOLD YOUR PARENTS YOU HAD EXTRA CHORES...
AND THEN MR. HALY SLIPPED ME HIS TRUCK KEYS.
WELL, ZANE'S PERSUASIVE.
REALLY??
WHOA.
SO I'M THINKING A MIDNIGHT MOVIE-- FIRST ONE TO THE TRUCK RIDES SHOTGUN.
ON IT!
OH COME ON, RAYMOND, YOU GOT A HEAD START!
THAT'S TOTALLY NOT FAIR...
HOLD ON A SECOND, DICK...
YOU KNOW SHE COULD OUTRUN 'EM BOTH IF SHE WANTED TO, RIGHT?
WHAT DO YOU MEAN?
I MEAN MAYBE SHE DOESN'T WANT TO SIT IN FRONT... SINCE SHE ALREADY KNOWS WHO'S GONNA BE LAST TO THE TRUCK.
YOU CATCH MY DRIFT?
HEY, YOU KNOW I'M ALWAYS LOOKING OUT FOR YOU, KIDDO...
It's funny how it's the little things you remember about a person.
A smile, a few kind words, the way they made you feel at a certain moment.
Right now I'm trying to remember Mr. Haly as the "fu uncle" I grew up with...

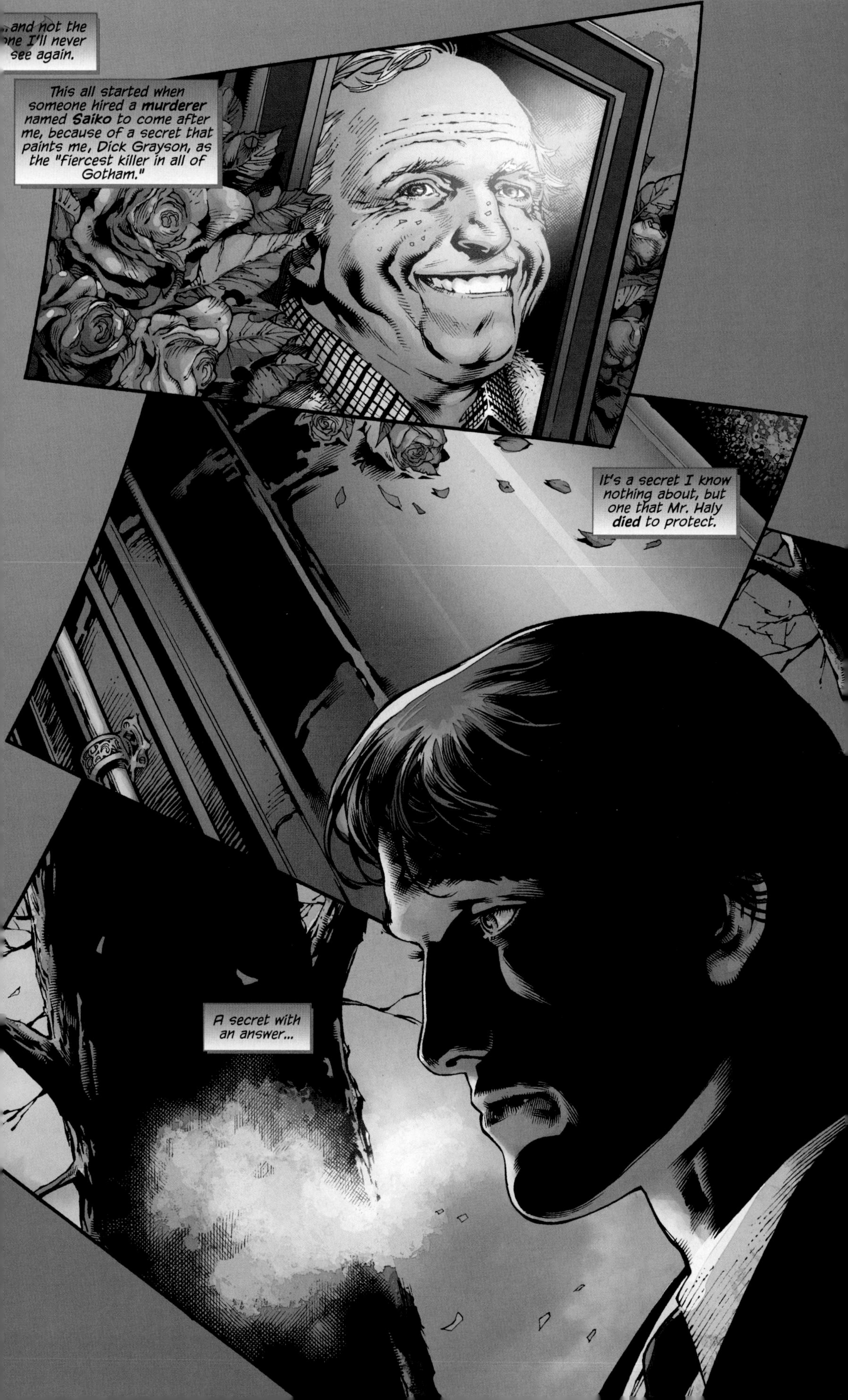
...and not the one I'll never see again.
This all started when someone hired a **murderer** named **Saiko** to come after me, because of a secret that paints me, Dick Grayson, as the "fiercest killer in all of Gotham."
It's a secret I know nothing about, but one that Mr. Haly **died** to protect.
A secret with an answer...

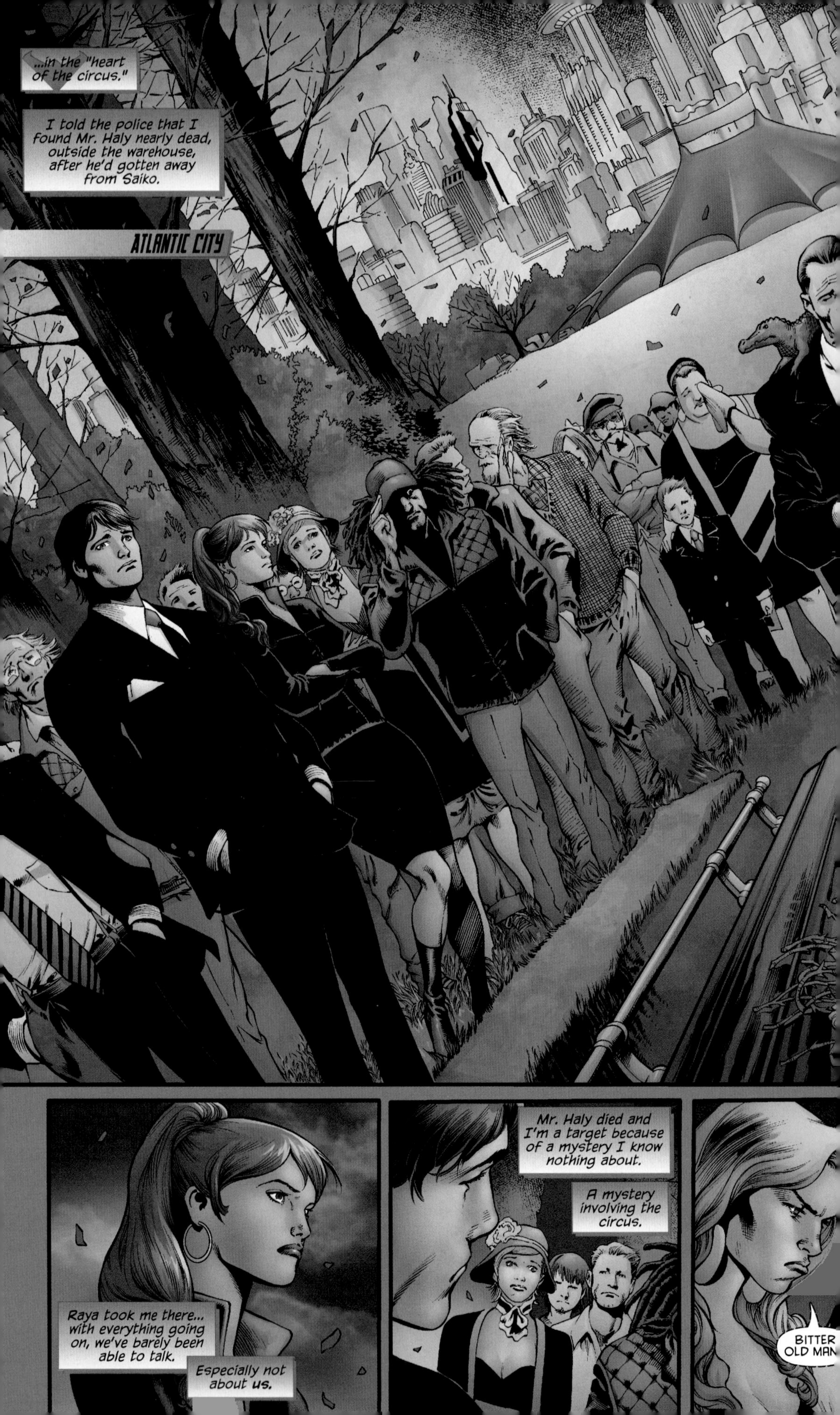
...in the "heart of the circus."
I told the police that I found Mr. Haly nearly dead, outside the warehouse, after he'd gotten away from Saiko.
ATLANTIC CITY
Raya took me there... with everything going on, we've barely been able to talk.
Especially not about us.
Mr. Haly died and I'm a target because of a mystery I know nothing about.
A mystery involving the circus.
BITTER OLD MAN

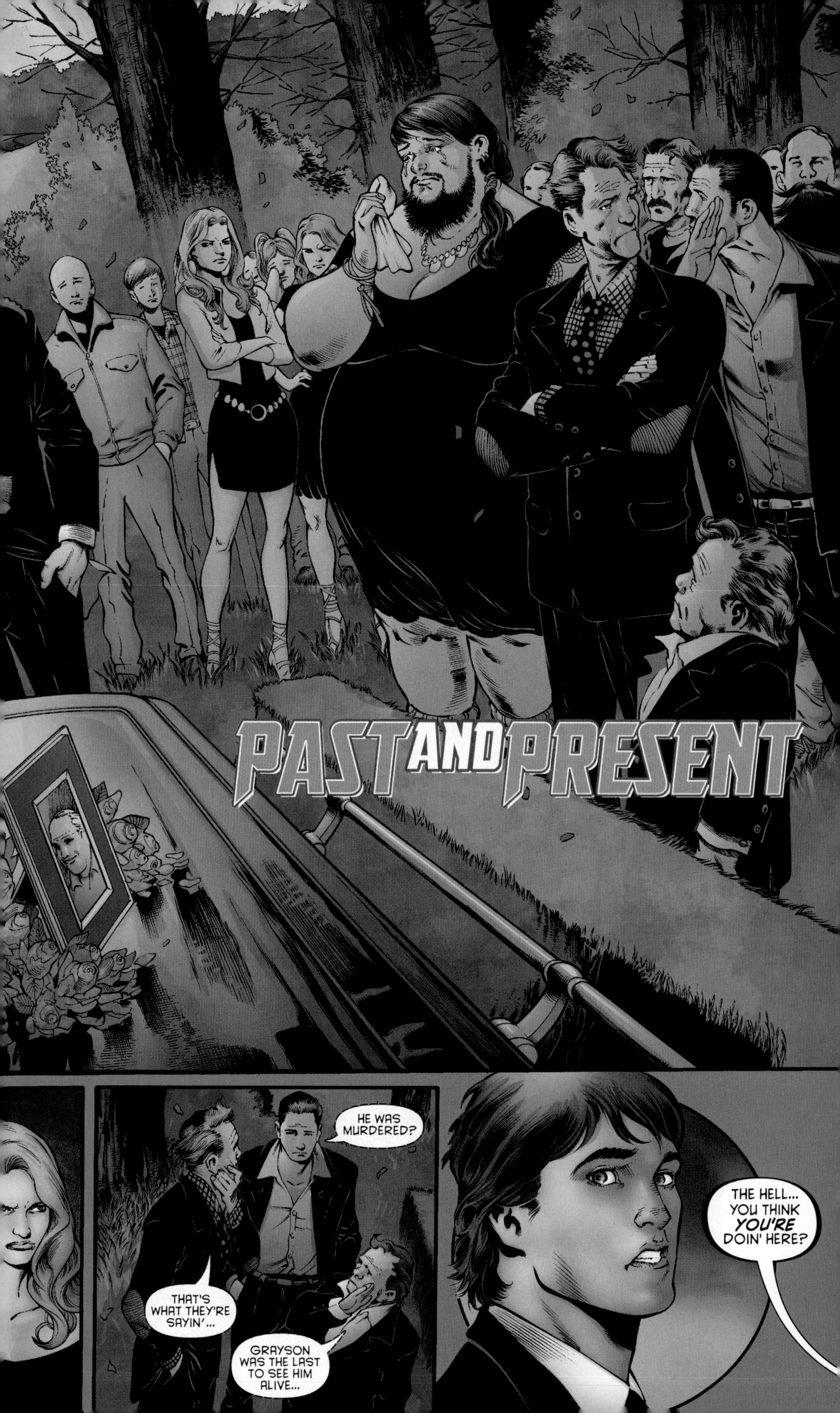
PAST AND PRESENT
HE WAS MURDERED?
THAT'S WHAT THEY'RE SAYIN'...
GRAYSON WAS THE LAST TO SEE HIM ALIVE...
THE HELL... YOU THINK *YOU'RE* DOIN' HERE?

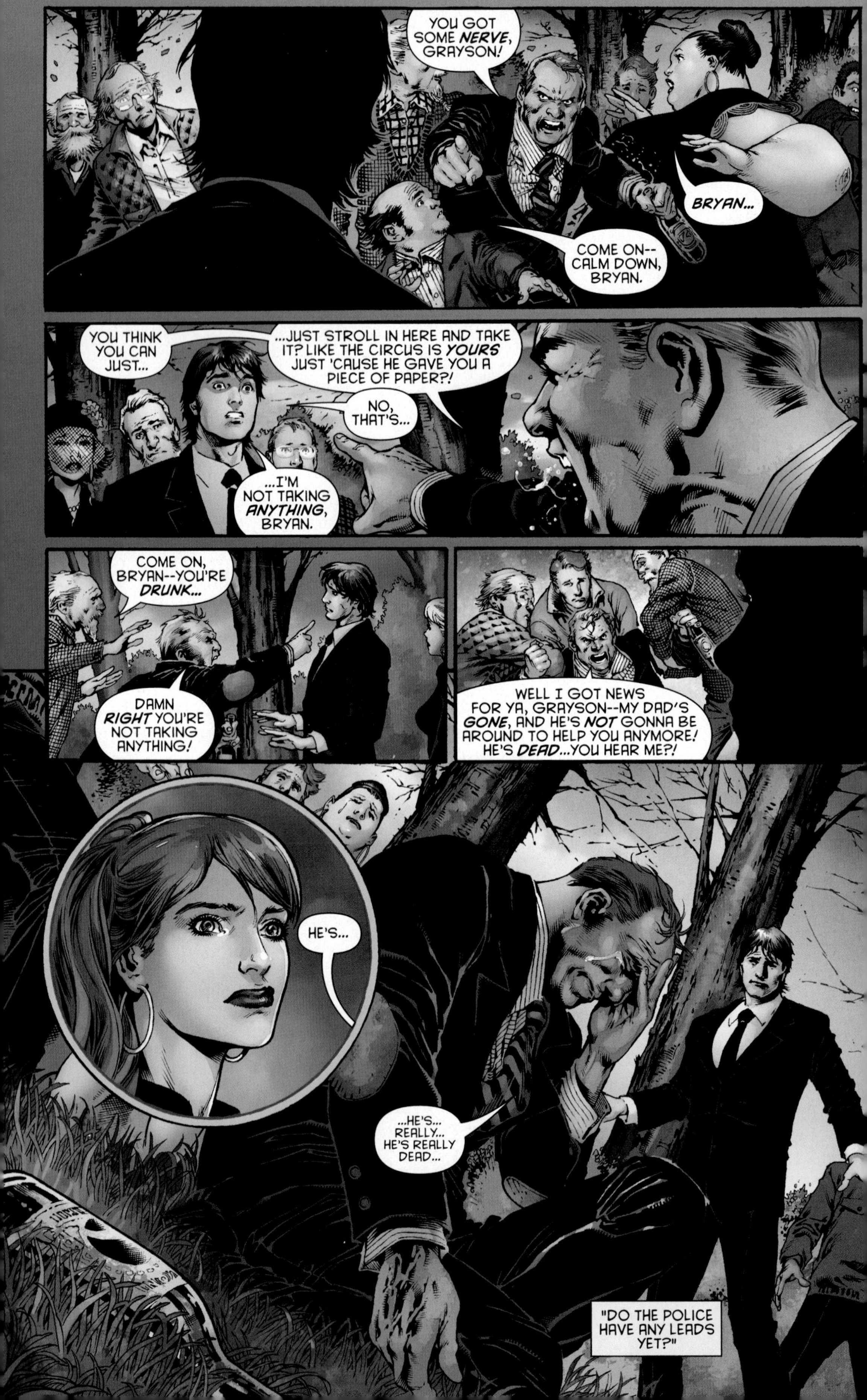

YOU GOT SOME NERVE, GRAYSON!
BRYAN...
COME ON-- CALM DOWN, BRYAN.
YOU THINK YOU CAN JUST...
...JUST STROLL IN HERE AND TAKE IT? LIKE THE CIRCUS IS YOURS JUST 'CAUSE HE GAVE YOU A PIECE OF PAPER?!
NO, THAT'S...
...I'M NOT TAKING ANYTHING, BRYAN.
COME ON, BRYAN--YOU'RE DRUNK...
DAMN RIGHT YOU'RE NOT TAKING ANYTHING!
WELL I GOT NEWS FOR YA, GRAYSON--MY DAD'S GONE, AND HE'S NOT GONNA BE AROUND TO HELP YOU ANYMORE! HE'S DEAD...YOU HEAR ME?!
HE'S...
...HE'S... REALLY... HE'S REALLY DEAD...
"DO THE POLICE HAVE ANY LEADS YET?"

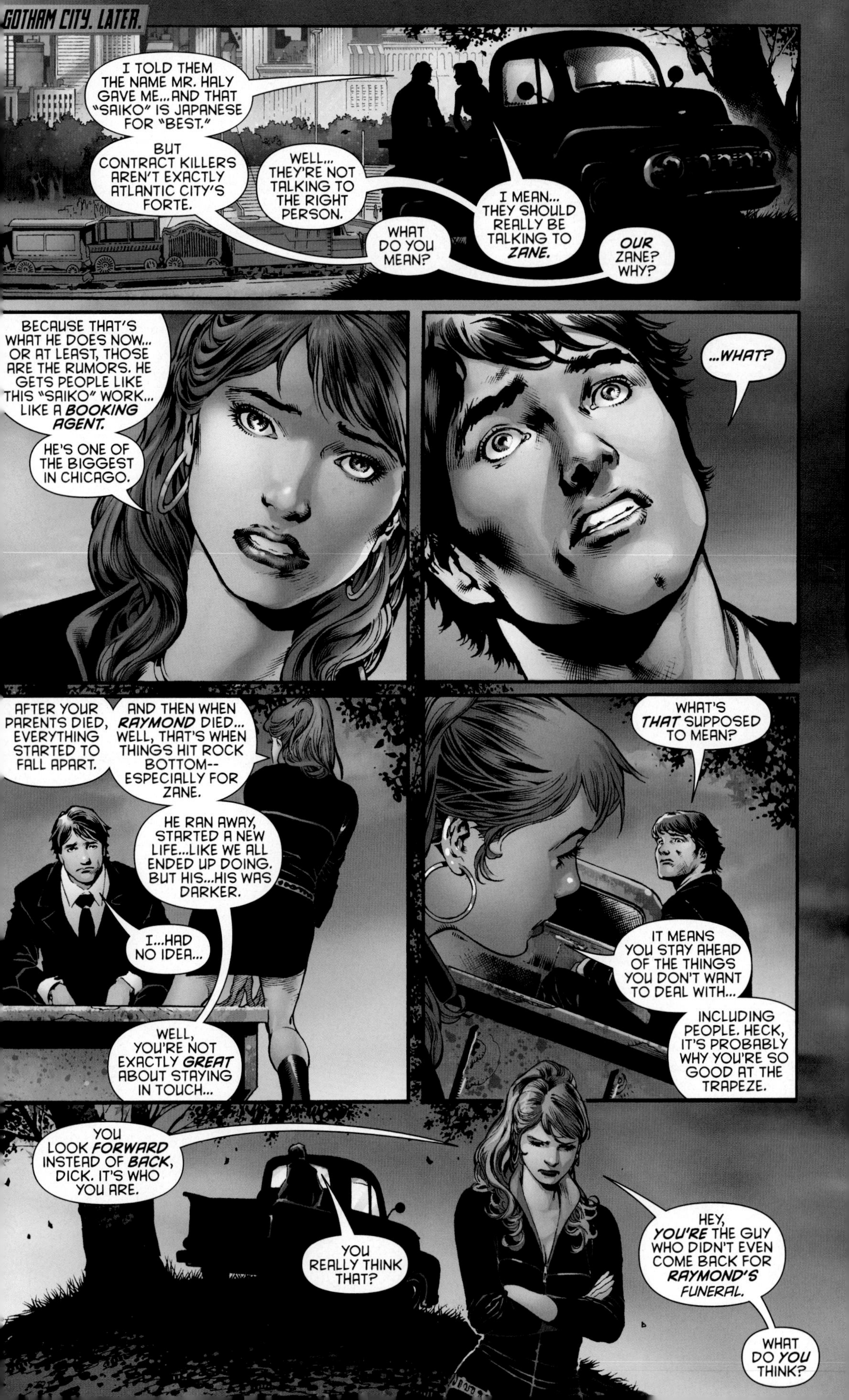
GOTHAM CITY. LATER.
I TOLD THEM THE NAME MR. HALY GAVE ME...AND THAT "SAIKO" IS JAPANESE FOR "BEST."
BUT CONTRACT KILLERS AREN'T EXACTLY ATLANTIC CITY'S FORTE.
WELL... THEY'RE NOT TALKING TO THE RIGHT PERSON.
I MEAN... THEY SHOULD REALLY BE TALKING TO ZANE.
WHAT DO YOU MEAN?
OUR ZANE? WHY?
BECAUSE THAT'S WHAT HE DOES NOW... OR AT LEAST, THOSE ARE THE RUMORS. HE GETS PEOPLE LIKE THIS "SAIKO" WORK... LIKE A BOOKING AGENT.
HE'S ONE OF THE BIGGEST IN CHICAGO.
...WHAT?
AFTER YOUR PARENTS DIED, EVERYTHING STARTED TO FALL APART.
AND THEN WHEN RAYMOND DIED... WELL, THAT'S WHEN THINGS HIT ROCK BOTTOM-- ESPECIALLY FOR ZANE.
HE RAN AWAY, STARTED A NEW LIFE...LIKE WE ALL ENDED UP DOING. BUT HIS...HIS WAS DARKER.
I...HAD NO IDEA...
WELL, YOU'RE NOT EXACTLY GREAT ABOUT STAYING IN TOUCH...
WHAT'S THAT SUPPOSED TO MEAN?
IT MEANS YOU STAY AHEAD OF THE THINGS YOU DON'T WANT TO DEAL WITH...
INCLUDING PEOPLE. HECK, IT'S PROBABLY WHY YOU'RE SO GOOD AT THE TRAPEZE.
YOU LOOK FORWARD INSTEAD OF BACK, DICK. IT'S WHO YOU ARE.
YOU REALLY THINK THAT?
HEY, YOU'RE THE GUY WHO DIDN'T EVEN COME BACK FOR RAYMOND'S FUNERAL.
WHAT DO YOU THINK?

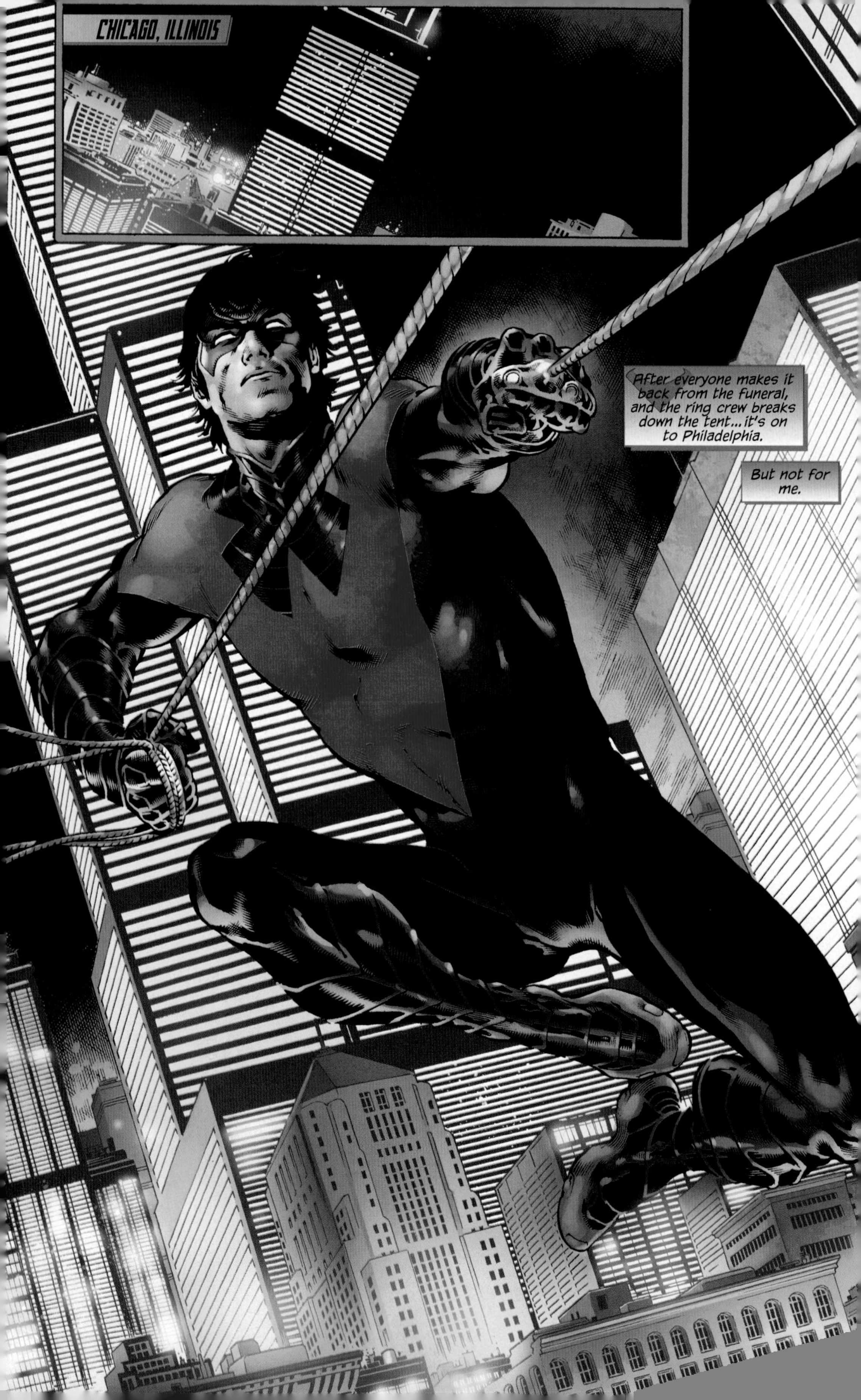
CHICAGO, ILLINOIS
After everyone makes it back from the funeral, and the ring crew breaks down the tent...it's on to Philadelphia.
But not for me.

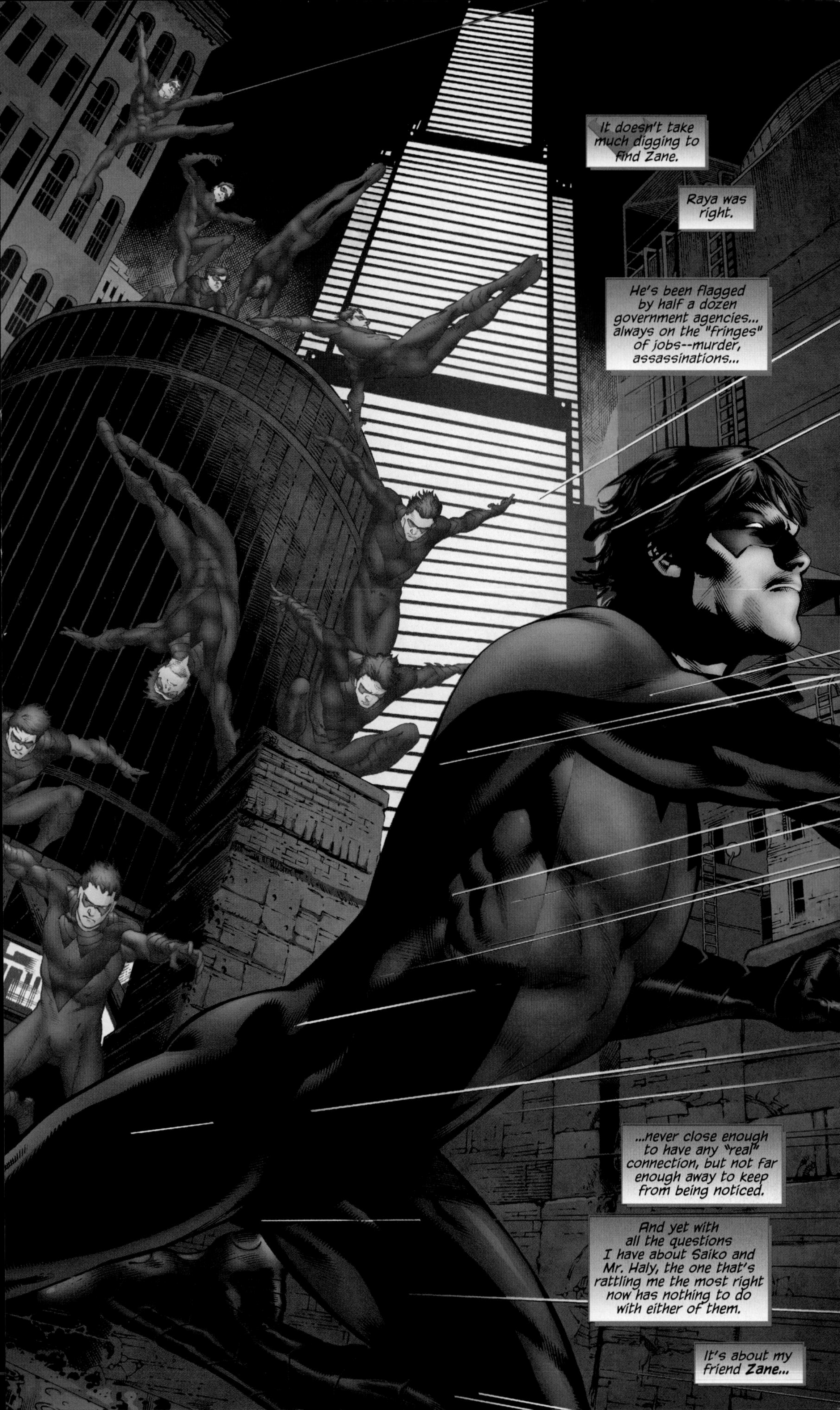
It doesn't take much digging to find Zane.
Raya was right.
He's been flagged by half a dozen government agencies... always on the "fringes" of jobs--murder, assassinations...
...never close enough to have any "real" connection, but not far enough away to keep from being noticed.
And yet with all the questions I have about Saiko and Mr. Haly, the one that's rattling me the most right now has nothing to do with either of them.
It's about my friend **Zane...**

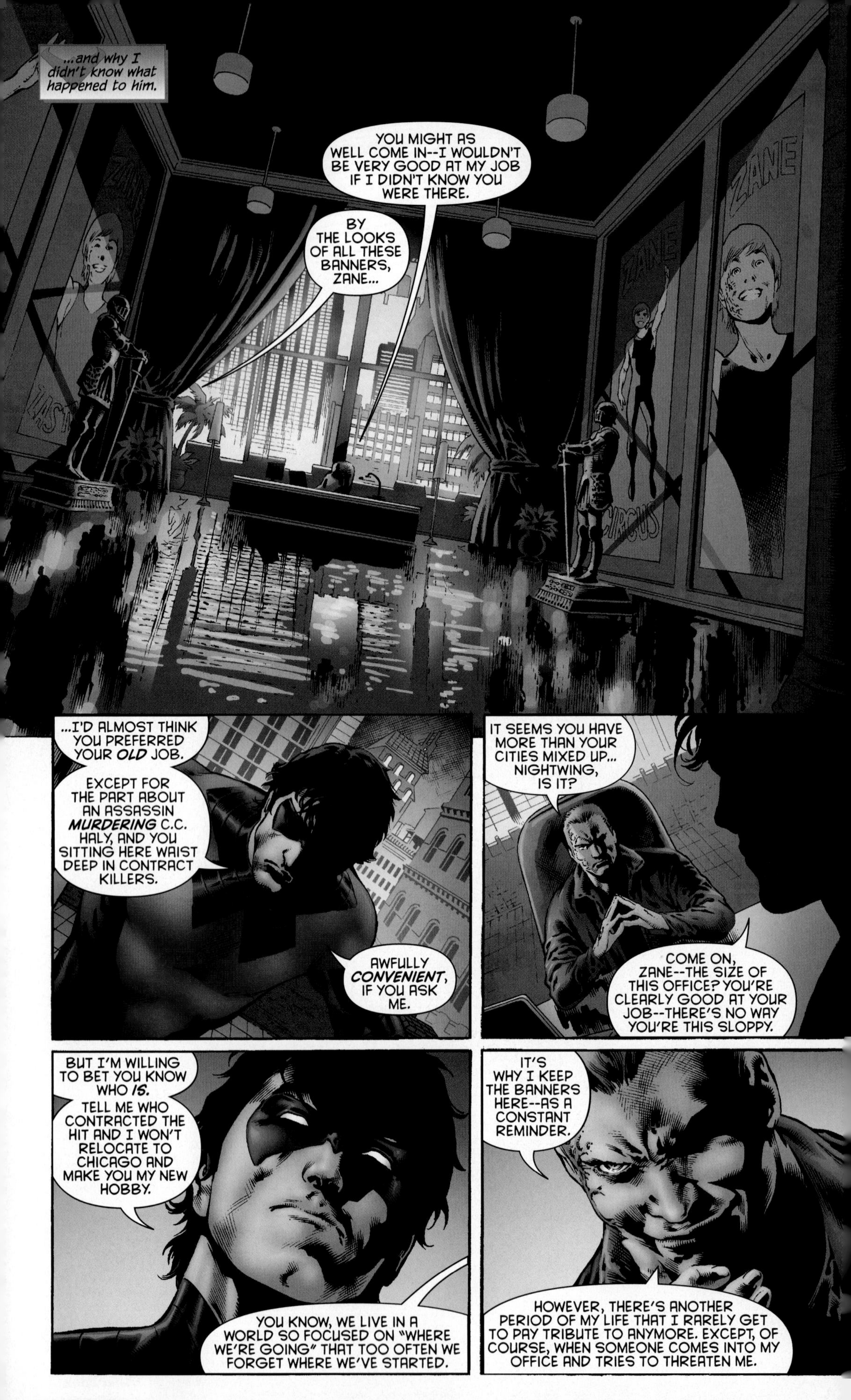
...and why I didn't know what happened to him.
YOU MIGHT AS WELL COME IN--I WOULDN'T BE VERY GOOD AT MY JOB IF I DIDN'T KNOW YOU WERE THERE.
BY THE LOOKS OF ALL THESE BANNERS, ZANE...
ZANE
ZANE
ZANE
CIRCUS
...I'D ALMOST THINK YOU PREFERRED YOUR OLD JOB.
EXCEPT FOR THE PART ABOUT AN ASSASSIN MURDERING C.C. HALY, AND YOU SITTING HERE WAIST DEEP IN CONTRACT KILLERS.
AWFULLY CONVENIENT, IF YOU ASK ME.
IT SEEMS YOU HAVE MORE THAN YOUR CITIES MIXED UP... NIGHTWING, IS IT?
COME ON, ZANE--THE SIZE OF THIS OFFICE? YOU'RE CLEARLY GOOD AT YOUR JOB--THERE'S NO WAY YOU'RE THIS SLOPPY.
BUT I'M WILLING TO BET YOU KNOW WHO IS.
TELL ME WHO CONTRACTED THE HIT AND I WON'T RELOCATE TO CHICAGO AND MAKE YOU MY NEW HOBBY.
YOU KNOW, WE LIVE IN A WORLD SO FOCUSED ON "WHERE WE'RE GOING" THAT TOO OFTEN WE FORGET WHERE WE'VE STARTED.
IT'S WHY I KEEP THE BANNERS HERE--AS A CONSTANT REMINDER.
HOWEVER, THERE'S ANOTHER PERIOD OF MY LIFE THAT I RARELY GET TO PAY TRIBUTE TO ANYMORE. EXCEPT, OF COURSE, WHEN SOMEONE COMES INTO MY OFFICE AND TRIES TO THREATEN ME.

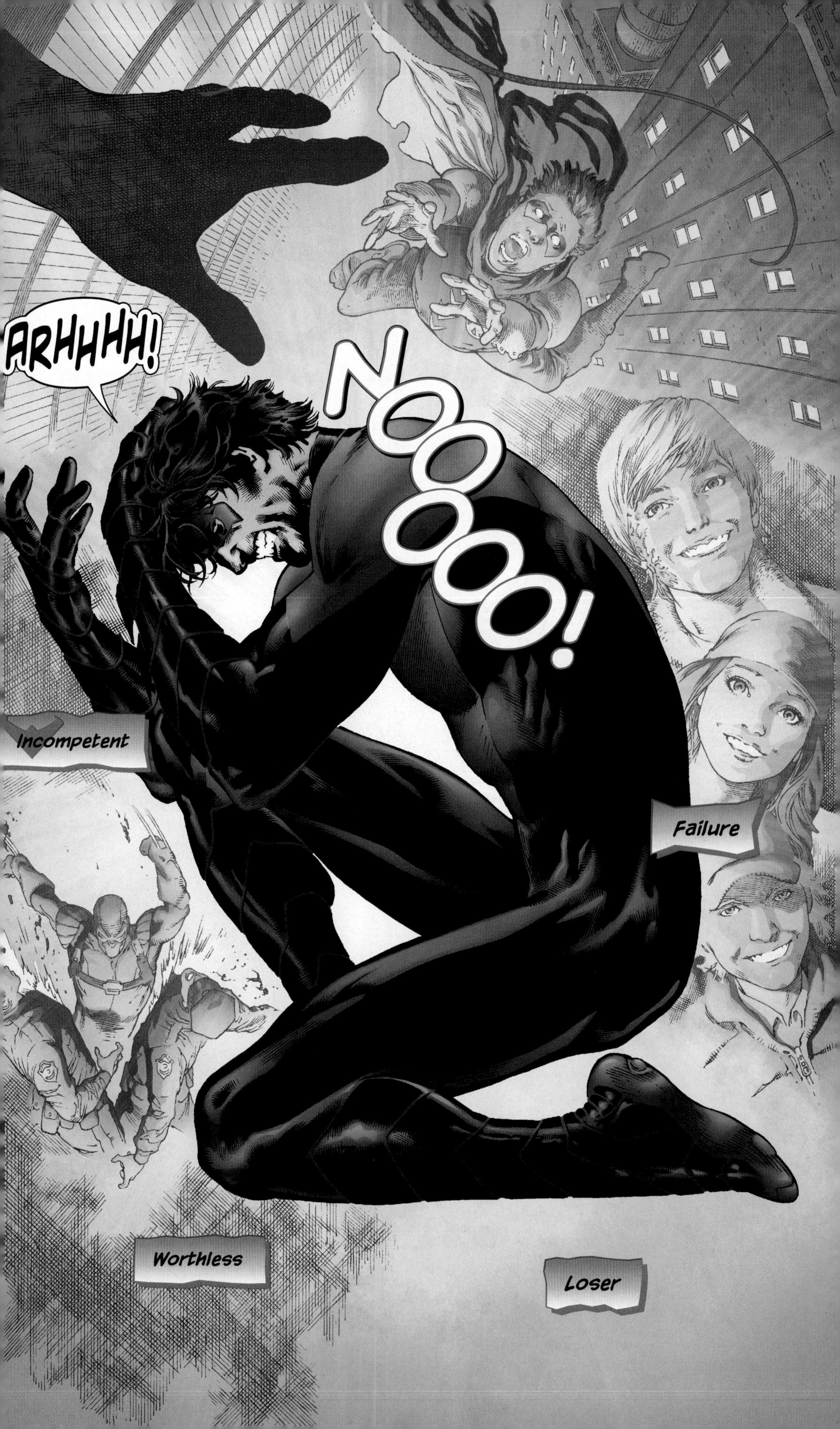
ARHHHH!
NOOOOO!
Incompetent
Failure
Worthless
Loser

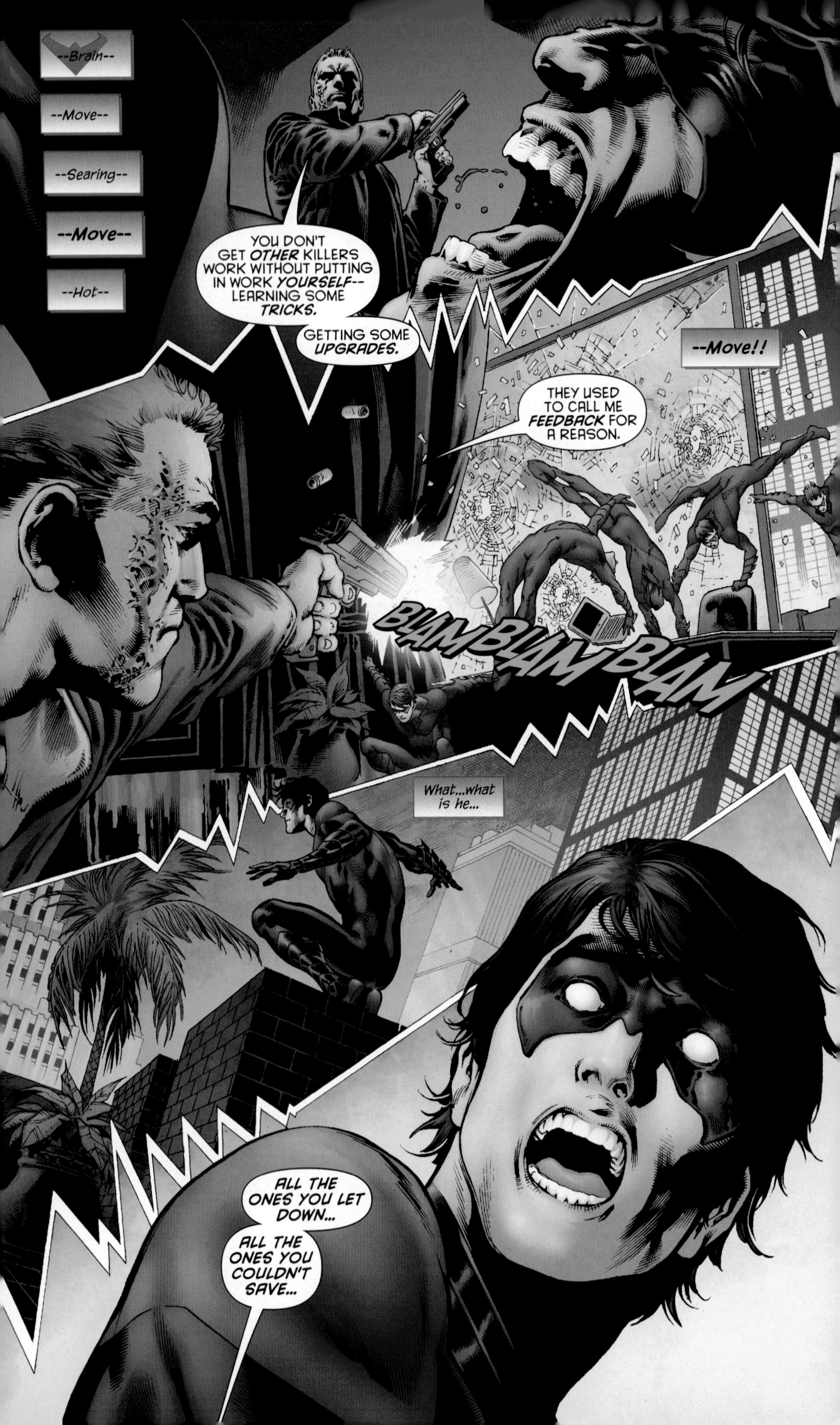

--Brain--
--Move--
--Searing--
--Move--
--Hot--
YOU DON'T GET OTHER KILLERS WORK WITHOUT PUTTING IN WORK YOURSELF-- LEARNING SOME TRICKS.
GETTING SOME UPGRADES.
--Move!!
THEY USED TO CALL ME FEEDBACK FOR A REASON.
BLAM BLAM BLAM BLAM
What...what is he...
ALL THE ONES YOU LET DOWN...
ALL THE ONES YOU COULDN'T SAVE...

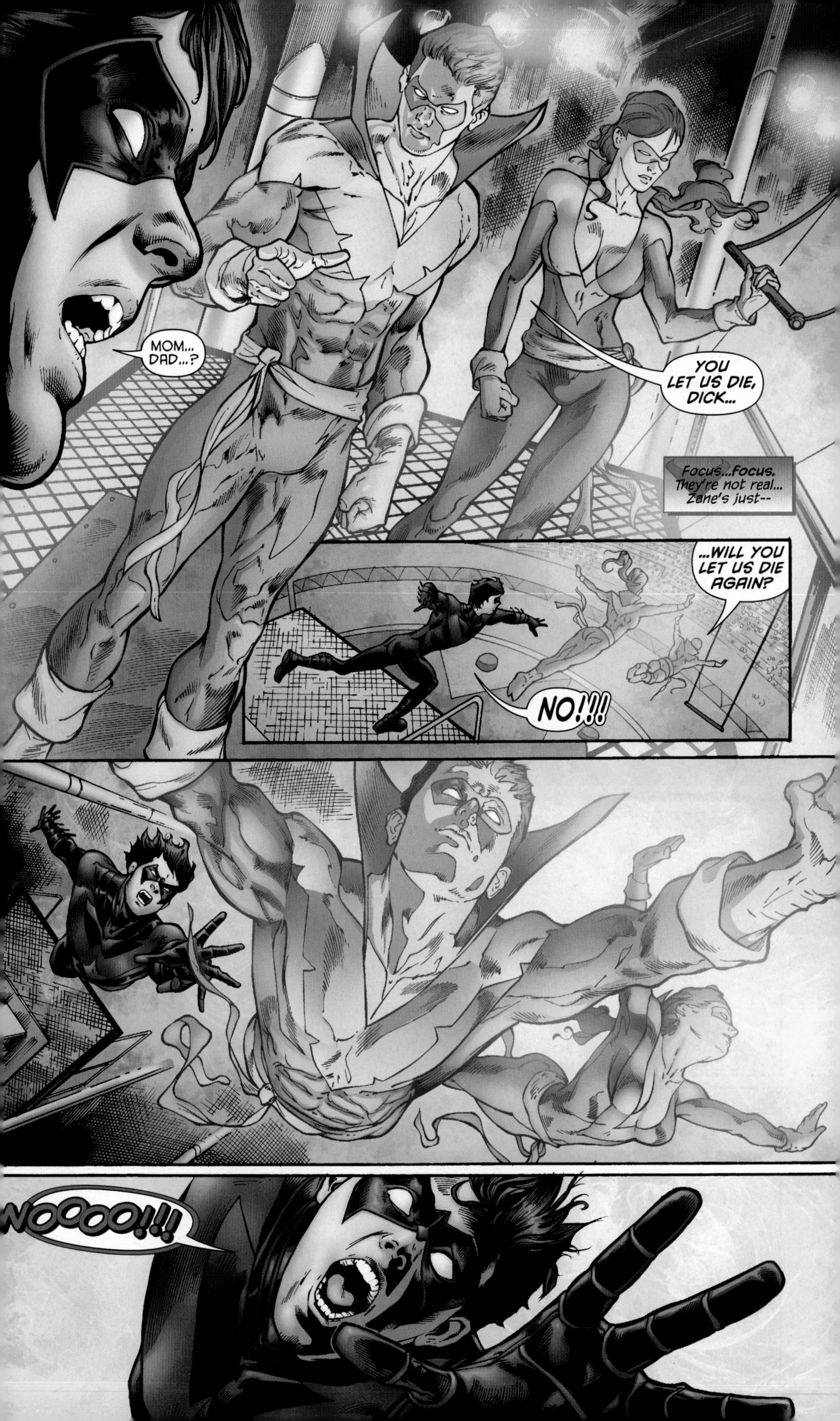
MOM... DAD...?
YOU LET US DIE, DICK...
Focus...Focus. They're not real... Zane's just--
...WILL YOU LET US DIE AGAIN?
NO!!!
NOOOO!!!

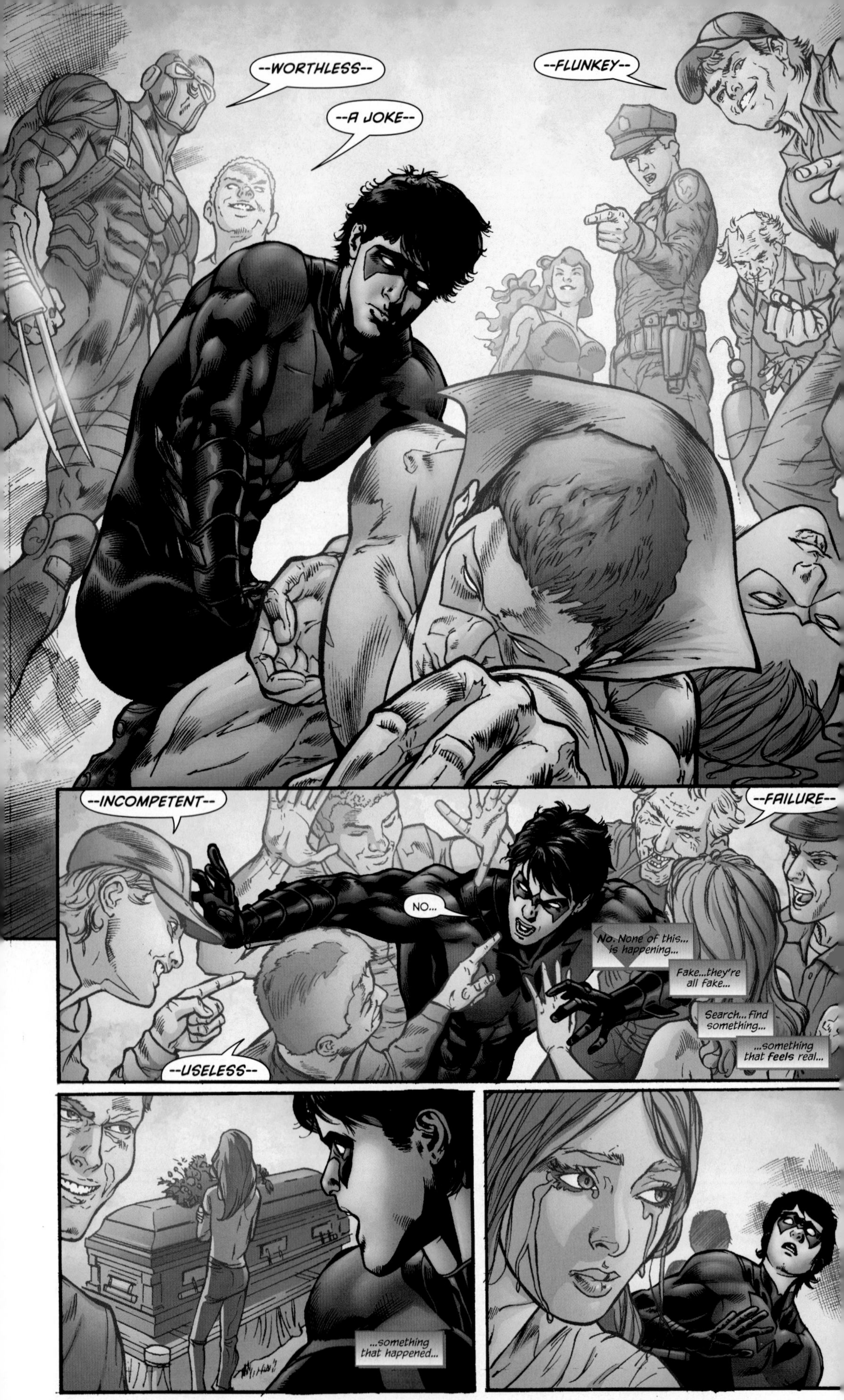
--WORTHLESS--
--A JOKE--
--FLUNKEY--
--INCOMPETENT--
--FAILURE--
NO...
No. None of this... is happening...
Fake...they're all fake...
Search...find something...
...something that feels real...
--USELESS--
...something that happened...

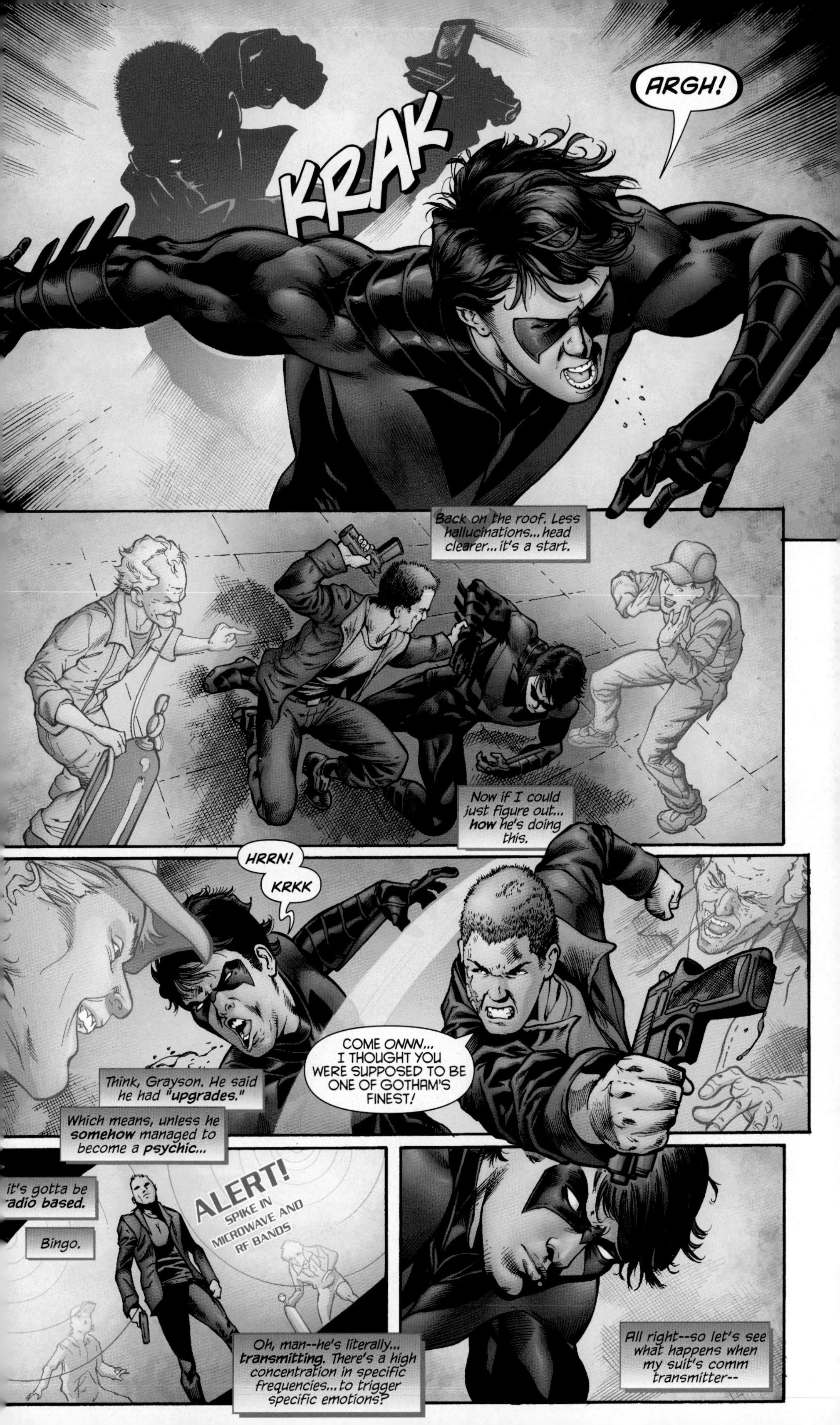
KRAK
ARGH!
Back on the roof. Less hallucinations... head clearer... it's a start.
Now if I could just figure out... how he's doing this.
HRRN!
KRKK
COME ONNN... I THOUGHT YOU WERE SUPPOSED TO BE ONE OF GOTHAM'S FINEST!
Think, Grayson. He said he had "upgrades."
Which means, unless he somehow managed to become a psychic...
it's gotta be radio based.
ALERT! SPIKE IN MICROWAVE AND RF BANDS
Bingo.
Oh, man--he's literally... transmitting. There's a high concentration in specific frequencies... to trigger specific emotions?
All right--so let's see what happens when my suit's comm transmitter--

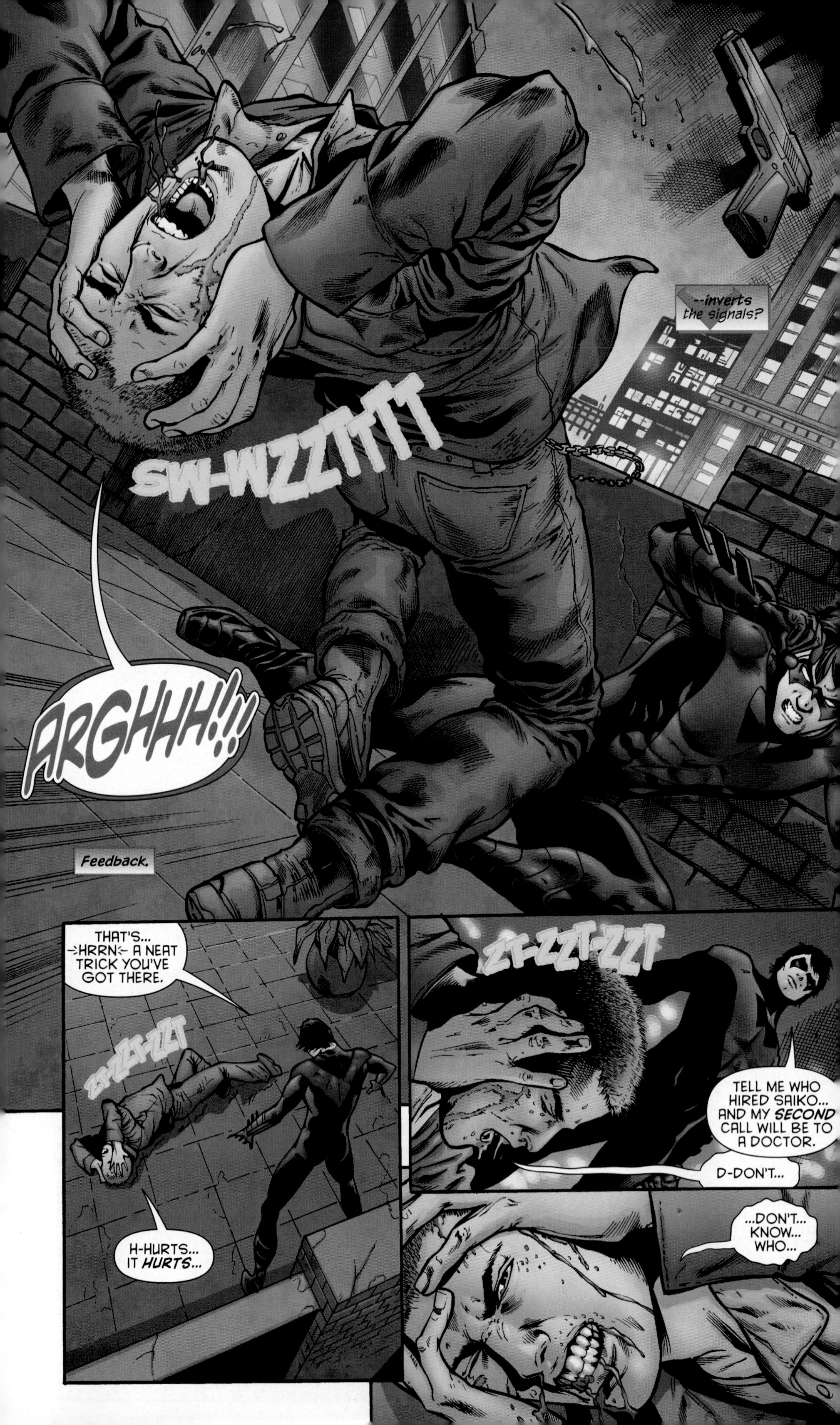
--inverts the signals?
SW-WZZTTTT
ARGHHH!!!
Feedback.
THAT'S... -HRRN- A NEAT TRICK YOU'VE GOT THERE.
ZT-ZZT-ZZT
H-HURTS... IT *HURTS*...
ZT-ZZT-ZZT
TELL ME WHO HIRED SAIKO... AND MY *SECOND* CALL WILL BE TO A DOCTOR.
D-DON'T...
...DON'T... KNOW... WHO...

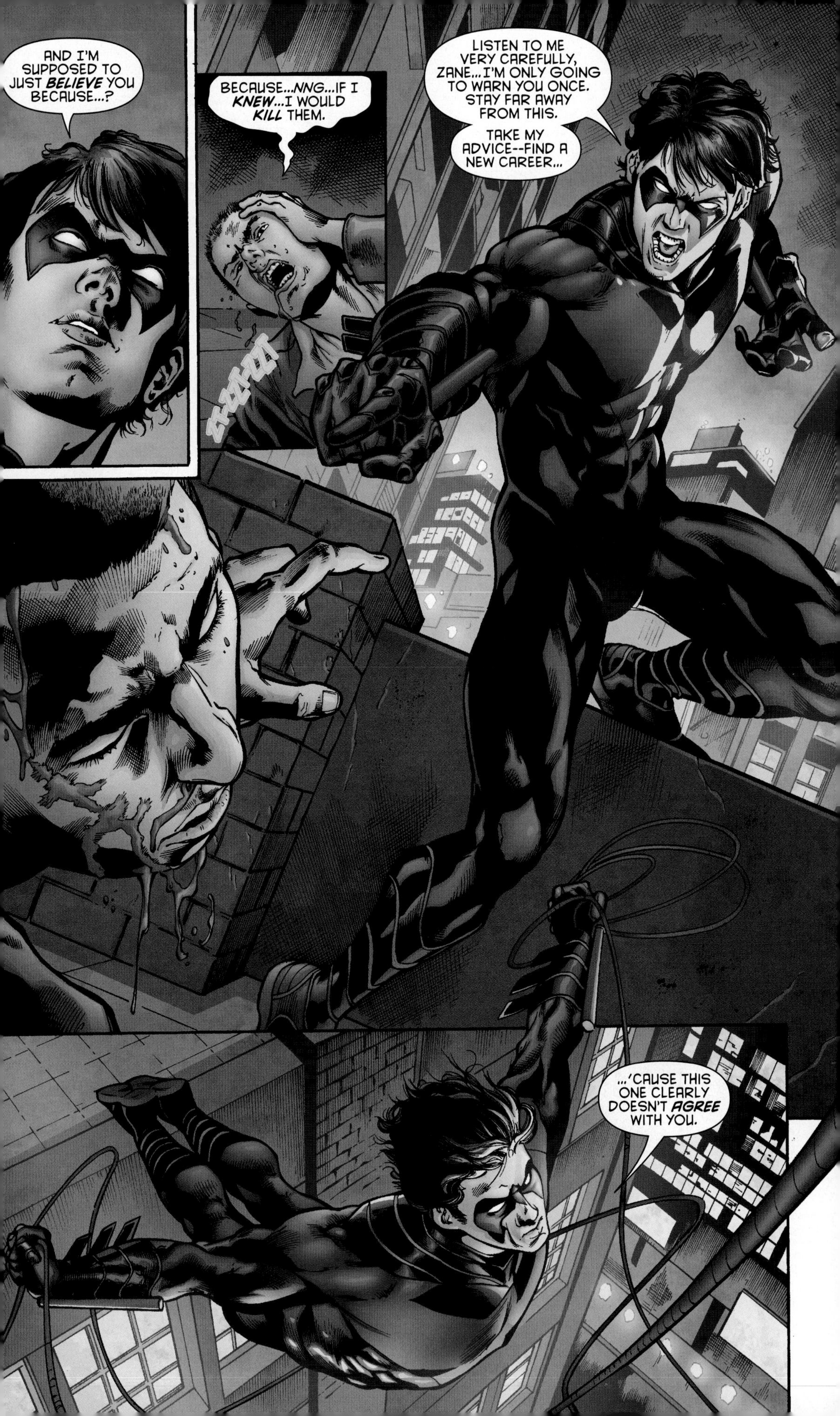
AND I'M SUPPOSED TO JUST BELIEVE YOU BECAUSE...?
BECAUSE...NNG...IF I KNEW...I WOULD KILL THEM.
ZZ-ZZ-ZZT
LISTEN TO ME VERY CAREFULLY, ZANE...I'M ONLY GOING TO WARN YOU ONCE. STAY FAR AWAY FROM THIS.
TAKE MY ADVICE--FIND A NEW CAREER...
...'CAUSE THIS ONE CLEARLY DOESN'T AGREE WITH YOU.

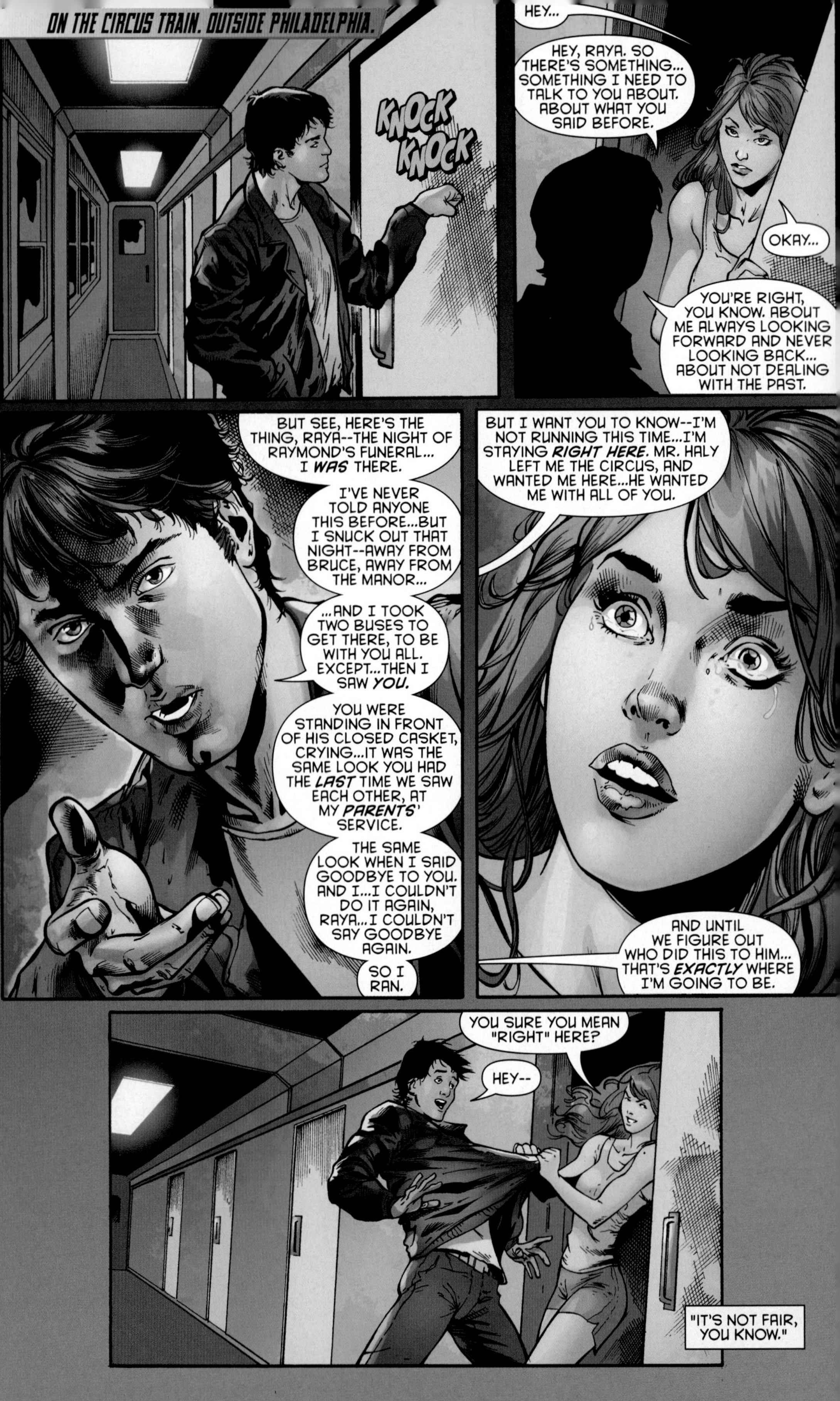
ON THE CIRCUS TRAIN. OUTSIDE PHILADELPHIA.
KNOCK KNOCK
HEY...
HEY, RAYA. SO THERE'S SOMETHING... SOMETHING I NEED TO TALK TO YOU ABOUT. ABOUT WHAT YOU SAID BEFORE.
OKAY...
YOU'RE RIGHT, YOU KNOW. ABOUT ME ALWAYS LOOKING FORWARD AND NEVER LOOKING BACK... ABOUT NOT DEALING WITH THE PAST.
BUT SEE, HERE'S THE THING, RAYA--THE NIGHT OF RAYMOND'S FUNERAL... I WAS THERE.
I'VE NEVER TOLD ANYONE THIS BEFORE...BUT I SNUCK OUT THAT NIGHT--AWAY FROM BRUCE, AWAY FROM THE MANOR...
...AND I TOOK TWO BUSES TO GET THERE, TO BE WITH YOU ALL. EXCEPT...THEN I SAW YOU.
YOU WERE STANDING IN FRONT OF HIS CLOSED CASKET, CRYING...IT WAS THE SAME LOOK YOU HAD THE LAST TIME WE SAW EACH OTHER, AT MY PARENTS' SERVICE.
THE SAME LOOK WHEN I SAID GOODBYE TO YOU. AND I...I COULDN'T DO IT AGAIN, RAYA...I COULDN'T SAY GOODBYE AGAIN.
SO I RAN.
BUT I WANT YOU TO KNOW--I'M NOT RUNNING THIS TIME...I'M STAYING RIGHT HERE. MR. HALY LEFT ME THE CIRCUS, AND WANTED ME HERE...HE WANTED ME WITH ALL OF YOU.
AND UNTIL WE FIGURE OUT WHO DID THIS TO HIM... THAT'S EXACTLY WHERE I'M GOING TO BE.
YOU SURE YOU MEAN "RIGHT" HERE?
HEY--
"IT'S NOT FAIR, YOU KNOW."

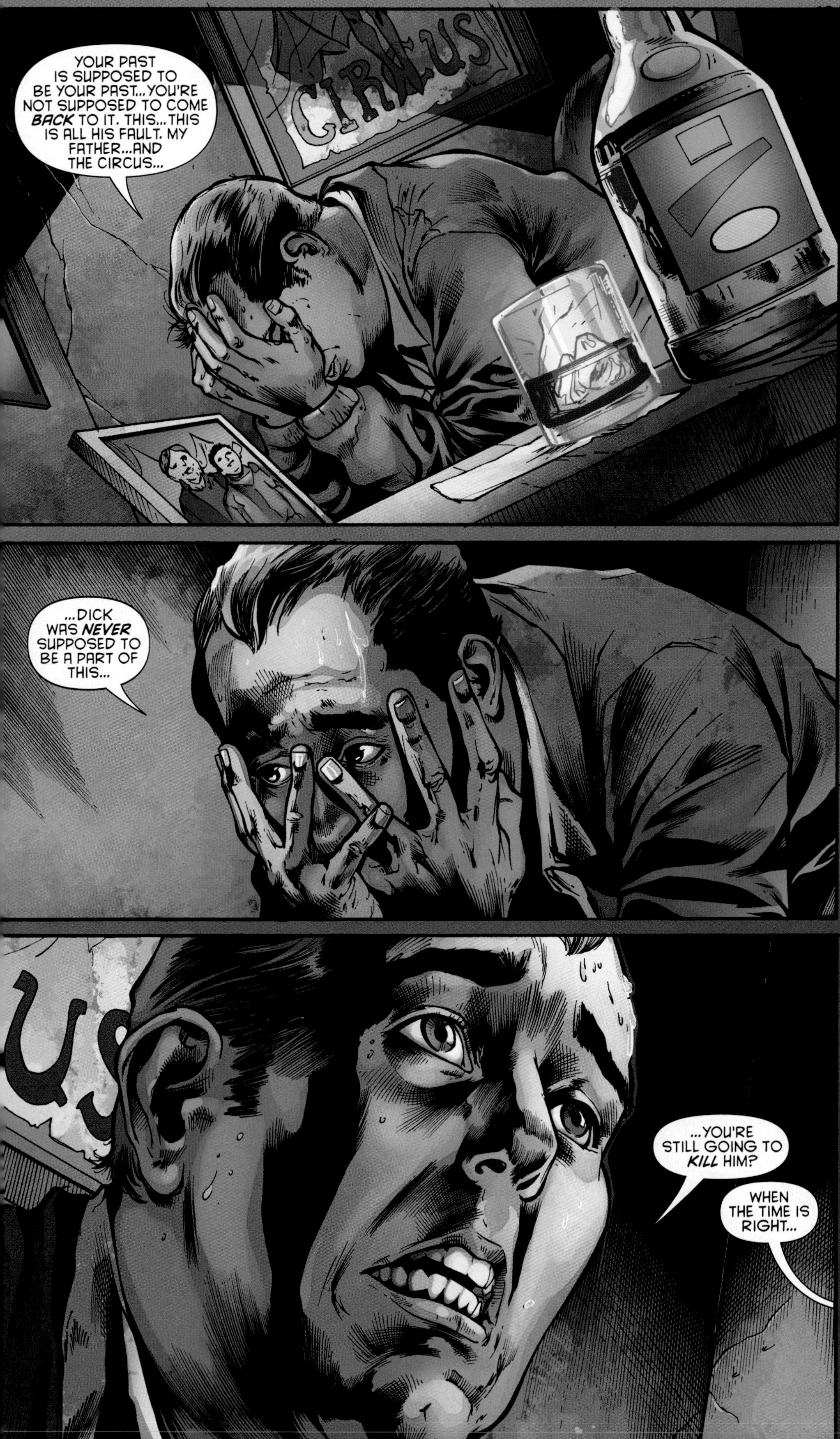

YOUR PAST IS SUPPOSED TO BE YOUR PAST...YOU'RE NOT SUPPOSED TO COME BACK TO IT. THIS...THIS IS ALL HIS FAULT. MY FATHER...AND THE CIRCUS...
CIRCUS
...DICK WAS NEVER SUPPOSED TO BE A PART OF THIS...
...YOU'RE STILL GOING TO KILL HIM?
WHEN THE TIME IS RIGHT...

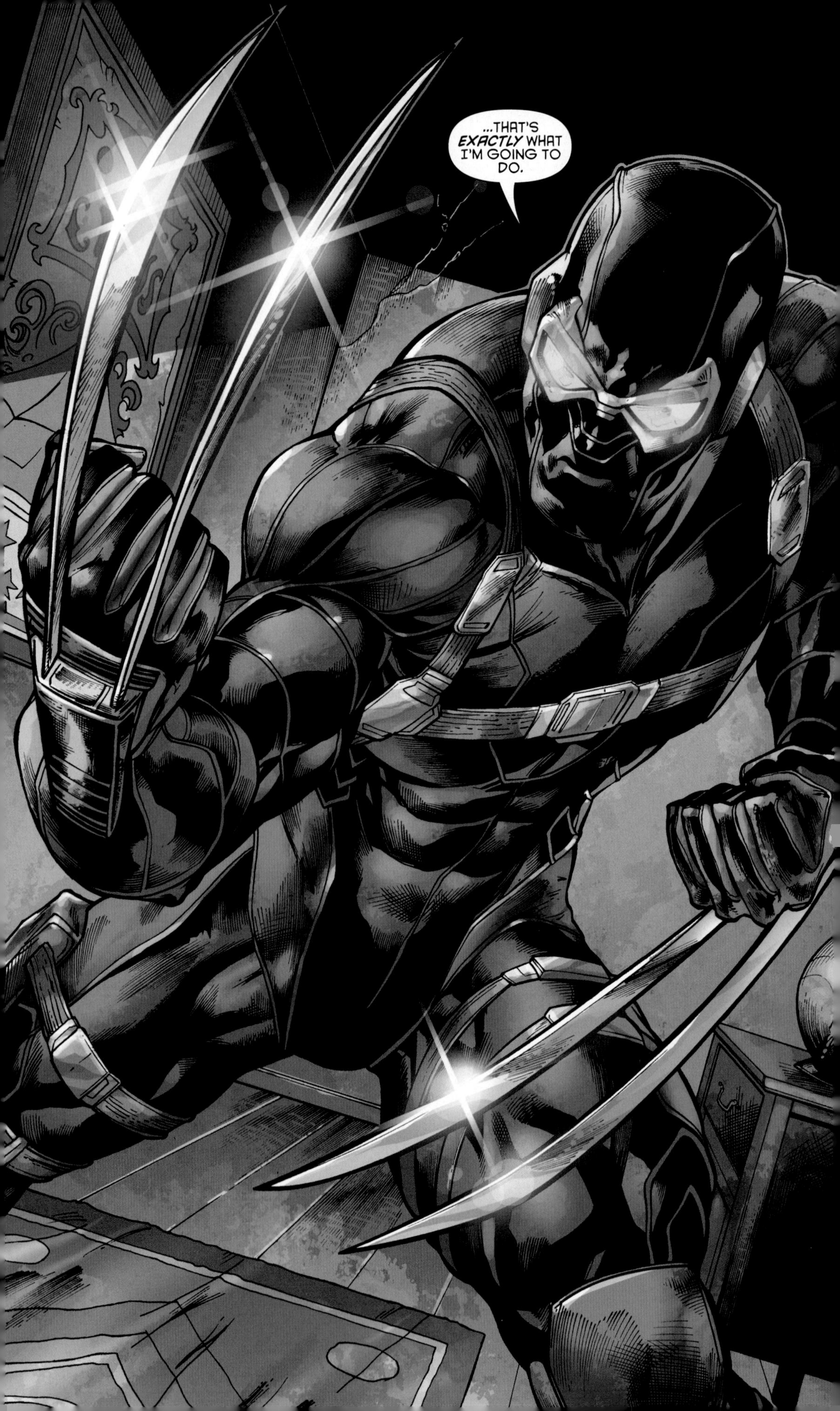
...THAT'S *EXACTLY* WHAT I'M GOING TO DO.

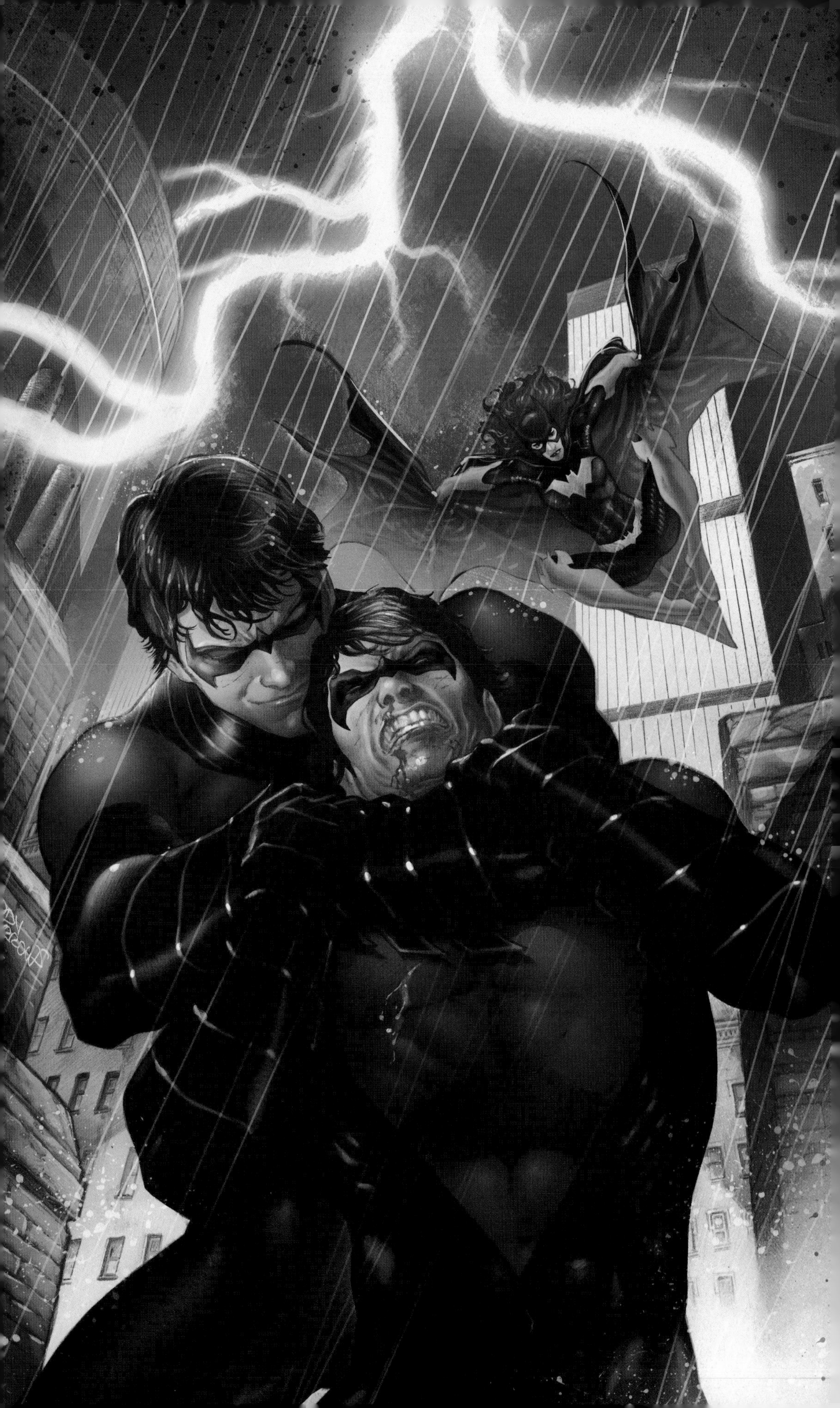

SOUTH BEACH CONNECTION

KYLE HIGGINS writer **TREVOR McCARTHY** artist cover art by Eddy Barrows & Rod Reis

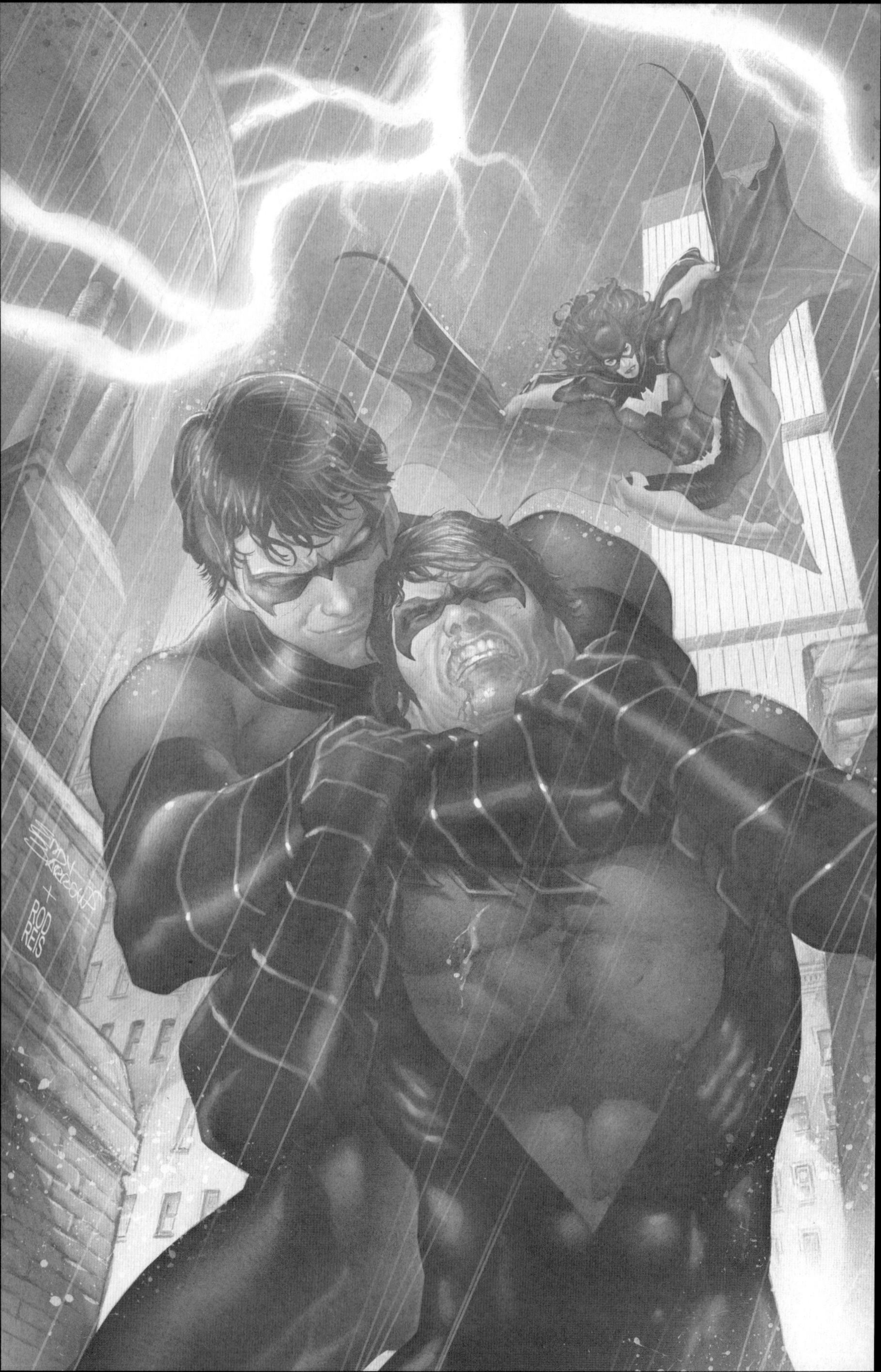

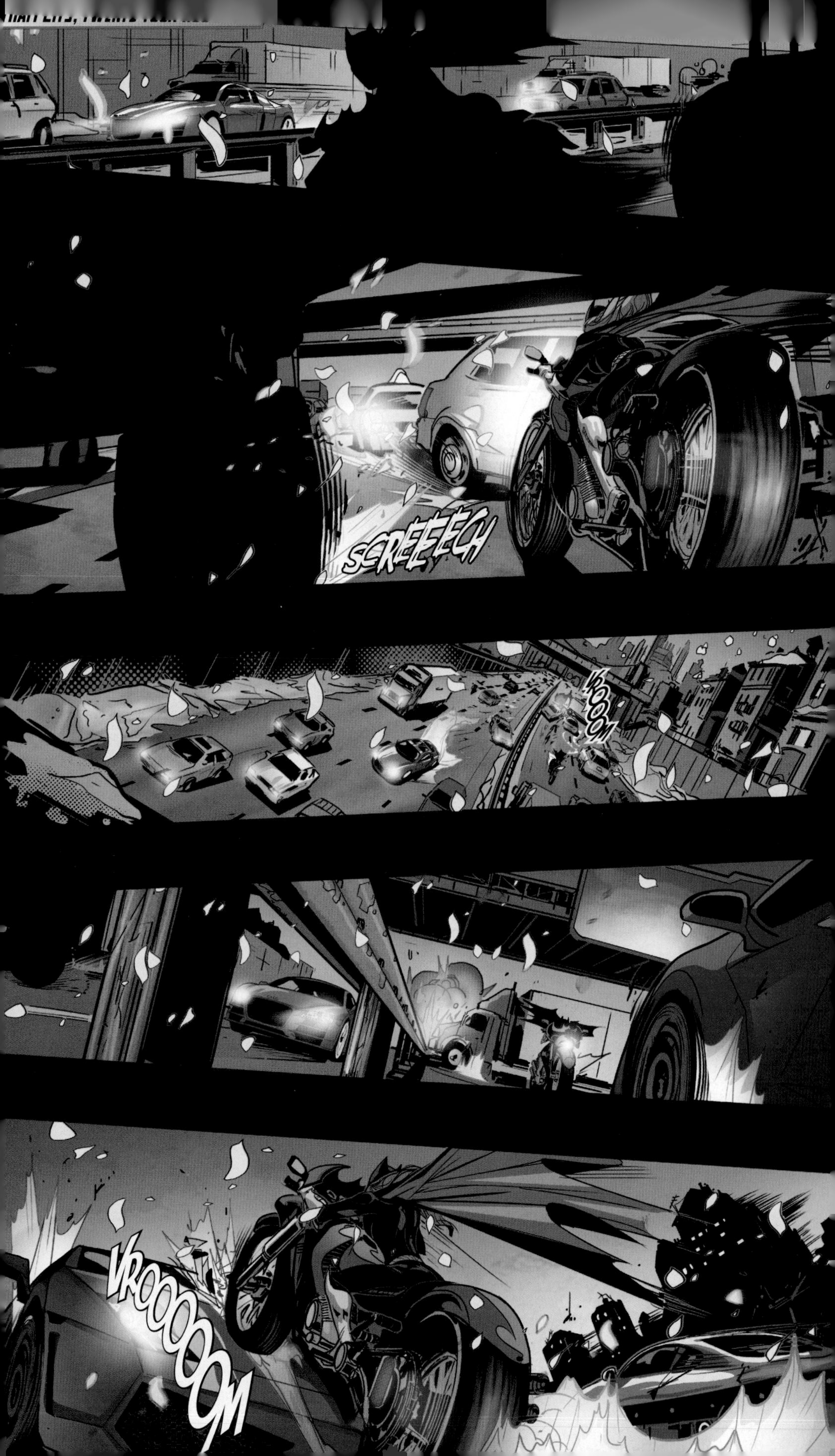
SCREEEECH
VROOOM
VROOOOOOM

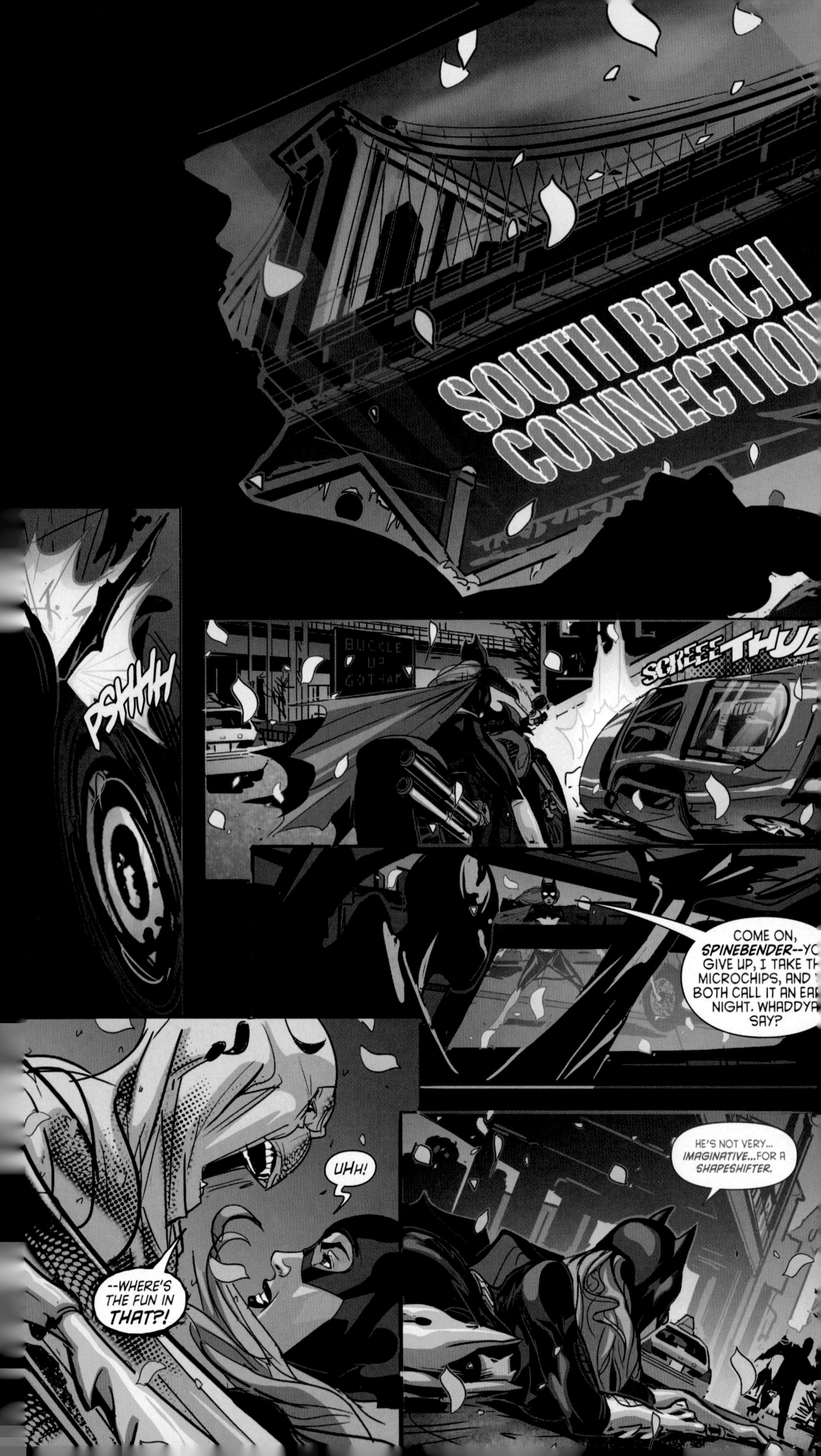
SOUTH BEACH
CONNECTION
PSHHH
BUCKLE UP GOTHAM
SCREEE
COME ON, *SPINEBENDER*--YO GIVE UP, I TAKE TH MICROCHIPS, AND BOTH CALL IT AN EA NIGHT. WHADDYA SAY?
UHH!
--WHERE'S THE FUN IN ***THAT?!***
HE'S NOT VERY... *IMAGINATIVE*...FOR A *SHAPESHIFTER.*

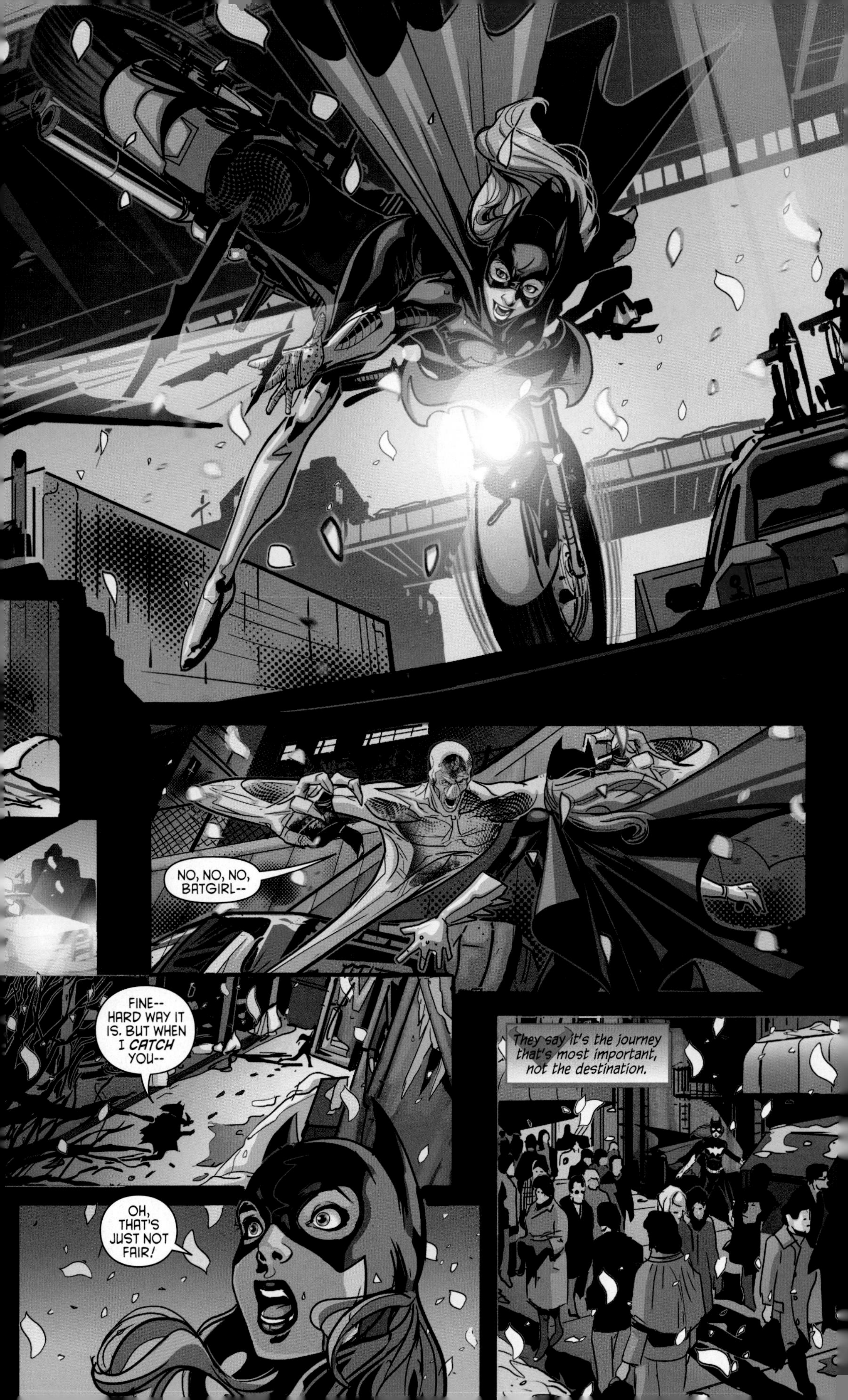
NO, NO, NO, BATGIRL--
FINE-- HARD WAY IT IS. BUT WHEN I CATCH YOU--
OH, THAT'S JUST NOT FAIR!
They say it's the journey that's most important, not the destination.

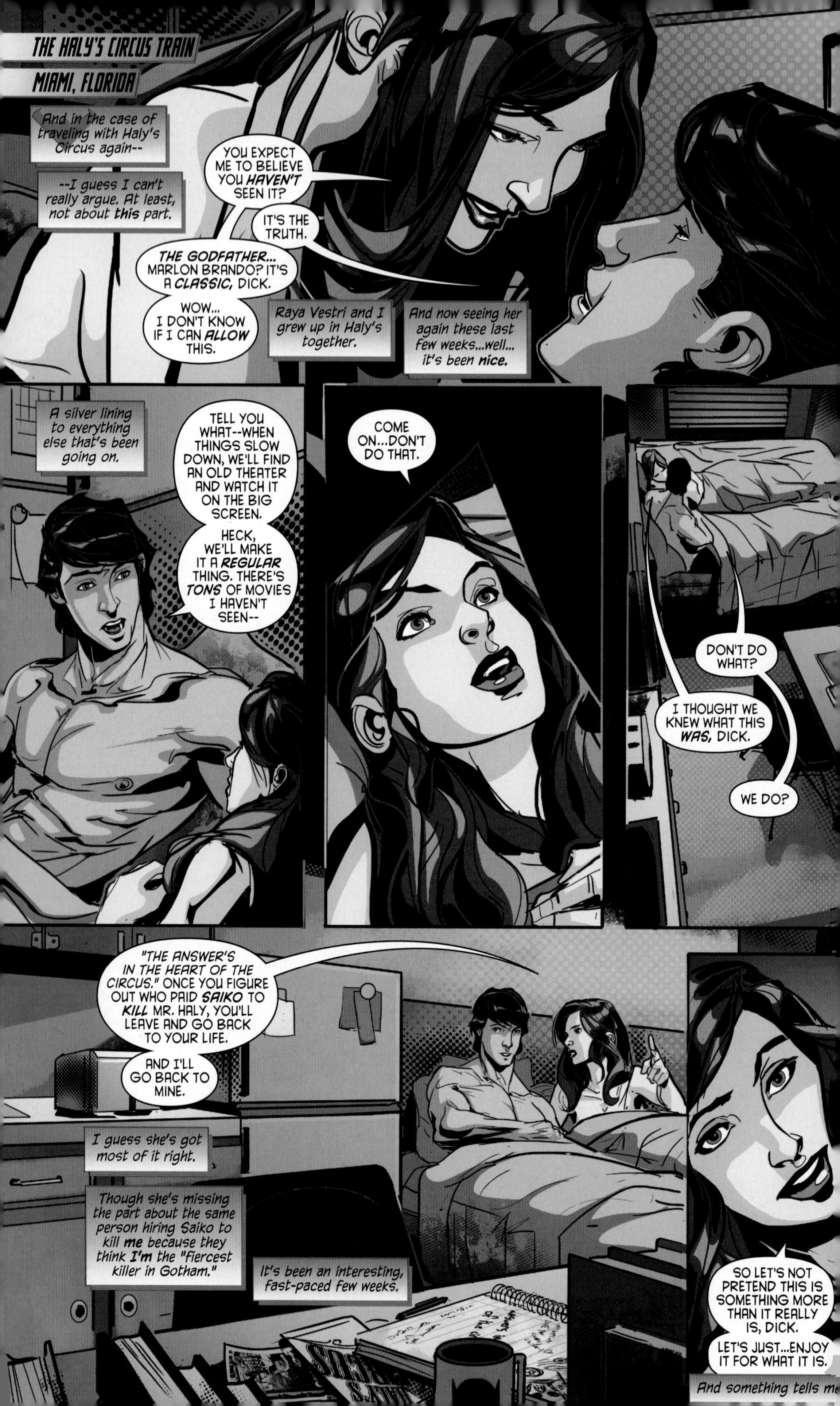
THE HALY'S CIRCUS TRAIN
MIAMI, FLORIDA
And in the case of traveling with Haly's Circus again--
--I guess I can't really argue. At least, not about this part.
YOU EXPECT ME TO BELIEVE YOU HAVEN'T SEEN IT?
IT'S THE TRUTH.
THE GODFATHER... MARLON BRANDO? IT'S A CLASSIC, DICK.
WOW... I DON'T KNOW IF I CAN ALLOW THIS.
Raya Vestri and I grew up in Haly's together.
And now seeing her again these last few weeks...well... it's been nice.
A silver lining to everything else that's been going on.
TELL YOU WHAT--WHEN THINGS SLOW DOWN, WE'LL FIND AN OLD THEATER AND WATCH IT ON THE BIG SCREEN.
HECK, WE'LL MAKE IT A REGULAR THING. THERE'S TONS OF MOVIES I HAVEN'T SEEN--
COME ON...DON'T DO THAT.
DON'T DO WHAT?
I THOUGHT WE KNEW WHAT THIS WAS, DICK.
WE DO?
"THE ANSWER'S IN THE HEART OF THE CIRCUS." ONCE YOU FIGURE OUT WHO PAID SAIKO TO KILL MR. HALY, YOU'LL LEAVE AND GO BACK TO YOUR LIFE.
AND I'LL GO BACK TO MINE.
I guess she's got most of it right.
Though she's missing the part about the same person hiring Saiko to kill me because they think I'm the "fiercest killer in Gotham."
It's been an interesting, fast-paced few weeks.
SO LET'S NOT PRETEND THIS IS SOMETHING MORE THAN IT REALLY IS, DICK.
LET'S JUST...ENJOY IT FOR WHAT IT IS.
And something tells me

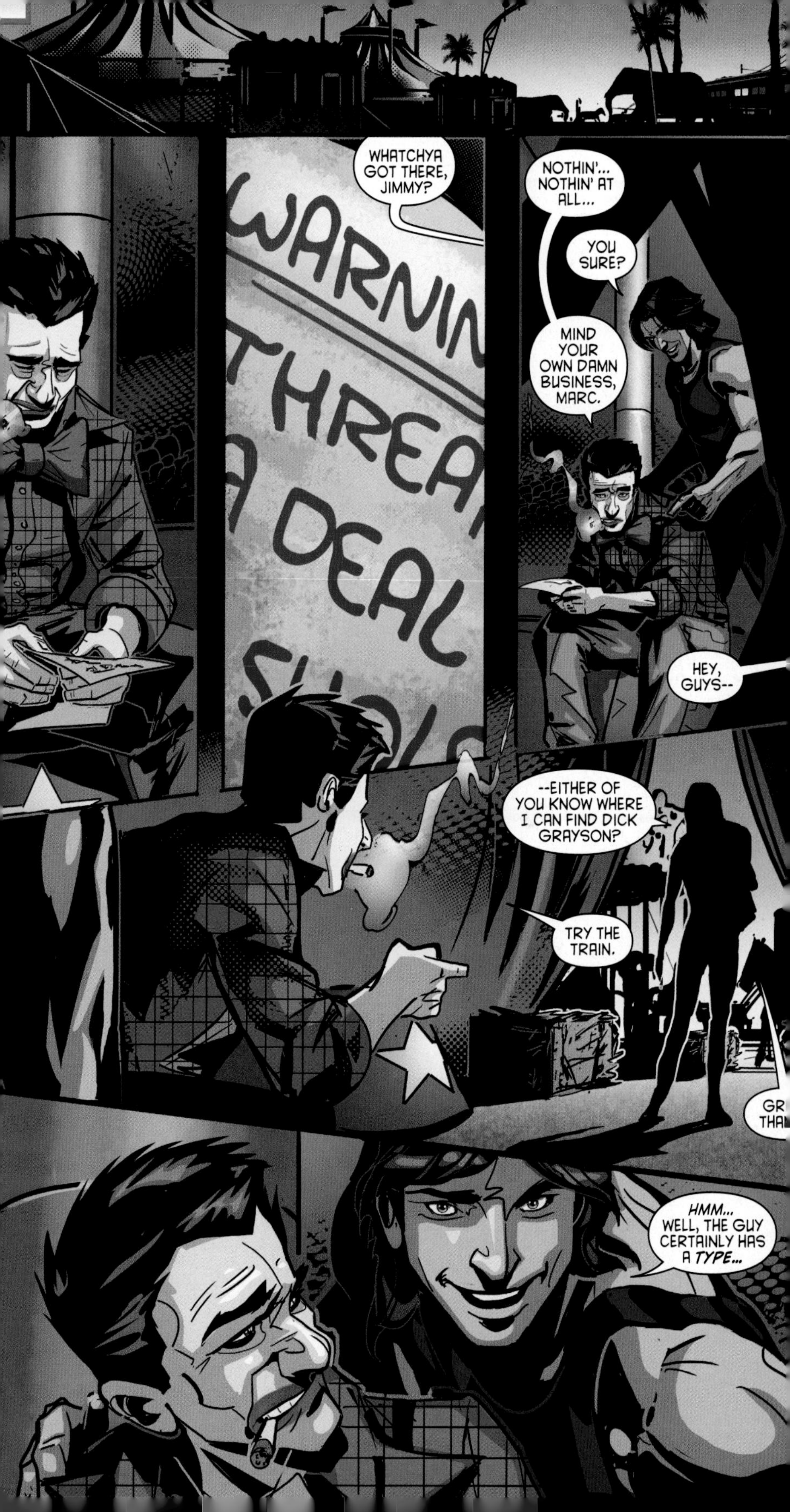
WHATCHYA GOT THERE, JIMMY?
NOTHIN'... NOTHIN' AT ALL...
YOU SURE?
MIND YOUR OWN DAMN BUSINESS, MARC.
HEY, GUYS--
--EITHER OF YOU KNOW WHERE I CAN FIND DICK GRAYSON?
TRY THE TRAIN.
HMM... WELL, THE GUY CERTAINLY HAS A *TYPE*...

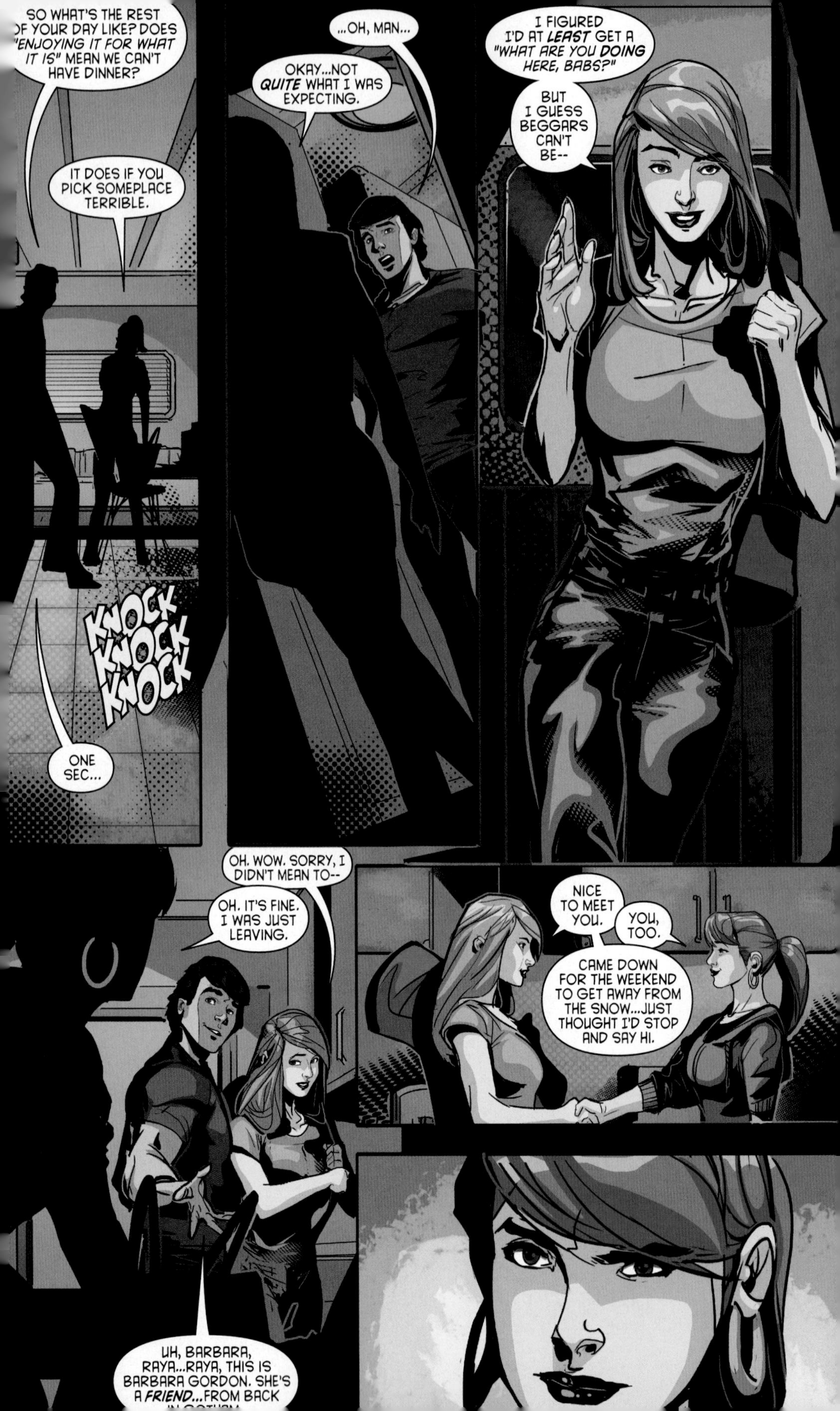

SO WHAT'S THE REST OF YOUR DAY LIKE? DOES "ENJOYING IT FOR WHAT IT IS" MEAN WE CAN'T HAVE DINNER?
IT DOES IF YOU PICK SOMEPLACE TERRIBLE.
KNOCK KNOCK KNOCK
ONE SEC...
...OH, MAN...
OKAY...NOT QUITE WHAT I WAS EXPECTING.
I FIGURED I'D AT LEAST GET A "WHAT ARE YOU DOING HERE, BABS?"
BUT I GUESS BEGGARS CAN'T BE--
OH. WOW. SORRY, I DIDN'T MEAN TO--
OH. IT'S FINE. I WAS JUST LEAVING.
UH, BARBARA, RAYA...RAYA, THIS IS BARBARA GORDON. SHE'S A FRIEND...FROM BACK
NICE TO MEET YOU.
YOU, TOO.
CAME DOWN FOR THE WEEKEND TO GET AWAY FROM THE SNOW...JUST THOUGHT I'D STOP AND SAY HI.

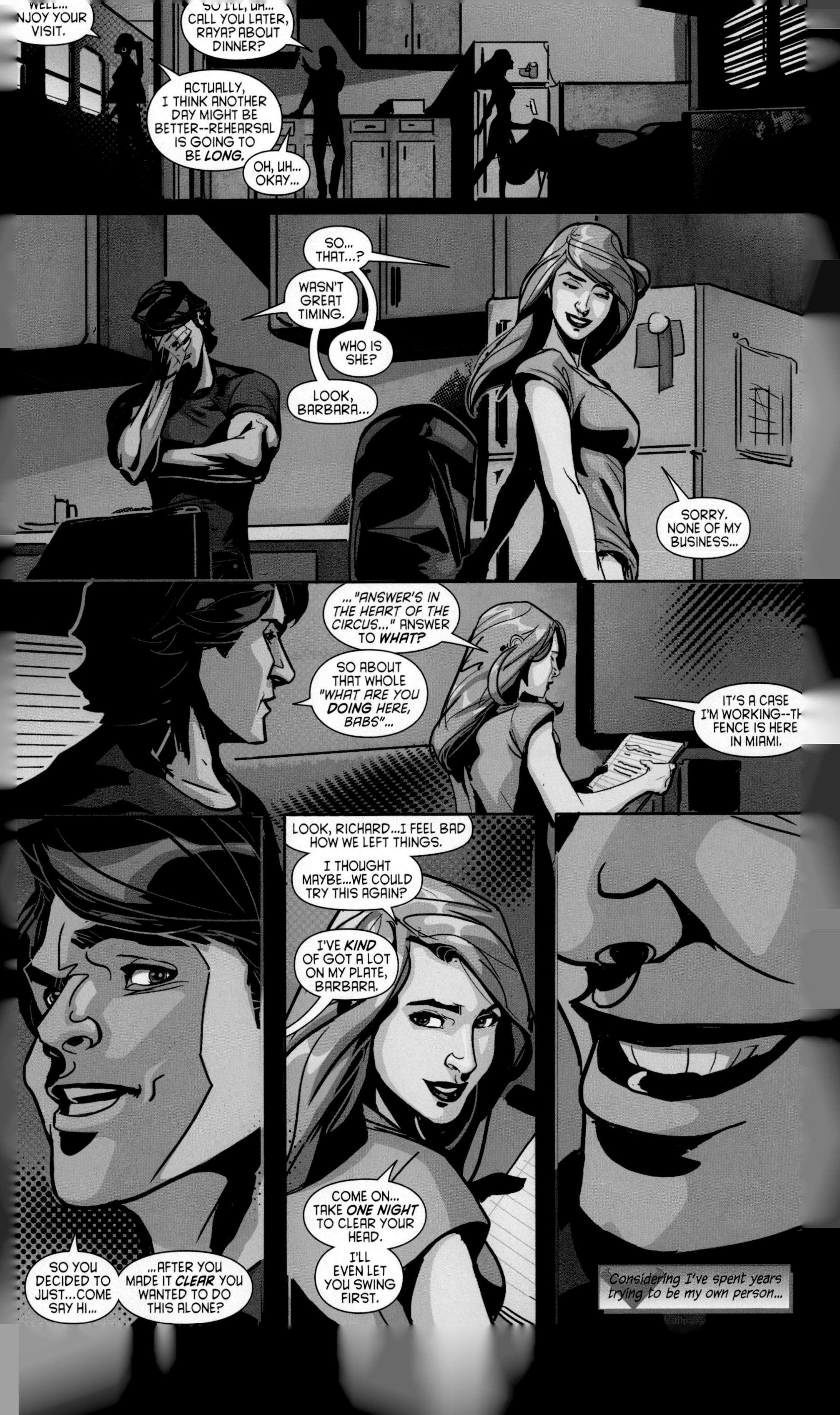
WELL... ENJOY YOUR VISIT.
SO I'LL, UH... CALL YOU LATER, RAYA? ABOUT DINNER?
ACTUALLY, I THINK ANOTHER DAY MIGHT BE BETTER--REHEARSAL IS GOING TO BE LONG.
OH, UH... OKAY...
SO... THAT...?
WASN'T GREAT TIMING.
WHO IS SHE?
LOOK, BARBARA...
SORRY. NONE OF MY BUSINESS...
..."ANSWER'S IN THE HEART OF THE CIRCUS..." ANSWER TO WHAT?
SO ABOUT THAT WHOLE "WHAT ARE YOU DOING HERE, BABS"...
IT'S A CASE I'M WORKING--TH FENCE IS HERE IN MIAMI.
LOOK, RICHARD...I FEEL BAD HOW WE LEFT THINGS.
I THOUGHT MAYBE...WE COULD TRY THIS AGAIN?
I'VE KIND OF GOT A LOT ON MY PLATE, BARBARA.
COME ON... TAKE ONE NIGHT TO CLEAR YOUR HEAD.
I'LL EVEN LET YOU SWING FIRST.
SO YOU DECIDED TO JUST...COME SAY HI...
...AFTER YOU MADE IT CLEAR YOU WANTED TO DO THIS ALONE?
Considering I've spent years trying to be my own person...

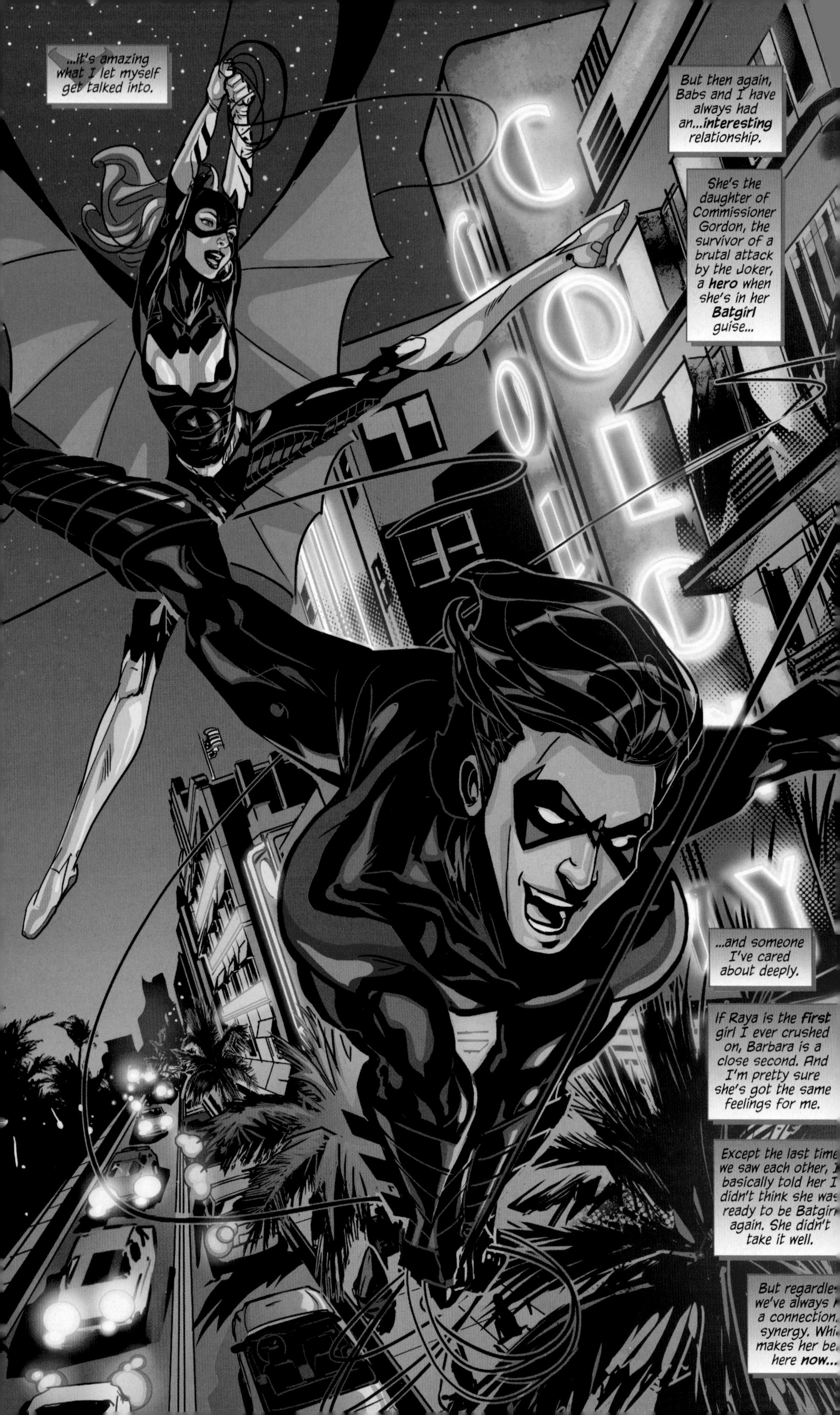
...it's amazing what I let myself get talked into.
But then again, Babs and I have always had an...interesting relationship.
She's the daughter of Commissioner Gordon, the survivor of a brutal attack by the Joker, a hero when she's in her Batgirl guise...
...and someone I've cared about deeply.
If Raya is the first girl I ever crushed on, Barbara is a close second. And I'm pretty sure she's got the same feelings for me.
Except the last time we saw each other, I basically told her I didn't think she was ready to be Batgirl again. She didn't take it well.
But regardle we've always a connection. synergy. Whi makes her be here now...

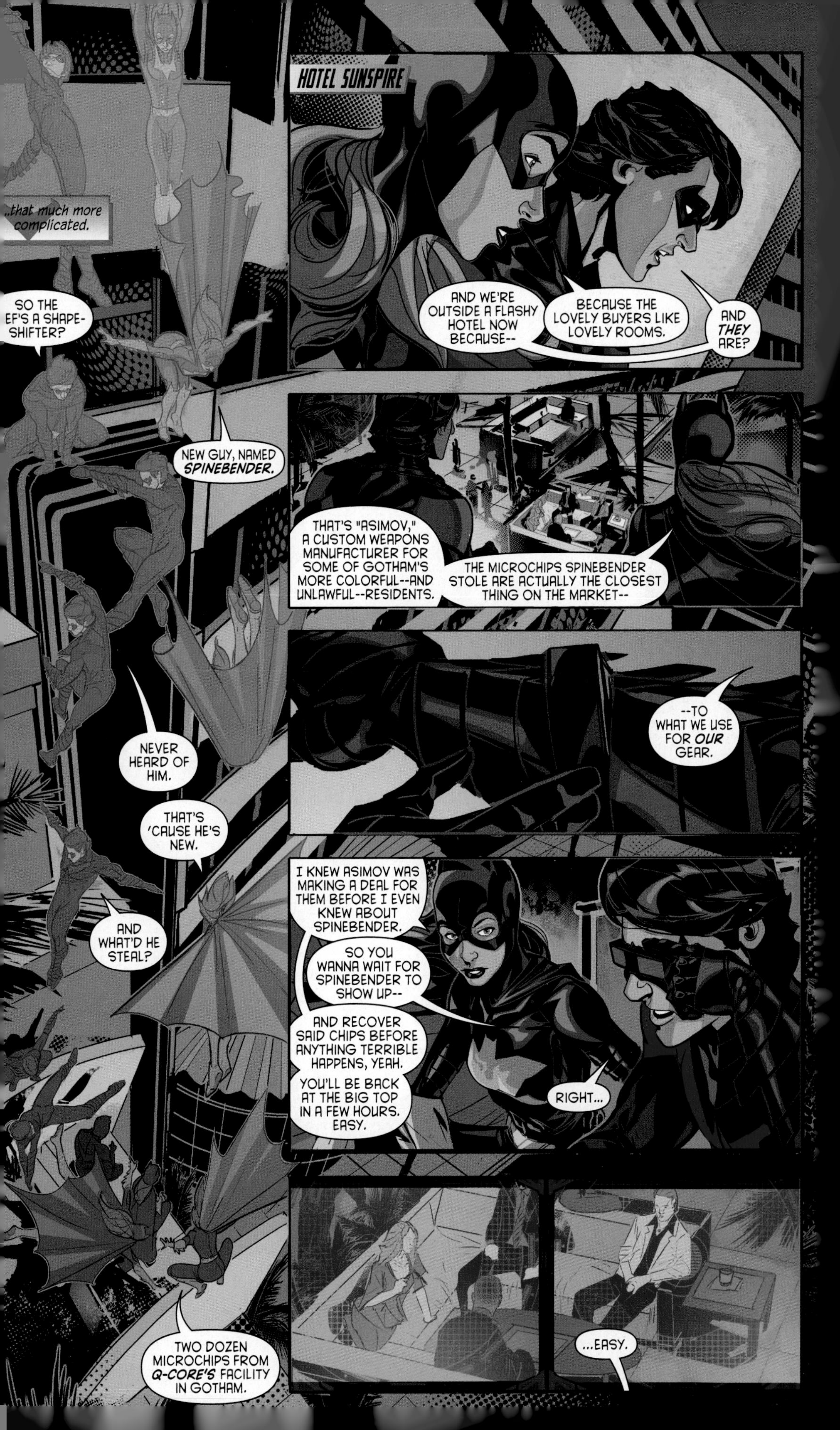
..that much more complicated.
SO THE EF'S A SHAPE-SHIFTER?
NEW GUY, NAMED SPINEBENDER.
NEVER HEARD OF HIM.
THAT'S 'CAUSE HE'S NEW.
AND WHAT'D HE STEAL?
TWO DOZEN MICROCHIPS FROM Q-CORE'S FACILITY IN GOTHAM.
HOTEL SUNSPIRE
AND WE'RE OUTSIDE A FLASHY HOTEL NOW BECAUSE--
BECAUSE THE LOVELY BUYERS LIKE LOVELY ROOMS.
AND THEY ARE?
THAT'S "ASIMOV," A CUSTOM WEAPONS MANUFACTURER FOR SOME OF GOTHAM'S MORE COLORFUL--AND UNLAWFUL--RESIDENTS.
THE MICROCHIPS SPINEBENDER STOLE ARE ACTUALLY THE CLOSEST THING ON THE MARKET--
--TO WHAT WE USE FOR OUR GEAR.
I KNEW ASIMOV WAS MAKING A DEAL FOR THEM BEFORE I EVEN KNEW ABOUT SPINEBENDER.
SO YOU WANNA WAIT FOR SPINEBENDER TO SHOW UP--
AND RECOVER SAID CHIPS BEFORE ANYTHING TERRIBLE HAPPENS, YEAH.
YOU'LL BE BACK AT THE BIG TOP IN A FEW HOURS. EASY.
RIGHT...
...EASY.

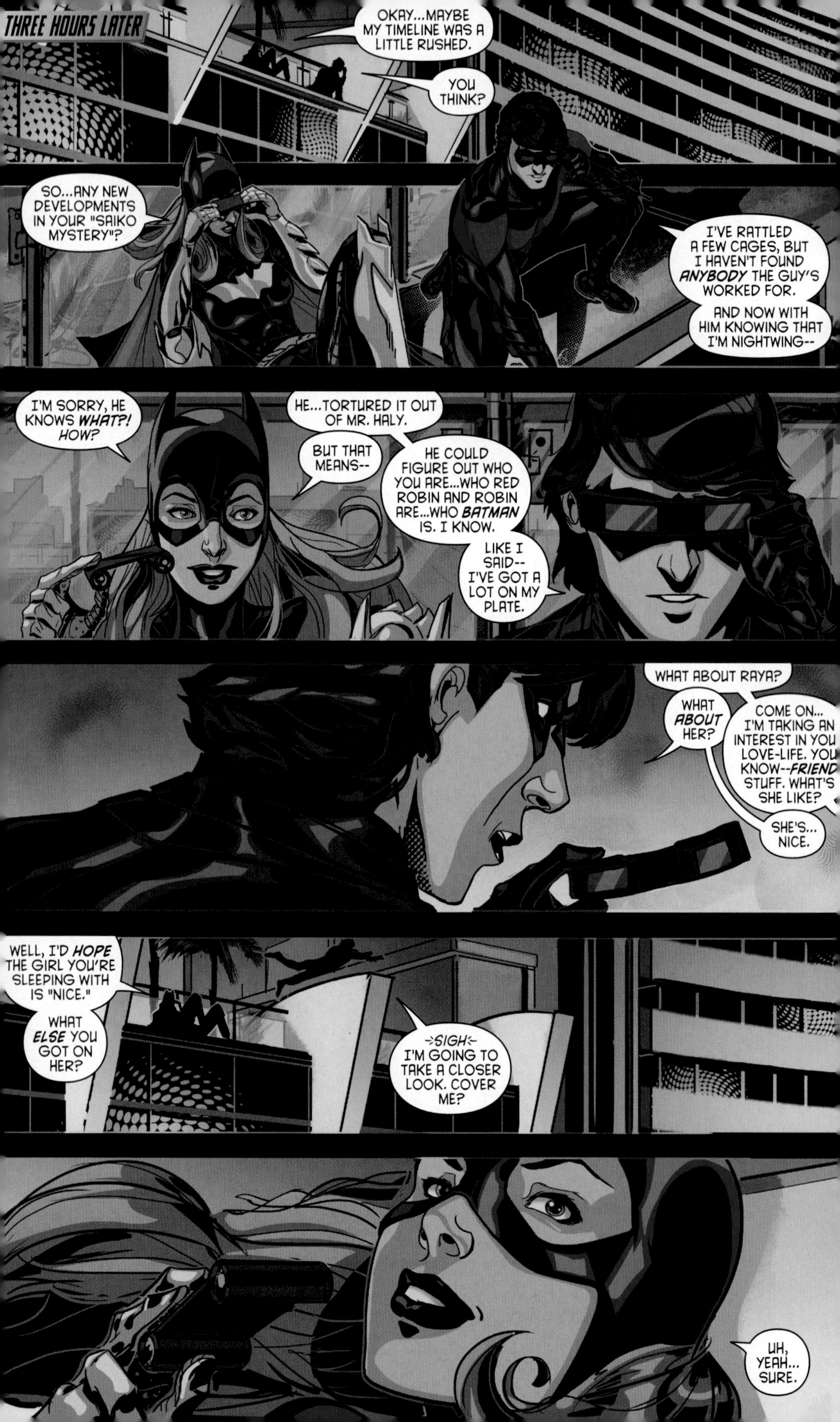
THREE HOURS LATER
OKAY...MAYBE MY TIMELINE WAS A LITTLE RUSHED.
YOU THINK?
SO...ANY NEW DEVELOPMENTS IN YOUR "SAIKO MYSTERY"?
I'VE RATTLED A FEW CAGES, BUT I HAVEN'T FOUND ANYBODY THE GUY'S WORKED FOR.
AND NOW WITH HIM KNOWING THAT I'M NIGHTWING--
I'M SORRY, HE KNOWS WHAT?! HOW?
HE...TORTURED IT OUT OF MR. HALY.
BUT THAT MEANS--
HE COULD FIGURE OUT WHO YOU ARE...WHO RED ROBIN AND ROBIN ARE...WHO BATMAN IS. I KNOW.
LIKE I SAID-- I'VE GOT A LOT ON MY PLATE.
WHAT ABOUT RAYA?
WHAT ABOUT HER?
COME ON... I'M TAKING AN INTEREST IN YOU LOVE-LIFE. YOU KNOW--FRIEND STUFF. WHAT'S SHE LIKE?
SHE'S... NICE.
WELL, I'D HOPE THE GIRL YOU'RE SLEEPING WITH IS "NICE."
WHAT ELSE YOU GOT ON HER?
SIGH
I'M GOING TO TAKE A CLOSER LOOK. COVER ME?
UH, YEAH... SURE.

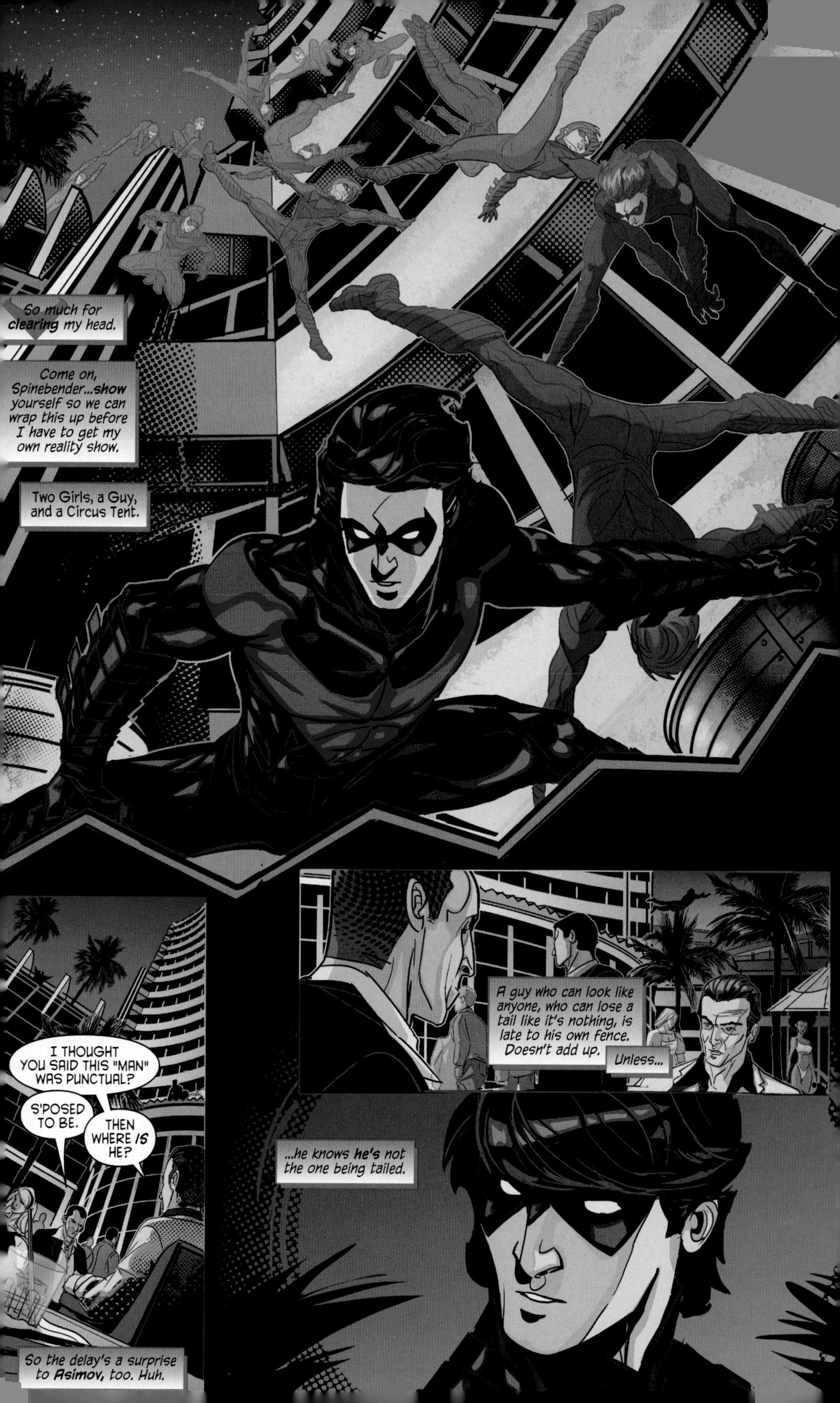
So much for clearing my head.
Come on, Spinebender...show yourself so we can wrap this up before I have to get my own reality show.
Two Girls, a Guy, and a Circus Tent.
I THOUGHT YOU SAID THIS "MAN" WAS PUNCTUAL?
S'POSED TO BE.
THEN WHERE IS HE?
So the delay's a surprise to Asimov, too. Huh.
A guy who can look like anyone, who can lose a tail like it's nothing, is late to his own fence. Doesn't add up.
Unless...
...he knows he's not the one being tailed.

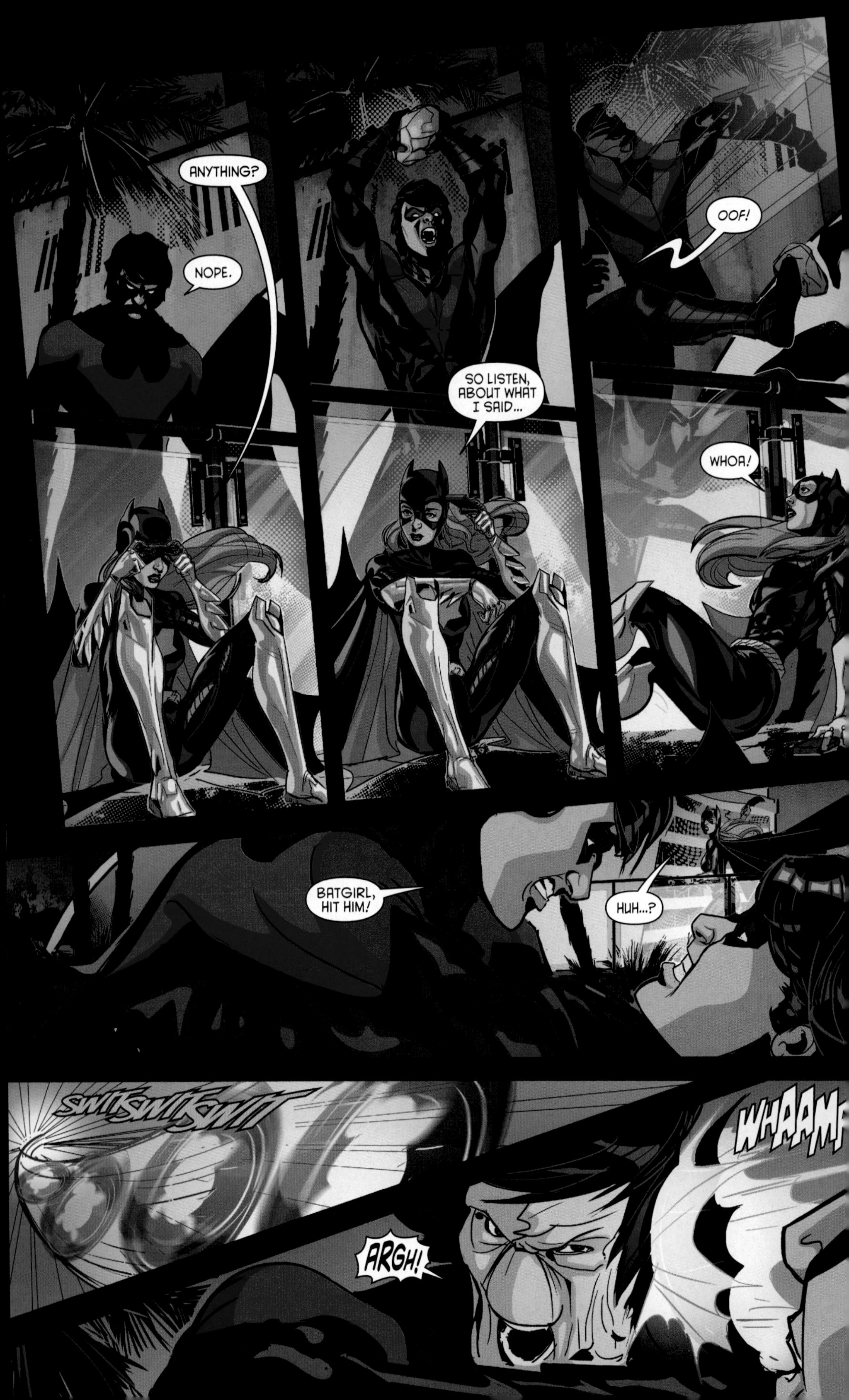
ANYTHING?
NOPE.
SO LISTEN, ABOUT WHAT I SAID...
OOF!
WHOA!
BATGIRL, HIT HIM!
HUH...?
SWISWISWIT
WHAAM!
ARGH!

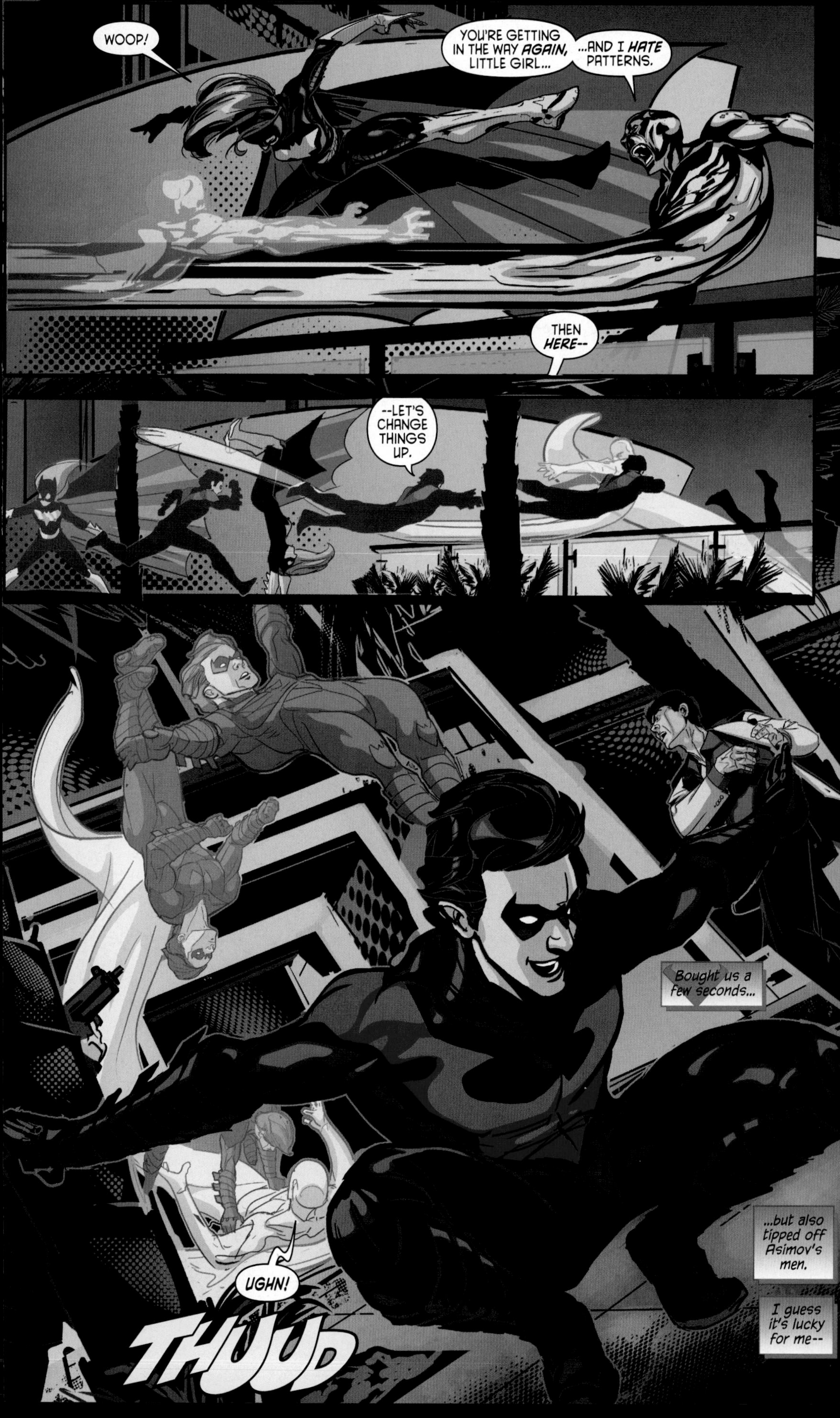
WOOP!
YOU'RE GETTING IN THE WAY AGAIN, LITTLE GIRL...
...AND I HATE PATTERNS.
THEN HERE--
--LET'S CHANGE THINGS UP.
Bought us a few seconds...
...but also tipped off Asimov's men.
I guess it's lucky for me--
UGHN!
THUUD

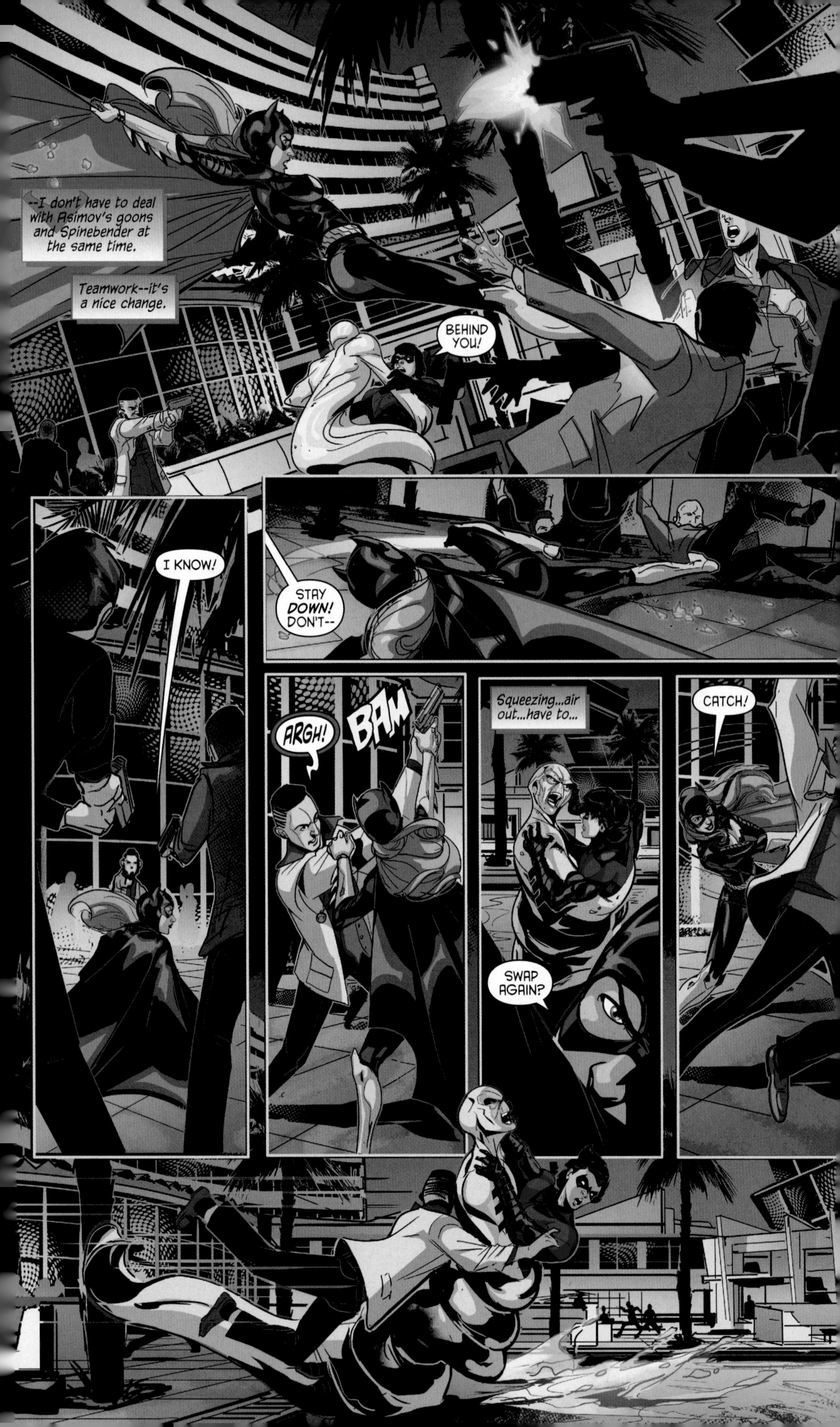
--I don't have to deal with Asimov's goons and Spinebender at the same time.
Teamwork--it's a nice change.
BEHIND YOU!
I KNOW!
STAY DOWN! DON'T--
ARGH!
BAM
Squeezing...air out...have to...
SWAP AGAIN?
CATCH!

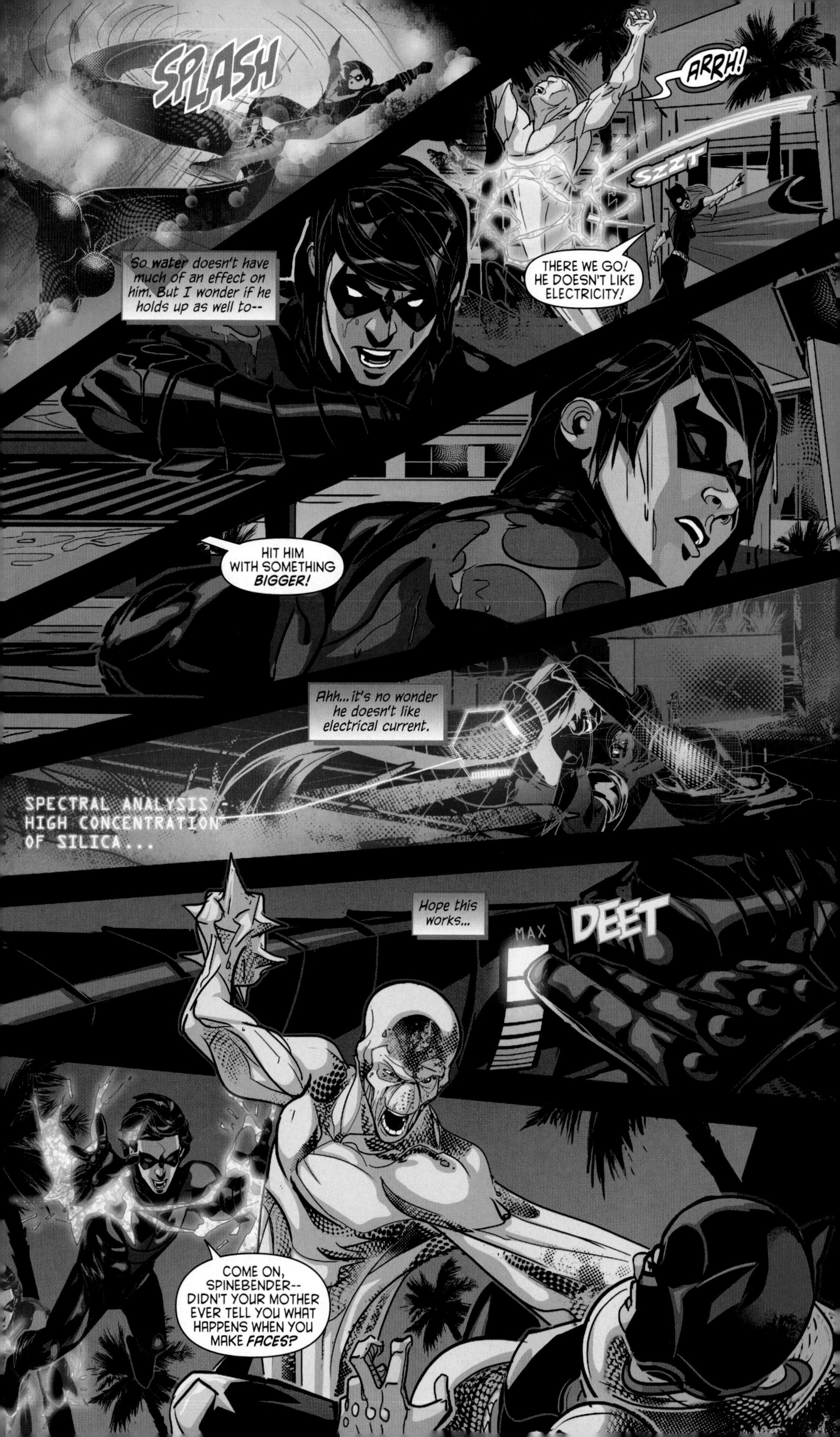
SPLASH
ARRH!
SZZT
So water doesn't have much of an effect on him. But I wonder if he holds up as well to--
THERE WE GO! HE DOESN'T LIKE ELECTRICITY!
HIT HIM WITH SOMETHING BIGGER!
Ahh...it's no wonder he doesn't like electrical current.
SPECTRAL ANALYSIS - HIGH CONCENTRATION OF SILICA...
Hope this works...
MAX
DEET
COME ON, SPINEBENDER-- DIDN'T YOUR MOTHER EVER TELL YOU WHAT HAPPENS WHEN YOU MAKE FACES?

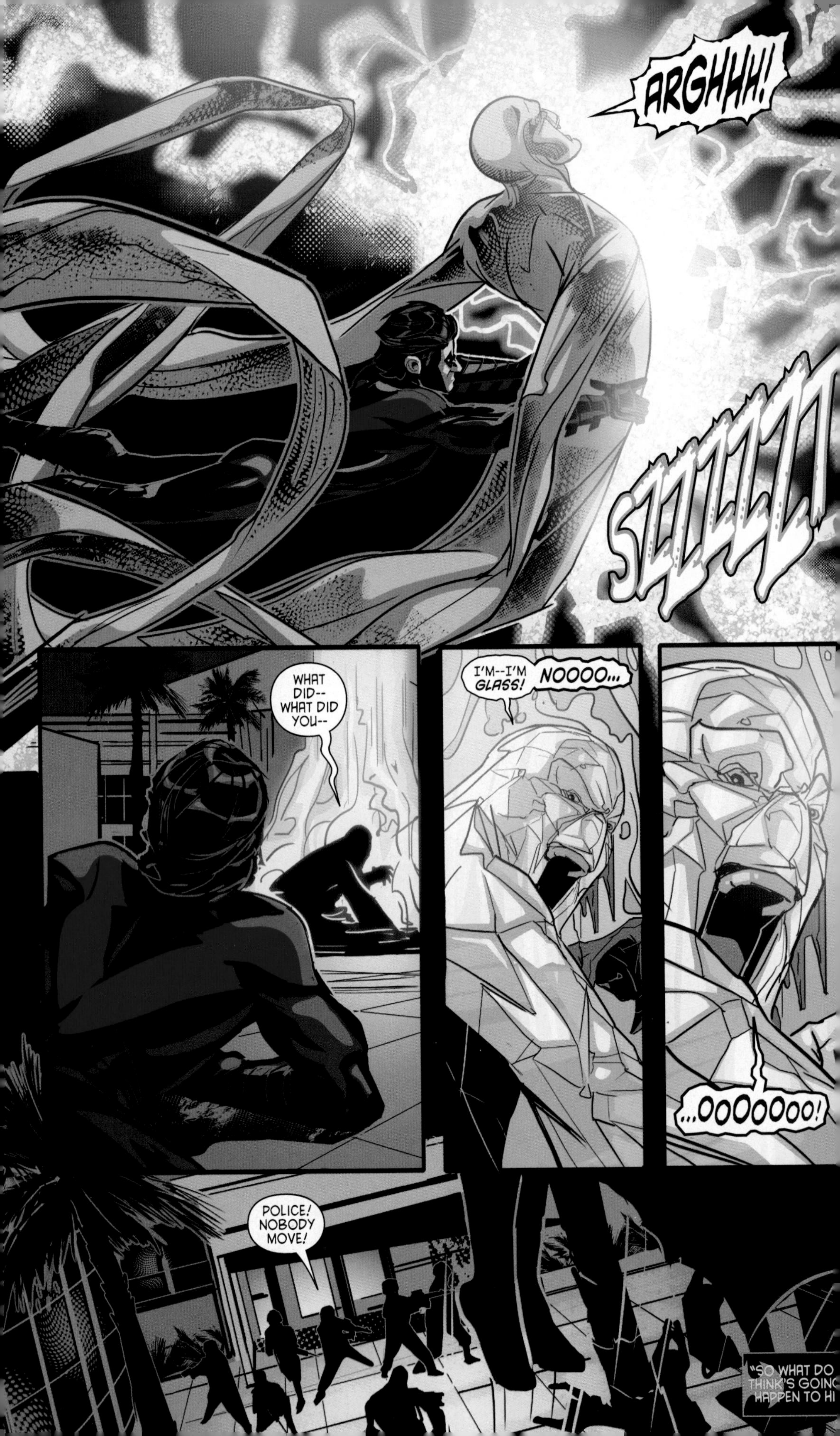
ARGHHH!
SZZZZZT
WHAT DID-- WHAT DID YOU--
I'M--I'M GLASS!
NOOOO...
...OOOOOOO!
POLICE! NOBODY MOVE!
"SO WHAT DO
THINK'S GOING
HAPPEN TO HI

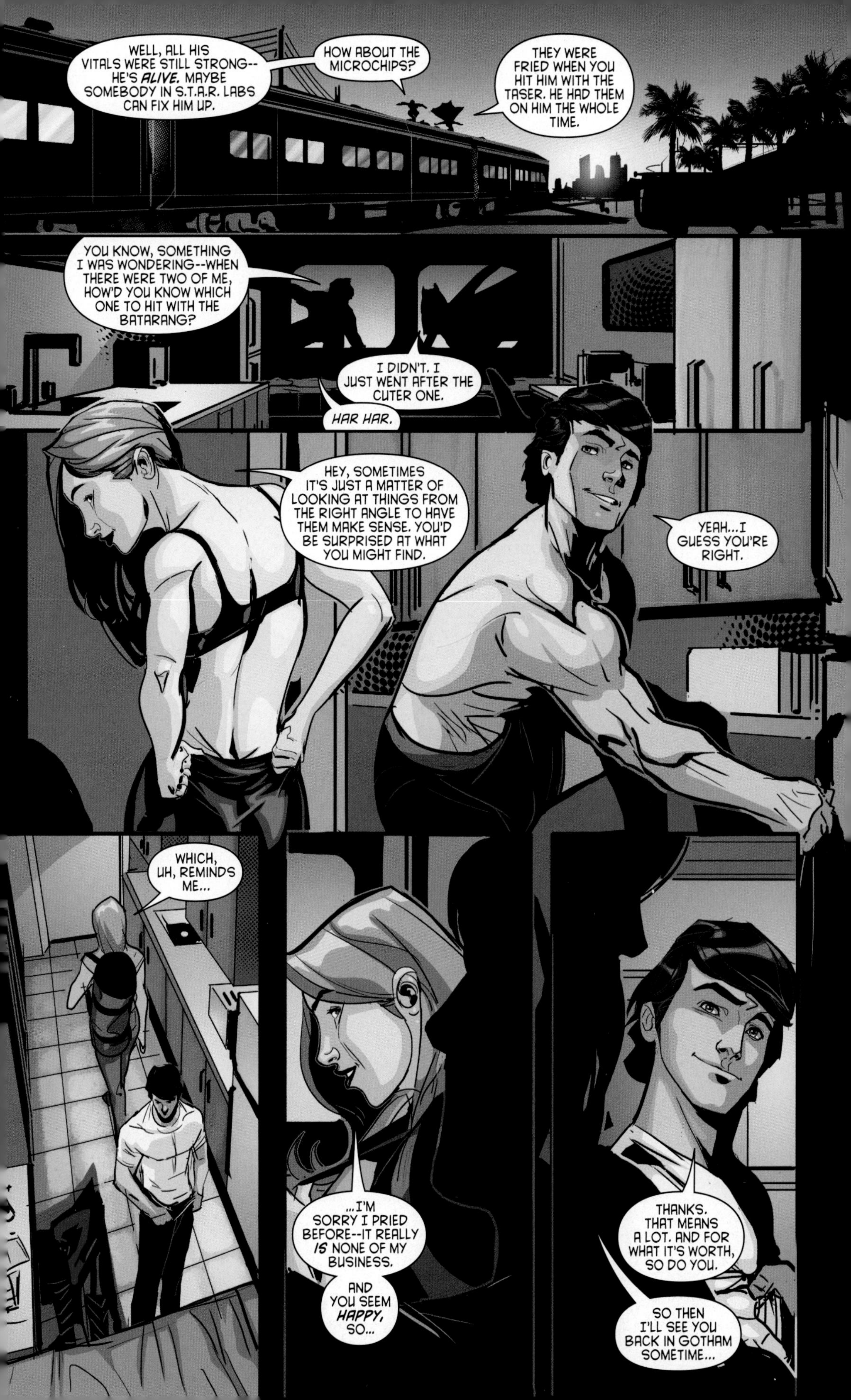
WELL, ALL HIS VITALS WERE STILL STRONG-- HE'S ALIVE. MAYBE SOMEBODY IN S.T.A.R. LABS CAN FIX HIM UP.
HOW ABOUT THE MICROCHIPS?
THEY WERE FRIED WHEN YOU HIT HIM WITH THE TASER. HE HAD THEM ON HIM THE WHOLE TIME.
YOU KNOW, SOMETHING I WAS WONDERING--WHEN THERE WERE TWO OF ME, HOW'D YOU KNOW WHICH ONE TO HIT WITH THE BATARANG?
I DIDN'T. I JUST WENT AFTER THE CUTER ONE.
HAR HAR.
HEY, SOMETIMES IT'S JUST A MATTER OF LOOKING AT THINGS FROM THE RIGHT ANGLE TO HAVE THEM MAKE SENSE. YOU'D BE SURPRISED AT WHAT YOU MIGHT FIND.
YEAH...I GUESS YOU'RE RIGHT.
WHICH, UH, REMINDS ME...
...I'M SORRY I PRIED BEFORE--IT REALLY IS NONE OF MY BUSINESS.
AND YOU SEEM HAPPY, SO...
THANKS. THAT MEANS A LOT. AND FOR WHAT IT'S WORTH, SO DO YOU.
SO THEN I'LL SEE YOU BACK IN GOTHAM SOMETIME...

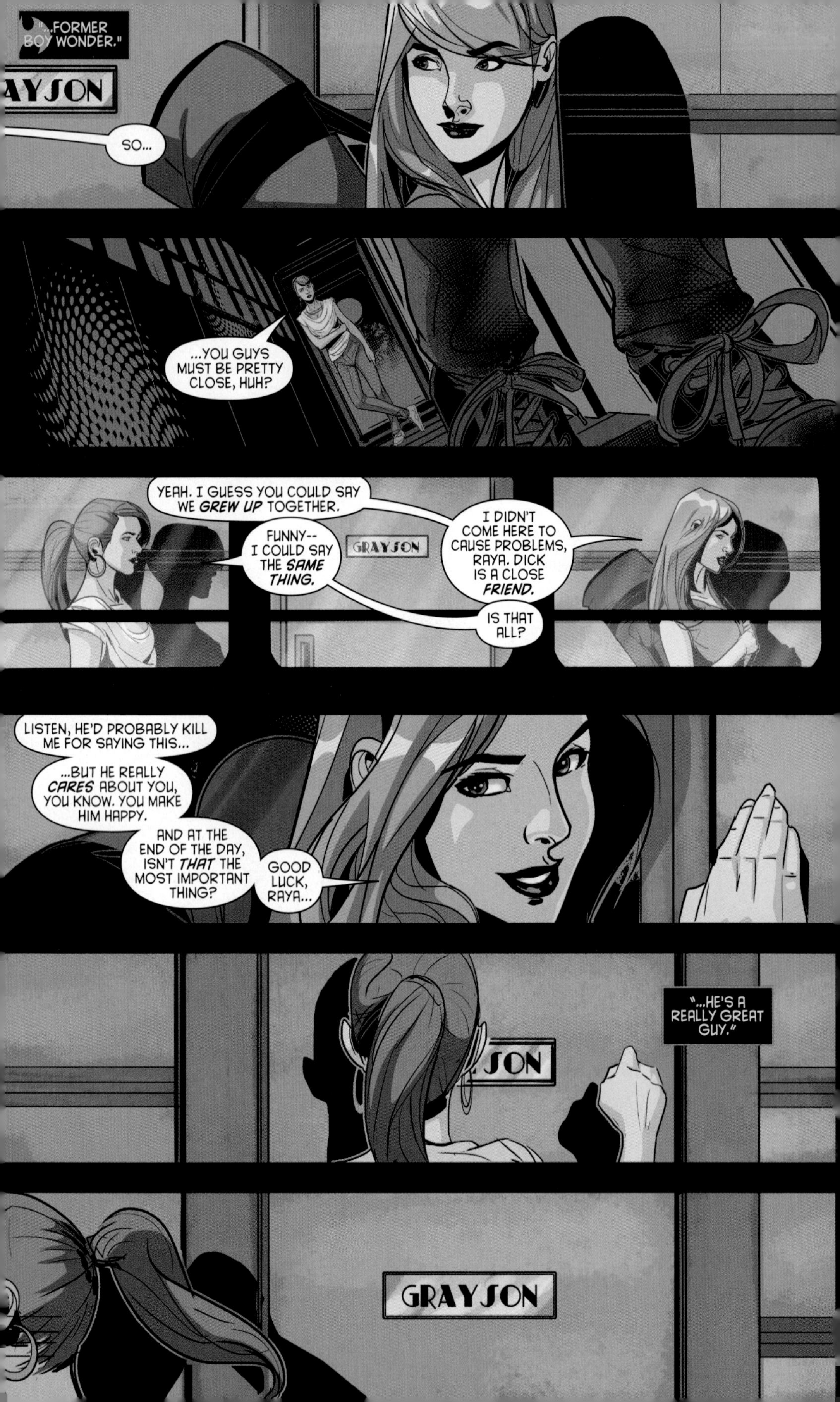
"...FORMER BOY WONDER."
AYSON
SO...
...YOU GUYS MUST BE PRETTY CLOSE, HUH?
YEAH. I GUESS YOU COULD SAY WE GREW UP TOGETHER.
GRAYSON
I DIDN'T COME HERE TO CAUSE PROBLEMS, RAYA. DICK IS A CLOSE FRIEND.
FUNNY-- I COULD SAY THE SAME THING.
IS THAT ALL?
LISTEN, HE'D PROBABLY KILL ME FOR SAYING THIS...
...BUT HE REALLY CARES ABOUT YOU, YOU KNOW. YOU MAKE HIM HAPPY.
AND AT THE END OF THE DAY, ISN'T THAT THE MOST IMPORTANT THING?
GOOD LUCK, RAYA...
SON
"...HE'S A REALLY GREAT GUY."
GRAYSON

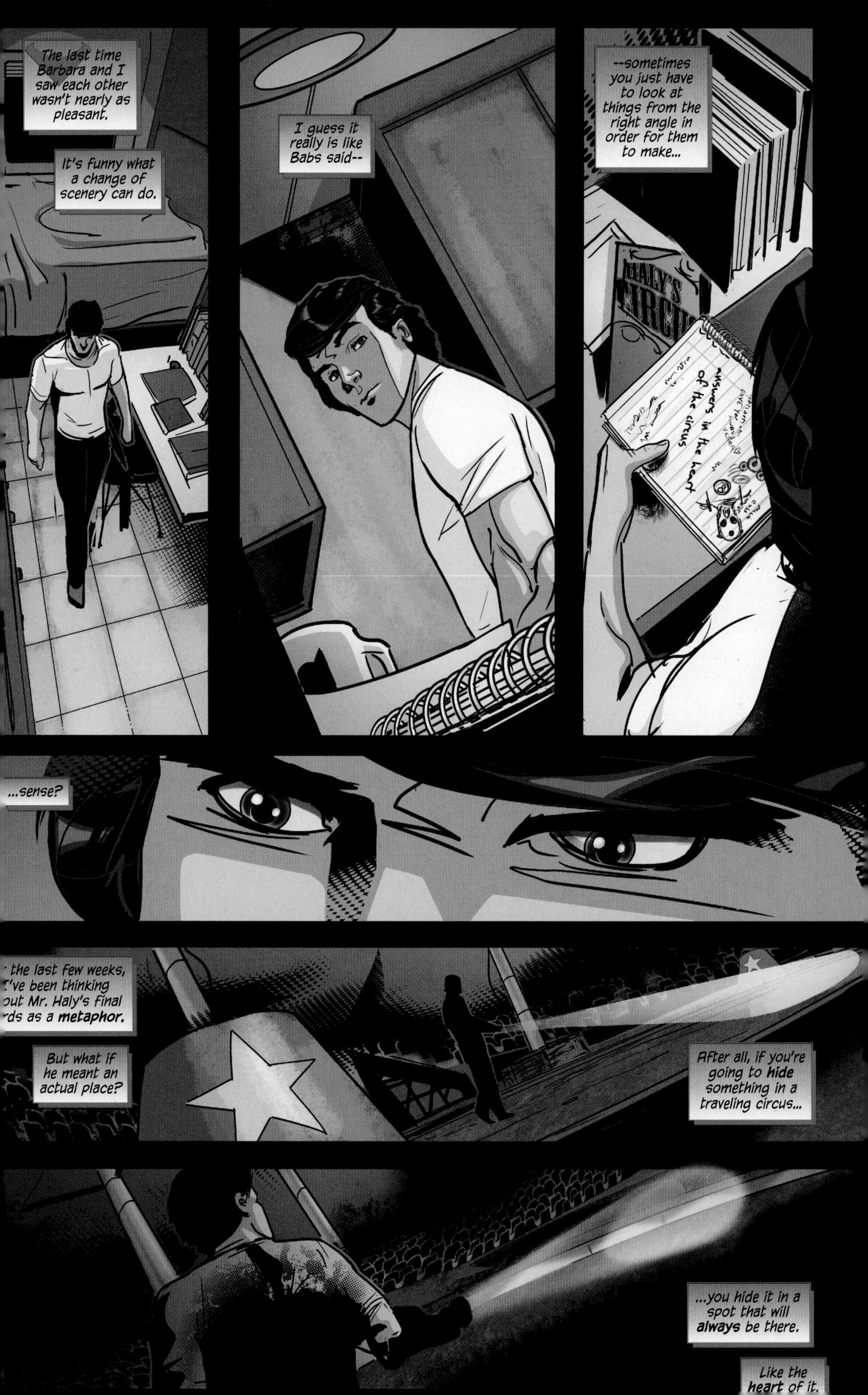
The last time Barbara and I saw each other wasn't nearly as pleasant.
It's funny what a change of scenery can do.
I guess it really is like Babs said--
--sometimes you just have to look at things from the right angle in order for them to make...
HALY'S CIRCUS
answers in the heart of the circus
...sense?
the last few weeks, I've been thinking out Mr. Haly's final rds as a **metaphor.**
But what if he meant an actual place?
After all, if you're going to **hide** something in a traveling circus...
...you hide it in a spot that will **always** be there.
Like the **heart** of it.

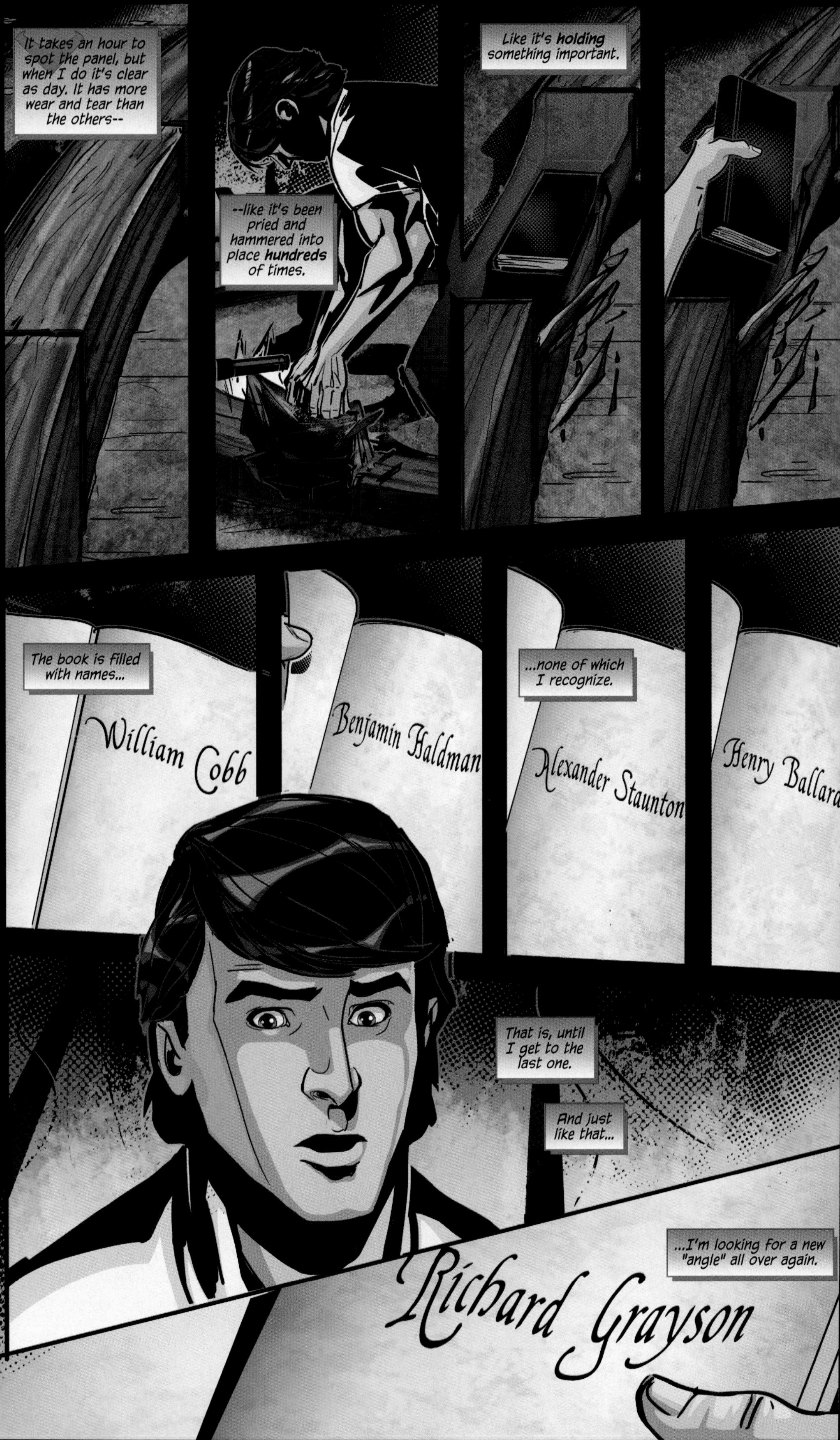

It takes an hour to spot the panel, but when I do it's clear as day. It has more wear and tear than the others--
--like it's been pried and hammered into place **hundreds** of times.
Like it's **holding** something important.
The book is filled with names...
William Cobb
Benjamin Haldman
...none of which I recognize.
Alexander Staunton
Henry Ballard
That is, until I get to the last one.
And just like that...
...I'm looking for a new "angle" all over again.
Richard Grayson

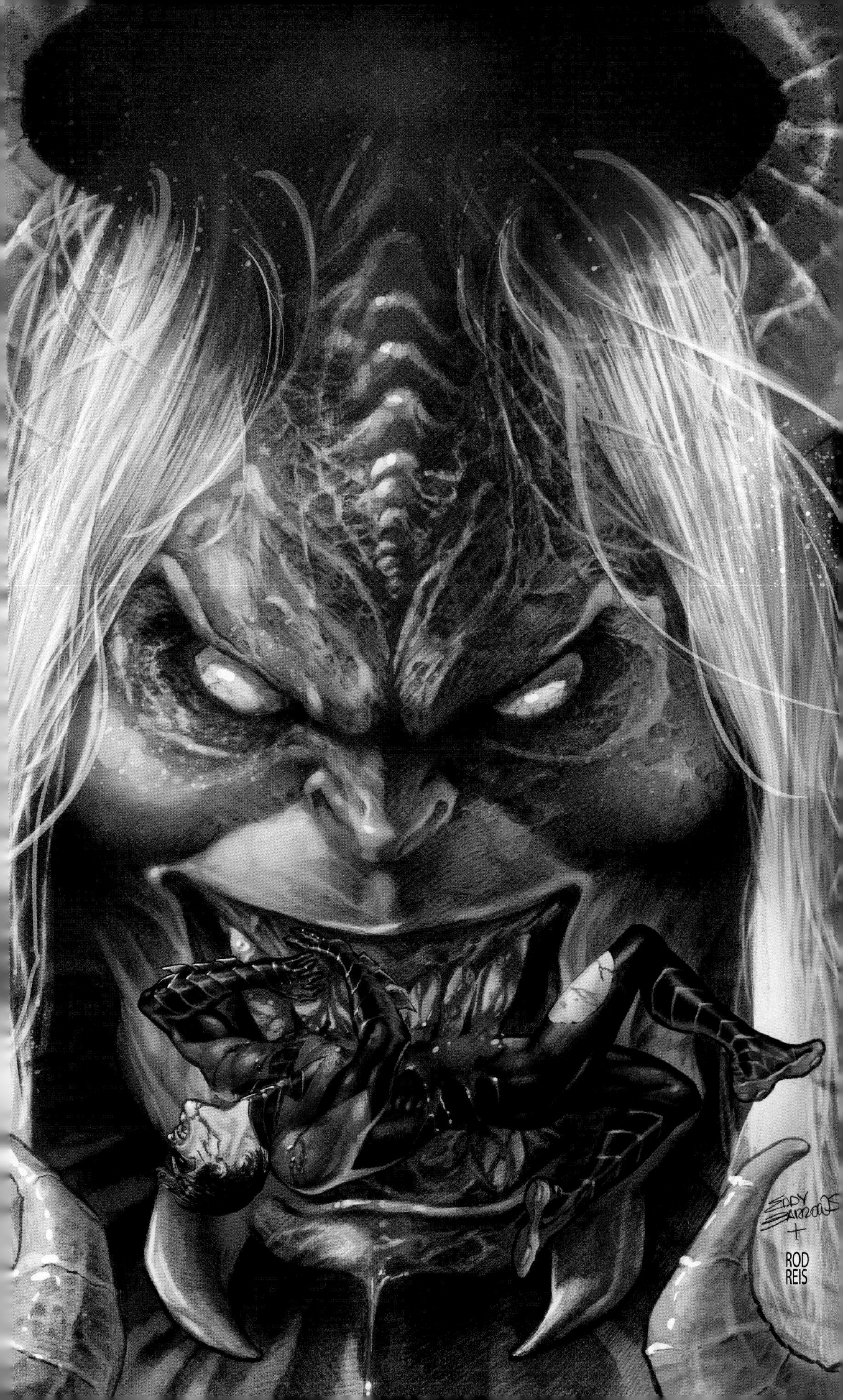

EDDY BARROWS
+
ROD REIS

'TIL DEATH DO US PART

KYLE HIGGINS writer **EDDY BARROWS** penciller **PAULO SIQUEIRA & EBER FERREIRA** inkers cover art by Eddy Barrows & Rod Reis

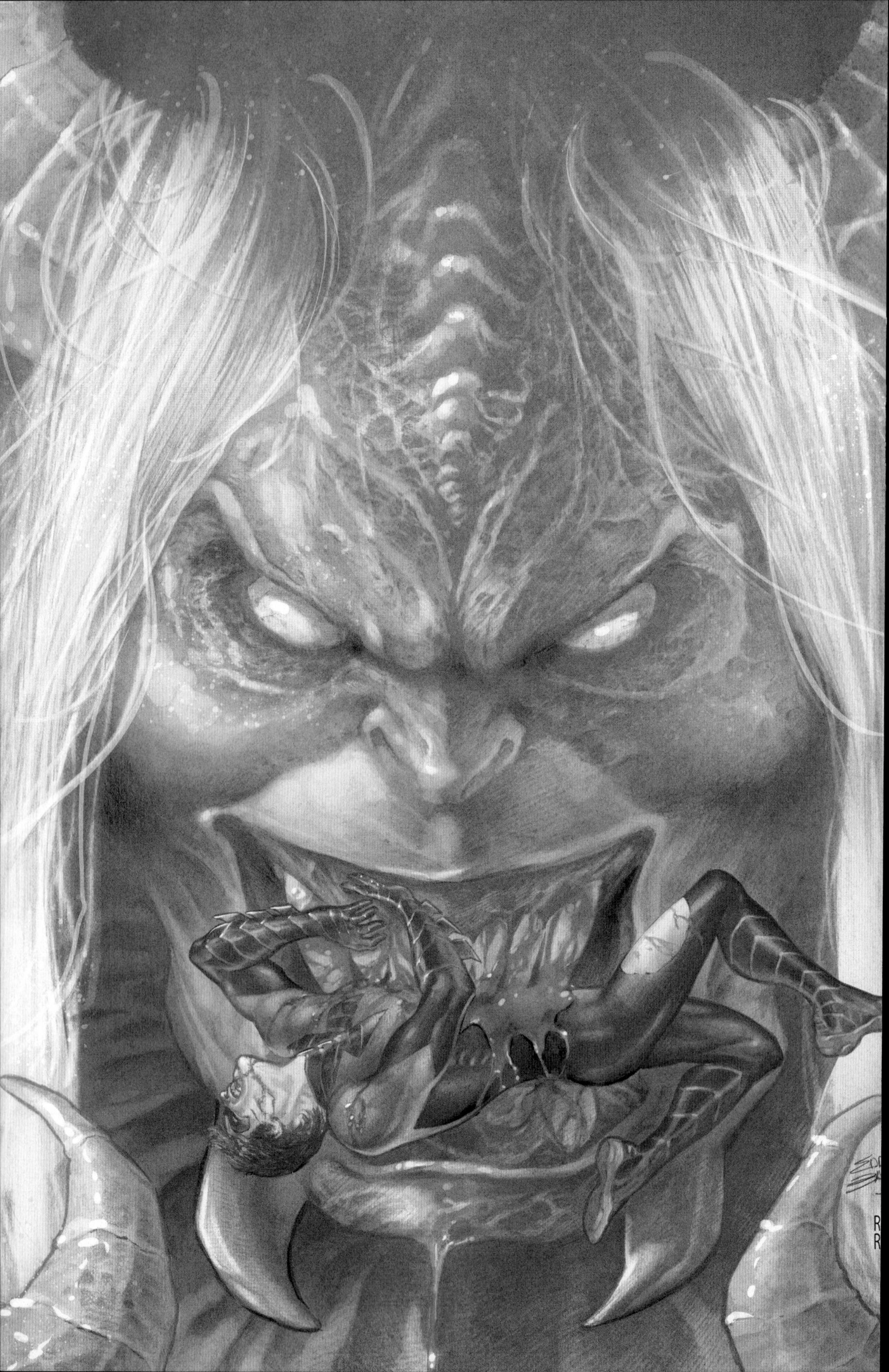

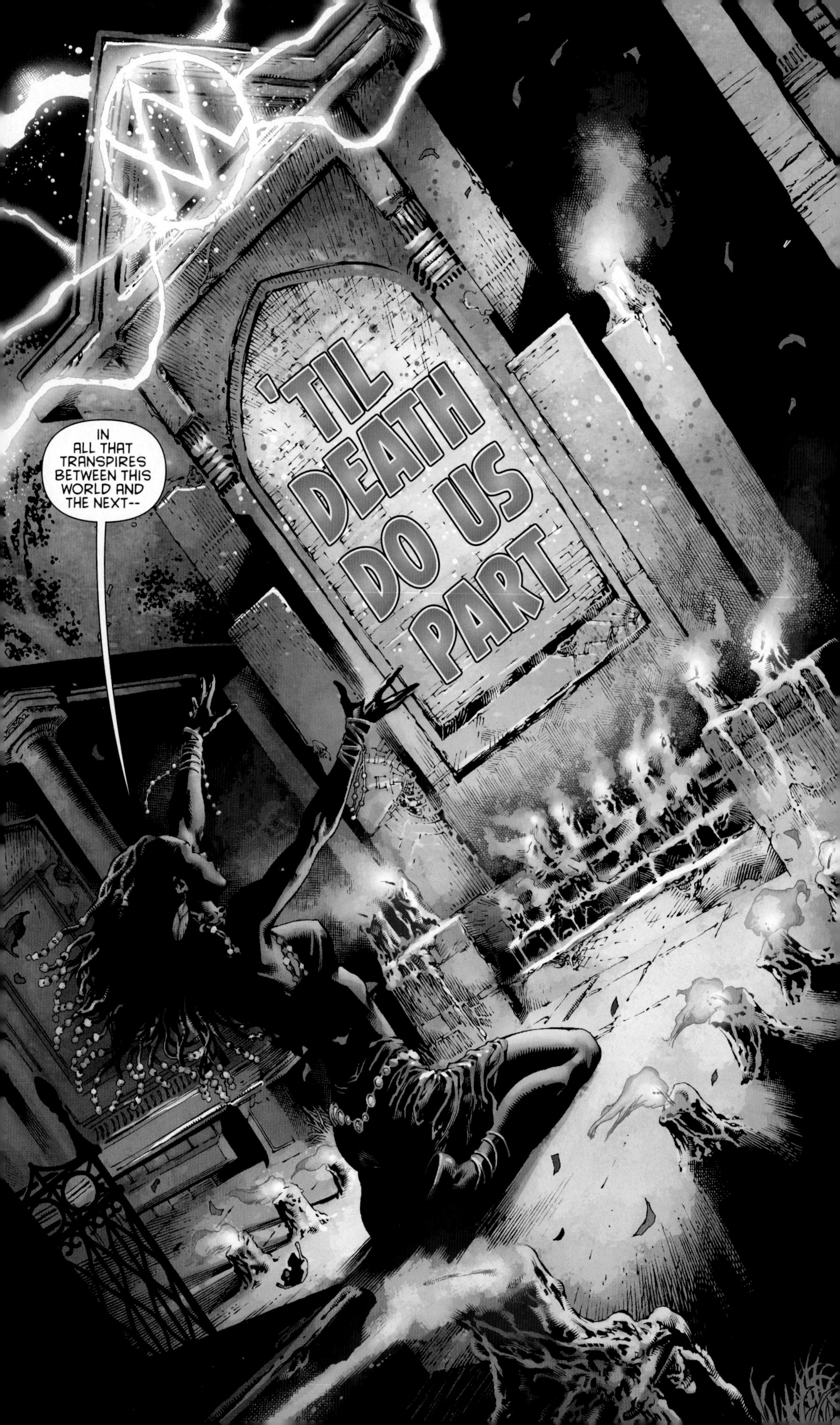
IN ALL THAT TRANSPIRES BETWEEN THIS WORLD AND THE NEXT--
'TIL DEATH DO US PART

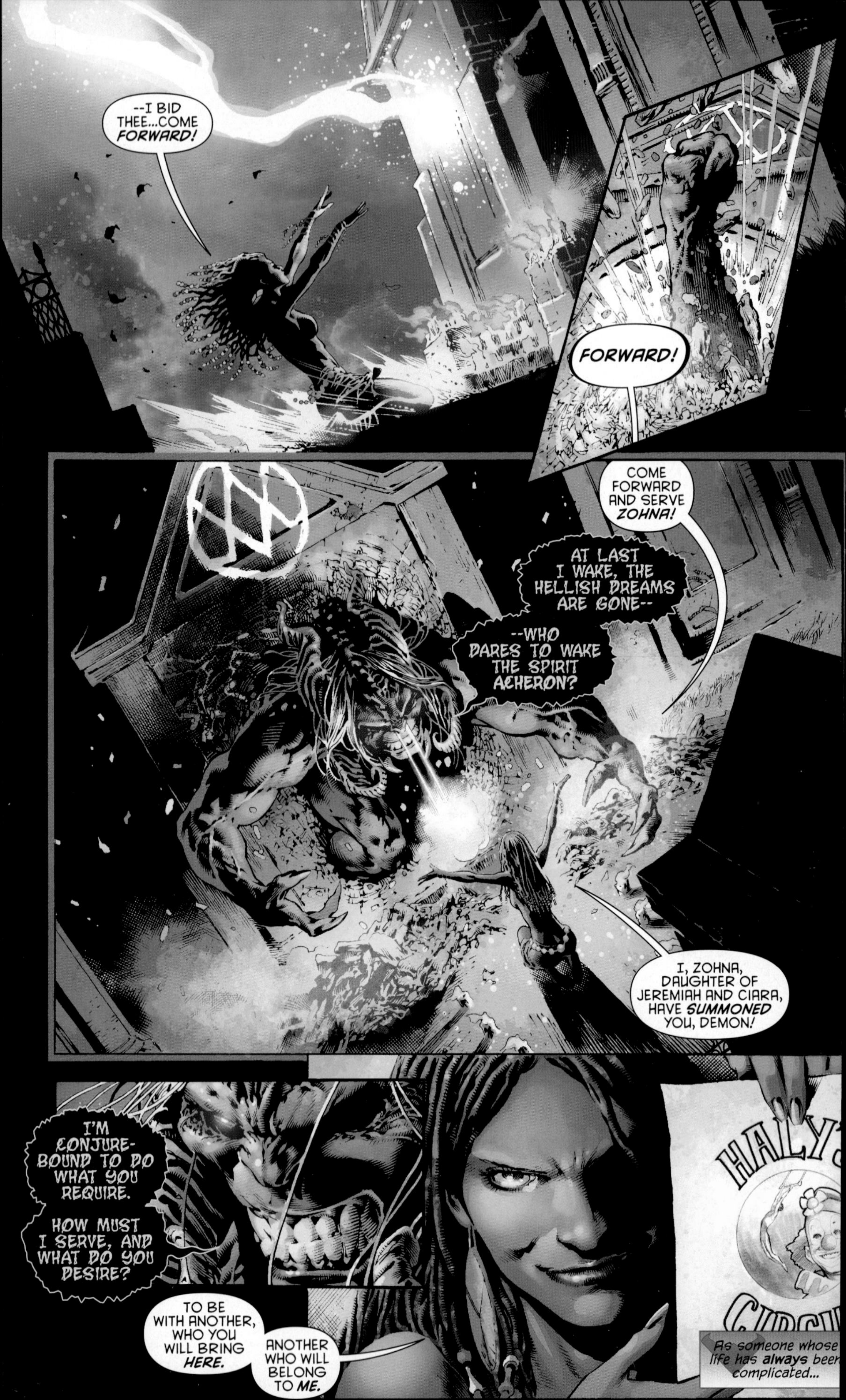
--I BID THEE...COME FORWARD!
FORWARD!
COME FORWARD AND SERVE ZOHNA!
AT LAST I WAKE, THE HELLISH DREAMS ARE GONE--
--WHO DARES TO WAKE THE SPIRIT ACHERON?
I, ZOHNA, DAUGHTER OF JEREMIAH AND CIARA, HAVE SUMMONED YOU, DEMON!
I'M CONJURE-BOUND TO DO WHAT YOU REQUIRE.
HOW MUST I SERVE, AND WHAT DO YOU DESIRE?
TO BE WITH ANOTHER, WHO YOU WILL BRING HERE.
ANOTHER WHO WILL BELONG TO ME.
As someone whose life has always been complicated...

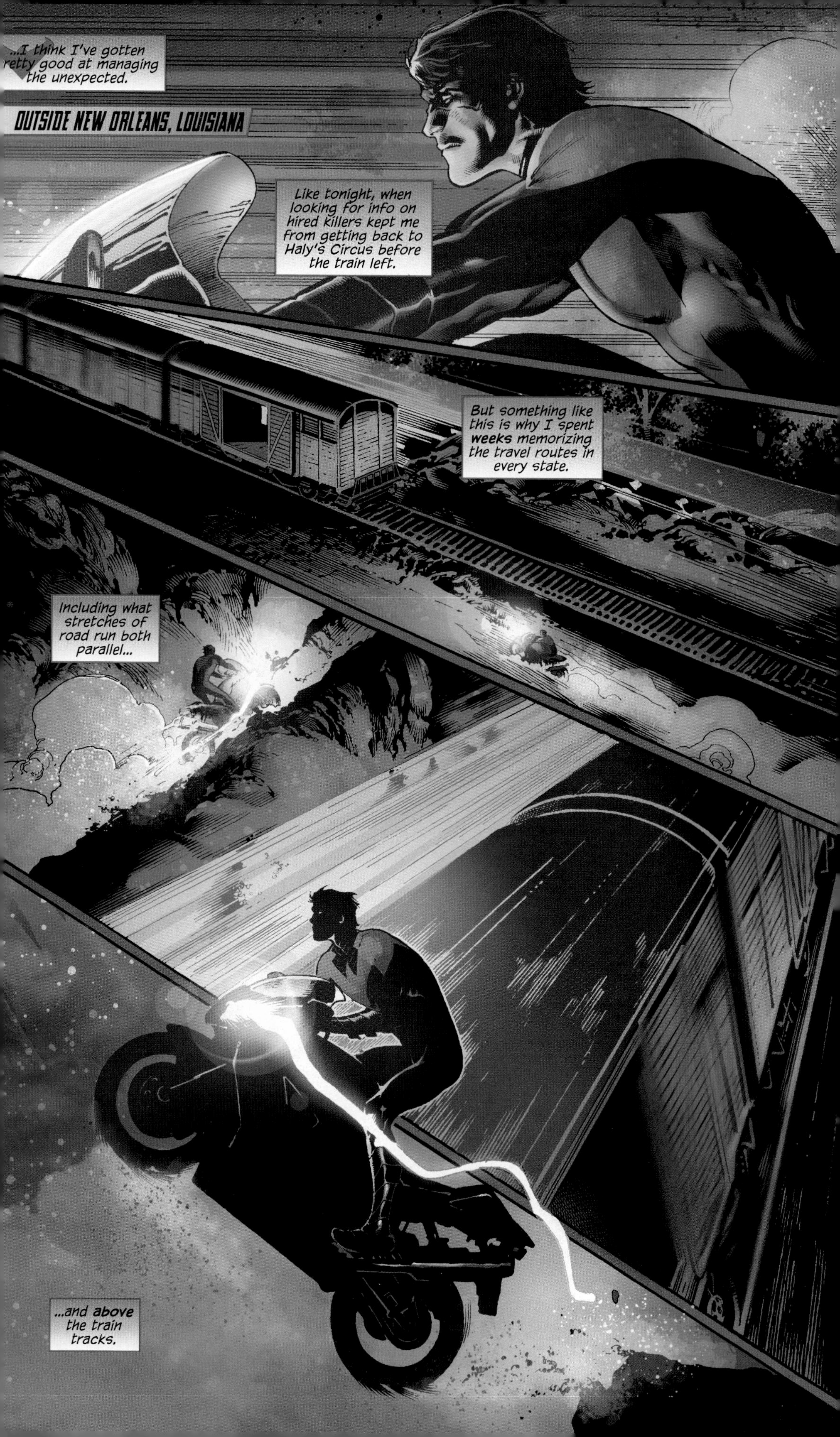
...I think I've gotten
retty good at managing
the unexpected.
OUTSIDE NEW ORLEANS, LOUISIANA
Like tonight, when looking for info on hired killers kept me from getting back to Haly's Circus before the train left.
But something like this is why I spent **weeks** memorizing the travel routes in every state.
Including what stretches of road run both parallel...
...and **above** the train tracks.

It's also why I asked the ring crew to run my "storage car" as the caboose--to limit the odds of someone seeing me duck in or out on the bike.

But of course, no matter how many plans you make, there'll always be **something** that catches you off guard.

Like the reason I'm here in the **first** place.

A few weeks ago, a hired gun named **Saiko** came after **Dick Grayson**, claiming **I** was the "fiercest killer in all of Gotham."

Which was actually **before** he murdered Mr. Haly and discovered that I'm **Nightwing.**

Mr. Haly left me the circus, a mystery about what it **really** is, and the responsibility to protect it.

But aside from putting pressure on the underworld in order to find Saiko--which hasn't gotten me **anywhere**...

...my only clue is an old book that was hidden in the center ring of the circus.

It's filled w names, inclu **mine**, and supposed t the answer whatever se this place holding.

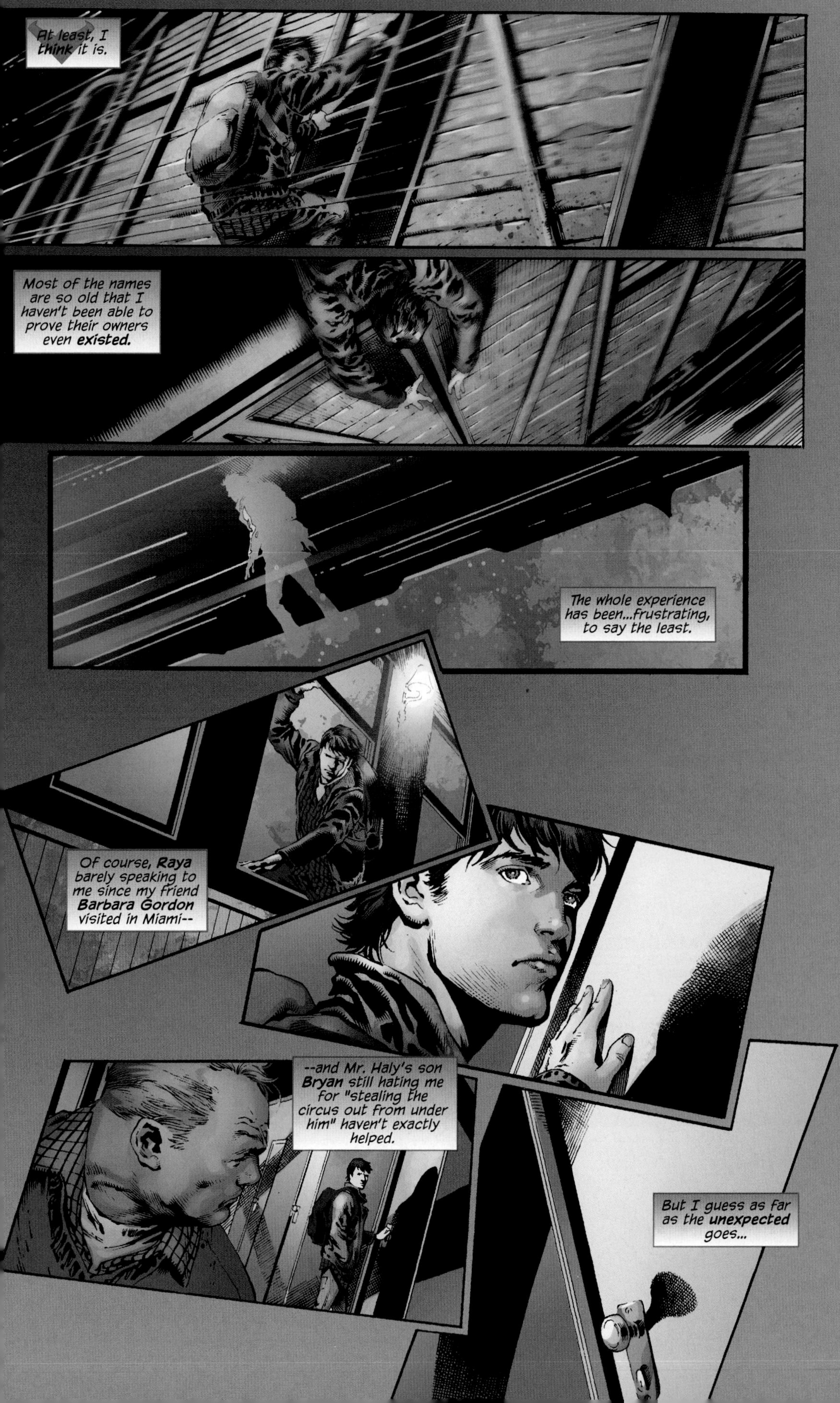
At least, I think it is.
Most of the names are so old that I haven't been able to prove their owners even existed.
The whole experience has been...frustrating, to say the least.
Of course, Raya barely speaking to me since my friend Barbara Gordon visited in Miami--
--and Mr. Haly's son Bryan still hating me for "stealing the circus out from under him" haven't exactly helped.
But I guess as far as the unexpected goes...

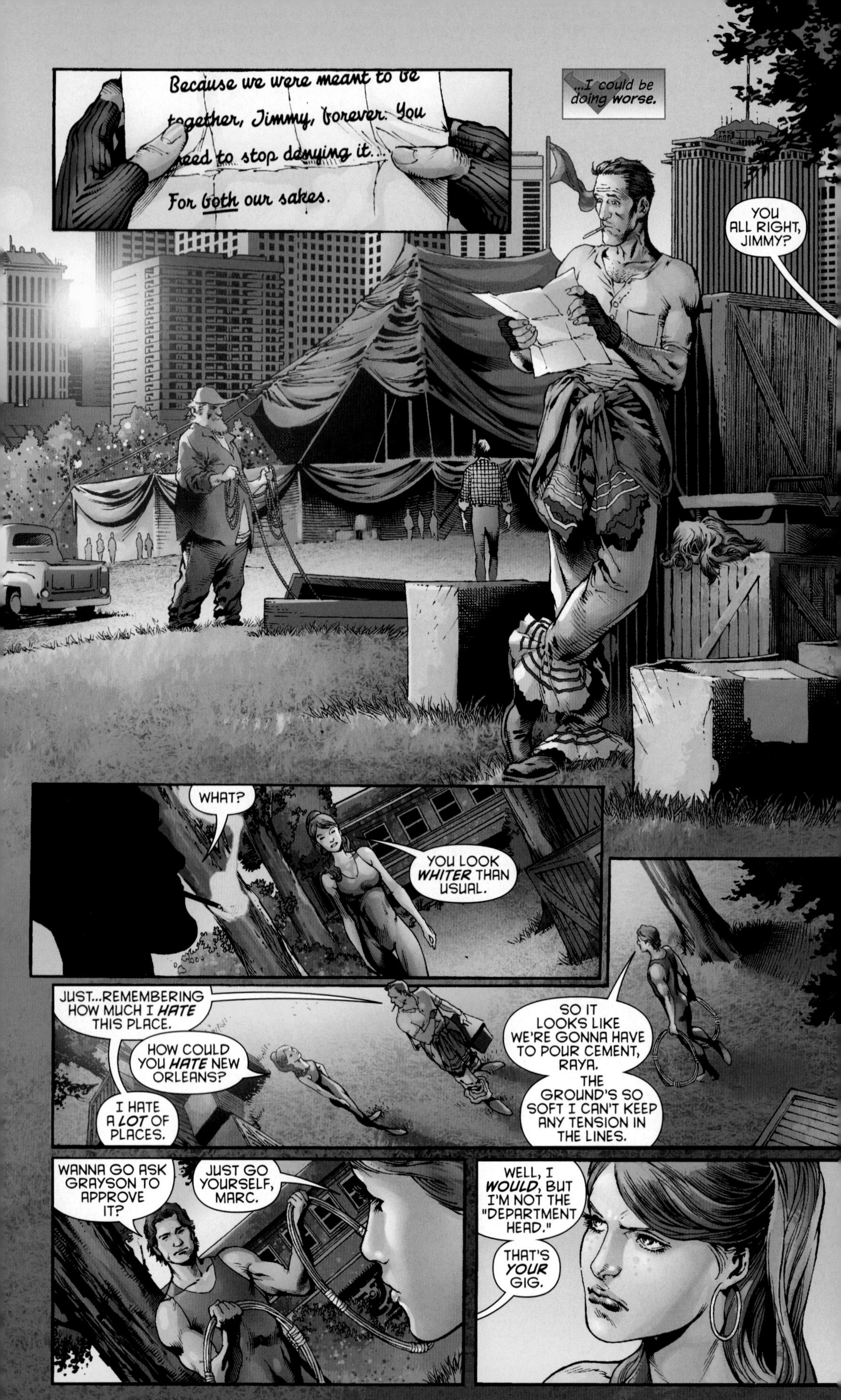
Because we were meant to be together, Jimmy, forever. You need to stop denying it...
For both our sakes.
...I could be doing worse.
YOU ALL RIGHT, JIMMY?
WHAT?
YOU LOOK WHITER THAN USUAL.
JUST...REMEMBERING HOW MUCH I HATE THIS PLACE.
HOW COULD YOU HATE NEW ORLEANS?
I HATE A LOT OF PLACES.
SO IT LOOKS LIKE WE'RE GONNA HAVE TO POUR CEMENT, RAYA.
THE GROUND'S SO SOFT I CAN'T KEEP ANY TENSION IN THE LINES.
WANNA GO ASK GRAYSON TO APPROVE IT?
JUST GO YOURSELF, MARC.
WELL, I WOULD, BUT I'M NOT THE "DEPARTMENT HEAD."
THAT'S YOUR GIG.

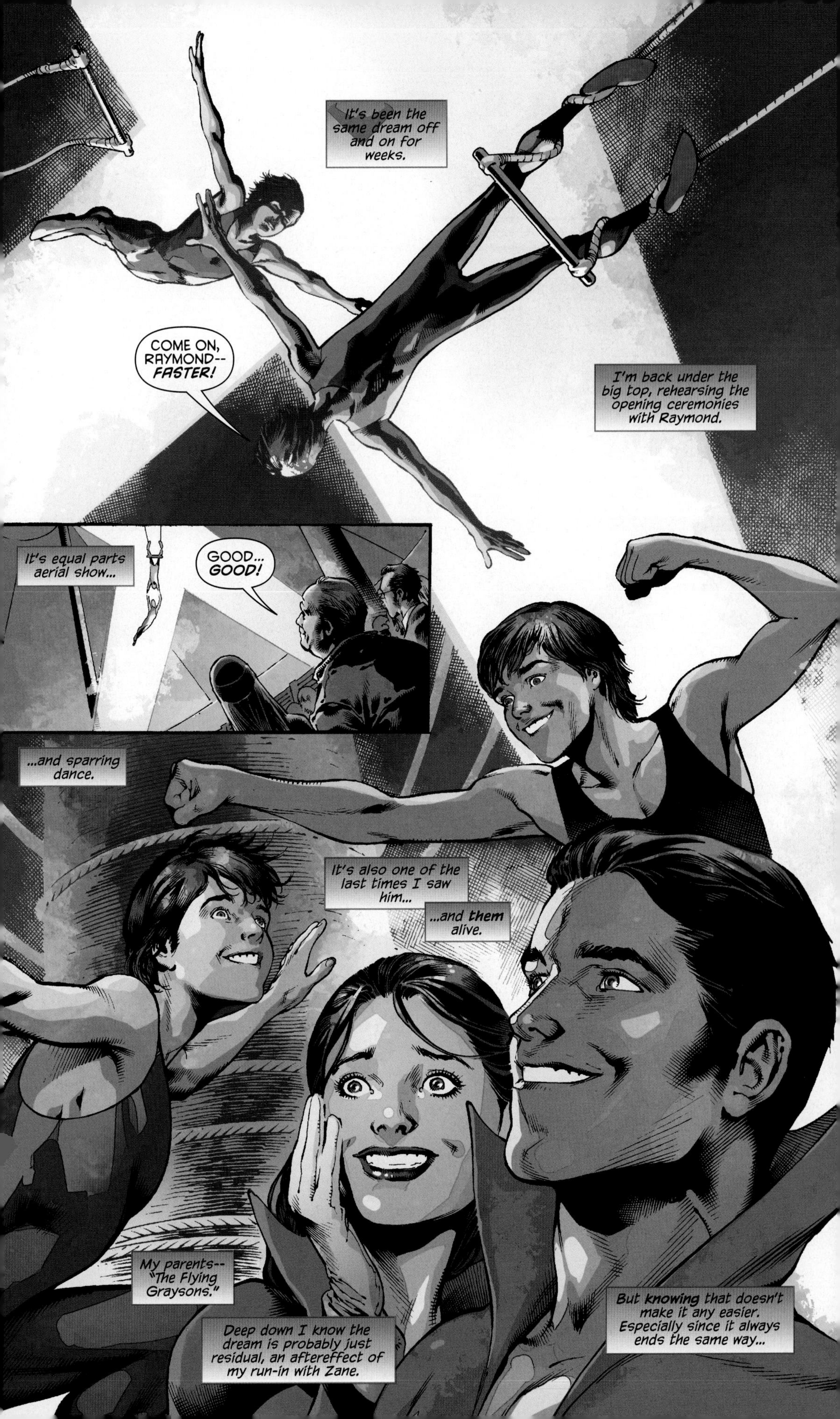
It's been the same dream off and on for weeks.
COME ON, RAYMOND-- FASTER!
I'm back under the big top, rehearsing the opening ceremonies with Raymond.
It's equal parts aerial show...
GOOD... GOOD!
...and sparring dance.
It's also one of the last times I saw him...
...and them alive.
My parents-- "The Flying Graysons."
Deep down I know the dream is probably just residual, an aftereffect of my run-in with Zane.
But knowing that doesn't make it any easier. Especially since it always ends the same way...

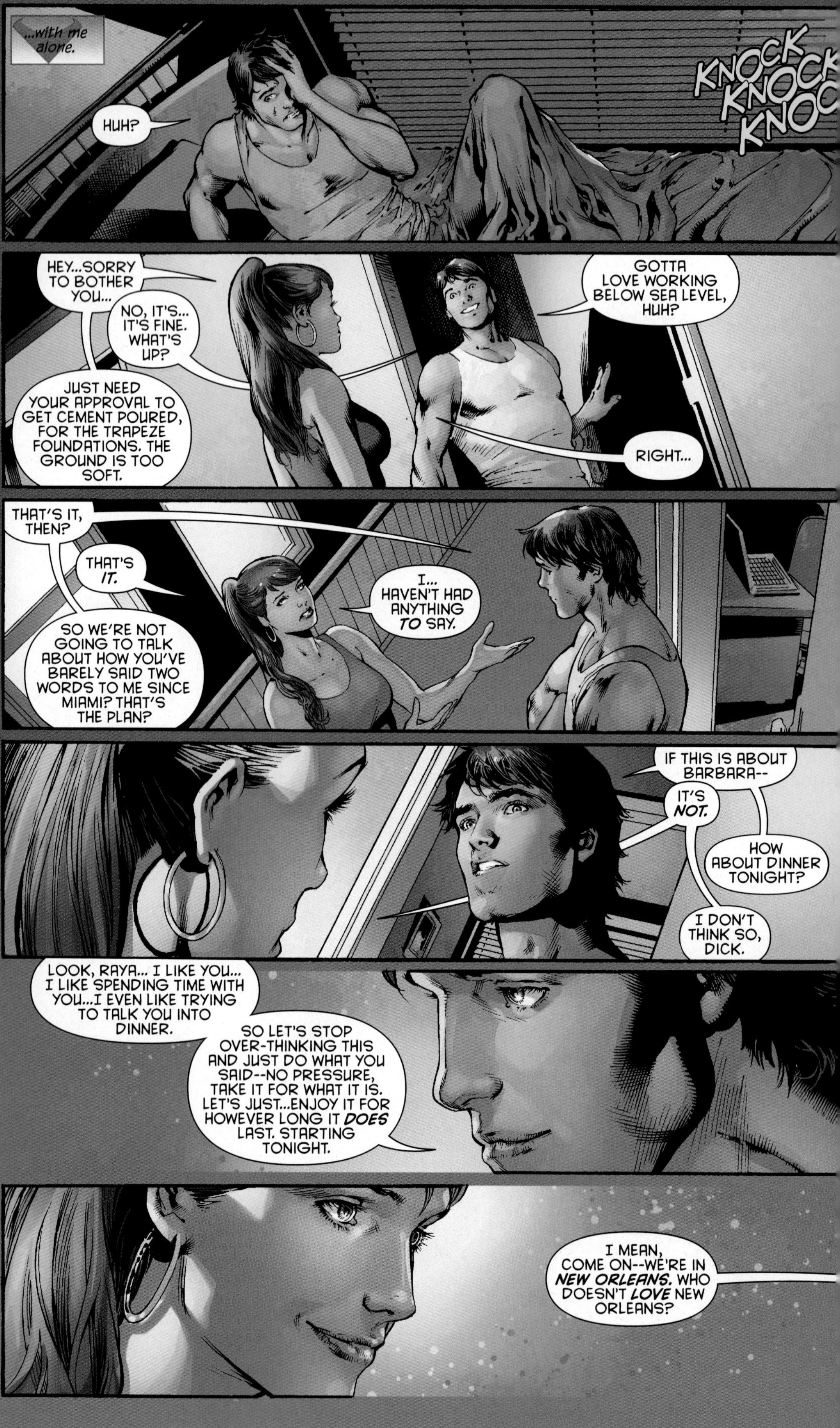

...with me alone.
KNOCK KNOCK KNOC
HUH?
HEY...SORRY TO BOTHER YOU...
NO, IT'S... IT'S FINE. WHAT'S UP?
GOTTA LOVE WORKING BELOW SEA LEVEL, HUH?
JUST NEED YOUR APPROVAL TO GET CEMENT POURED, FOR THE TRAPEZE FOUNDATIONS. THE GROUND IS TOO SOFT.
RIGHT...
THAT'S IT, THEN?
THAT'S *IT.*
SO WE'RE NOT GOING TO TALK ABOUT HOW YOU'VE BARELY SAID TWO WORDS TO ME SINCE MIAMI? THAT'S THE PLAN?
I... HAVEN'T HAD ANYTHING *TO* SAY.
IF THIS IS ABOUT BARBARA--
IT'S *NOT.*
HOW ABOUT DINNER TONIGHT?
I DON'T THINK SO, DICK.
LOOK, RAYA... I LIKE YOU... I LIKE SPENDING TIME WITH YOU...I EVEN LIKE TRYING TO TALK YOU INTO DINNER.
SO LET'S STOP OVER-THINKING THIS AND JUST DO WHAT YOU SAID--NO PRESSURE, TAKE IT FOR WHAT IT IS. LET'S JUST...ENJOY IT FOR HOWEVER LONG IT *DOES* LAST. STARTING TONIGHT.
I MEAN, COME ON--WE'RE IN *NEW ORLEANS.* WHO DOESN'T *LOVE* NEW ORLEANS?

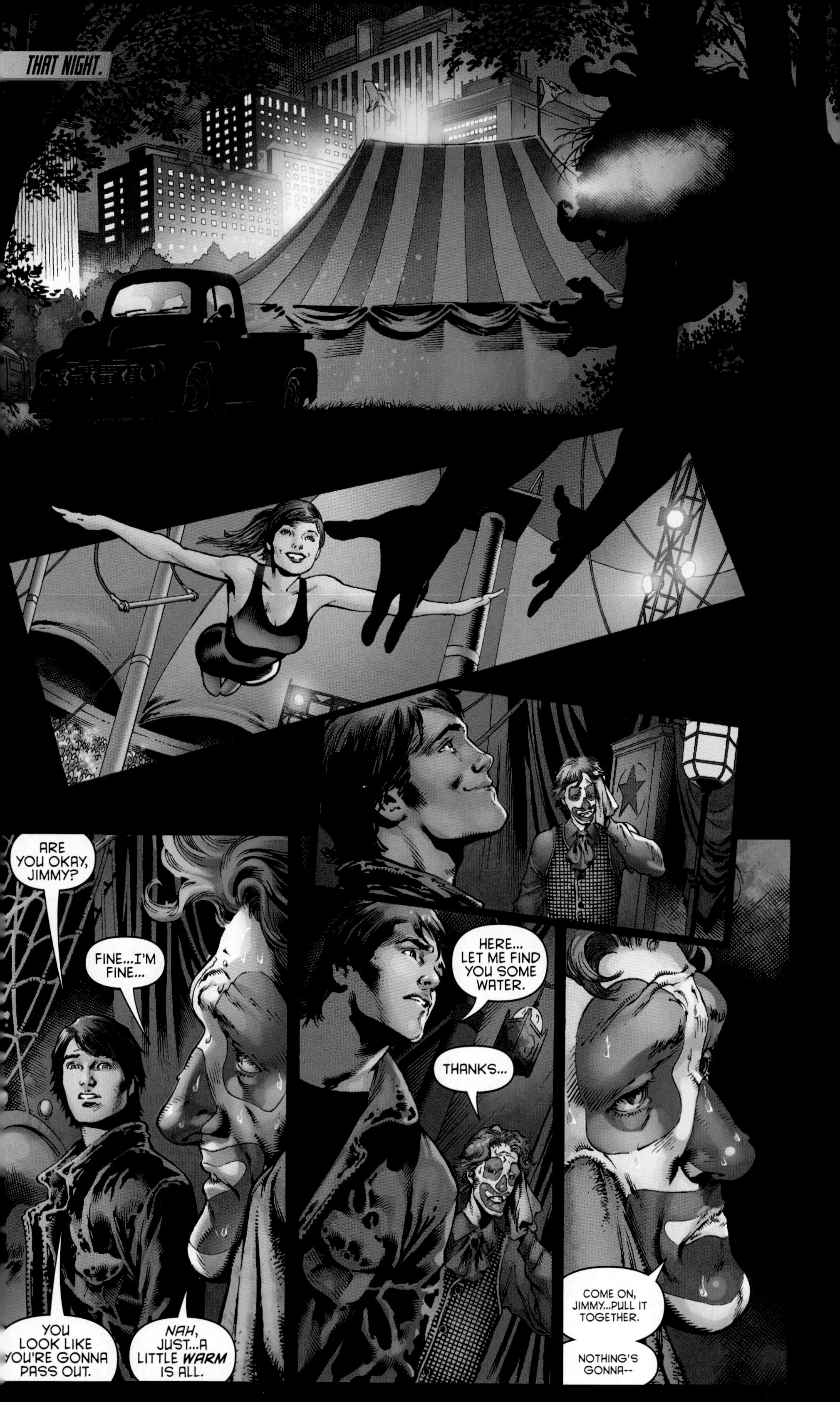
THAT NIGHT.
ARE YOU OKAY, JIMMY?
FINE...I'M FINE...
YOU LOOK LIKE YOU'RE GONNA PASS OUT.
NAH, JUST...A LITTLE WARM IS ALL.
HERE... LET ME FIND YOU SOME WATER.
THANKS...
COME ON, JIMMY...PULL IT TOGETHER.
NOTHING'S GONNA--

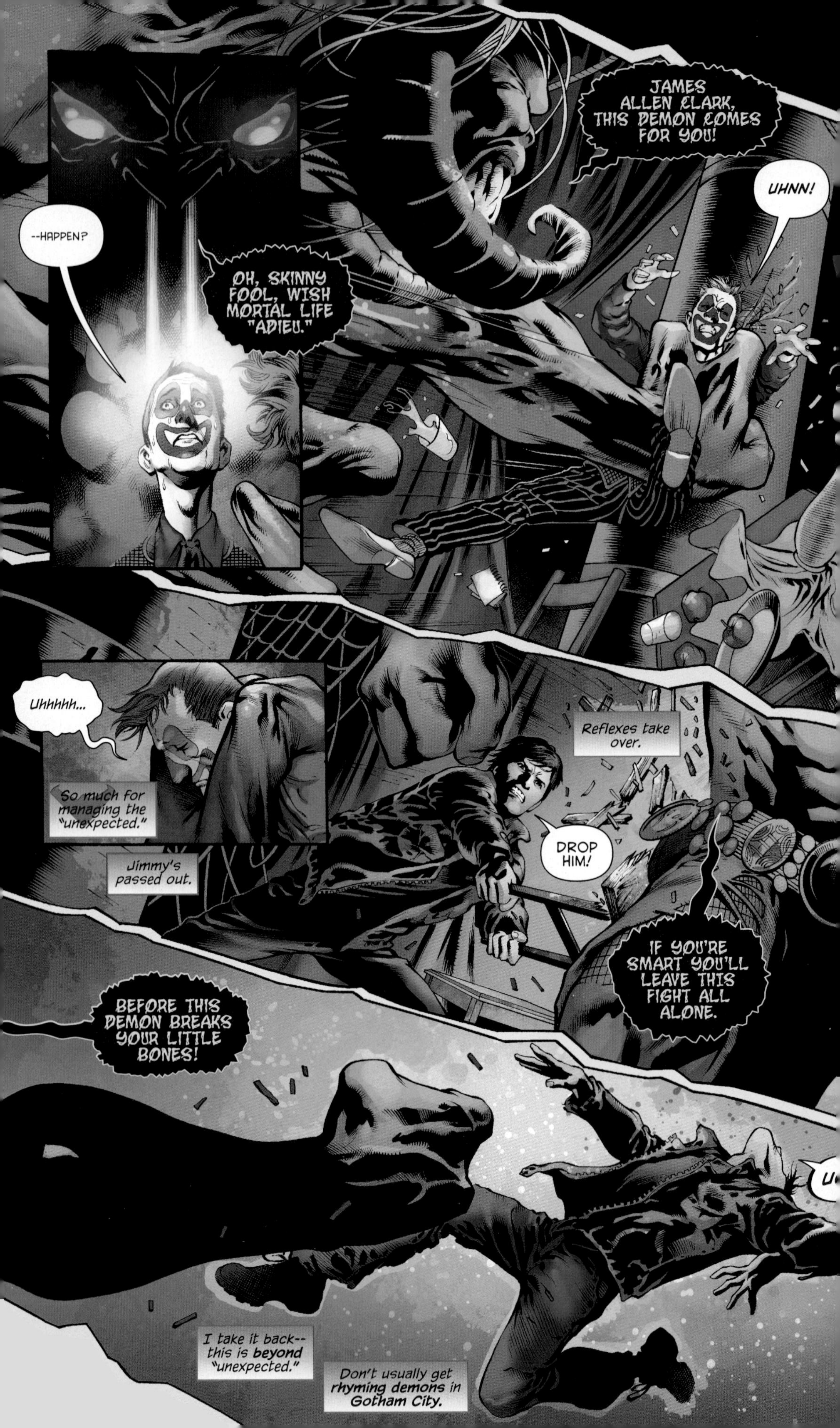
--HAPPEN?
OH, SKINNY FOOL, WISH MORTAL LIFE "ADIEU."
JAMES ALLEN CLARK, THIS DEMON COMES FOR YOU!
UHNN!
Uhhhhh...
So much for managing the "unexpected."
Jimmy's passed out.
Reflexes take over.
DROP HIM!
IF YOU'RE SMART YOU'LL LEAVE THIS FIGHT ALL ALONE.
BEFORE THIS DEMON BREAKS YOUR LITTLE BONES!
I take it back-- this is beyond "unexpected."
Don't usually get rhyming demons in Gotham City.

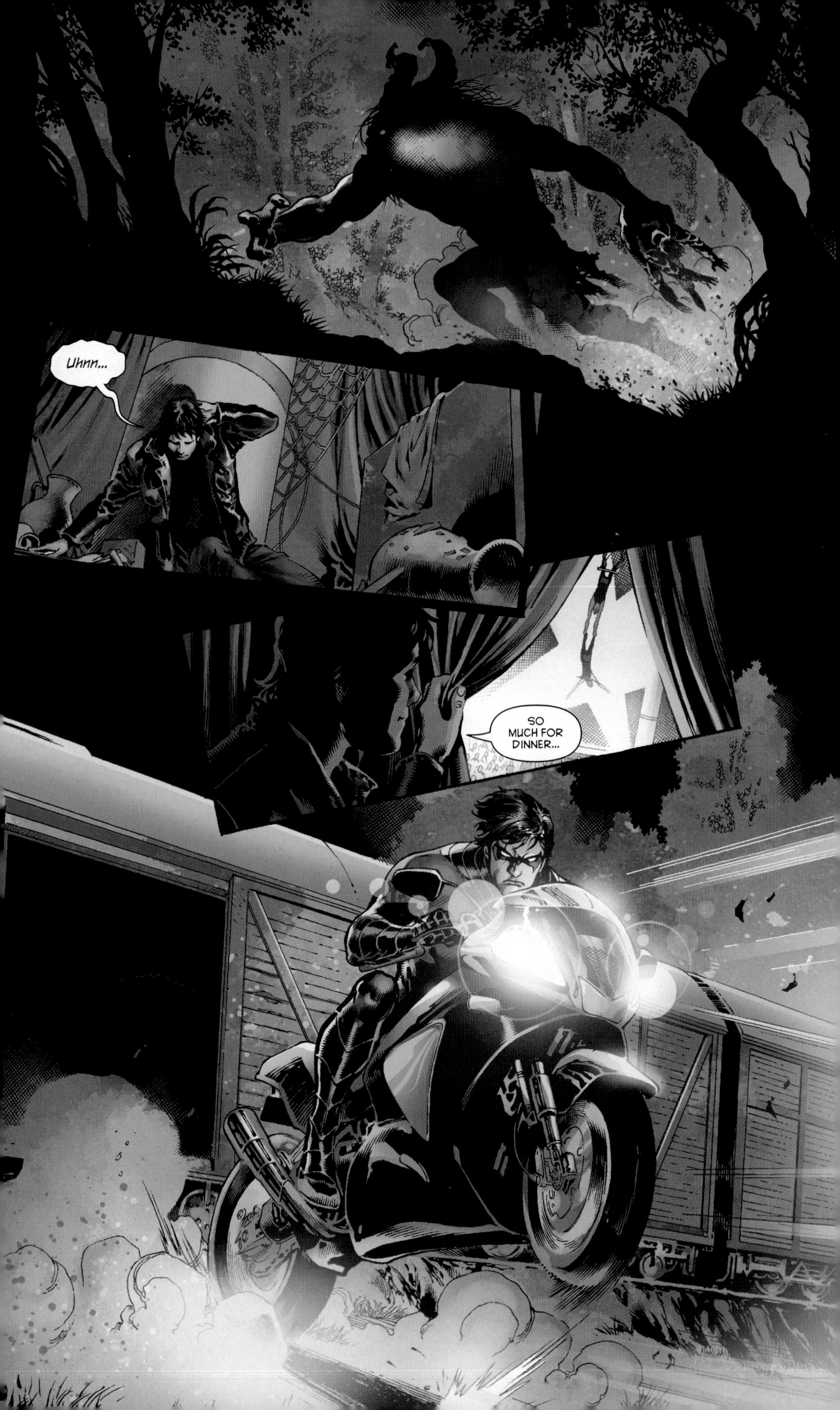
Uhnn...
SO MUCH FOR DINNER...

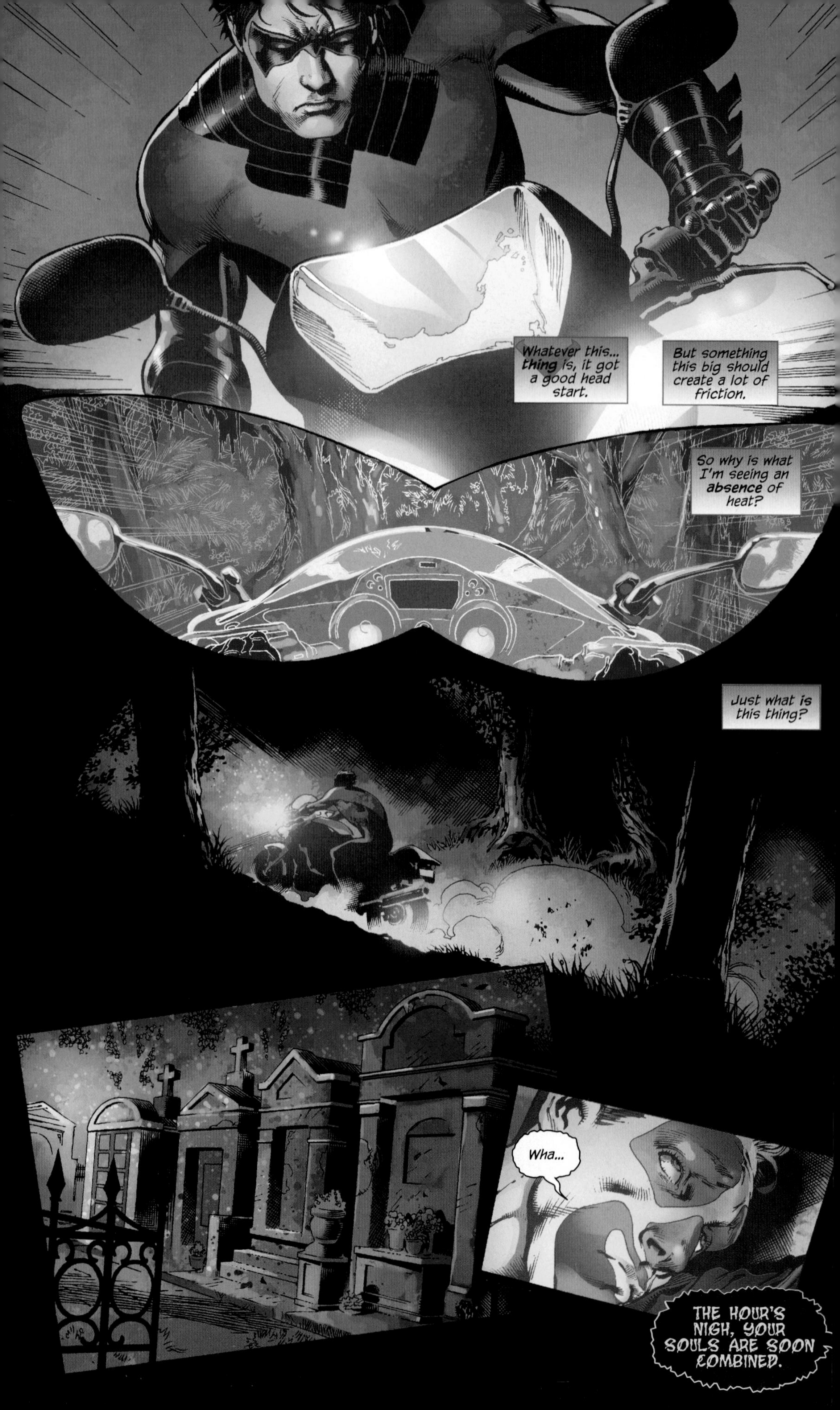
Whatever this... thing is, it got a good head start.
But something this big should create a lot of friction.
So why is what I'm seeing an absence of heat?
Just what is this thing?
Wha...
THE HOUR'S NIGH, YOUR SOULS ARE SOON COMBINED.

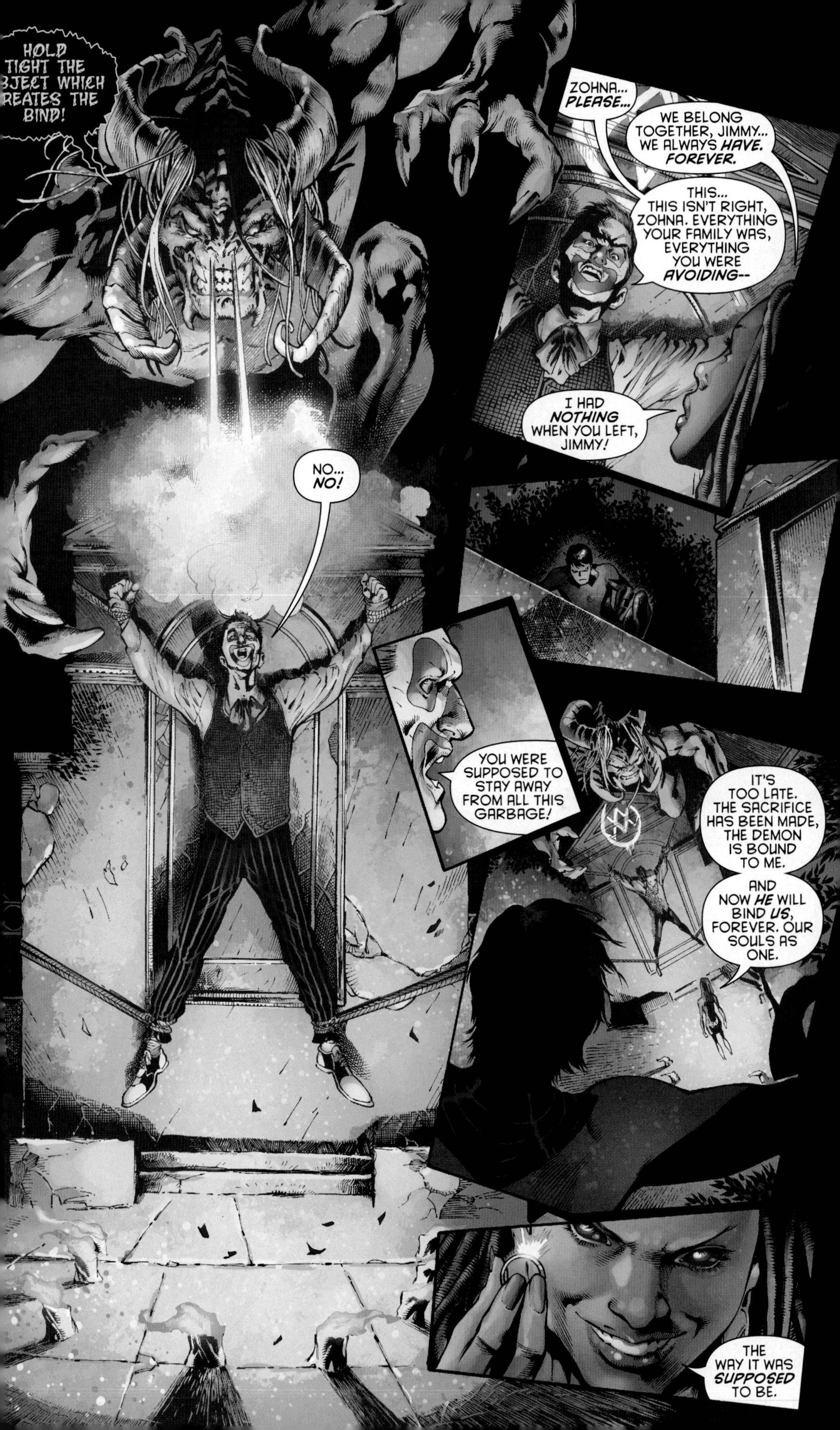
HOLD TIGHT THE BJECT WHICH REATES THE BIND!
ZOHNA... PLEASE...
WE BELONG TOGETHER, JIMMY... WE ALWAYS HAVE. FOREVER.
THIS... THIS ISN'T RIGHT, ZOHNA. EVERYTHING YOUR FAMILY WAS, EVERYTHING YOU WERE AVOIDING--
I HAD NOTHING WHEN YOU LEFT, JIMMY!
NO... NO!
YOU WERE SUPPOSED TO STAY AWAY FROM ALL THIS GARBAGE!
IT'S TOO LATE. THE SACRIFICE HAS BEEN MADE, THE DEMON IS BOUND TO ME.
AND NOW HE WILL BIND US, FOREVER. OUR SOULS AS ONE.
THE WAY IT WAS SUPPOSED TO BE.

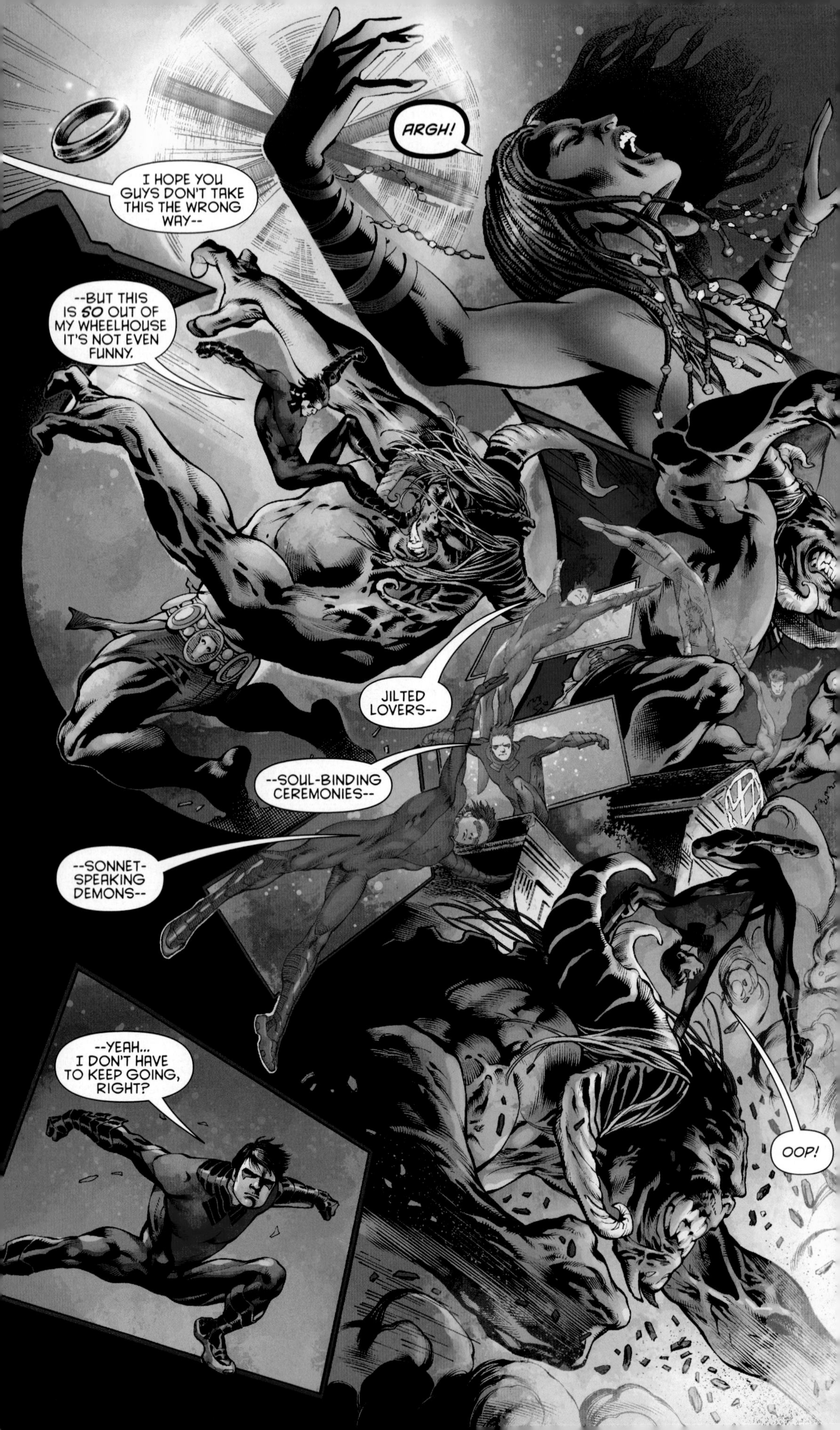
ARGH!
I HOPE YOU GUYS DON'T TAKE THIS THE WRONG WAY--
--BUT THIS IS *SO* OUT OF MY WHEELHOUSE IT'S NOT EVEN FUNNY.
JILTED LOVERS--
--SOUL-BINDING CEREMONIES--
--SONNET-SPEAKING DEMONS--
--YEAH... I DON'T HAVE TO KEEP GOING, RIGHT?
OOP!

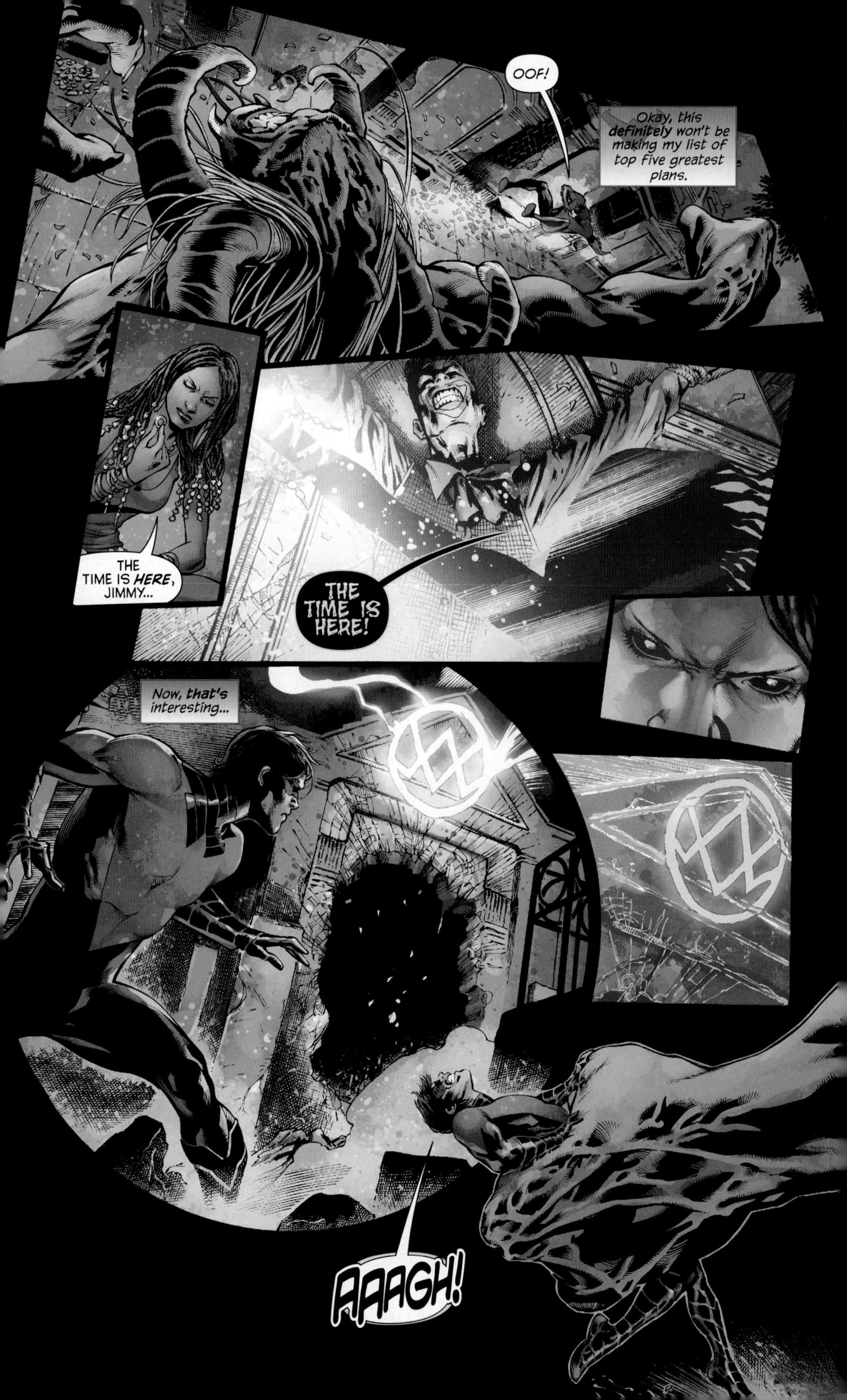
OOF!
Okay, this definitely won't be making my list of top five greatest plans.
THE TIME IS HERE, JIMMY...
THE TIME IS HERE!
Now, that's interesting...
AAAGH!

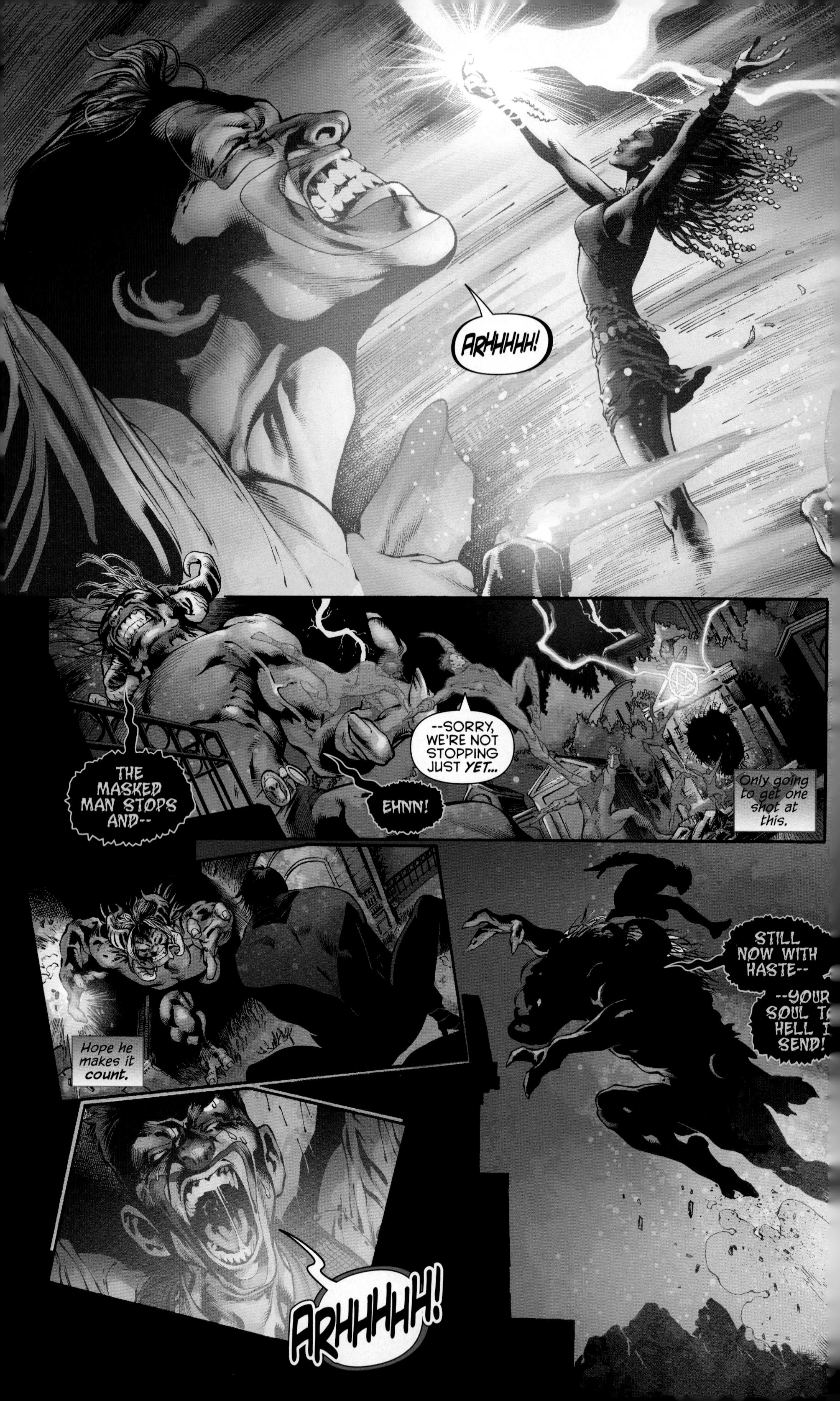
ARHHHHH!
THE MASKED MAN STOPS AND--
--SORRY, WE'RE NOT STOPPING JUST YET...
EHNN!
Only going to get one shot at this.
Hope he makes it count.
STILL NOW WITH HASTE--
ARHHHHH!

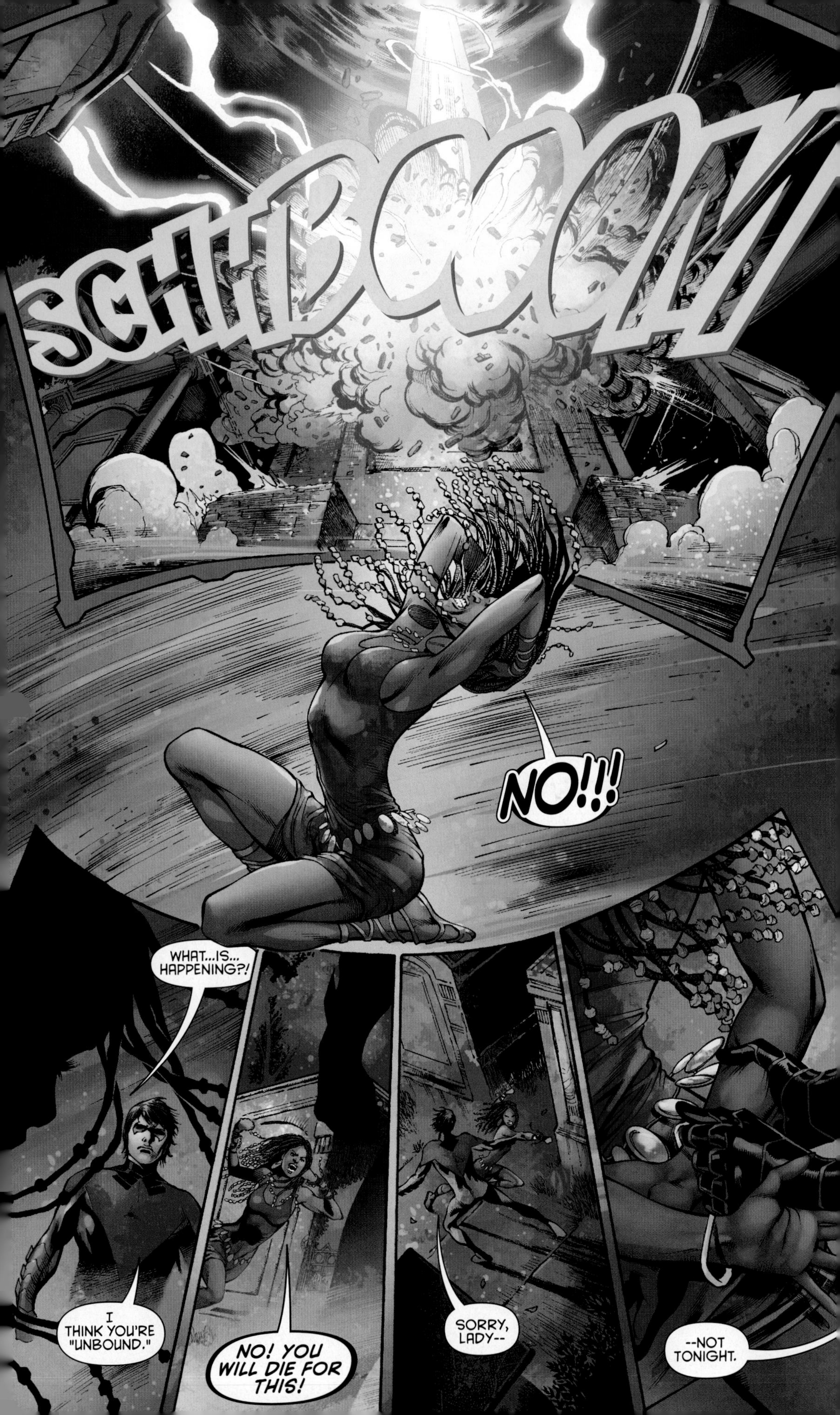
SCHHBOOOM
NO!!!
WHAT...IS... HAPPENING?!
I THINK YOU'RE "UNBOUND."
NO! YOU WILL DIE FOR THIS!
SORRY, LADY--
--NOT TONIGHT.

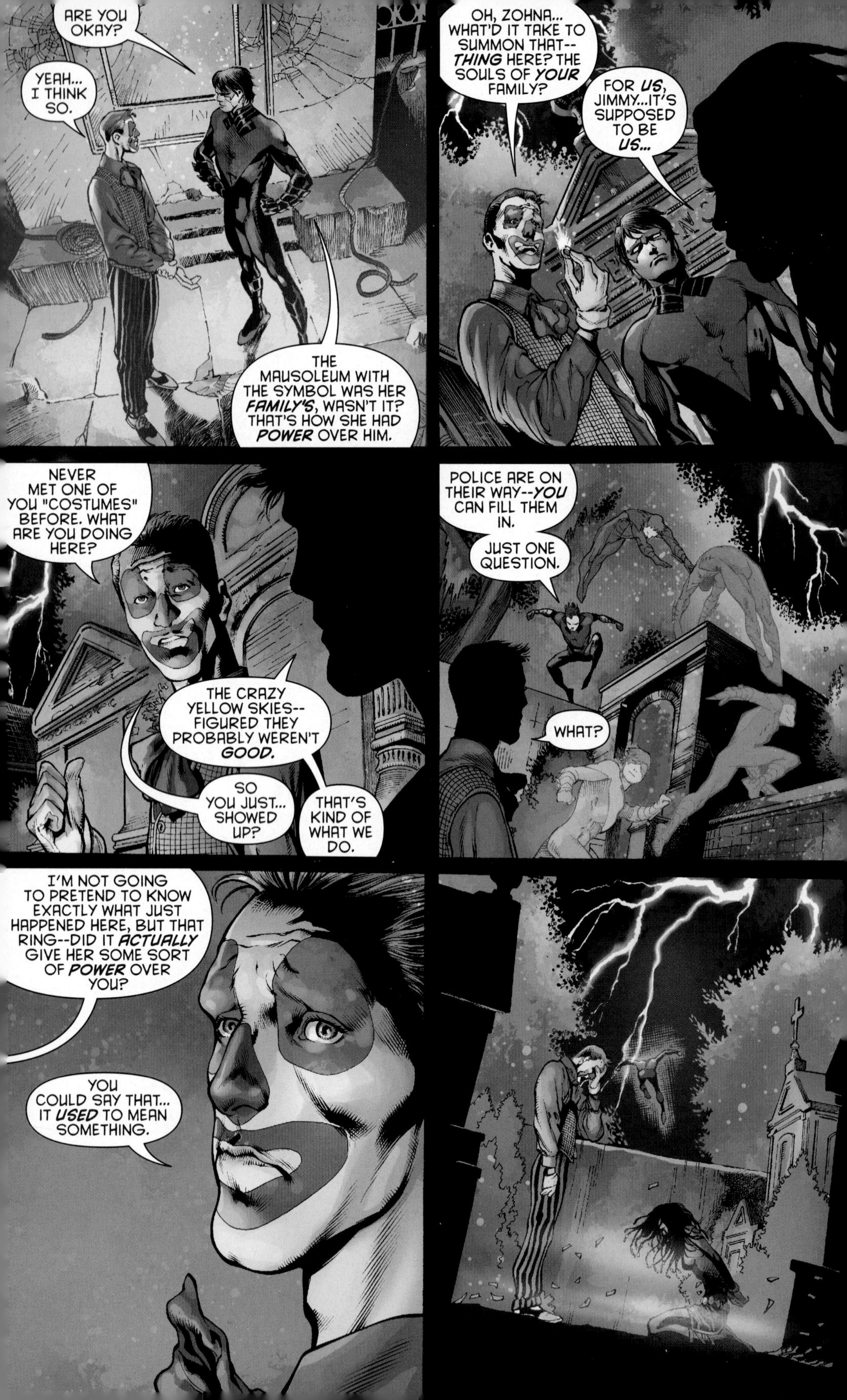
ARE YOU OKAY?
YEAH... I THINK SO.
THE MAUSOLEUM WITH THE SYMBOL WAS HER *FAMILY'S*, WASN'T IT? THAT'S HOW SHE HAD *POWER* OVER HIM.
OH, ZOHNA... WHAT'D IT TAKE TO SUMMON THAT-- *THING* HERE? THE SOULS OF *YOUR* FAMILY?
FOR *US*, JIMMY...IT'S SUPPOSED TO BE *US*...
NEVER MET ONE OF YOU "COSTUMES" BEFORE. WHAT ARE YOU DOING HERE?
THE CRAZY YELLOW SKIES-- FIGURED THEY PROBABLY WEREN'T *GOOD.*
SO YOU JUST... SHOWED UP?
THAT'S KIND OF WHAT WE DO.
POLICE ARE ON THEIR WAY--*YOU* CAN FILL THEM IN.
JUST ONE QUESTION.
WHAT?
I'M NOT GOING TO PRETEND TO KNOW EXACTLY WHAT JUST HAPPENED HERE, BUT THAT RING--DID IT *ACTUALLY* GIVE HER SOME SORT OF *POWER* OVER YOU?
YOU COULD SAY THAT... IT *USED* TO MEAN SOMETHING.

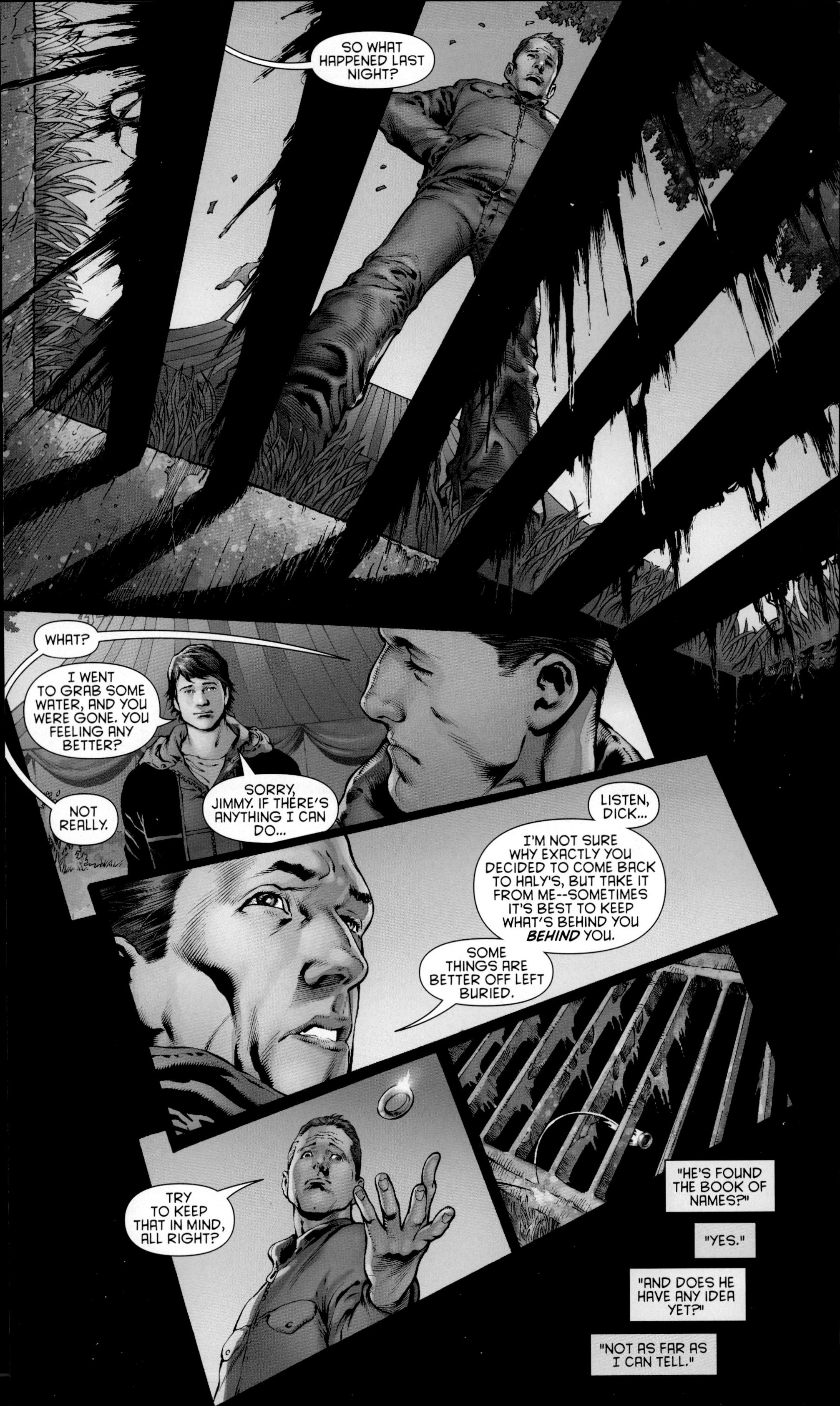

SO WHAT HAPPENED LAST NIGHT?
WHAT?
I WENT TO GRAB SOME WATER, AND YOU WERE GONE. YOU FEELING ANY BETTER?
NOT REALLY.
SORRY, JIMMY. IF THERE'S ANYTHING I CAN DO...
LISTEN, DICK...
I'M NOT SURE WHY EXACTLY YOU DECIDED TO COME BACK TO HALY'S, BUT TAKE IT FROM ME--SOMETIMES IT'S BEST TO KEEP WHAT'S BEHIND YOU *BEHIND* YOU.
SOME THINGS ARE BETTER OFF LEFT BURIED.
TRY TO KEEP THAT IN MIND, ALL RIGHT?
"HE'S FOUND THE BOOK OF NAMES?"
"YES."
"AND DOES HE HAVE ANY IDEA YET?"
"NOT AS FAR AS I CAN TELL."

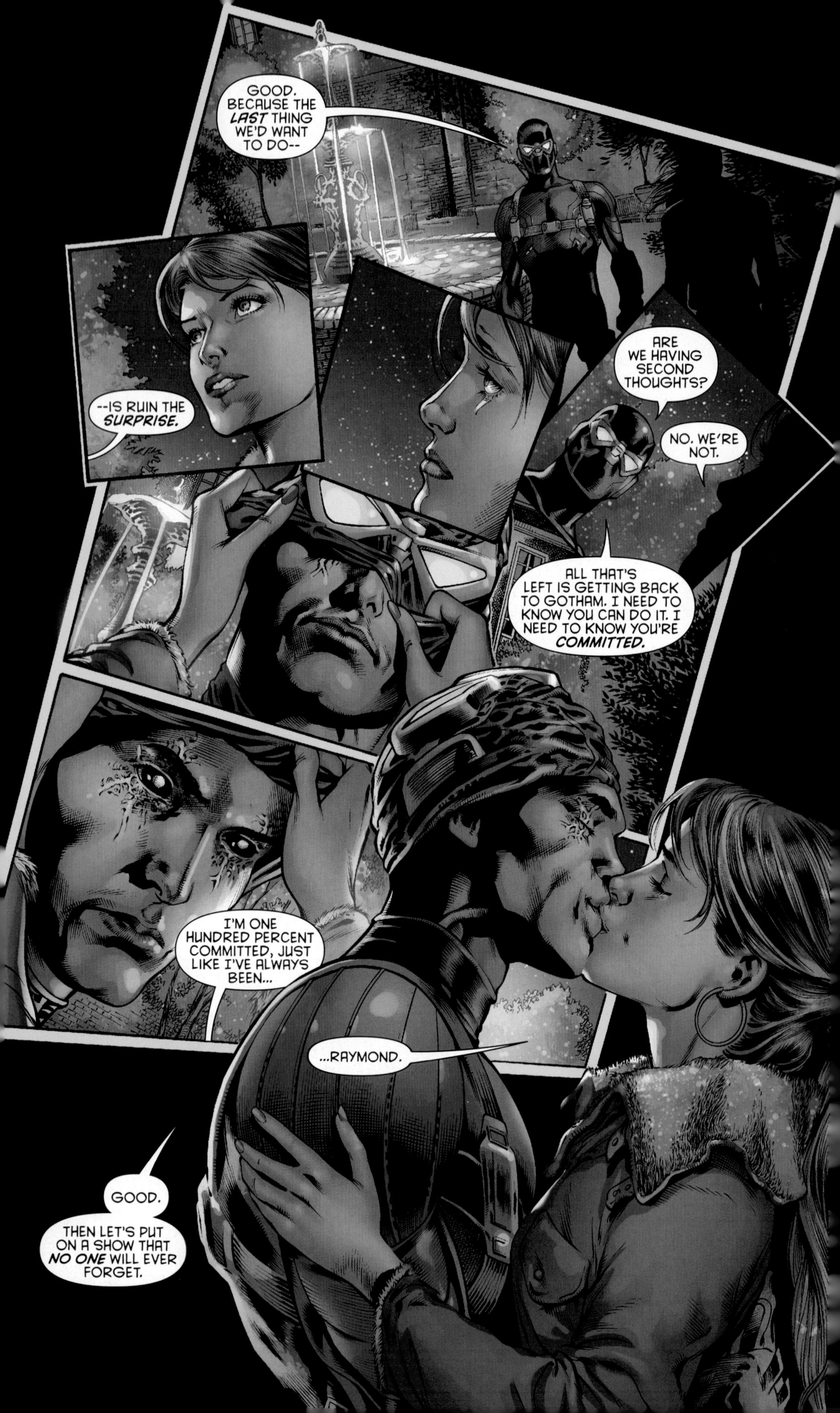
GOOD. BECAUSE THE *LAST* THING WE'D WANT TO DO--
--IS RUIN THE ***SURPRISE.***
ARE WE HAVING SECOND THOUGHTS?
NO. WE'RE NOT.
ALL THAT'S LEFT IS GETTING BACK TO GOTHAM. I NEED TO KNOW YOU CAN DO IT. I NEED TO KNOW YOU'RE ***COMMITTED.***
I'M ONE HUNDRED PERCENT COMMITTED, JUST LIKE I'VE ALWAYS BEEN...
...RAYMOND.
GOOD.
THEN LET'S PUT ON A SHOW THAT ***NO ONE*** WILL EVER FORGET.

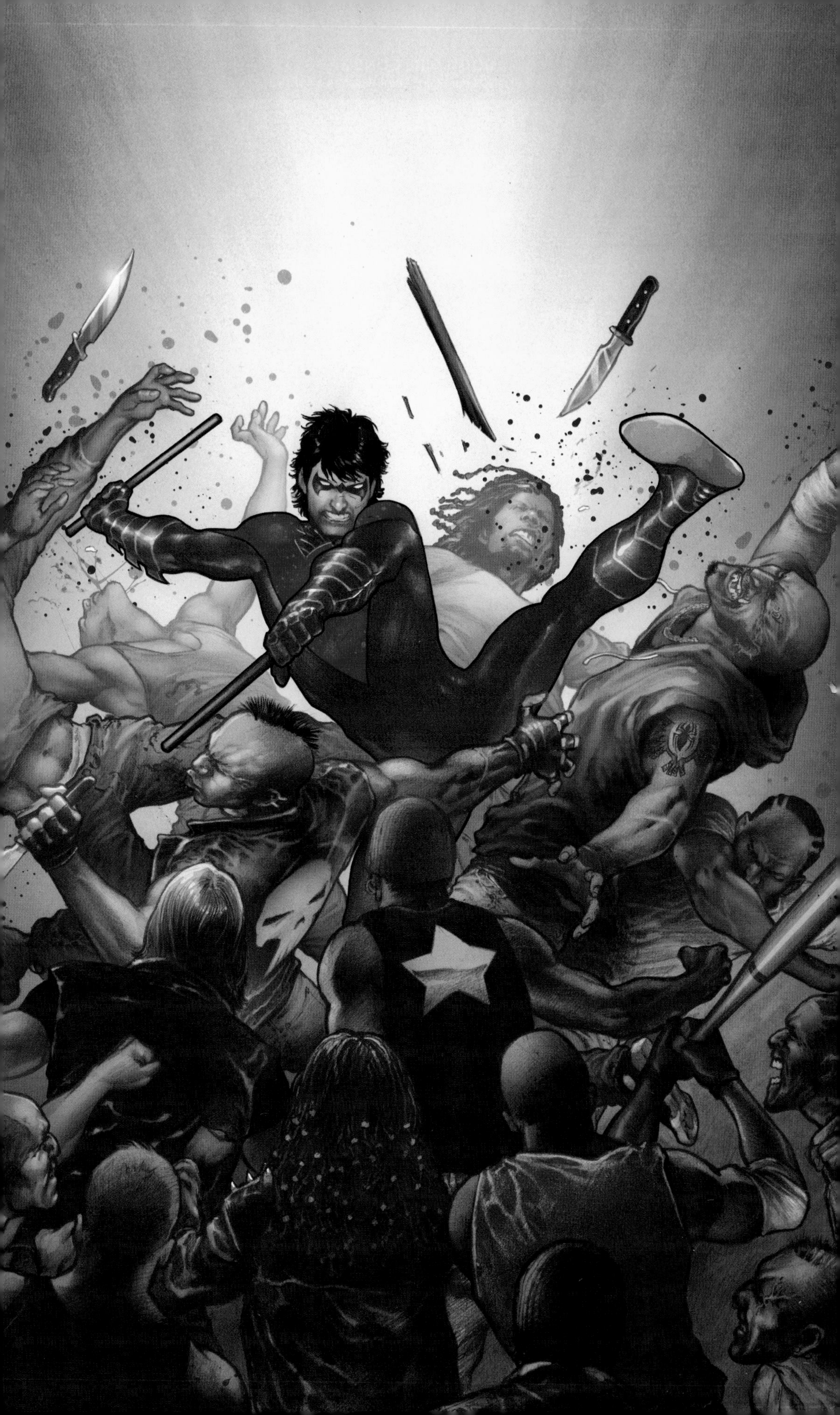

GOOD GIRL GONE BAD

KYLE HIGGINS writer **EDDY BARROWS & GERALDO BORGES** pencillers **EBER FERREIRA & RUY JOSÉ** inkers cover art by Eddy Barrows & Rod Rei

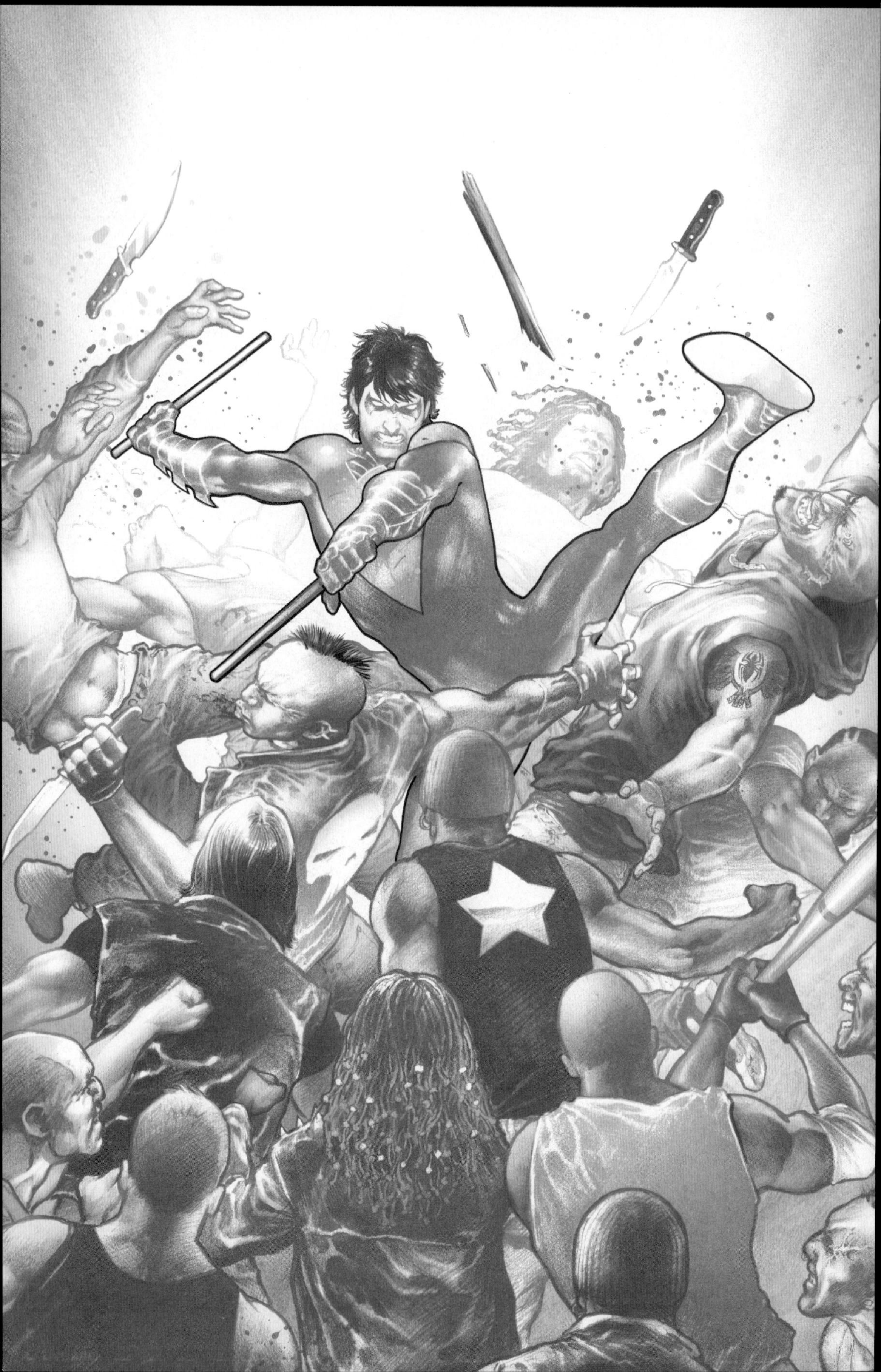

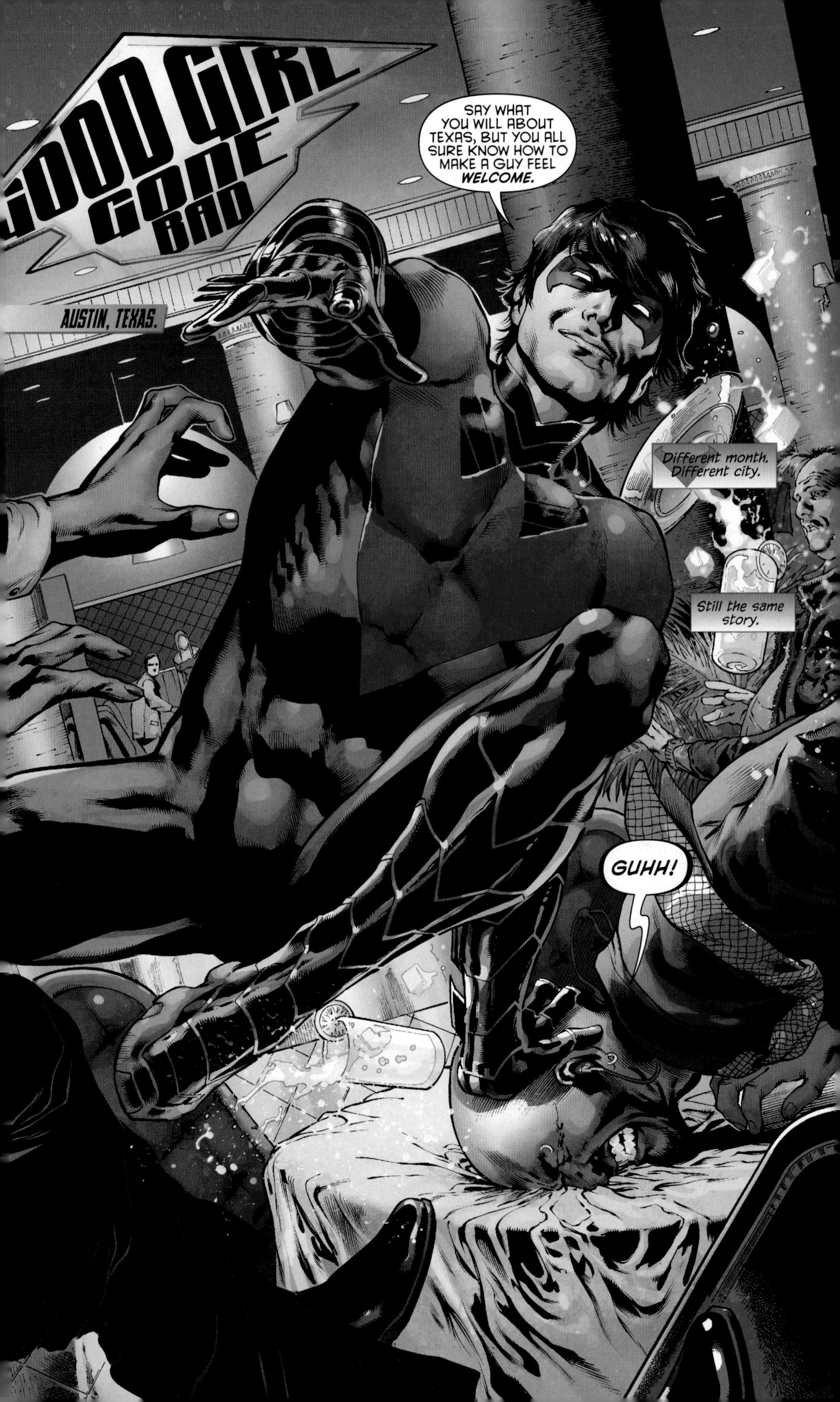
GOOD GIRL GONE BAD
AUSTIN, TEXAS.
SAY WHAT YOU WILL ABOUT TEXAS, BUT YOU ALL SURE KNOW HOW TO MAKE A GUY FEEL WELCOME.
Different month. Different city.
Still the same story.
GUHH!

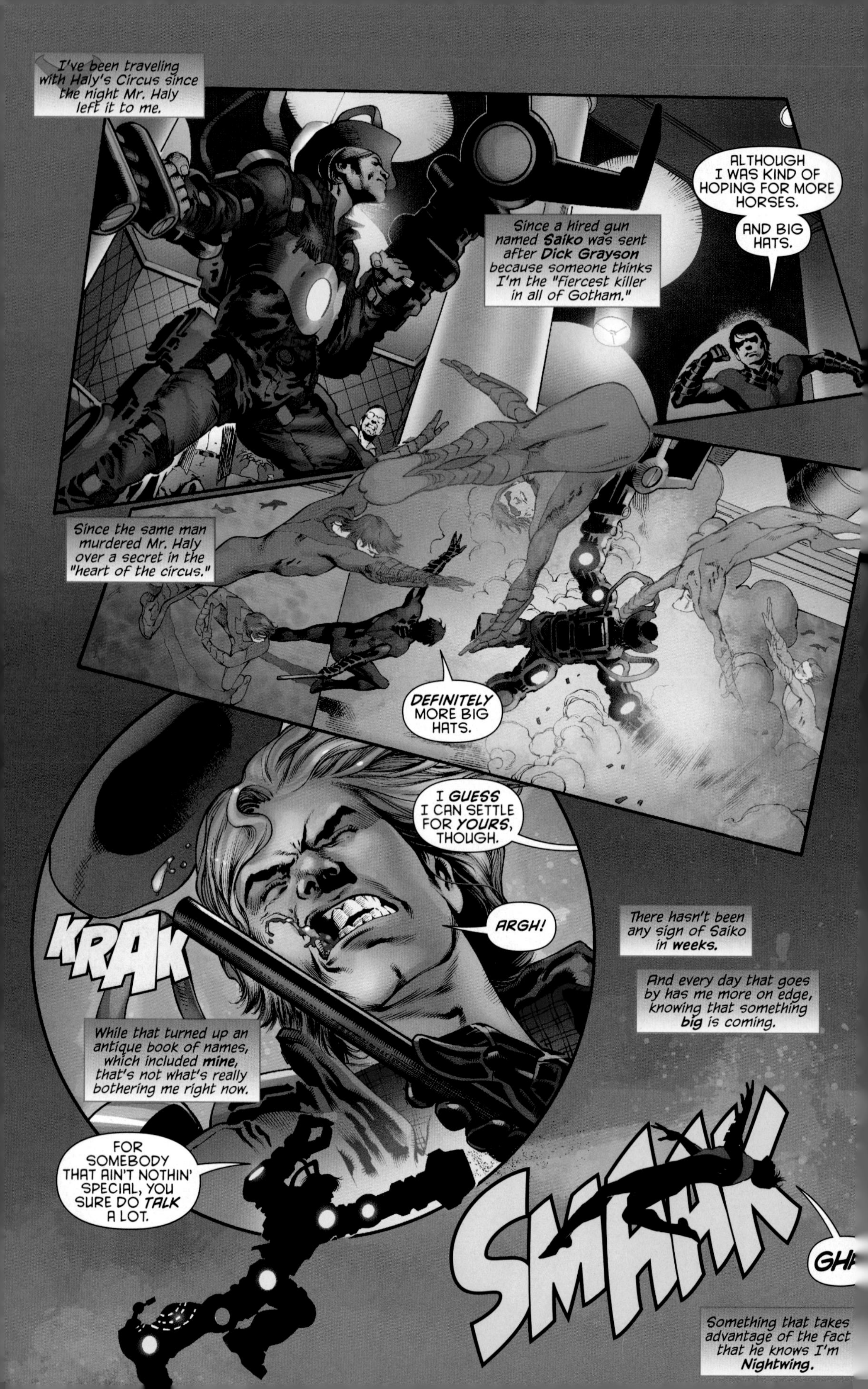
I've been traveling with Haly's Circus since the night Mr. Haly left it to me.
Since a hired gun named Saiko was sent after Dick Grayson because someone thinks I'm the "fiercest killer in all of Gotham."
ALTHOUGH I WAS KIND OF HOPING FOR MORE HORSES.
AND BIG HATS.
Since the same man murdered Mr. Haly over a secret in the "heart of the circus."
DEFINITELY MORE BIG HATS.
I GUESS I CAN SETTLE FOR YOURS, THOUGH.
KRAK
ARGH!
There hasn't been any sign of Saiko in weeks.
And every day that goes by has me more on edge, knowing that something big is coming.
While that turned up an antique book of names, which included mine, that's not what's really bothering me right now.
FOR SOMEBODY THAT AIN'T NOTHIN' SPECIAL, YOU SURE DO TALK A LOT.
SMAAK
GH
Something that takes advantage of the fact that he knows I'm Nightwing.

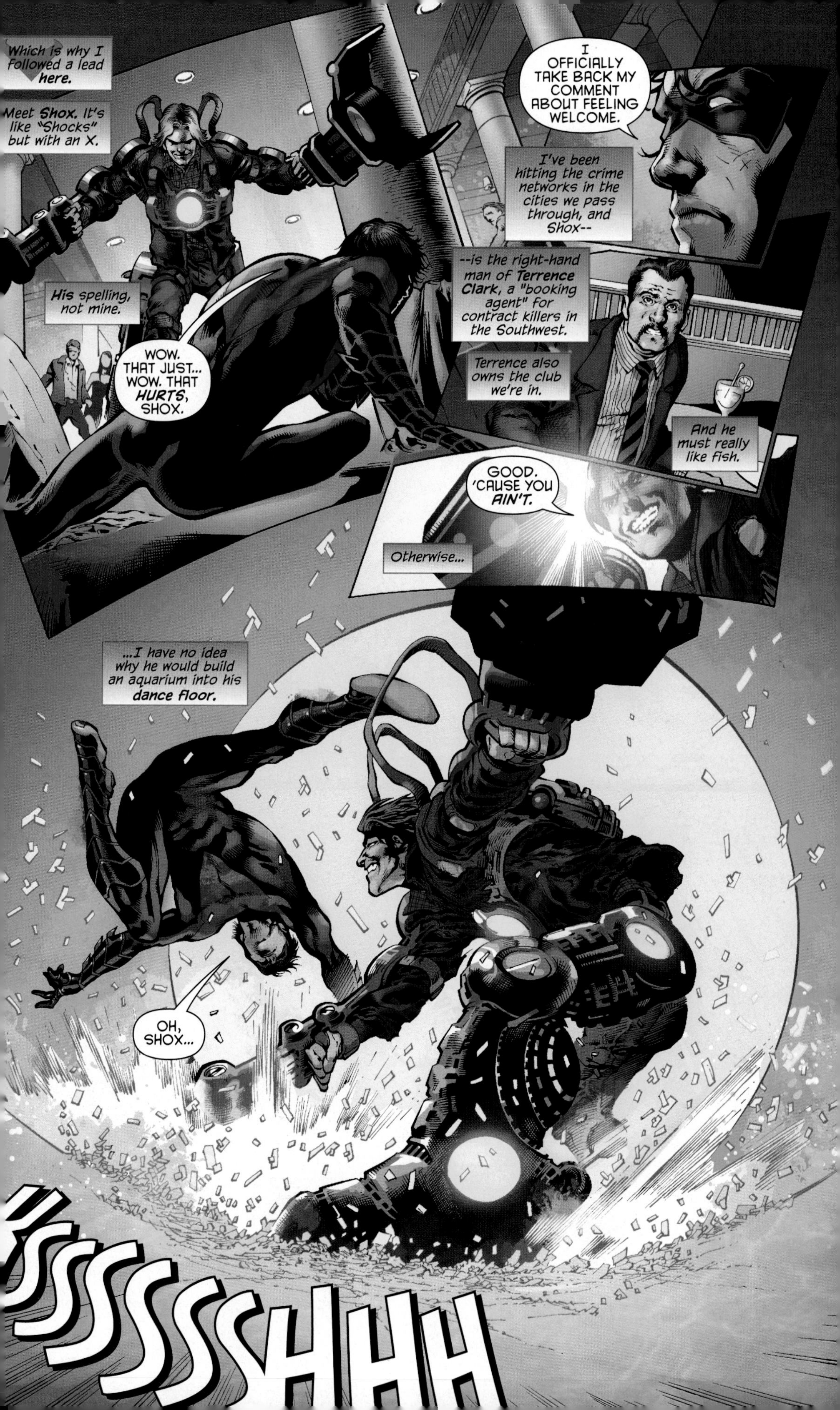

Which is why I followed a lead here.
Meet Shox. It's like "Shocks" but with an X.
His spelling, not mine.
WOW. THAT JUST... WOW. THAT HURTS, SHOX.
I OFFICIALLY TAKE BACK MY COMMENT ABOUT FEELING WELCOME.
I've been hitting the crime networks in the cities we pass through, and Shox--
--is the right-hand man of Terrence Clark, a "booking agent" for contract killers in the Southwest.
Terrence also owns the club we're in.
And he must really like fish.
GOOD. 'CAUSE YOU AIN'T.
Otherwise...
...I have no idea why he would build an aquarium into his dance floor.
OH, SHOX...
SSSSSHHH

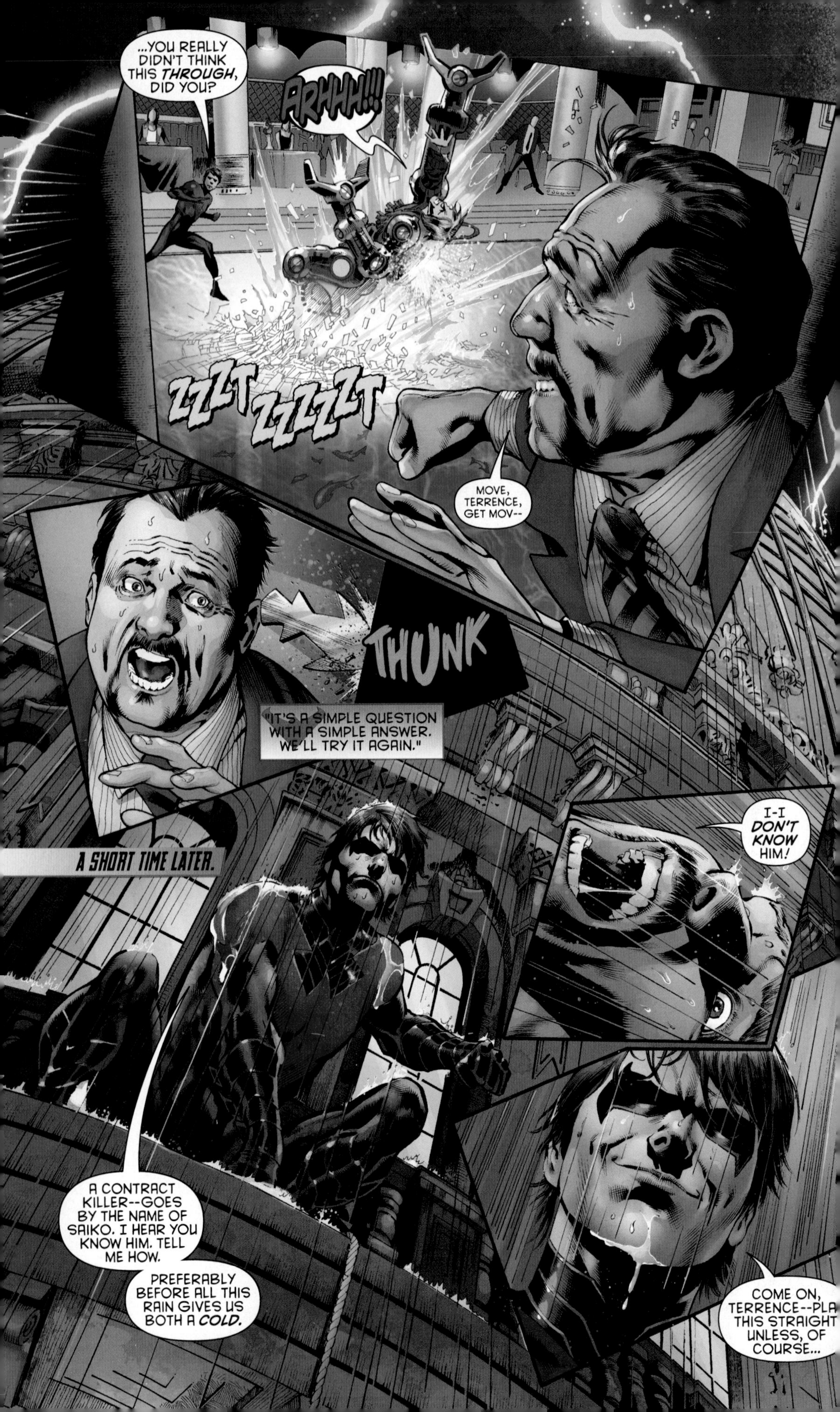
...YOU REALLY DIDN'T THINK THIS *THROUGH*, DID YOU?
ARHHH!!!
ZZZT ZZZZZT
MOVE, TERRENCE, GET MOV--
THUNK
"IT'S A SIMPLE QUESTION WITH A SIMPLE ANSWER. WE'LL TRY IT AGAIN."
A SHORT TIME LATER.
A CONTRACT KILLER--GOES BY THE NAME OF SAIKO. I HEAR YOU KNOW HIM. TELL ME HOW.
PREFERABLY BEFORE ALL THIS RAIN GIVES US BOTH A *COLD.*
I-I *DON'T KNOW* HIM!
COME ON, TERRENCE--PLA THIS STRAIGHT UNLESS, OF COURSE...

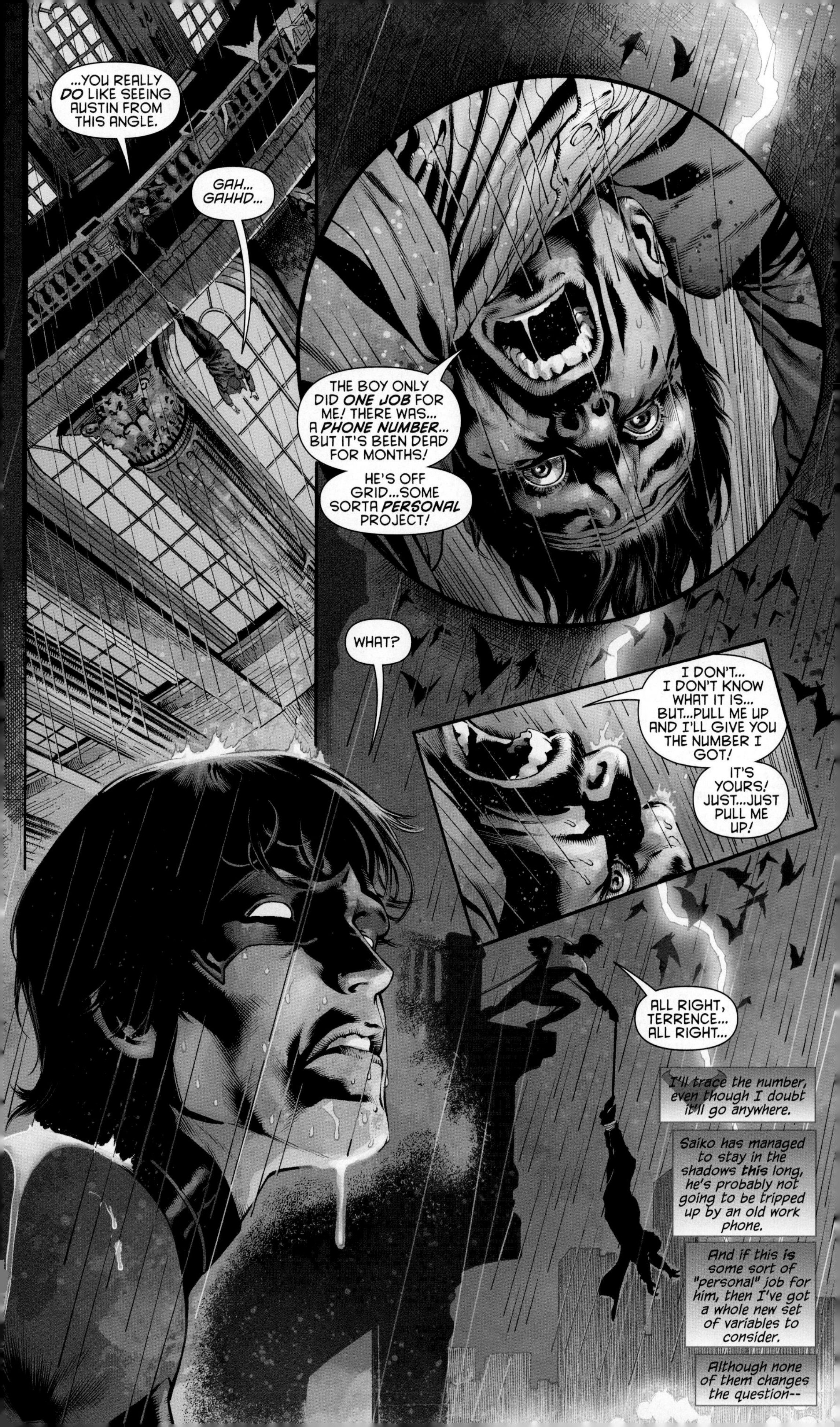
...YOU REALLY DO LIKE SEEING AUSTIN FROM THIS ANGLE.
GAH... GAHHD...
THE BOY ONLY DID ONE JOB FOR ME! THERE WAS... A PHONE NUMBER... BUT IT'S BEEN DEAD FOR MONTHS!
HE'S OFF GRID...SOME SORTA PERSONAL PROJECT!
WHAT?
I DON'T... I DON'T KNOW WHAT IT IS... BUT...PULL ME UP AND I'LL GIVE YOU THE NUMBER I GOT!
IT'S YOURS! JUST...JUST PULL ME UP!
ALL RIGHT, TERRENCE... ALL RIGHT...
I'll trace the number, even though I doubt it'll go anywhere.
Saiko has managed to stay in the shadows this long, he's probably not going to be tripped up by an old work phone.
And if this is some sort of "personal" job for him, then I've got a whole new set of variables to consider.
Although none of them changes the question--

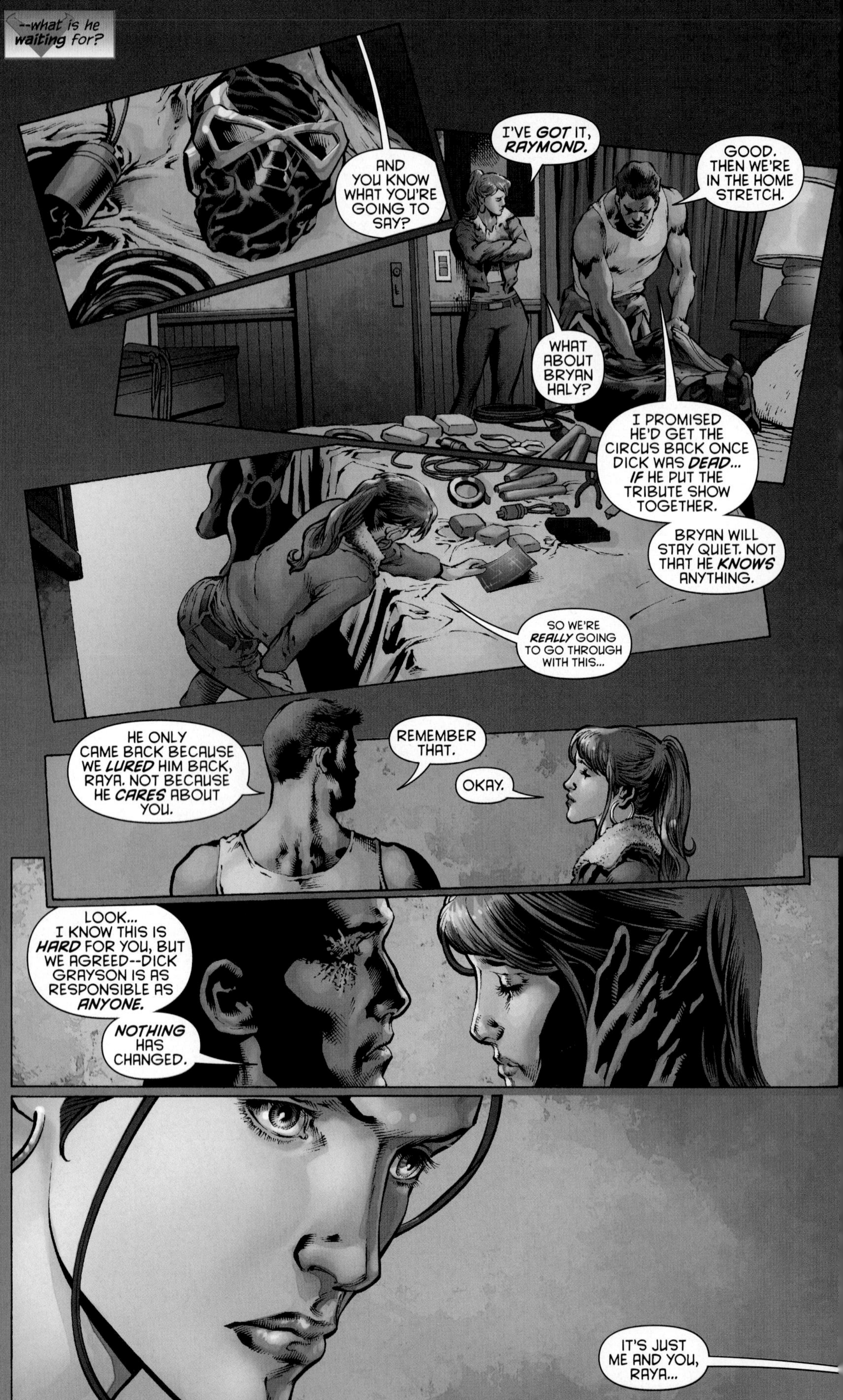
--what is he waiting for?
AND YOU KNOW WHAT YOU'RE GOING TO SAY?
I'VE GOT IT, RAYMOND.
GOOD. THEN WE'RE IN THE HOME STRETCH.
WHAT ABOUT BRYAN HALY?
I PROMISED HE'D GET THE CIRCUS BACK ONCE DICK WAS DEAD... IF HE PUT THE TRIBUTE SHOW TOGETHER.
BRYAN WILL STAY QUIET. NOT THAT HE KNOWS ANYTHING.
SO WE'RE REALLY GOING TO GO THROUGH WITH THIS...
HE ONLY CAME BACK BECAUSE WE LURED HIM BACK, RAYA. NOT BECAUSE HE CARES ABOUT YOU.
REMEMBER THAT.
OKAY.
LOOK... I KNOW THIS IS HARD FOR YOU, BUT WE AGREED--DICK GRAYSON IS AS RESPONSIBLE AS ANYONE.
NOTHING HAS CHANGED.
IT'S JUST ME AND YOU, RAYA...

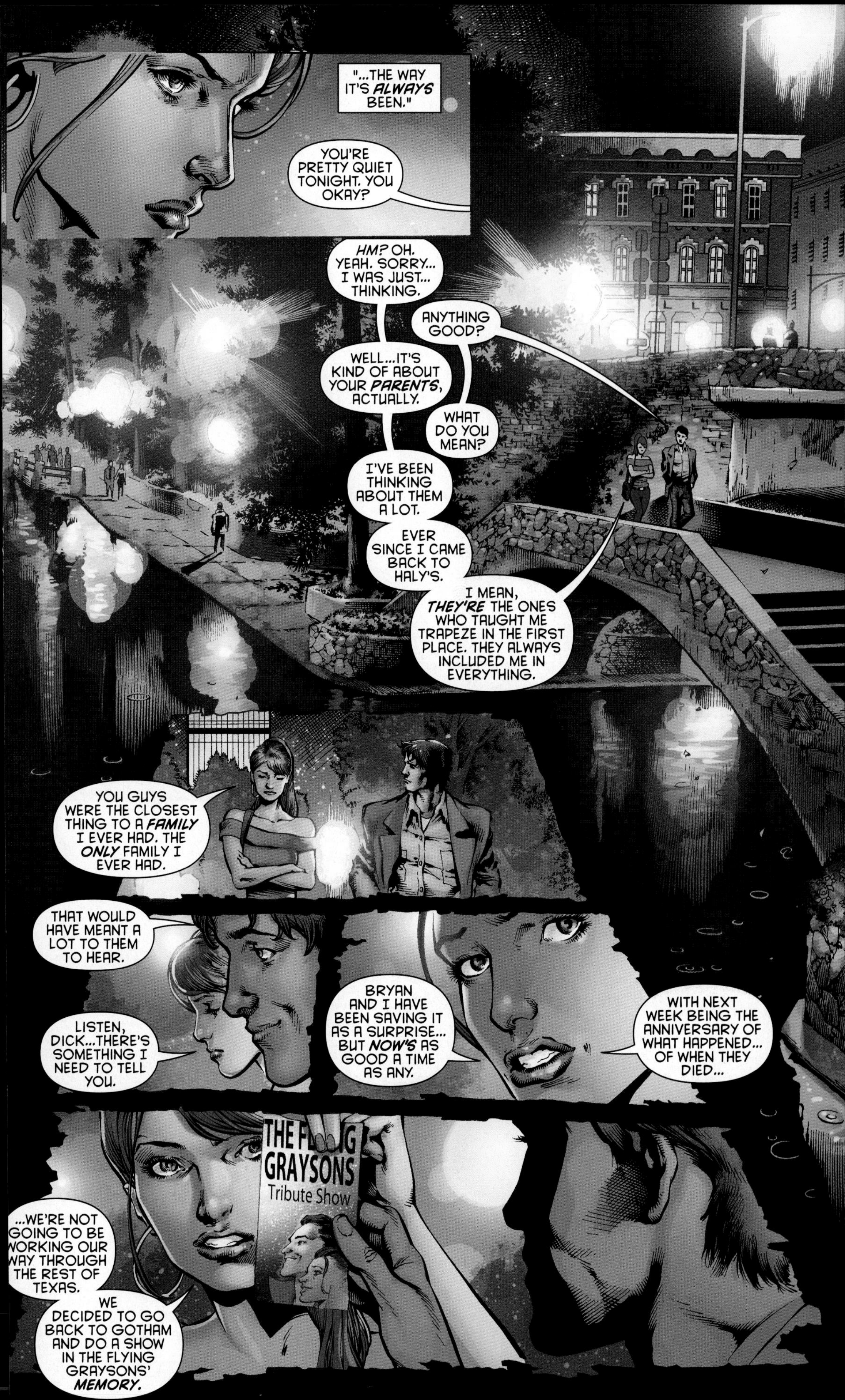
"...THE WAY IT'S ALWAYS BEEN."
YOU'RE PRETTY QUIET TONIGHT. YOU OKAY?
HM? OH. YEAH. SORRY... I WAS JUST... THINKING.
ANYTHING GOOD?
WELL...IT'S KIND OF ABOUT YOUR PARENTS, ACTUALLY.
WHAT DO YOU MEAN?
I'VE BEEN THINKING ABOUT THEM A LOT.
EVER SINCE I CAME BACK TO HALY'S.
I MEAN, THEY'RE THE ONES WHO TAUGHT ME TRAPEZE IN THE FIRST PLACE. THEY ALWAYS INCLUDED ME IN EVERYTHING.
YOU GUYS WERE THE CLOSEST THING TO A FAMILY I EVER HAD. THE ONLY FAMILY I EVER HAD.
THAT WOULD HAVE MEANT A LOT TO THEM TO HEAR.
LISTEN, DICK...THERE'S SOMETHING I NEED TO TELL YOU.
BRYAN AND I HAVE BEEN SAVING IT AS A SURPRISE... BUT NOW'S AS GOOD A TIME AS ANY.
WITH NEXT WEEK BEING THE ANNIVERSARY OF WHAT HAPPENED... OF WHEN THEY DIED...
GRAYSONS
Tribute Show
...WE'RE NOT GOING TO BE WORKING OUR WAY THROUGH THE REST OF TEXAS.
WE DECIDED TO GO BACK TO GOTHAM AND DO A SHOW IN THE FLYING GRAYSONS' MEMORY.

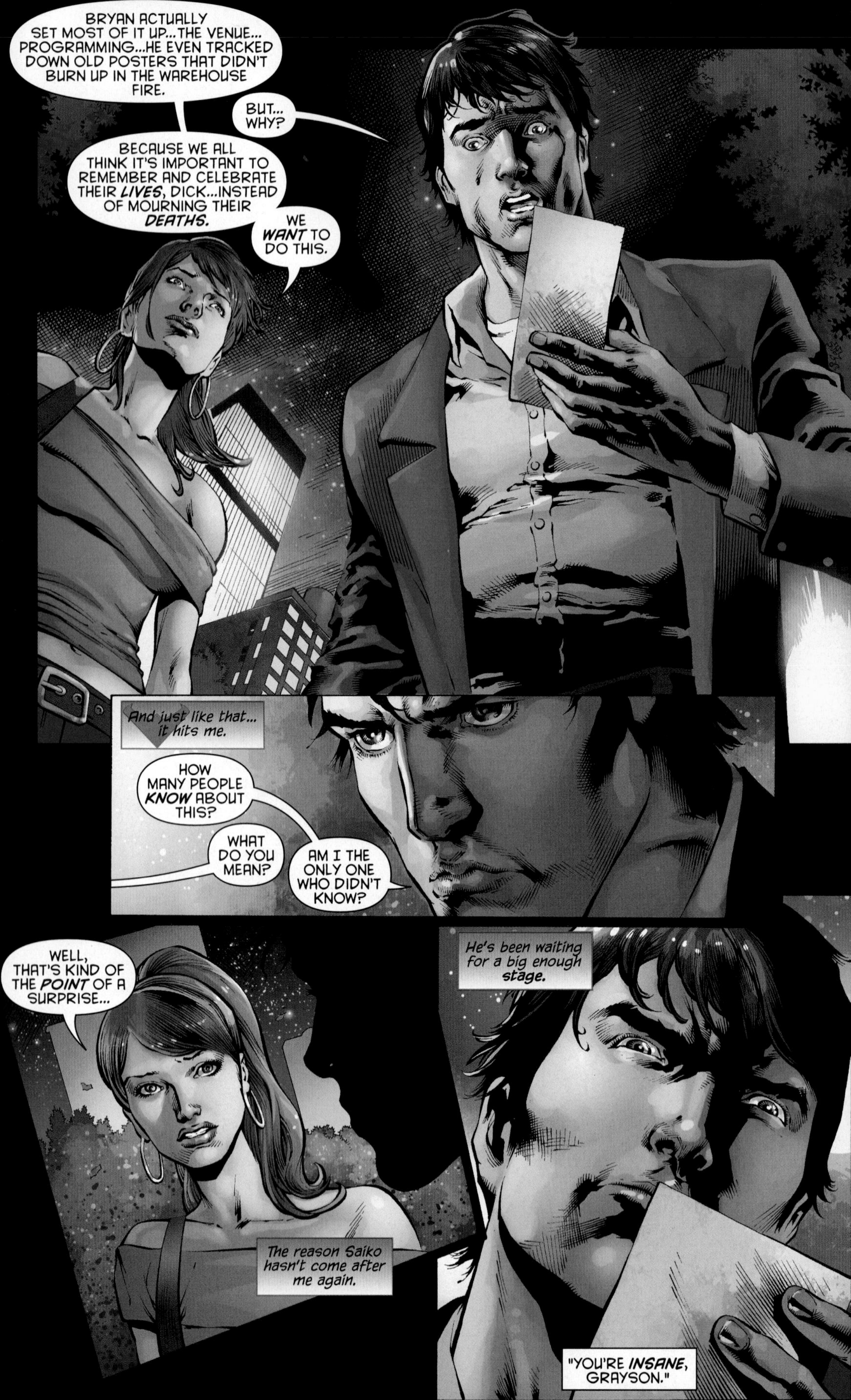
BRYAN ACTUALLY SET MOST OF IT UP...THE VENUE... PROGRAMMING...HE EVEN TRACKED DOWN OLD POSTERS THAT DIDN'T BURN UP IN THE WAREHOUSE FIRE.
BUT... WHY?
BECAUSE WE ALL THINK IT'S IMPORTANT TO REMEMBER AND CELEBRATE THEIR *LIVES*, DICK...INSTEAD OF MOURNING THEIR *DEATHS.*
WE *WANT* TO DO THIS.
And just like that... it hits me.
HOW MANY PEOPLE *KNOW* ABOUT THIS?
WHAT DO YOU MEAN?
AM I THE ONLY ONE WHO DIDN'T KNOW?
WELL, THAT'S KIND OF THE *POINT* OF A SURPRISE...
He's been waiting for a big enough *stage.*
The reason Saiko hasn't come after me again.
"YOU'RE *INSANE*, GRAYSON."

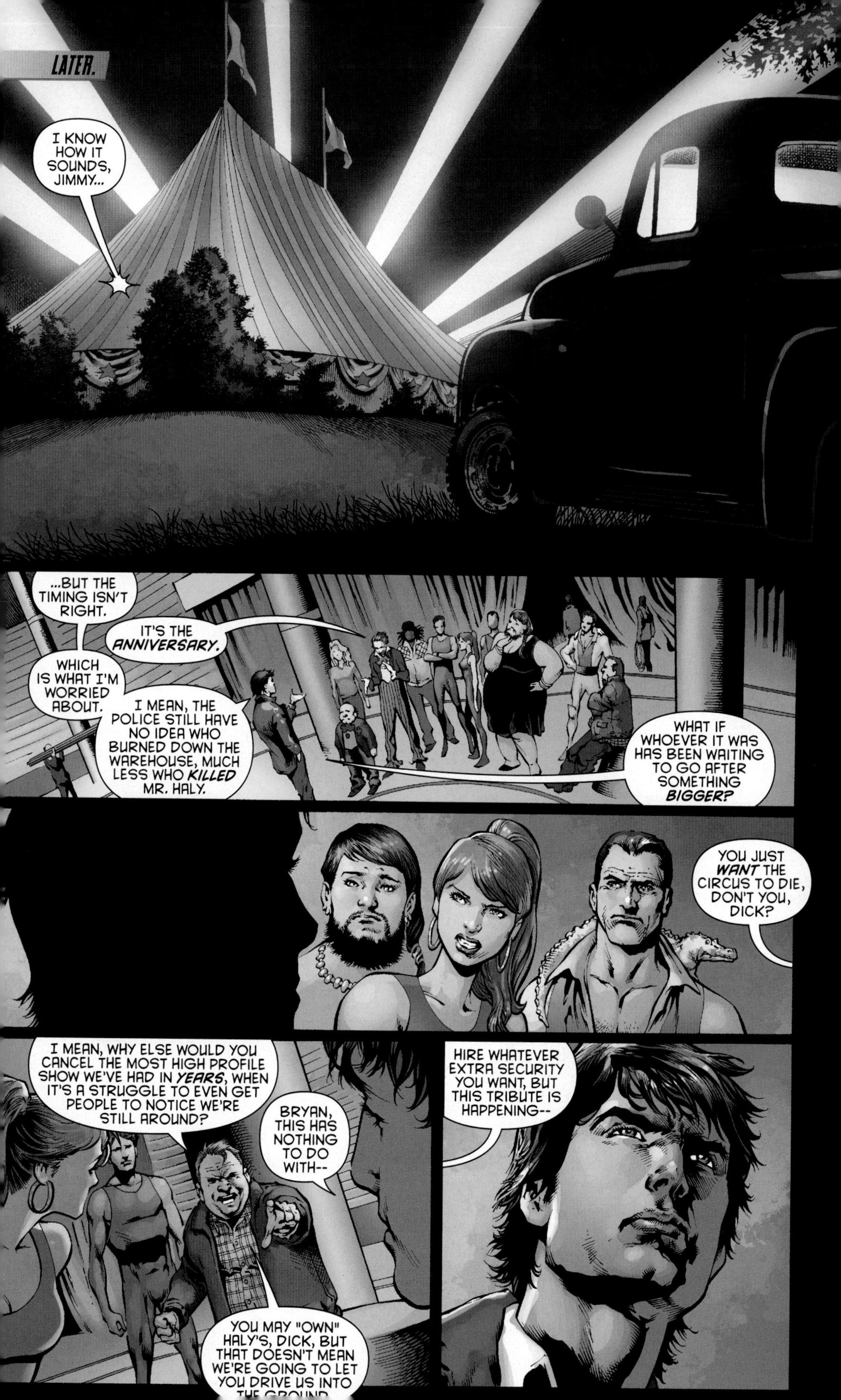
LATER.
I KNOW HOW IT SOUNDS, JIMMY...
...BUT THE TIMING ISN'T RIGHT.
IT'S THE ANNIVERSARY.
WHICH IS WHAT I'M WORRIED ABOUT.
I MEAN, THE POLICE STILL HAVE NO IDEA WHO BURNED DOWN THE WAREHOUSE, MUCH LESS WHO KILLED MR. HALY.
WHAT IF WHOEVER IT WAS HAS BEEN WAITING TO GO AFTER SOMETHING BIGGER?
YOU JUST WANT THE CIRCUS TO DIE, DON'T YOU, DICK?
I MEAN, WHY ELSE WOULD YOU CANCEL THE MOST HIGH PROFILE SHOW WE'VE HAD IN YEARS, WHEN IT'S A STRUGGLE TO EVEN GET PEOPLE TO NOTICE WE'RE STILL AROUND?
BRYAN, THIS HAS NOTHING TO DO WITH--
YOU MAY "OWN" HALY'S, DICK, BUT THAT DOESN'T MEAN WE'RE GOING TO LET YOU DRIVE US INTO
HIRE WHATEVER EXTRA SECURITY YOU WANT, BUT THIS TRIBUTE IS HAPPENING--

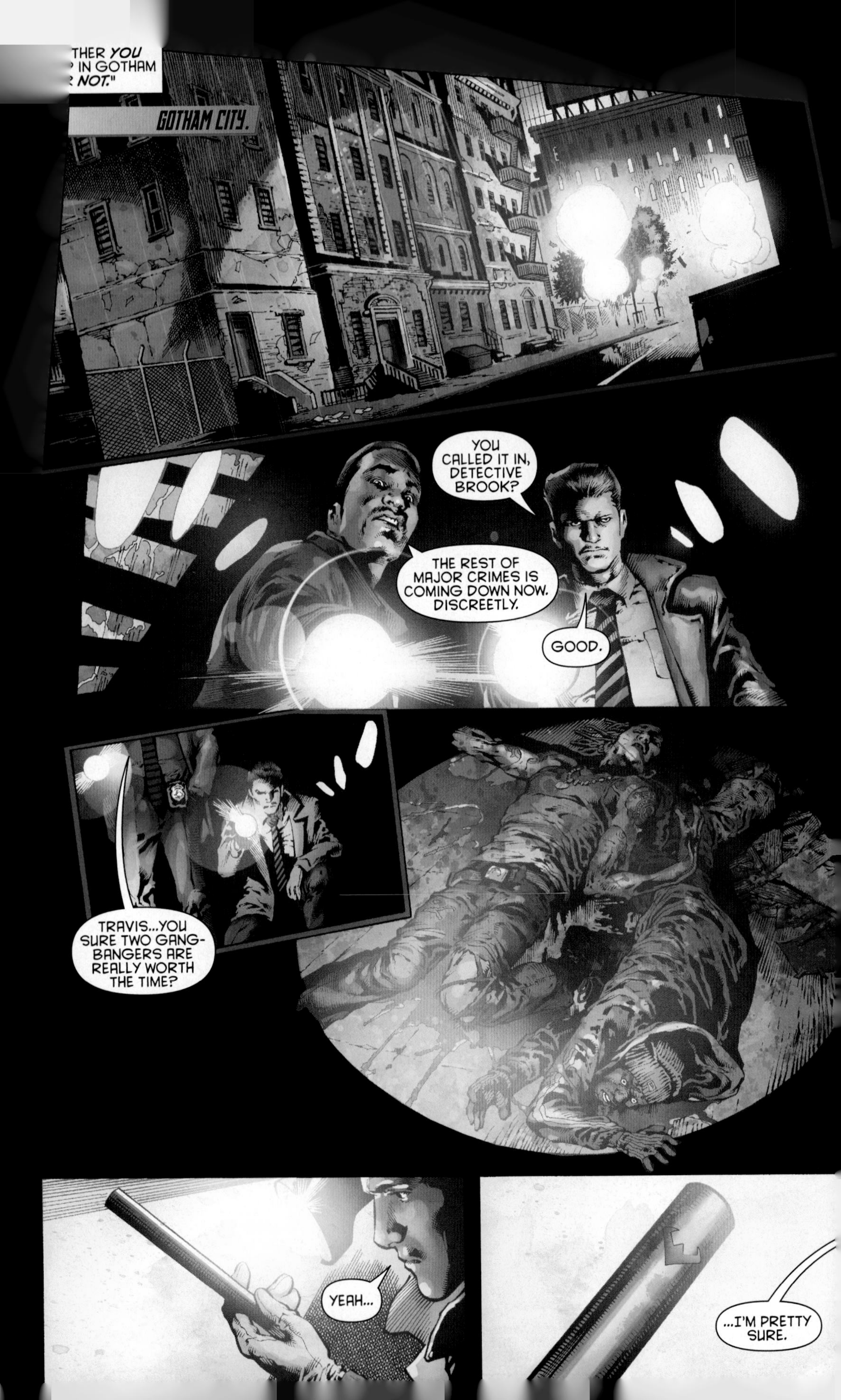

THER YOU
P IN GOTHAM
R NOT."
GOTHAM CITY.
YOU CALLED IT IN, DETECTIVE BROOK?
THE REST OF MAJOR CRIMES IS COMING DOWN NOW. DISCREETLY.
GOOD.
TRAVIS...YOU SURE TWO GANG-BANGERS ARE REALLY WORTH THE TIME?
YEAH...
...I'M PRETTY SURE.

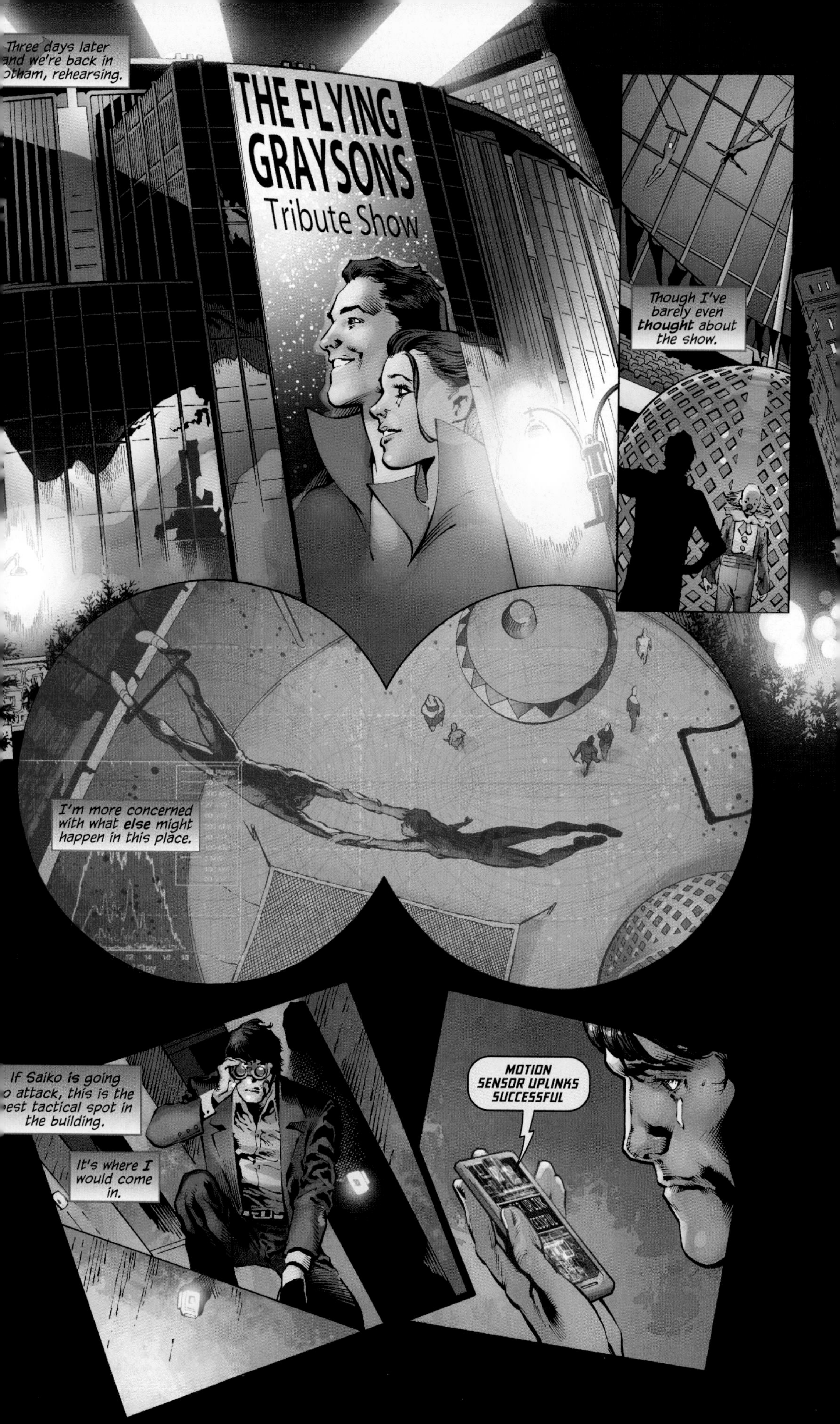
Three days later and we're back in otham, rehearsing.
THE FLYING GRAYSONS
Tribute Show
Though I've barely even thought about the show.
I'm more concerned with what else might happen in this place.
If Saiko is going o attack, this is the est tactical spot in the building.
It's where I would come in.
MOTION SENSOR UPLINKS SUCCESSFUL

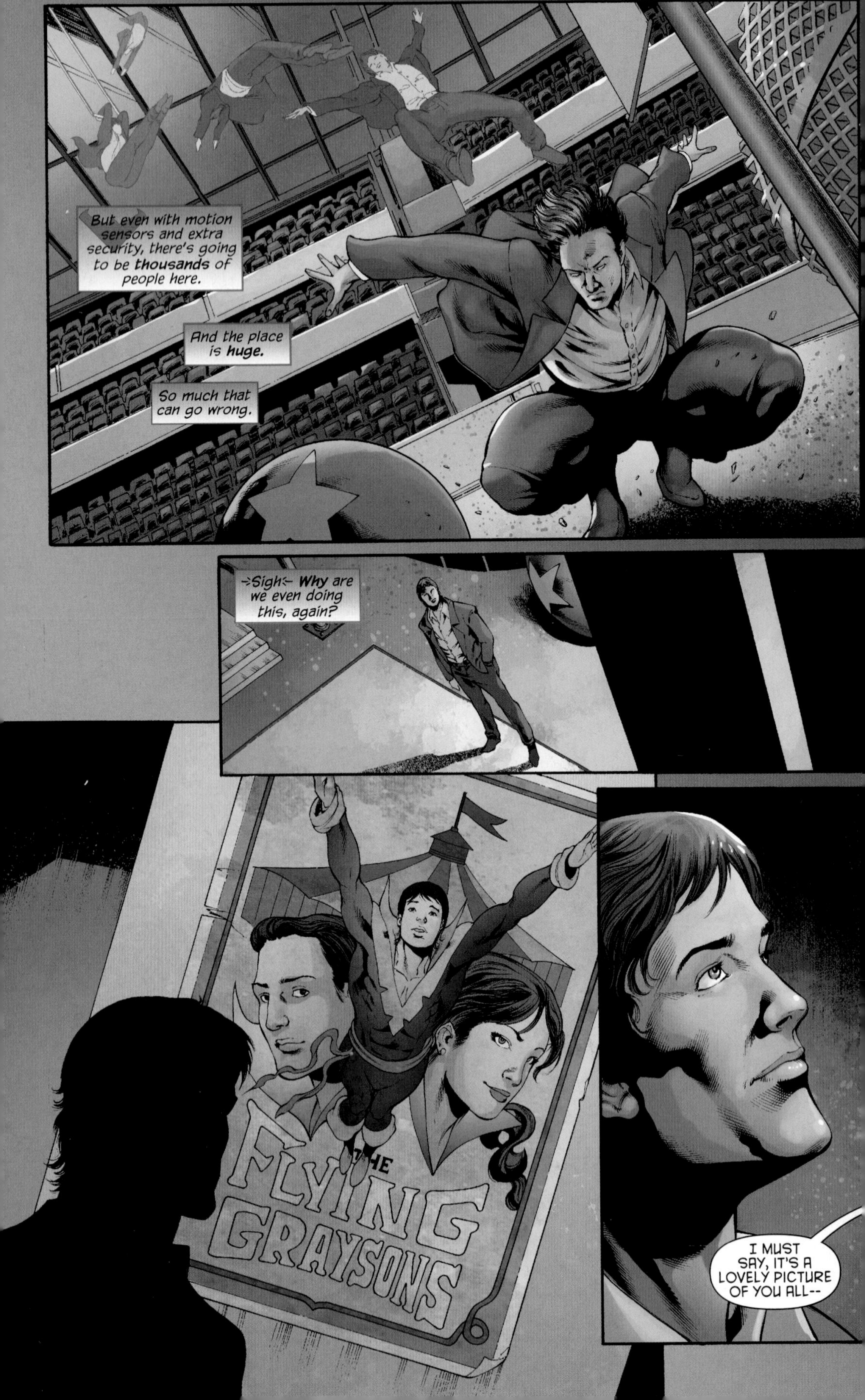
But even with motion sensors and extra security, there's going to be **thousands** of people here.
And the place is **huge.**
So much that can go wrong.
→Sigh← **Why** are we even doing this, again?
THE FLYING GRAYSONS
I MUST SAY, IT'S A LOVELY PICTURE OF YOU ALL--

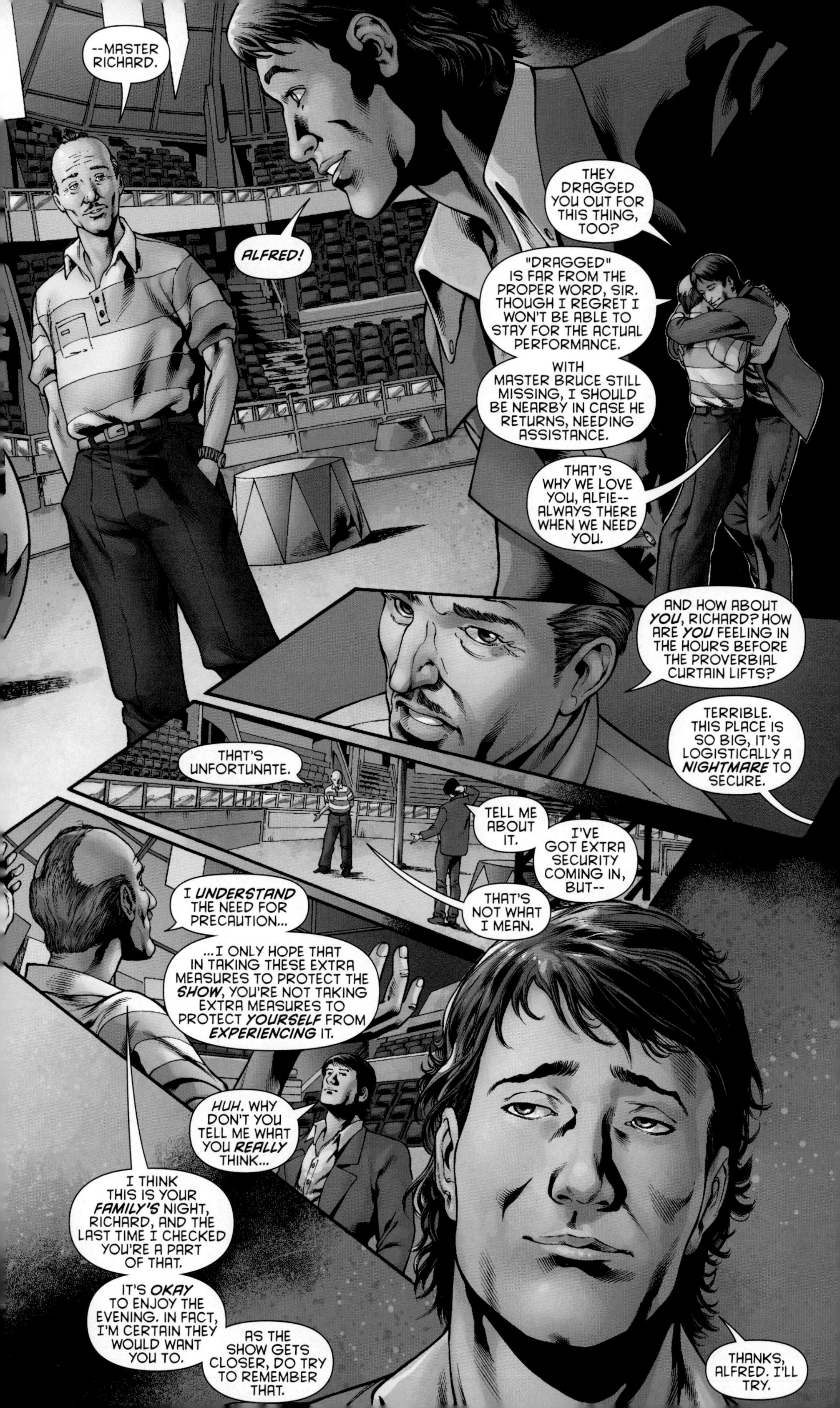
--MASTER RICHARD.
ALFRED!
THEY DRAGGED YOU OUT FOR THIS THING, TOO?
"DRAGGED" IS FAR FROM THE PROPER WORD, SIR. THOUGH I REGRET I WON'T BE ABLE TO STAY FOR THE ACTUAL PERFORMANCE.
WITH MASTER BRUCE STILL MISSING, I SHOULD BE NEARBY IN CASE HE RETURNS, NEEDING ASSISTANCE.
THAT'S WHY WE LOVE YOU, ALFIE--ALWAYS THERE WHEN WE NEED YOU.
AND HOW ABOUT YOU, RICHARD? HOW ARE YOU FEELING IN THE HOURS BEFORE THE PROVERBIAL CURTAIN LIFTS?
TERRIBLE. THIS PLACE IS SO BIG, IT'S LOGISTICALLY A NIGHTMARE TO SECURE.
THAT'S UNFORTUNATE.
TELL ME ABOUT IT.
I'VE GOT EXTRA SECURITY COMING IN, BUT--
THAT'S NOT WHAT I MEAN.
I UNDERSTAND THE NEED FOR PRECAUTION...
...I ONLY HOPE THAT IN TAKING THESE EXTRA MEASURES TO PROTECT THE SHOW, YOU'RE NOT TAKING EXTRA MEASURES TO PROTECT YOURSELF FROM EXPERIENCING IT.
HUH. WHY DON'T YOU TELL ME WHAT YOU REALLY THINK...
I THINK THIS IS YOUR FAMILY'S NIGHT, RICHARD, AND THE LAST TIME I CHECKED YOU'RE A PART OF THAT.
IT'S OKAY TO ENJOY THE EVENING. IN FACT, I'M CERTAIN THEY WOULD WANT YOU TO.
AS THE SHOW GETS CLOSER, DO TRY TO REMEMBER THAT.
THANKS, ALFRED. I'LL TRY.

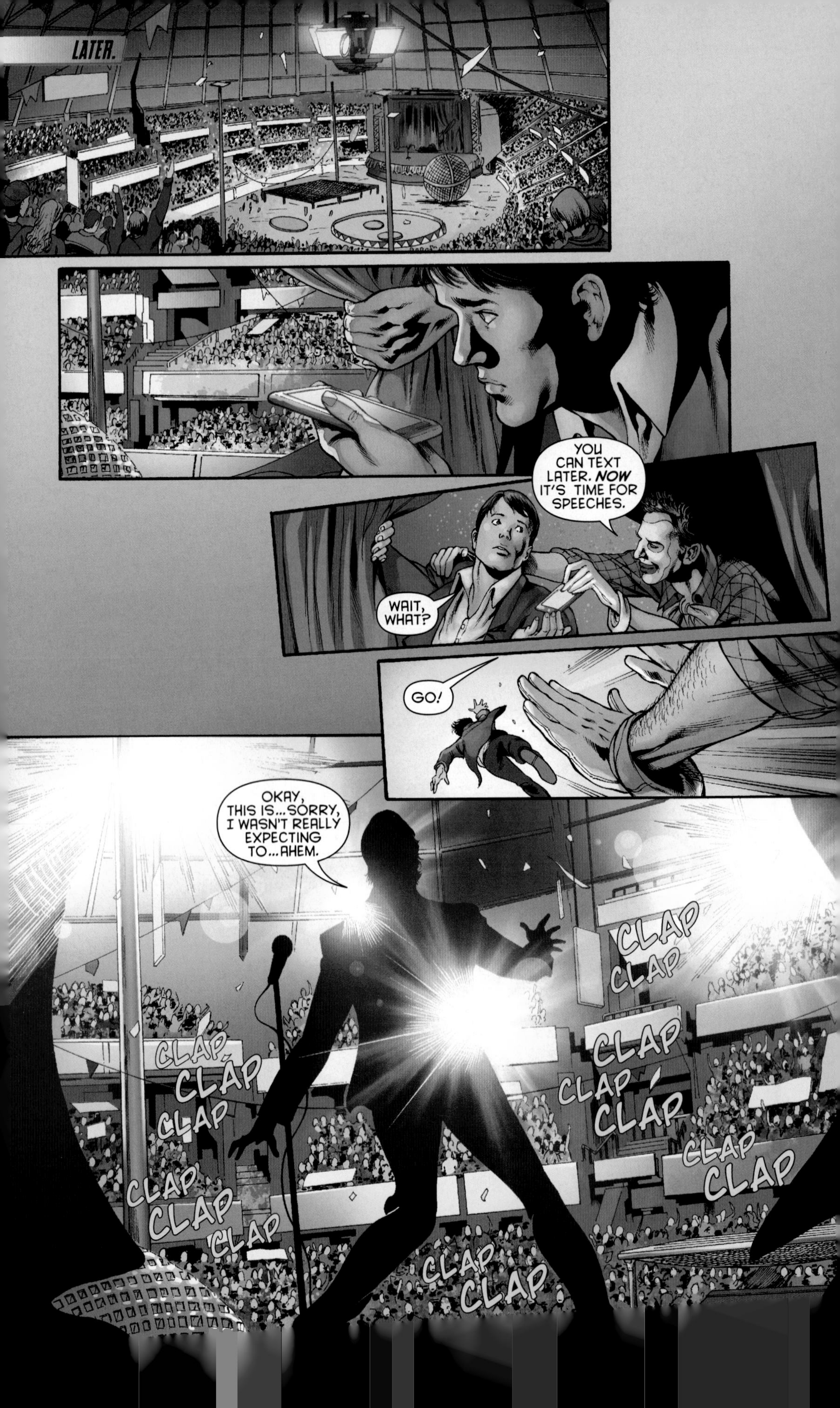
LATER.
YOU CAN TEXT LATER. NOW IT'S TIME FOR SPEECHES.
WAIT, WHAT?
GO!
OKAY, THIS IS...SORRY, I WASN'T REALLY EXPECTING TO...AHEM.
CLAP CLAP CLAP
CLAP CLAP CLAP
CLAP CLAP
CLAP CLAP
CLAP CLAP CLAP
CLAP CLAP

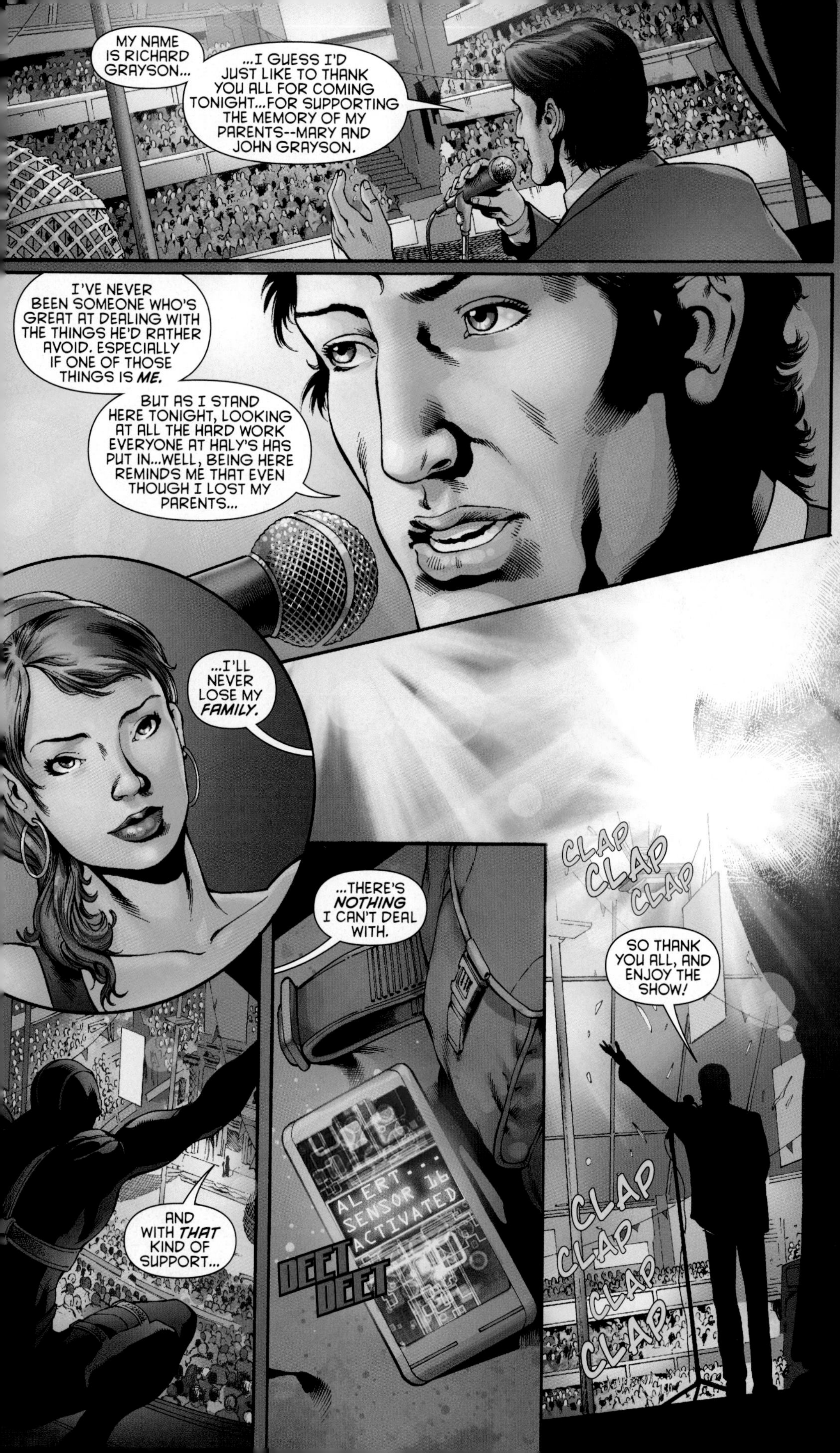
MY NAME IS RICHARD GRAYSON...
...I GUESS I'D JUST LIKE TO THANK YOU ALL FOR COMING TONIGHT...FOR SUPPORTING THE MEMORY OF MY PARENTS--MARY AND JOHN GRAYSON.
I'VE NEVER BEEN SOMEONE WHO'S GREAT AT DEALING WITH THE THINGS HE'D RATHER AVOID. ESPECIALLY IF ONE OF THOSE THINGS IS ME.
BUT AS I STAND HERE TONIGHT, LOOKING AT ALL THE HARD WORK EVERYONE AT HALY'S HAS PUT IN...WELL, BEING HERE REMINDS ME THAT EVEN THOUGH I LOST MY PARENTS...
...I'LL NEVER LOSE MY FAMILY.
AND WITH THAT KIND OF SUPPORT...
...THERE'S NOTHING I CAN'T DEAL WITH.
ALERT SENSOR 16 ACTIVATED
DEET DEET
CLAP CLAP CLAP
SO THANK YOU ALL, AND ENJOY THE SHOW!
CLAP CLAP CLAP CLAP

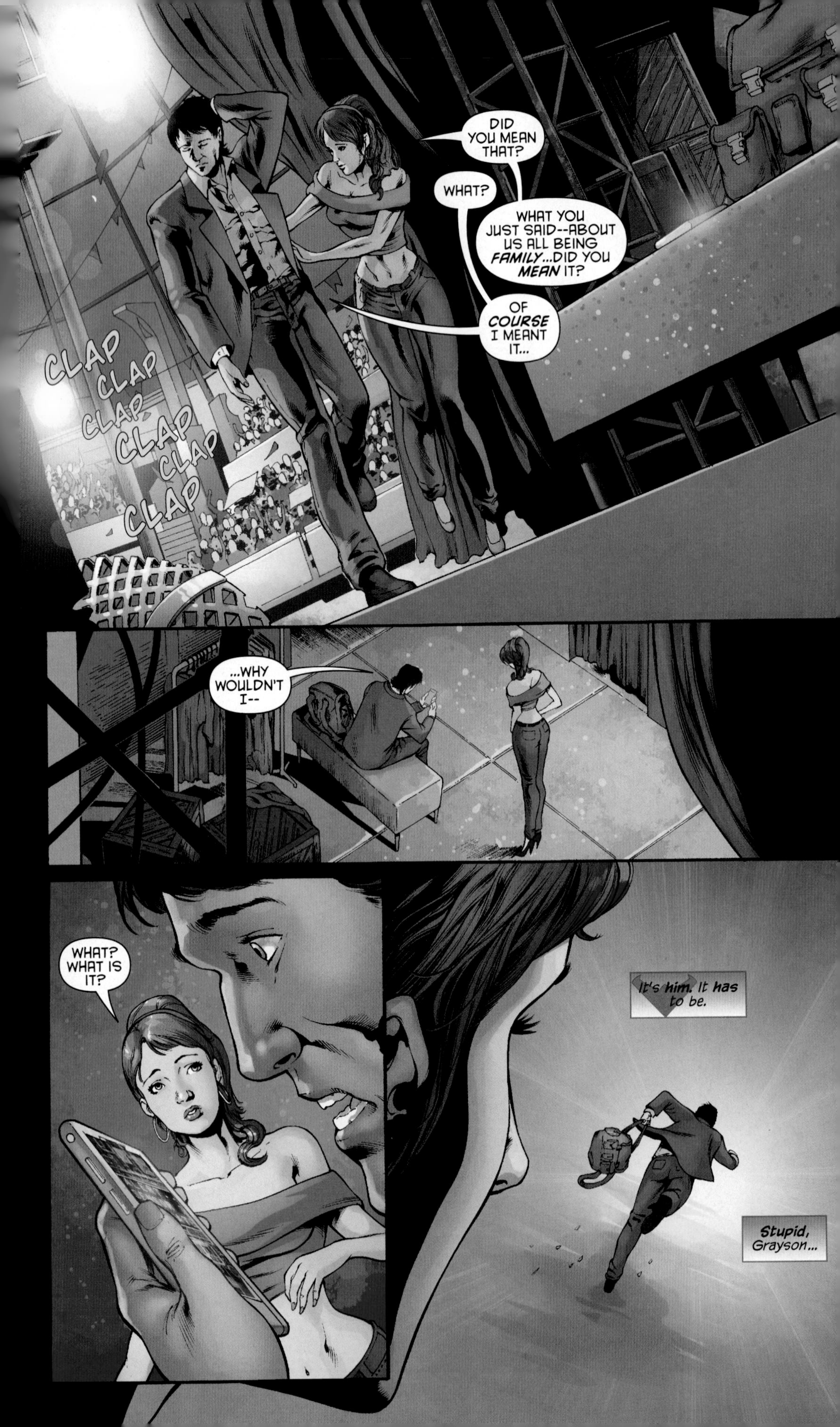
DID YOU MEAN THAT?
WHAT?
WHAT YOU JUST SAID--ABOUT US ALL BEING *FAMILY*...DID YOU *MEAN* IT?
OF *COURSE* I MEANT IT...
CLAP CLAP CLAP CLAP CLAP CLAP
...WHY WOULDN'T I--
WHAT? WHAT IS IT?
It's **him**. It **has** to be.
Stupid, Grayson...

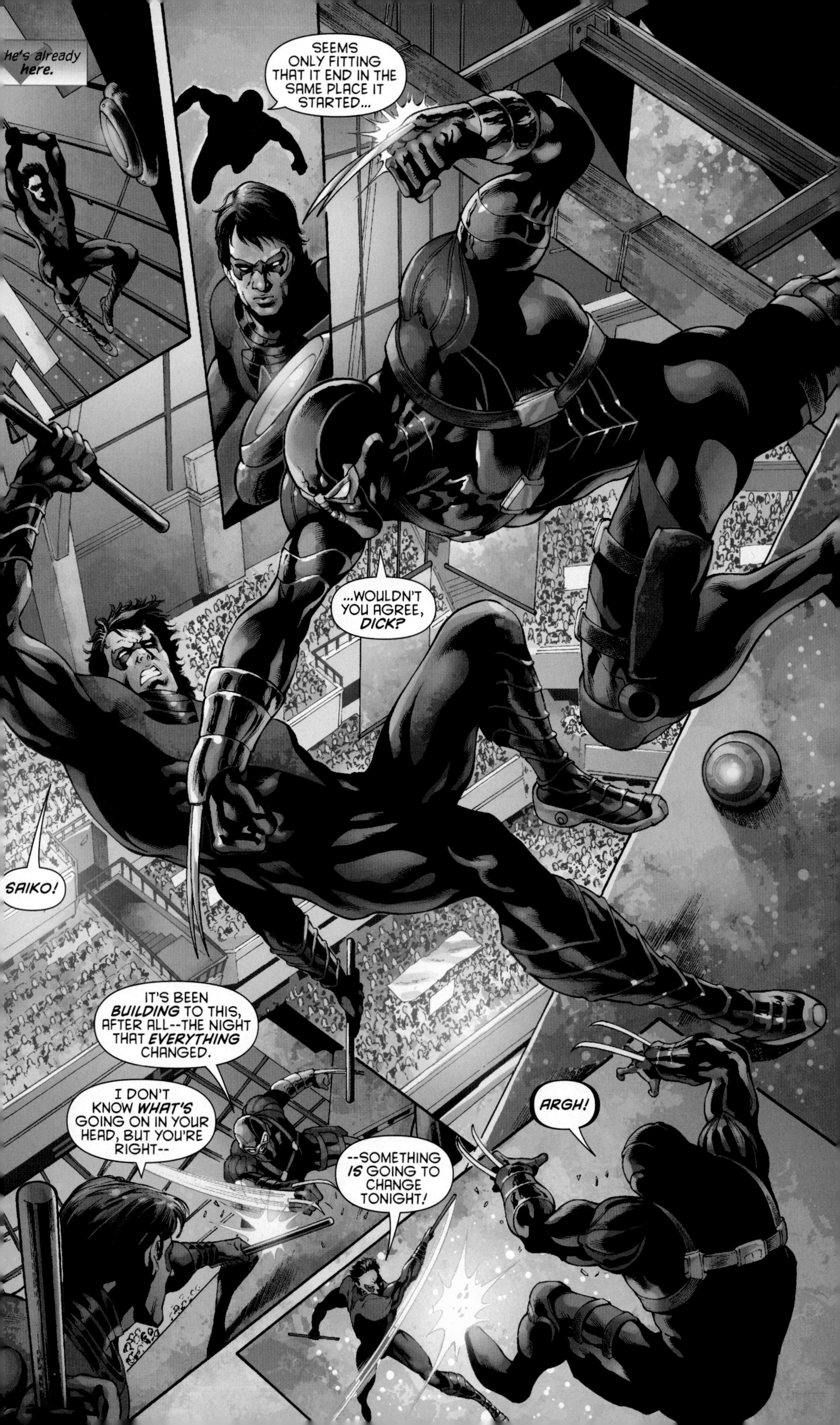
he's already here.
SEEMS ONLY FITTING THAT IT END IN THE SAME PLACE IT STARTED...
...WOULDN'T YOU AGREE, DICK?
SAIKO!
IT'S BEEN BUILDING TO THIS, AFTER ALL--THE NIGHT THAT EVERYTHING CHANGED.
I DON'T KNOW WHAT'S GOING ON IN YOUR HEAD, BUT YOU'RE RIGHT--
--SOMETHING IS GOING TO CHANGE TONIGHT!
ARGH!

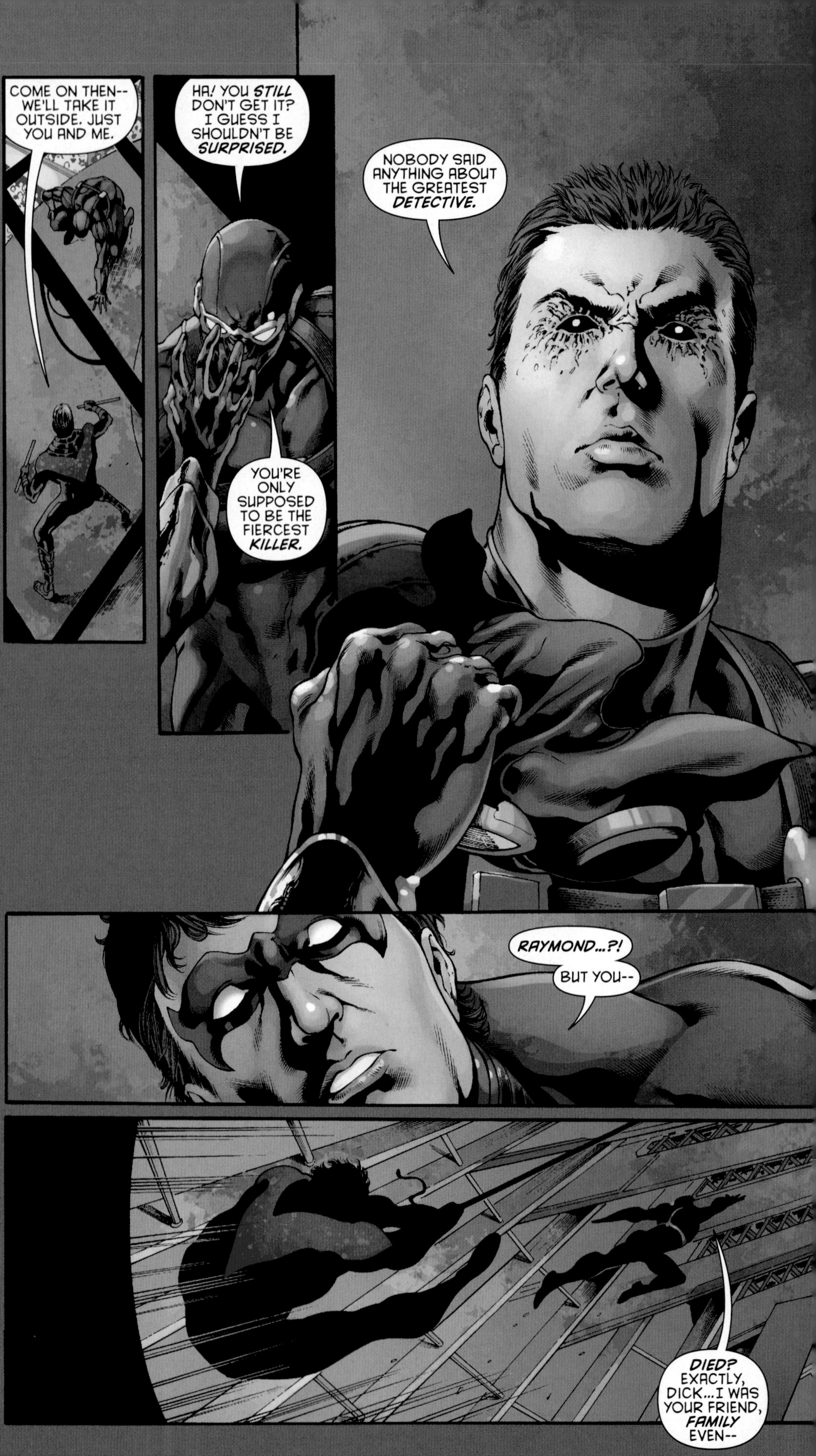
COME ON THEN-- WE'LL TAKE IT OUTSIDE. JUST YOU AND ME.
HA! YOU STILL DON'T GET IT? I GUESS I SHOULDN'T BE SURPRISED.
YOU'RE ONLY SUPPOSED TO BE THE FIERCEST KILLER.
NOBODY SAID ANYTHING ABOUT THE GREATEST DETECTIVE.
RAYMOND...?!
BUT YOU--
DIED? EXACTLY, DICK...I WAS YOUR FRIEND, FAMILY EVEN--

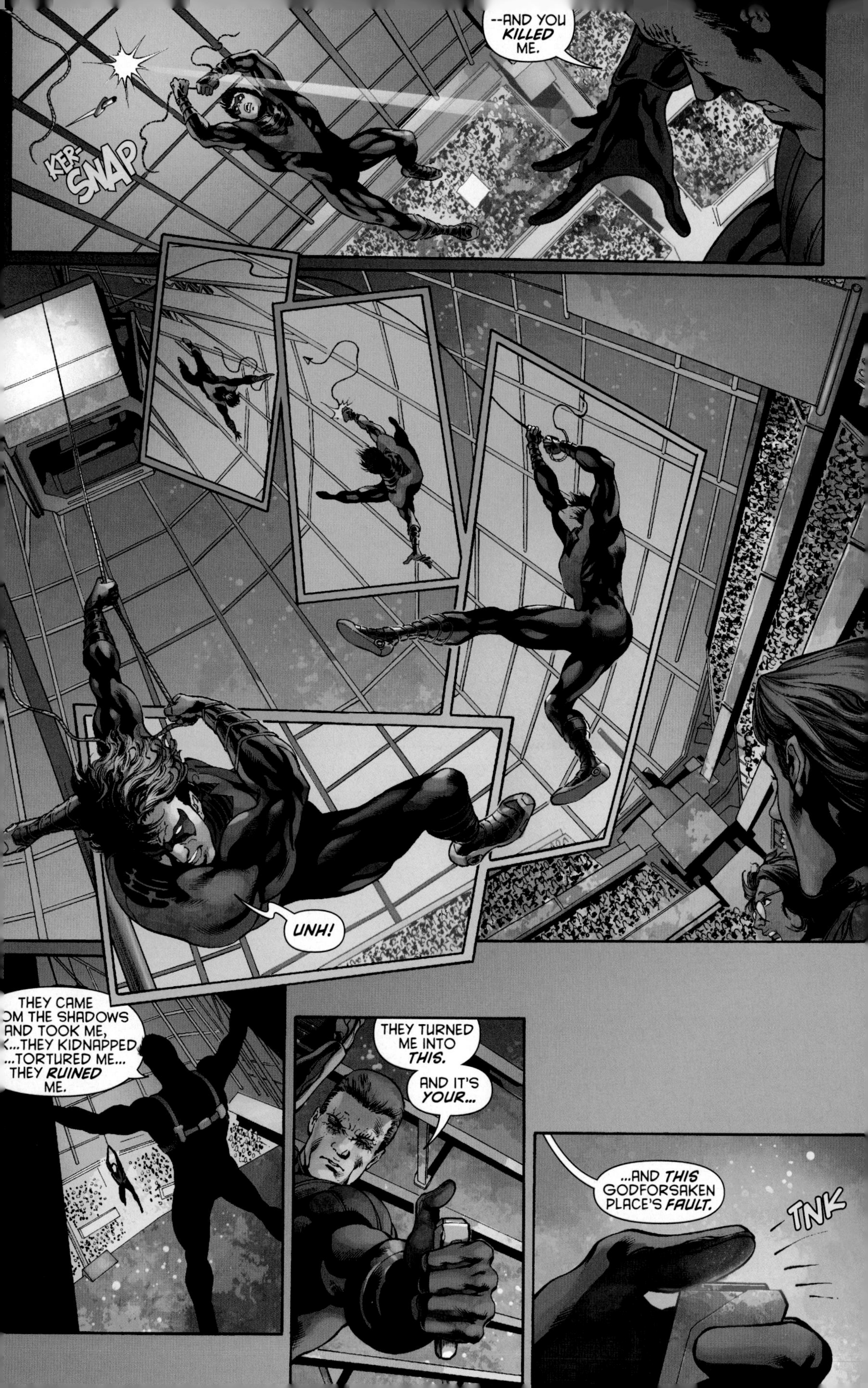

--AND YOU KILLED ME.
KER-SNAP
UNH!
THEY CAME OM THE SHADOWS AND TOOK ME, ...THEY KIDNAPPED ...TORTURED ME... THEY RUINED ME.
THEY TURNED ME INTO THIS.
AND IT'S YOUR...
...AND THIS GODFORSAKEN PLACE'S FAULT.
TNK

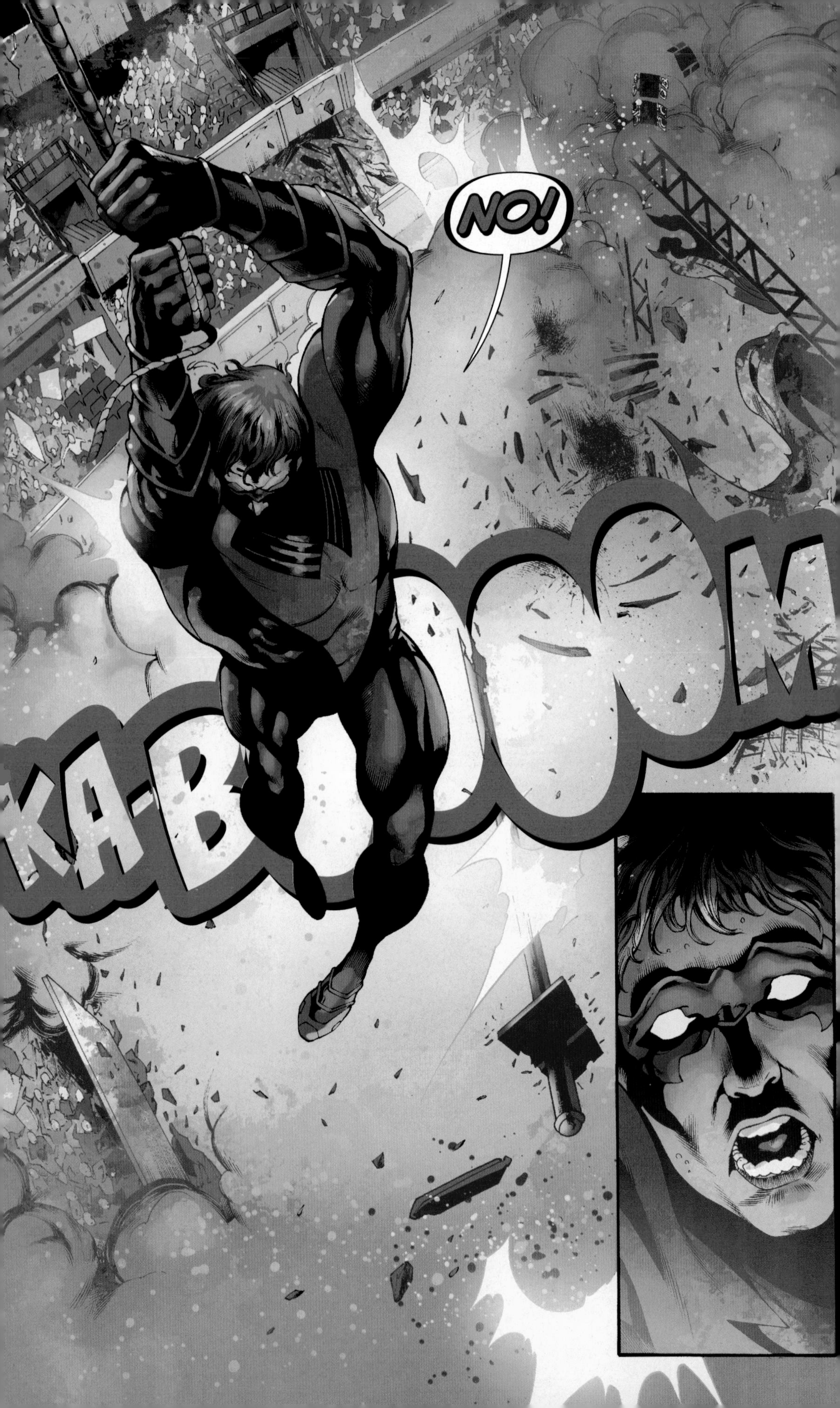
NO!
KA-BOOOOM

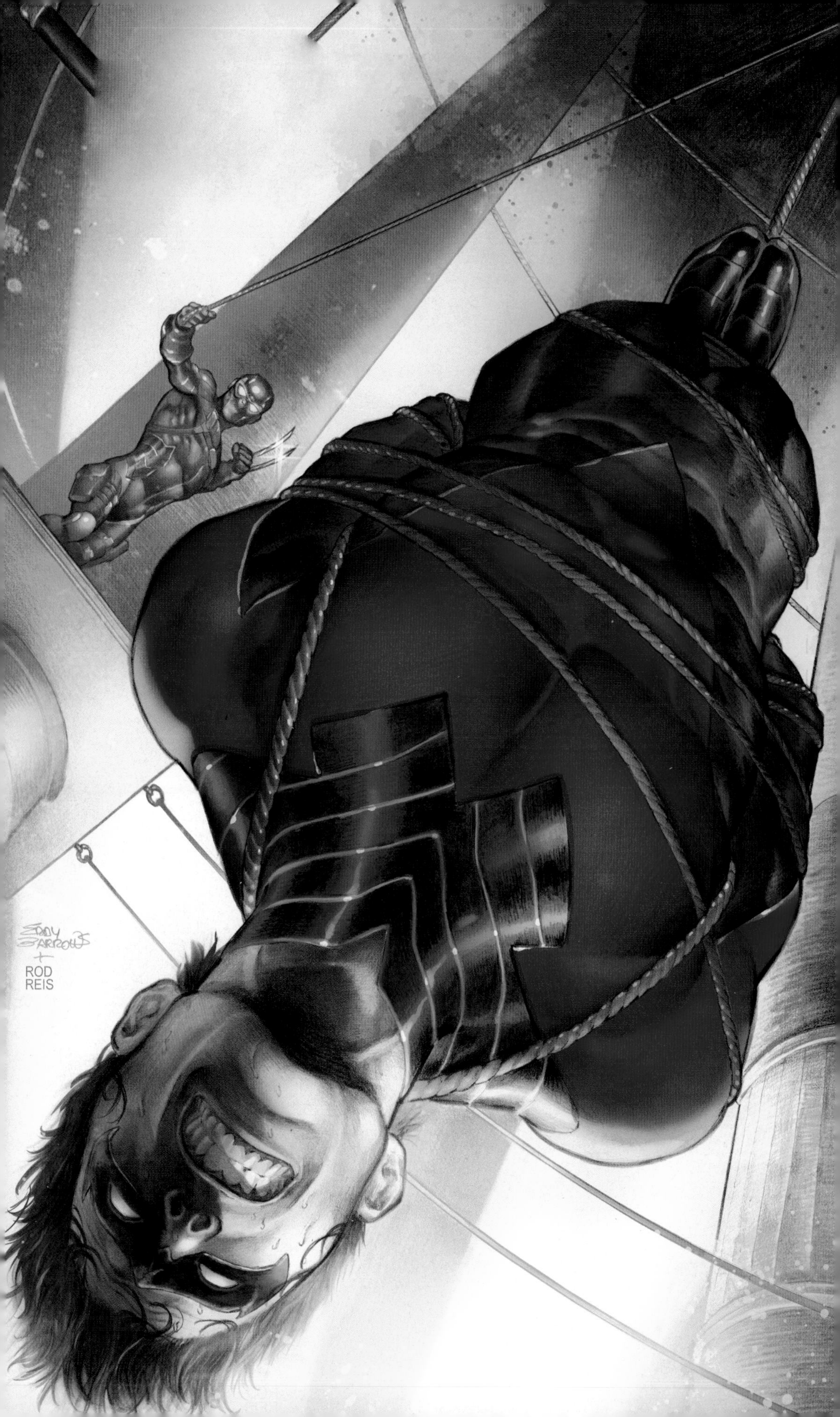
EDDY BARROWS
+
ROD REIS

cover art by Eddy Barrows & Rod Reis

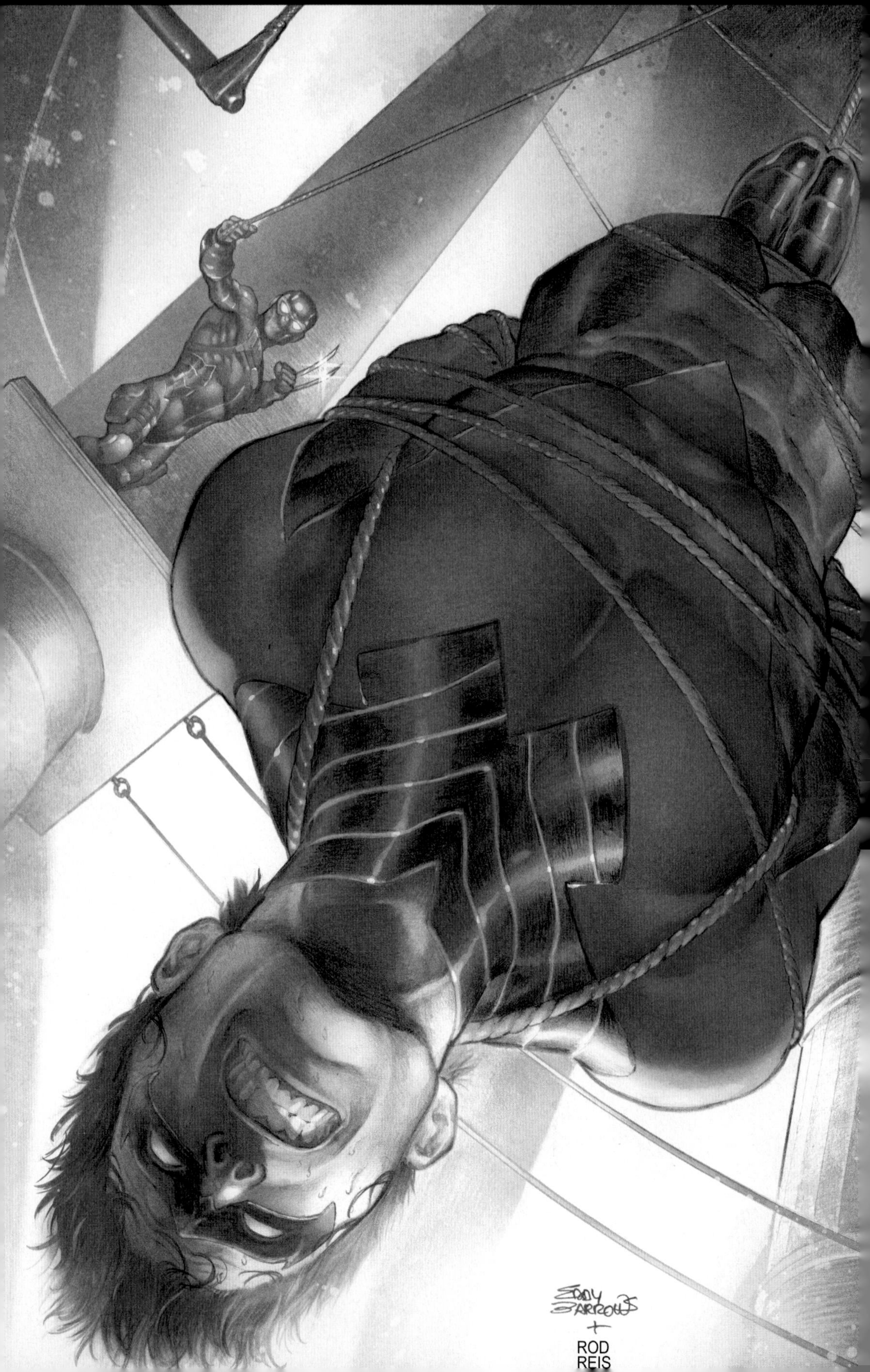
ROD
REIS

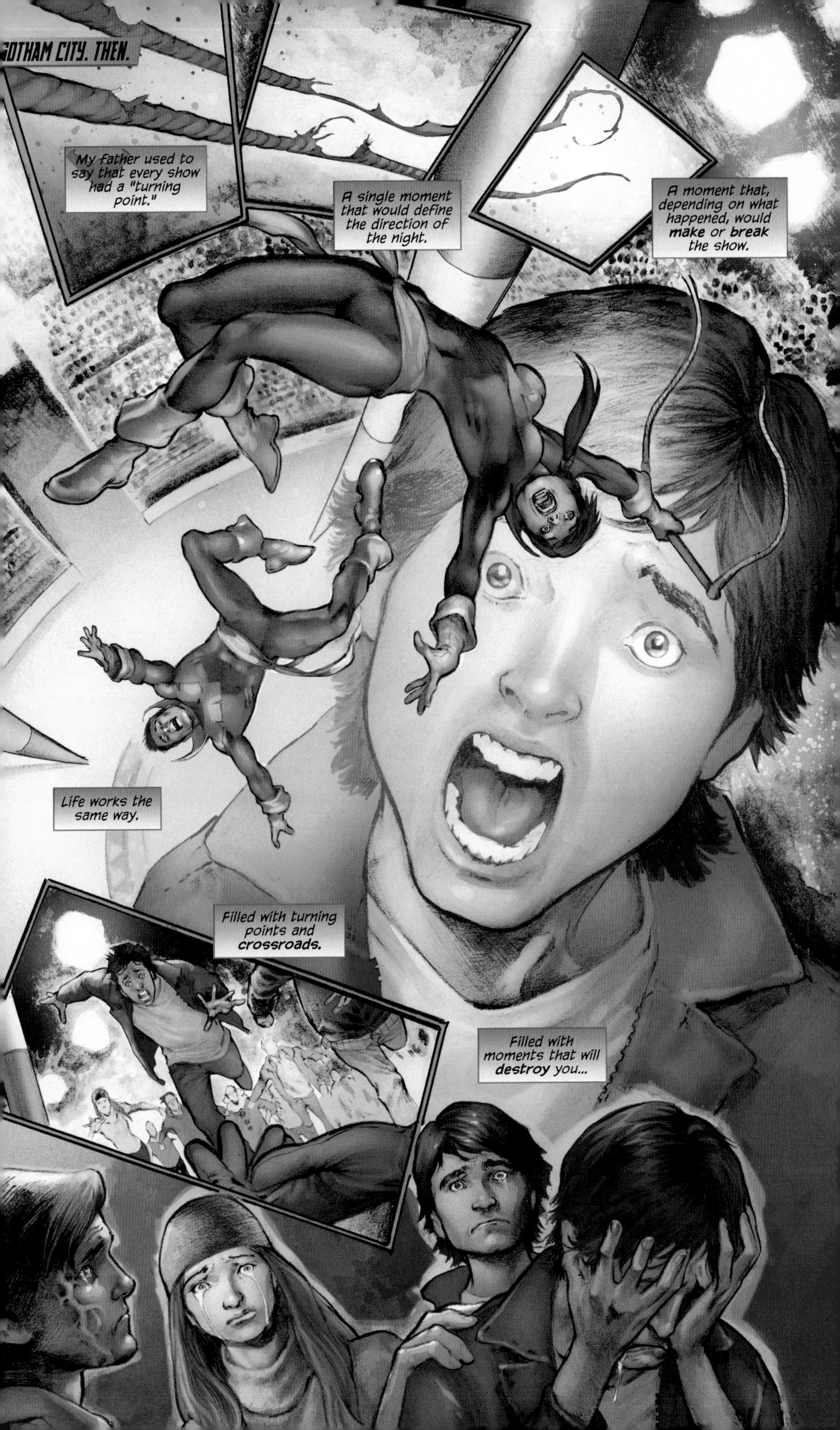
GOTHAM CITY. THEN.
My father used to say that every show had a "turning point."
A single moment that would define the direction of the night.
A moment that, depending on what happened, would **make** or **break** the show.
Life works the same way.
Filled with turning points and **crossroads.**
Filled with moments that will **destroy** you...

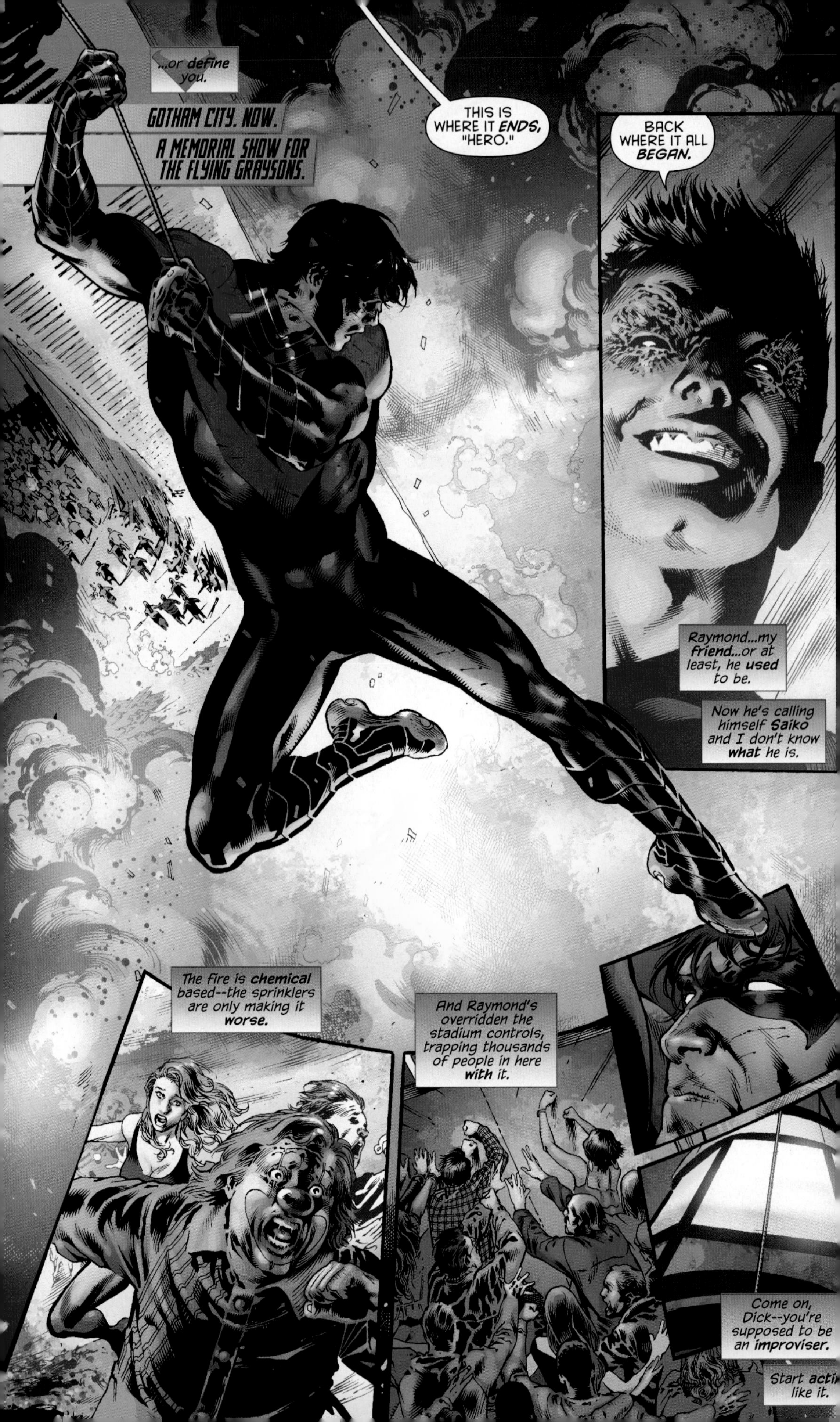

...or define you.
GOTHAM CITY. NOW.
A MEMORIAL SHOW FOR THE FLYING GRAYSONS.
THIS IS WHERE IT ENDS, "HERO."
BACK WHERE IT ALL BEGAN.
Raymond...my friend...or at least, he used to be.
Now he's calling himself Saiko and I don't know what he is.
The fire is chemical based--the sprinklers are only making it worse.
And Raymond's overridden the stadium controls, trapping thousands of people in here with it.
Come on, Dick--you're supposed to be an improviser.
Start acti like it.

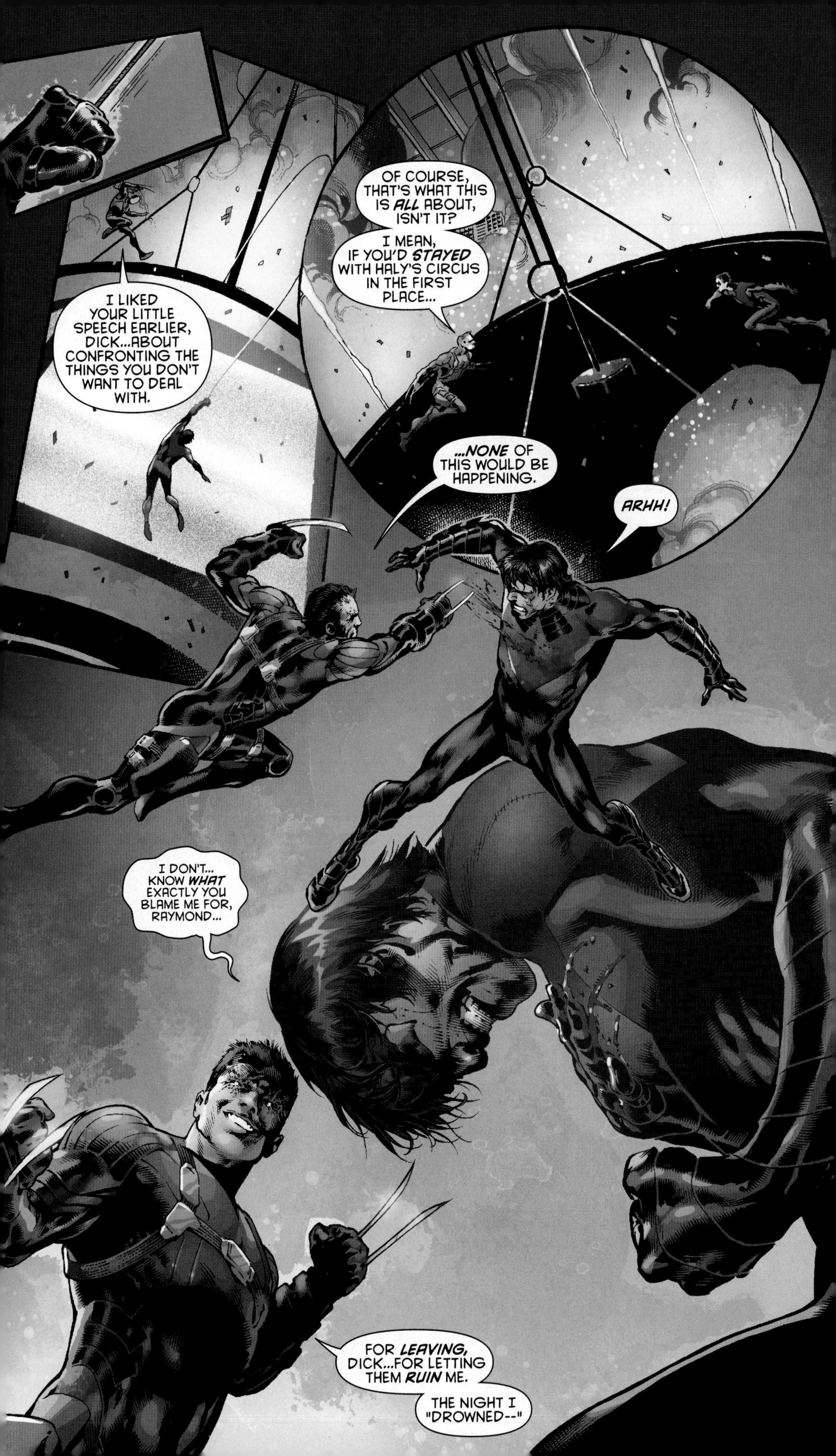
I LIKED YOUR LITTLE SPEECH EARLIER, DICK...ABOUT CONFRONTING THE THINGS YOU DON'T WANT TO DEAL WITH.
OF COURSE, THAT'S WHAT THIS IS ALL ABOUT, ISN'T IT?
I MEAN, IF YOU'D STAYED WITH HALY'S CIRCUS IN THE FIRST PLACE...
...NONE OF THIS WOULD BE HAPPENING.
ARHH!
I DON'T... KNOW WHAT EXACTLY YOU BLAME ME FOR, RAYMOND...
FOR LEAVING, DICK...FOR LETTING THEM RUIN ME.
THE NIGHT I "DROWNED--"

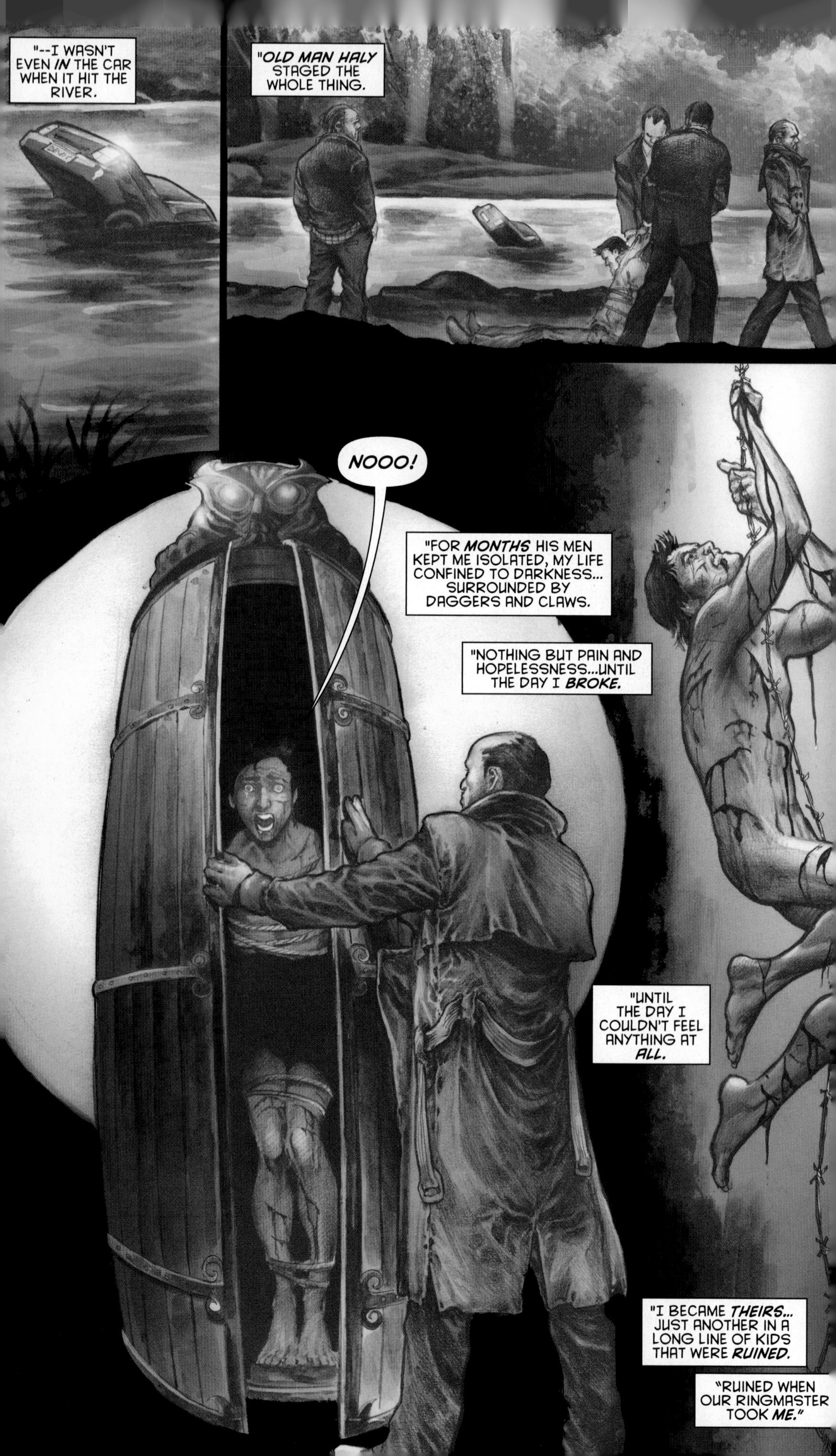
"--I WASN'T EVEN *IN* THE CAR WHEN IT HIT THE RIVER.
"*OLD MAN HALY* STAGED THE WHOLE THING.
NOOO!
"FOR *MONTHS* HIS MEN KEPT ME ISOLATED, MY LIFE CONFINED TO DARKNESS... SURROUNDED BY DAGGERS AND CLAWS.
"NOTHING BUT PAIN AND HOPELESSNESS...UNTIL THE DAY I *BROKE.*
"UNTIL THE DAY I COULDN'T FEEL ANYTHING AT *ALL.*
"I BECAME *THEIRS*... JUST ANOTHER IN A LONG LINE OF KIDS THAT WERE *RUINED.*
"RUINED WHEN OUR RINGMASTER TOOK *ME.*"

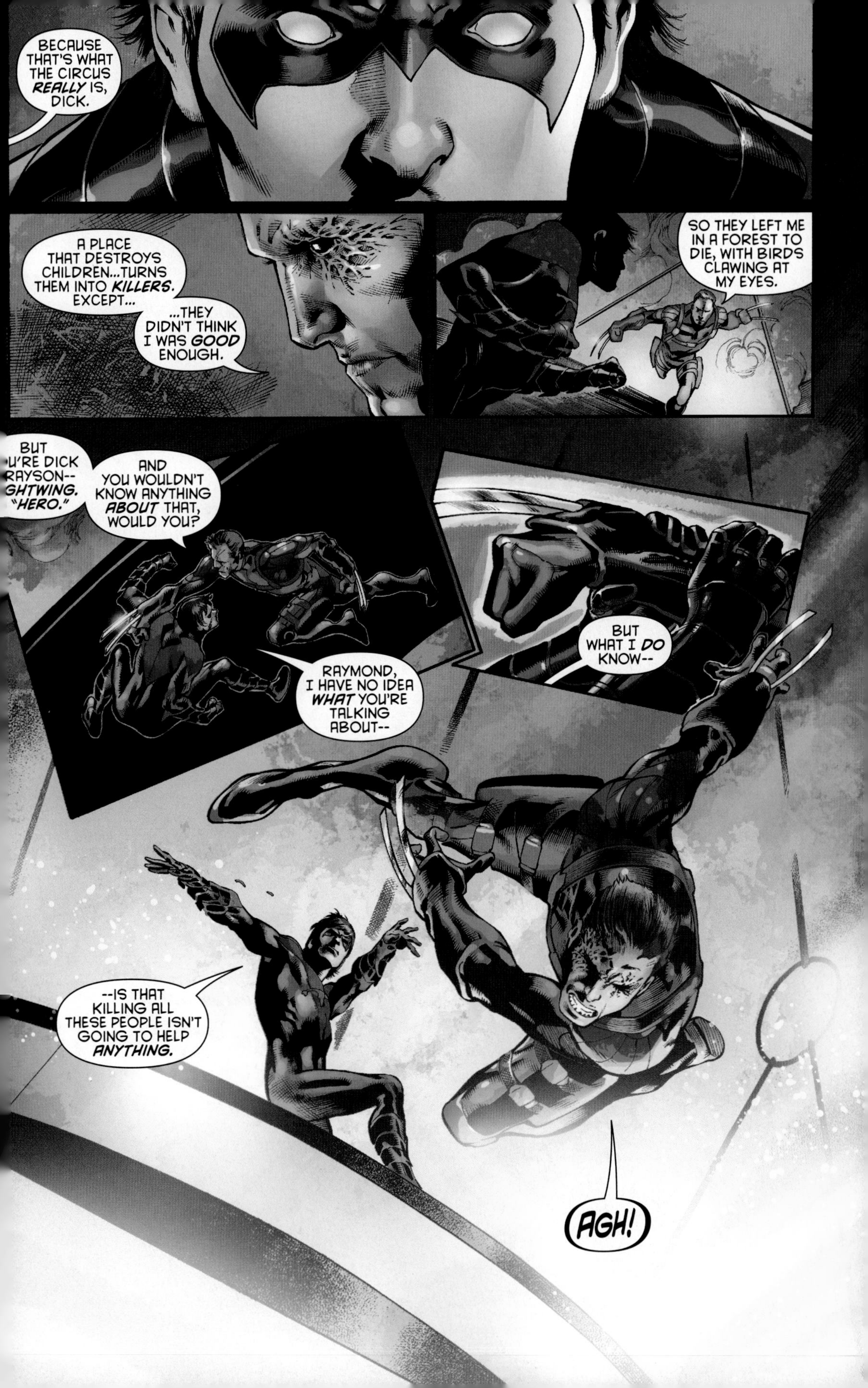
BECAUSE THAT'S WHAT THE CIRCUS REALLY IS, DICK.
A PLACE THAT DESTROYS CHILDREN...TURNS THEM INTO KILLERS. EXCEPT...
...THEY DIDN'T THINK I WAS GOOD ENOUGH.
SO THEY LEFT ME IN A FOREST TO DIE, WITH BIRDS CLAWING AT MY EYES.
BUT U'RE DICK RAYSON-- GHTWING. "HERO."
AND YOU WOULDN'T KNOW ANYTHING ABOUT THAT, WOULD YOU?
RAYMOND, I HAVE NO IDEA WHAT YOU'RE TALKING ABOUT--
BUT WHAT I DO KNOW--
--IS THAT KILLING ALL THESE PEOPLE ISN'T GOING TO HELP ANYTHING.
AGH!

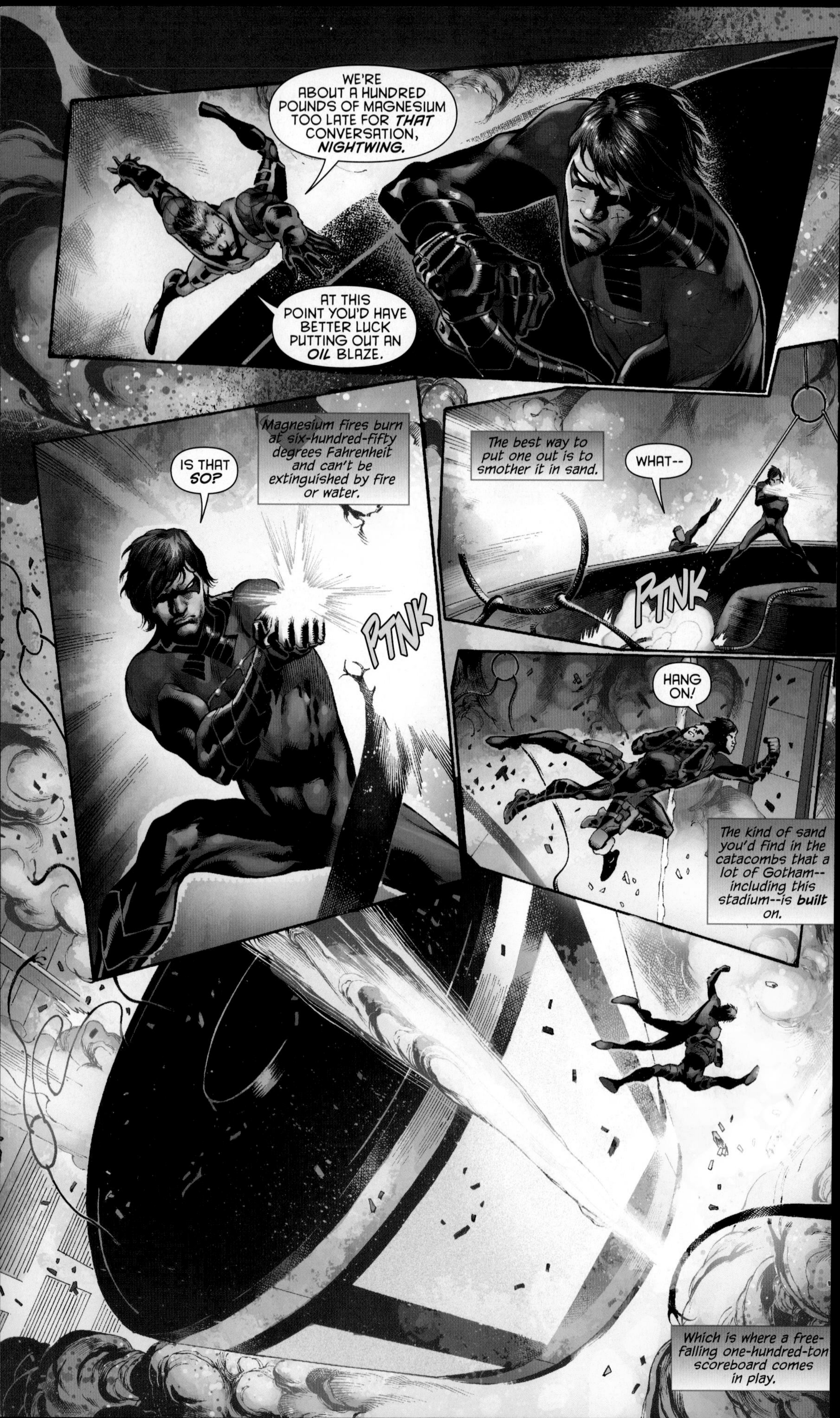
WE'RE ABOUT A HUNDRED POUNDS OF MAGNESIUM TOO LATE FOR THAT CONVERSATION, NIGHTWING.
AT THIS POINT YOU'D HAVE BETTER LUCK PUTTING OUT AN OIL BLAZE.
Magnesium fires burn at six-hundred-fifty degrees Fahrenheit and can't be extinguished by fire or water.
IS THAT SO?
PTNK
The best way to put one out is to smother it in sand.
WHAT--
PTNK
HANG ON!
The kind of sand you'd find in the catacombs that a lot of Gotham--including this stadium--is built on.
Which is where a free-falling one-hundred-ton scoreboard comes in play.

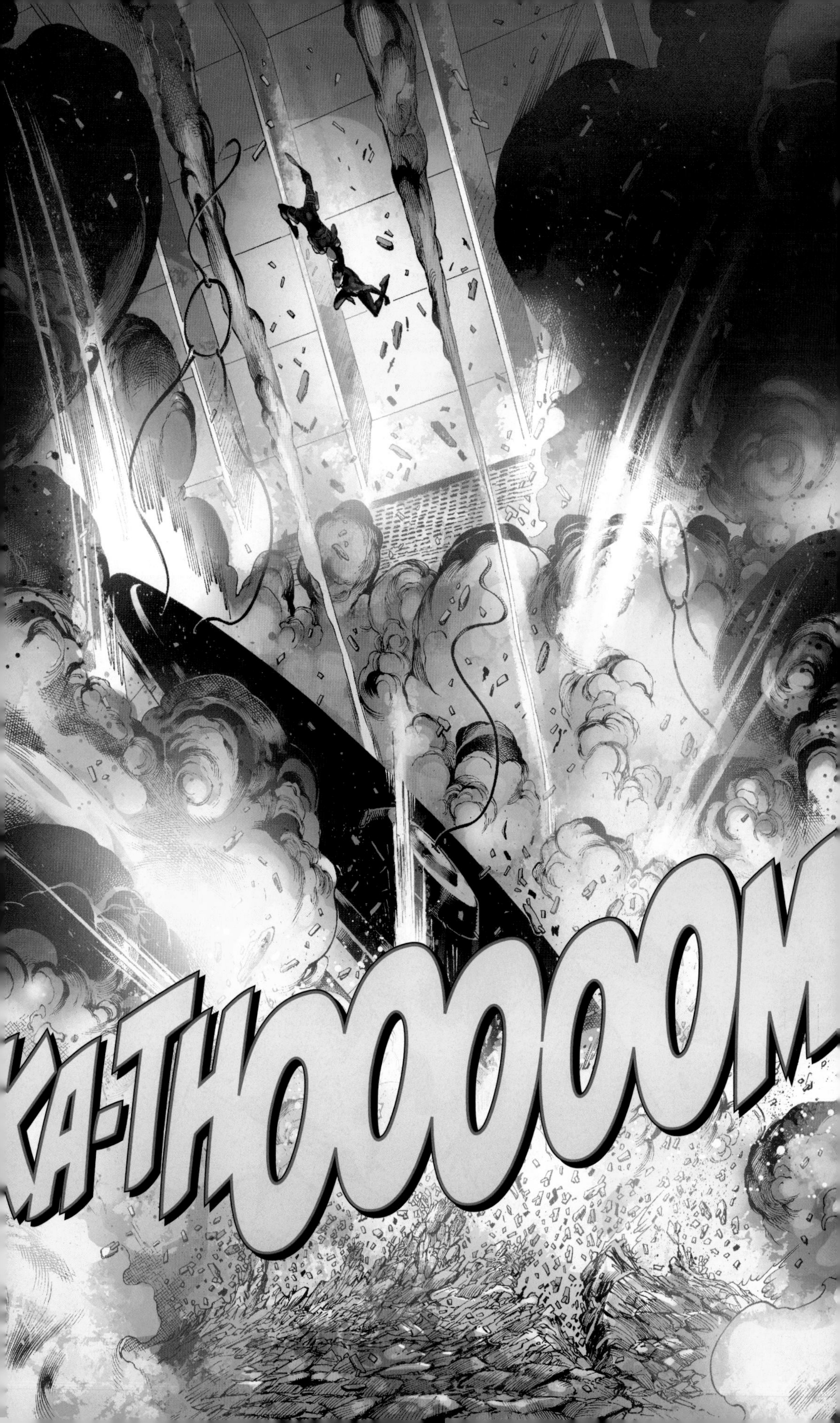
A-THOOOOOM

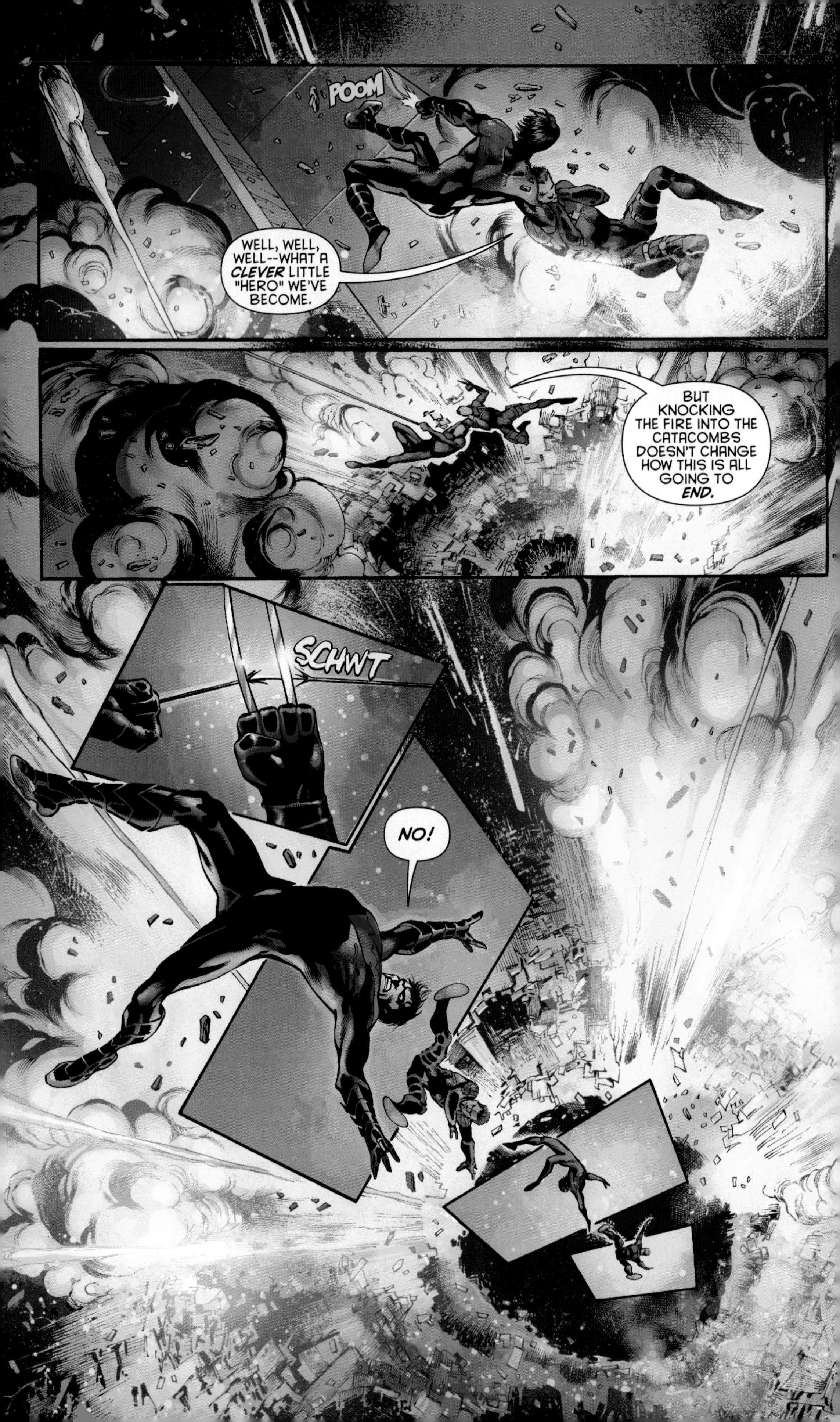
POOM
WELL, WELL, WELL--WHAT A CLEVER LITTLE "HERO" WE'VE BECOME.
BUT KNOCKING THE FIRE INTO THE CATACOMBS DOESN'T CHANGE HOW THIS IS ALL GOING TO END.
SCHWT
NO!

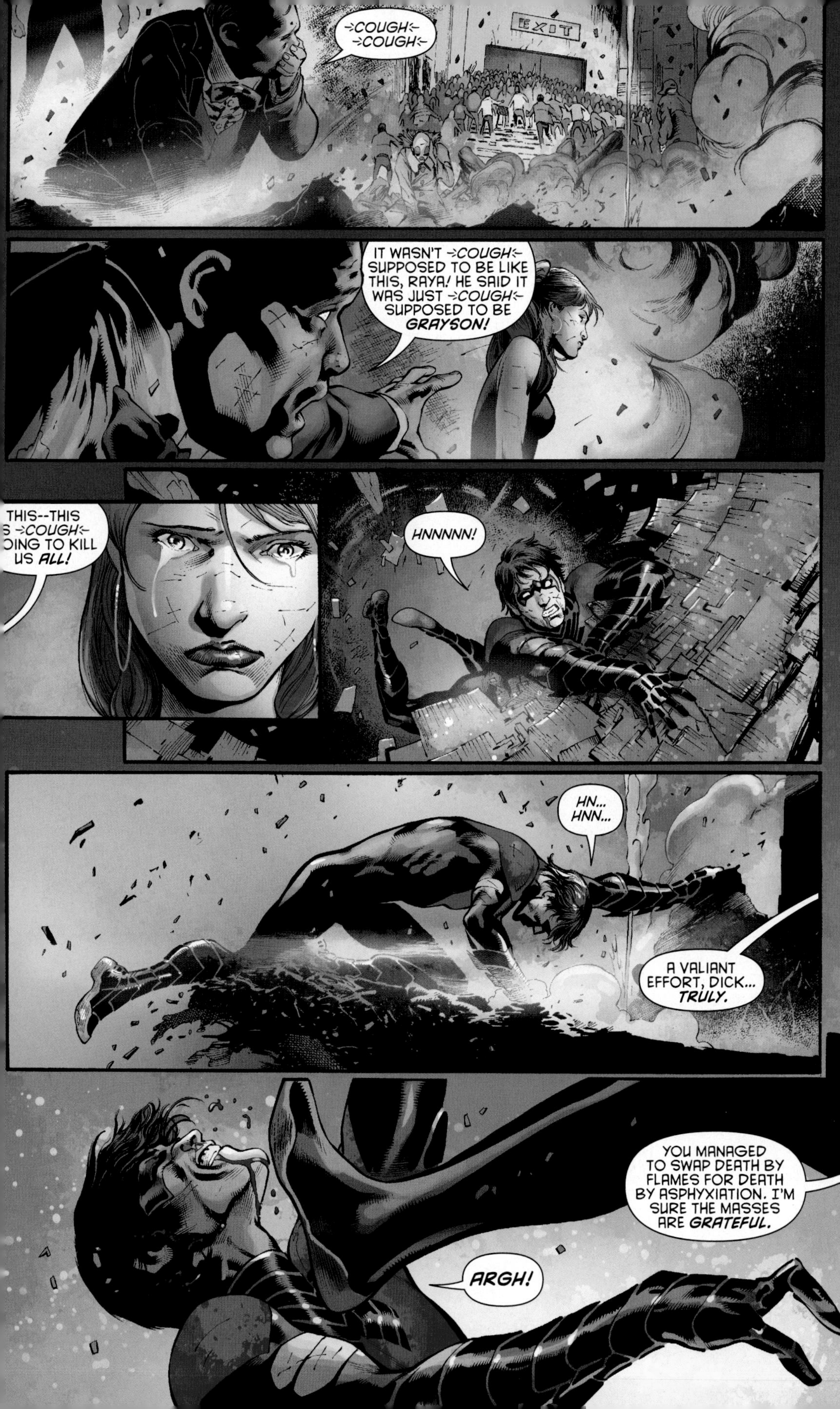

-COUGH-
-COUGH-
IT WASN'T -COUGH- SUPPOSED TO BE LIKE THIS, RAYA! HE SAID IT WAS JUST -COUGH- SUPPOSED TO BE GRAYSON!
THIS--THIS S -COUGH- OING TO KILL US ALL!
HNNNNN!
HN... HNN...
A VALIANT EFFORT, DICK... TRULY.
YOU MANAGED TO SWAP DEATH BY FLAMES FOR DEATH BY ASPHYXIATION. I'M SURE THE MASSES ARE GRATEFUL.
ARGH!

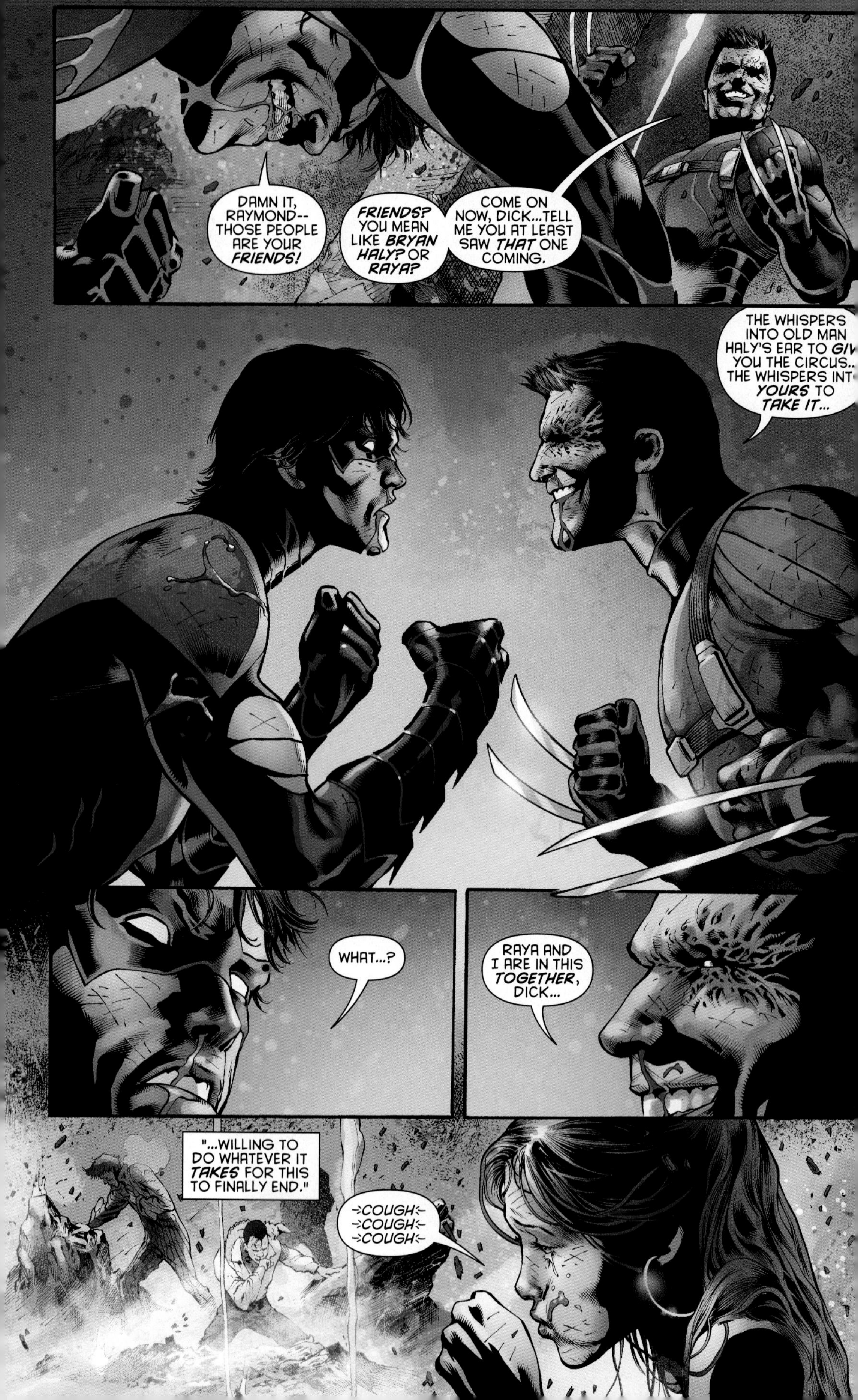
DAMN IT, RAYMOND-- THOSE PEOPLE ARE YOUR *FRIENDS!*
FRIENDS? YOU MEAN LIKE *BRYAN HALY?* OR *RAYA?*
COME ON NOW, DICK...TELL ME YOU AT LEAST SAW *THAT* ONE COMING.
THE WHISPERS INTO OLD MAN HALY'S EAR TO *GIV* YOU THE CIRCUS.. THE WHISPERS INT *YOURS* TO *TAKE IT*...
WHAT...?
RAYA AND I ARE IN THIS *TOGETHER*, DICK...
"...WILLING TO DO WHATEVER IT *TAKES* FOR THIS TO FINALLY END."
-COUGH- -COUGH- -COUGH-

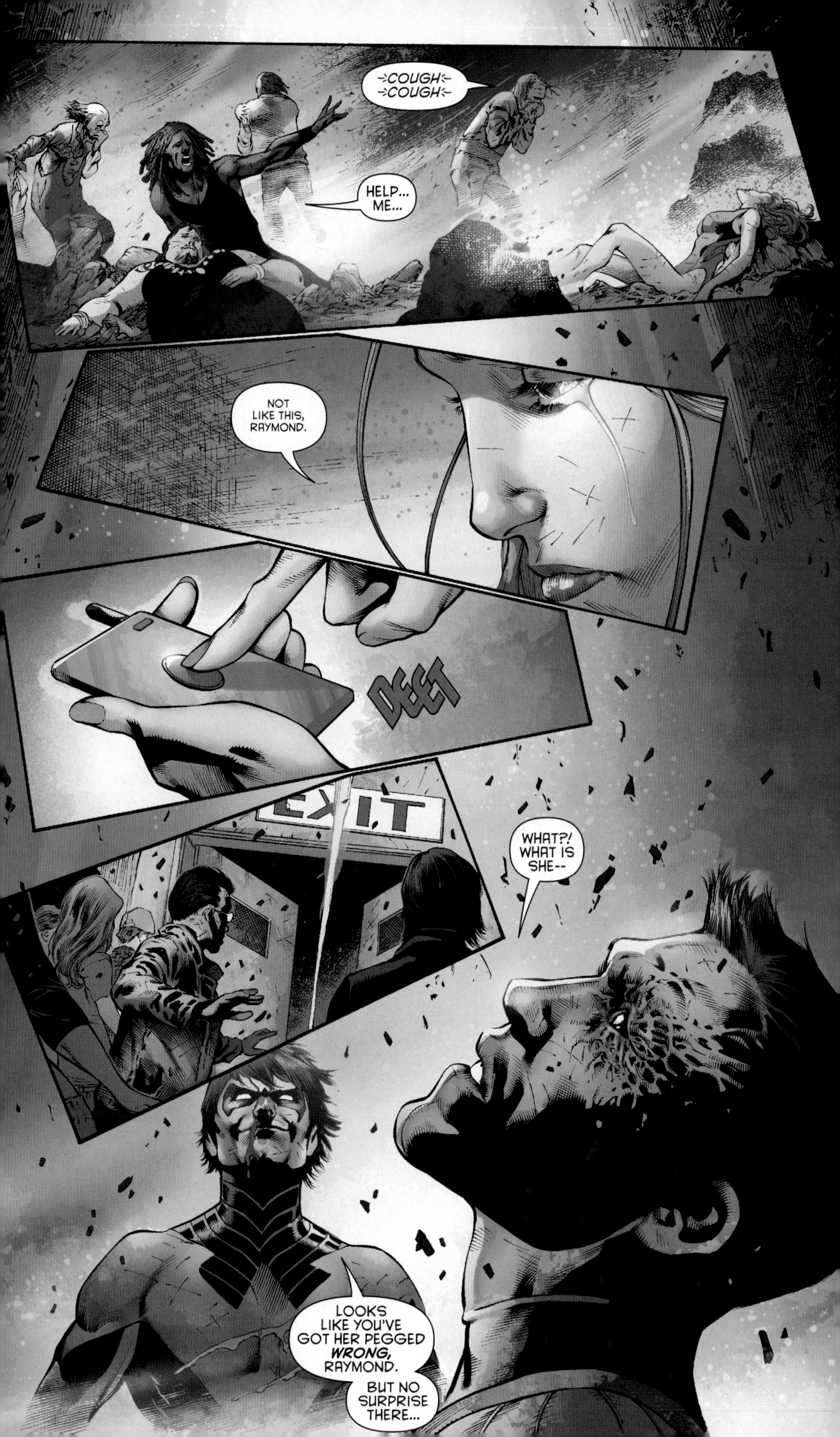

-COUGH-
-COUGH-
HELP... ME...
NOT LIKE THIS, RAYMOND.
DEET
EXIT
WHAT?! WHAT IS SHE--
LOOKS LIKE YOU'VE GOT HER PEGGED WRONG, RAYMOND.
BUT NO SURPRISE THERE...

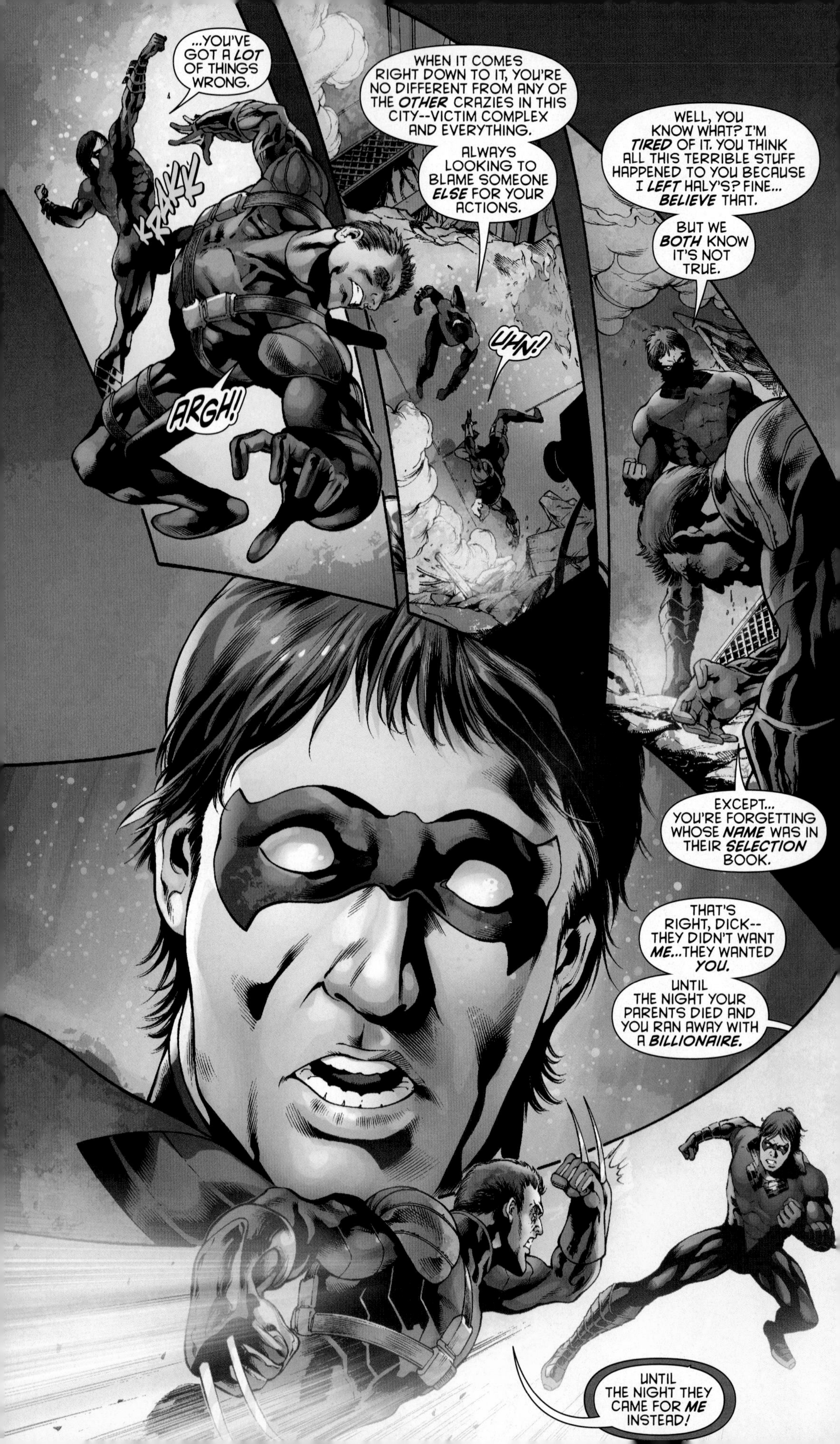

...YOU'VE GOT A *LOT* OF THINGS WRONG.
KRAKK
ARGH!
WHEN IT COMES RIGHT DOWN TO IT, YOU'RE NO DIFFERENT FROM ANY OF THE *OTHER* CRAZIES IN THIS CITY--VICTIM COMPLEX AND EVERYTHING.
ALWAYS LOOKING TO BLAME SOMEONE *ELSE* FOR YOUR ACTIONS.
UHN!
WELL, YOU KNOW WHAT? I'M *TIRED* OF IT. YOU THINK ALL THIS TERRIBLE STUFF HAPPENED TO YOU BECAUSE I *LEFT* HALY'S? FINE... *BELIEVE* THAT.
BUT WE *BOTH* KNOW IT'S NOT TRUE.
EXCEPT... YOU'RE FORGETTING WHOSE *NAME* WAS IN THEIR *SELECTION* BOOK.
THAT'S RIGHT, DICK-- THEY DIDN'T WANT *ME*...THEY WANTED *YOU*.
UNTIL THE NIGHT YOUR PARENTS DIED AND YOU RAN AWAY WITH A *BILLIONAIRE.*
UNTIL THE NIGHT THEY CAME FOR *ME* INSTEAD!

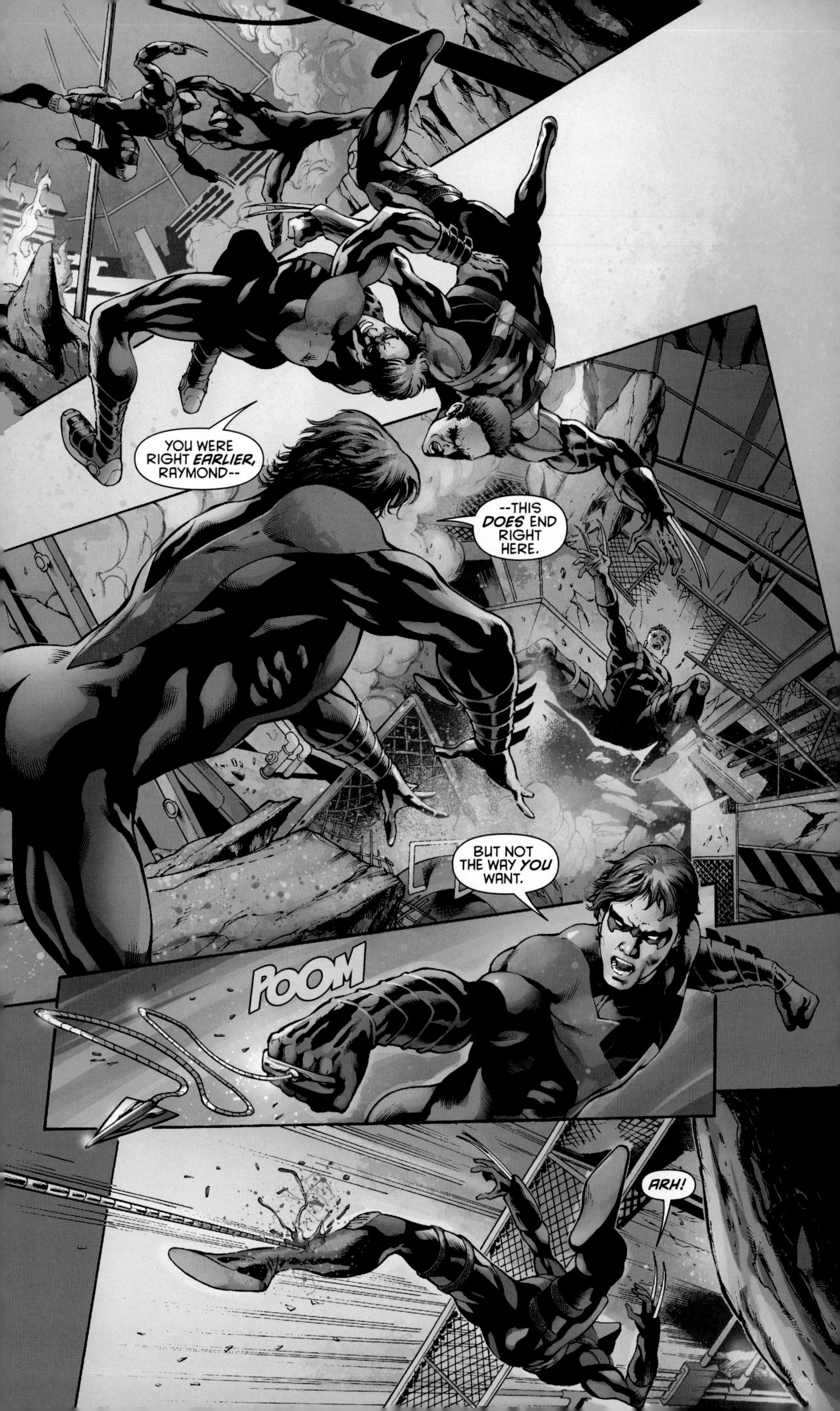
YOU WERE RIGHT EARLIER, RAYMOND--
--THIS DOES END RIGHT HERE.
BUT NOT THE WAY YOU WANT.
POOM
ARH!

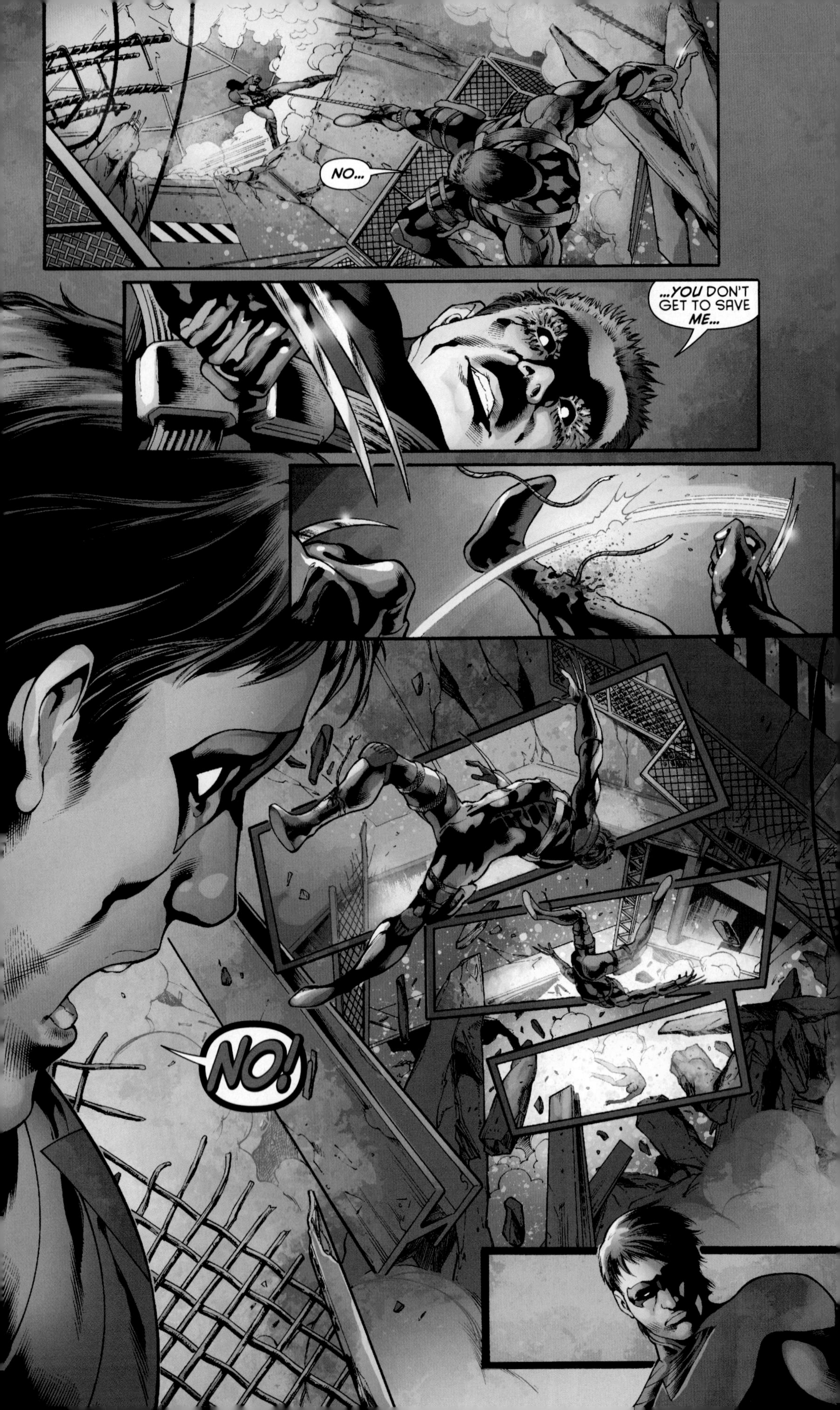
NO...
...YOU DON'T GET TO SAVE ME...
NO!

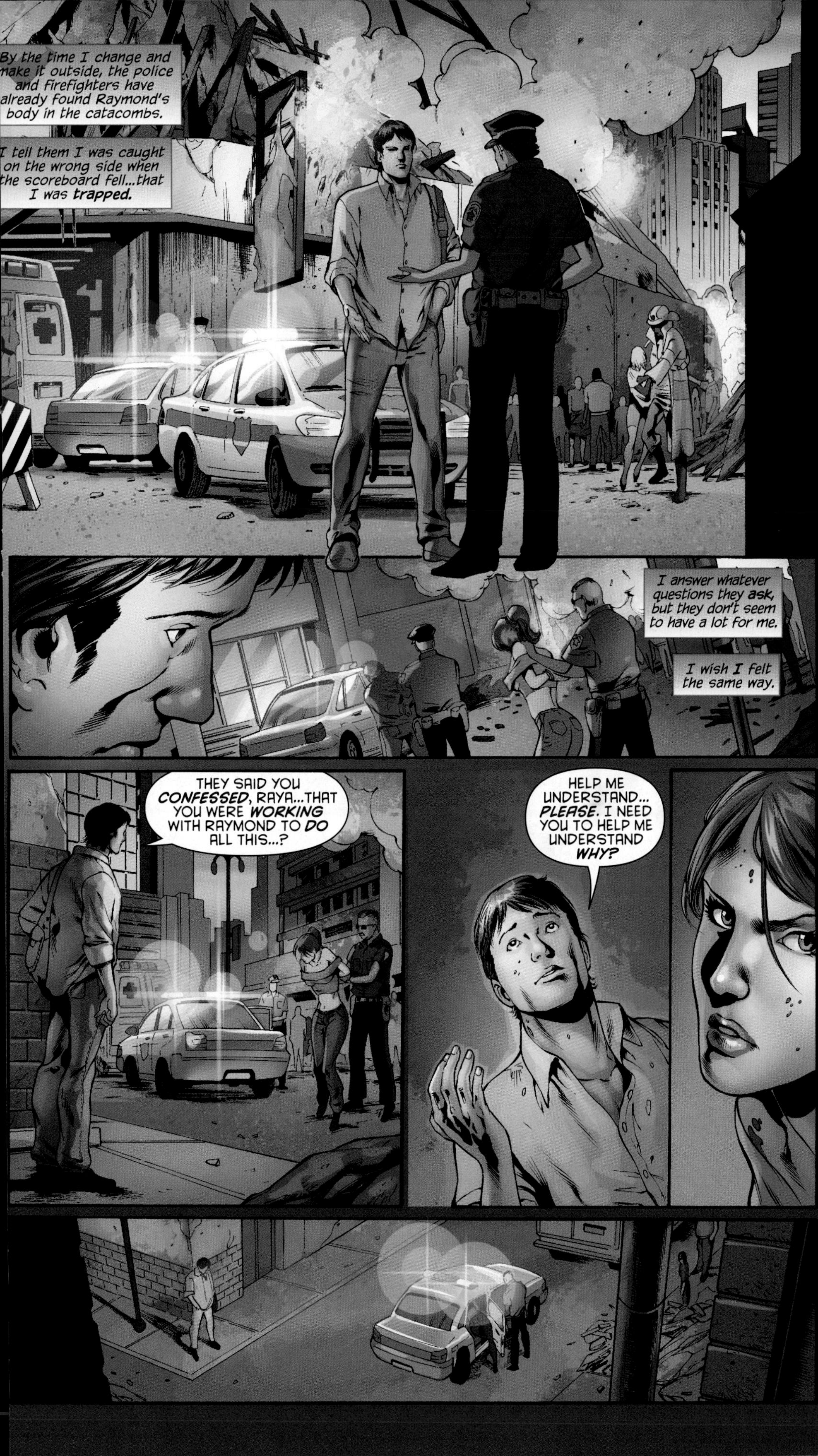

By the time I change and make it outside, the police and firefighters have already found Raymond's body in the catacombs.
I tell them I was caught on the wrong side when the scoreboard fell...that I was **trapped.**
I answer whatever questions they **ask**, but they don't seem to have a lot for me.
I wish **I** felt the same way.
THEY SAID YOU ***CONFESSED***, RAYA...THAT YOU WERE ***WORKING*** WITH RAYMOND TO ***DO*** ALL THIS...?
HELP ME UNDERSTAND... ***PLEASE***. I NEED YOU TO HELP ME UNDERSTAND ***WHY?***

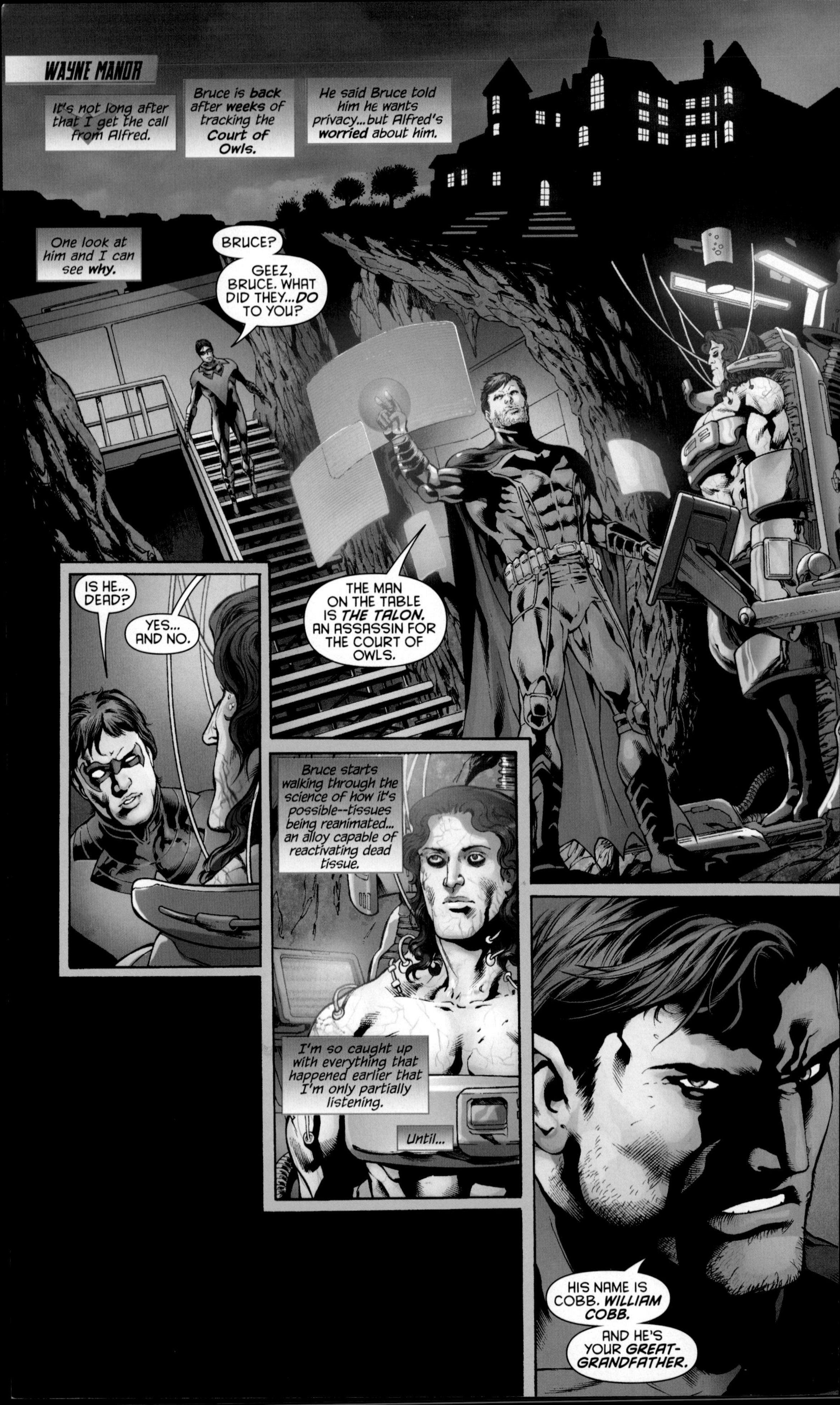

WAYNE MANOR
It's not long after that I get the call from Alfred.
Bruce is back after weeks of tracking the Court of Owls.
He said Bruce told him he wants privacy...but Alfred's worried about him.
One look at him and I can see why.
BRUCE?
GEEZ, BRUCE. WHAT DID THEY...DO TO YOU?
THE MAN ON THE TABLE IS THE TALON. AN ASSASSIN FOR THE COURT OF OWLS.
IS HE... DEAD?
YES... AND NO.
Bruce starts walking through the science of how it's possible--tissues being reanimated... an alloy capable of reactivating dead tissue.
I'm so caught up with everything that happened earlier that I'm only partially listening.
Until...
HIS NAME IS COBB. WILLIAM COBB.
AND HE'S YOUR GREAT-GRANDFATHER.

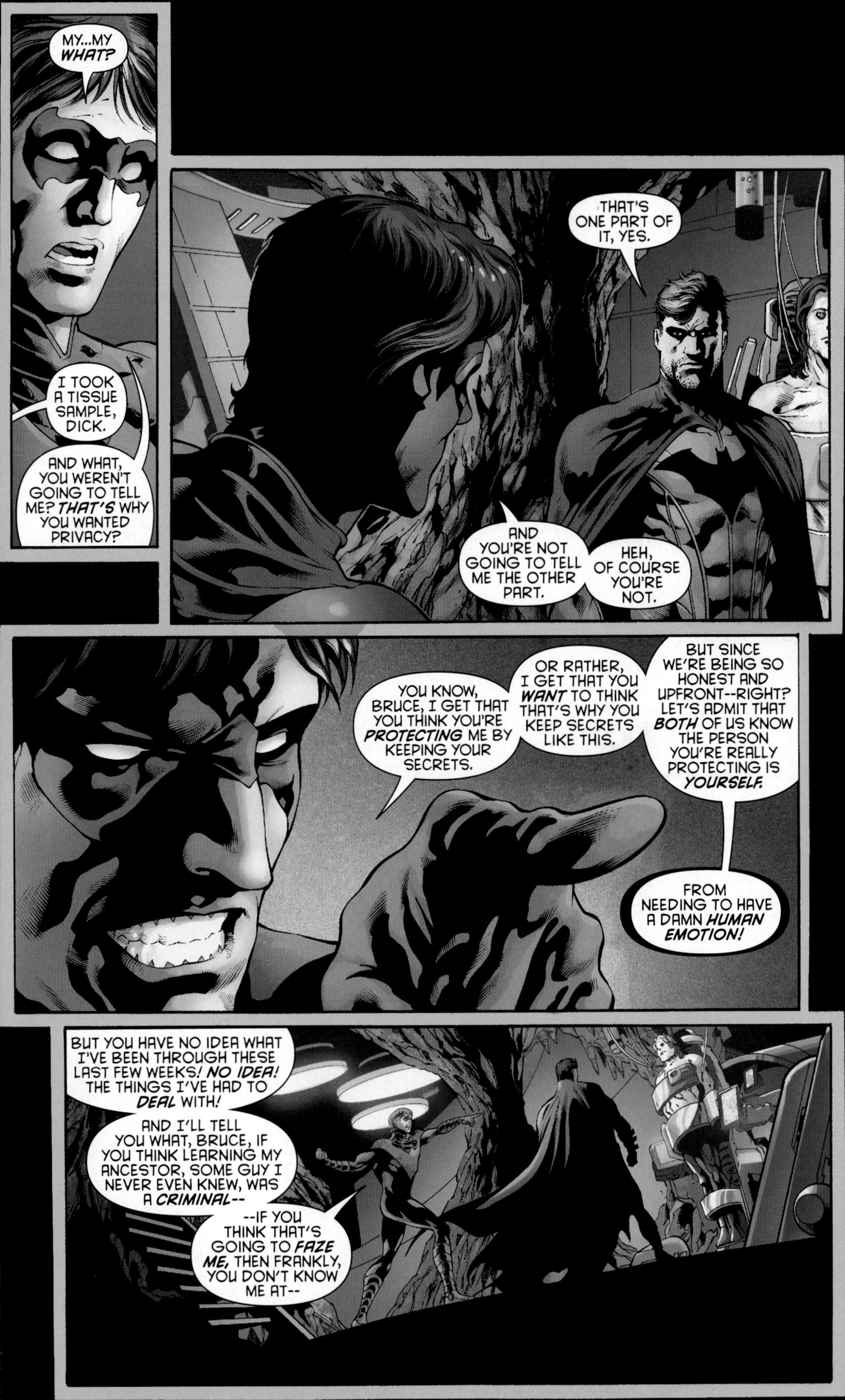
MY...MY WHAT?
THAT'S ONE PART OF IT, YES.
I TOOK A TISSUE SAMPLE, DICK.
AND WHAT, YOU WEREN'T GOING TO TELL ME? THAT'S WHY YOU WANTED PRIVACY?
AND YOU'RE NOT GOING TO TELL ME THE OTHER PART.
HEH, OF COURSE YOU'RE NOT.
YOU KNOW, BRUCE, I GET THAT YOU THINK YOU'RE PROTECTING ME BY KEEPING YOUR SECRETS.
OR RATHER, I GET THAT YOU WANT TO THINK THAT'S WHY YOU KEEP SECRETS LIKE THIS.
BUT SINCE WE'RE BEING SO HONEST AND UPFRONT--RIGHT? LET'S ADMIT THAT BOTH OF US KNOW THE PERSON YOU'RE REALLY PROTECTING IS YOURSELF.
FROM NEEDING TO HAVE A DAMN HUMAN EMOTION!
BUT YOU HAVE NO IDEA WHAT I'VE BEEN THROUGH THESE LAST FEW WEEKS! NO IDEA! THE THINGS I'VE HAD TO DEAL WITH!
AND I'LL TELL YOU WHAT, BRUCE, IF YOU THINK LEARNING MY ANCESTOR, SOME GUY I NEVER EVEN KNEW, WAS A CRIMINAL--
--IF YOU THINK THAT'S GOING TO FAZE ME, THEN FRANKLY, YOU DON'T KNOW ME AT--

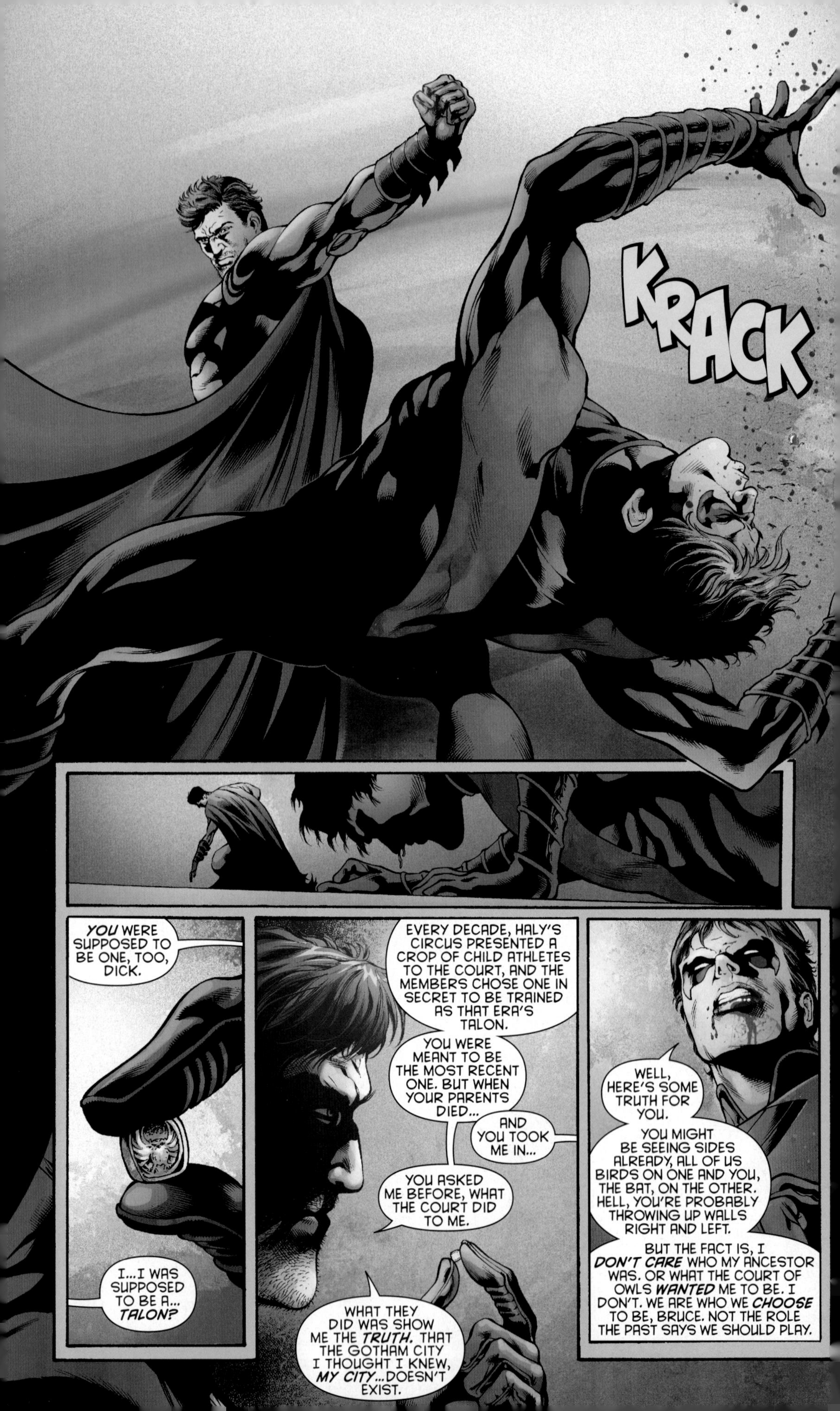

KRACK
YOU WERE SUPPOSED TO BE ONE, TOO, DICK.
I...I WAS SUPPOSED TO BE A... TALON?
EVERY DECADE, HALY'S CIRCUS PRESENTED A CROP OF CHILD ATHLETES TO THE COURT, AND THE MEMBERS CHOSE ONE IN SECRET TO BE TRAINED AS THAT ERA'S TALON.
YOU WERE MEANT TO BE THE MOST RECENT ONE. BUT WHEN YOUR PARENTS DIED...
AND YOU TOOK ME IN...
YOU ASKED ME BEFORE, WHAT THE COURT DID TO ME.
WHAT THEY DID WAS SHOW ME THE TRUTH. THAT THE GOTHAM CITY I THOUGHT I KNEW, MY CITY...DOESN'T EXIST.
WELL, HERE'S SOME TRUTH FOR YOU.
YOU MIGHT BE SEEING SIDES ALREADY, ALL OF US BIRDS ON ONE AND YOU, THE BAT, ON THE OTHER. HELL, YOU'RE PROBABLY THROWING UP WALLS RIGHT AND LEFT.
BUT THE FACT IS, I DON'T CARE WHO MY ANCESTOR WAS. OR WHAT THE COURT OF OWLS WANTED ME TO BE. I DON'T. WE ARE WHO WE CHOOSE TO BE, BRUCE. NOT THE ROLE THE PAST SAYS WE SHOULD PLAY.

"THE COURT OF OWLS IS JUST ANOTHER *BAD GUY*, BRUCE. THEY'RE A LITTLE GRAYER AROUND THE TEMPLES IS ALL.

"YES, YOU MADE A MISTAKE AND UNDERESTIMATED THEM...

"...BUT THEY'RE *NOT* GOTHAM CITY, BRUCE.

"AND NEITHER ARE YOU."

The *Book of Names*... a list of every Talon Haly's has ever produced. *Except* one.

Richard Grayson

I suppose it's fitting that it all comes back to Gotham City.

The place that takes the things you love and twists them against you.

The place that takes your greatest strengths and tries to use them to *break* you.

I used to think my past was *my* greatest strength, tragedy and all, because it's what *defined* me.

But I realize now that's not true-- not exactly.

MASTER RICHARD...THERE'S SOMETHING ELSE YOU NEED TO SEE.

WHAT IS IT, ALFRED?

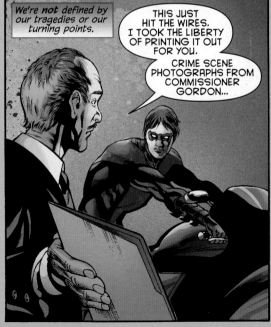

We're *not* defined by our tragedies or our turning points.

THIS JUST HIT THE WIRES. I TOOK THE LIBERTY OF PRINTING IT OUT FOR YOU. CRIME SCENE PHOTOGRAPHS FROM COMMISSIONER GORDON...

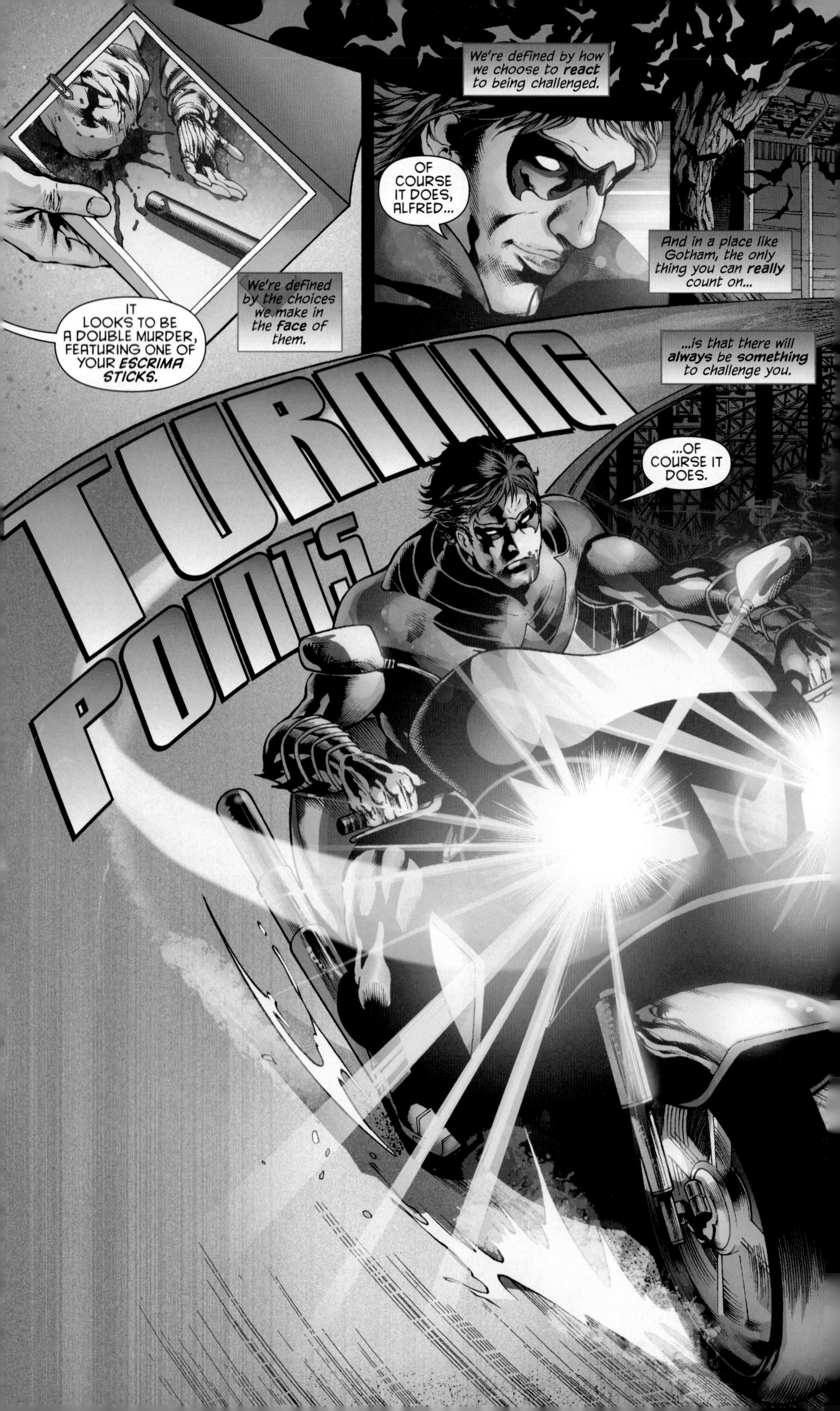

IT LOOKS TO BE A DOUBLE MURDER, FEATURING ONE OF YOUR ESCRIMA STICKS.
We're defined by the choices we make in the face of them.
We're defined by how we choose to react to being challenged.
OF COURSE IT DOES, ALFRED...
And in a place like Gotham, the only thing you can really count on...
...is that there will always be something to challenge you.
TURNING POINTS
...OF COURSE IT DOES.